Judaism and the Philosophy of Religion

Analytic philosophy of religion is a vibrant area of inquiry, but it has generally focused on generic forms of theism or on Christianity. David Shatz here offers a new and fresh approach to the field in a wide-ranging and engaging introduction to the analytic philosophy of religion from the perspective of Judaism. Exploring classical Jewish texts about philosophical topics in light of the concepts and arguments at the heart of analytic philosophy, he demonstrates how each tradition illuminates the other, yielding a deeper understanding of both Jewish sources and general philosophical issues. Shatz also advances growing efforts to imagine Jewish philosophy not only as an engrossing, invaluable part of Jewish intellectual history but also as a creative, constructive enterprise that mines the methods and literature of contemporary philosophy. His book offers new pathways to think deeply about God, evil, morality, freedom, ethics, and religious diversity, among other topics.

David Shatz is the Ronald P. Stanton University Professor of Philosophy, Ethics, and Religious Thought at Yeshiva University in New York. He is the author of *Jewish Thought in Dialogue* and the editor of *Philosophy and Faith*, and is included in Brill's Library of Contemporary Jewish Philosophers series.

Cambridge Studies in Religion, Philosophy, and Society

Series Editors

Paul K. Moser, *Loyola University, Chicago*
Chad Meister, *Bethel College, Indiana*

This is a series of interdisciplinary texts devoted to major-level courses in religion, philosophy, and related fields. It includes original, current, and wide-spanning contributions by leading scholars from various disciplines that (a) focus on the central academic topics in religion and philosophy, (b) are seminal and up-to-date regarding recent developments in scholarship on the various key topics, and (c) incorporate, with needed precision and depth, the major differing perspectives and backgrounds – the central voices on the major religions and the religious, philosophical, and sociological viewpoints that cover the intellectual landscape today. Cambridge Studies in Religion, Philosophy, and Society is a direct response to this recent and widespread interest and need.

Recent Books in the Series

Michael McGhee
Spirituality for the Godless: Buddhism, Humanism, and Religion

William B. Parsons
Freud and Religion

Charles Taliaferro and Jil Evans
Is God Invisible?: An Essay on Religion and Aesthetics

David Wenham
Jesus in Context: Making Sense of the Historical Figure

Paul W. Gooch
Paul and Religion: Unfinished Conversations

Herman Philipse
Reason and Religion: Evaluating and Explaining Belief in Gods

Phillip H. Wiebe
Religious Experience: Implications for What Is Real

Norman Russell
Theosis and Religion: Participation in Divine Life in the Eastern and Western Traditions

Amy E. Black and Douglas L. Koopman
Civil Religion and the Renewal of American Politics

Lenn E. Goodman
God and Truth

Judaism and the Philosophy of Religion

DAVID SHATZ
Yeshiva University

Shaftesbury Road, Cambridge CB2 8EA, United Kingdom

One Liberty Plaza, 20th Floor, New York, NY 10006, USA

477 Williamstown Road, Port Melbourne, VIC 3207, Australia

314–321, 3rd Floor, Plot 3, Splendor Forum, Jasola District Centre,
New Delhi – 110025, India

103 Penang Road, #05–06/07, Visioncrest Commercial, Singapore 238467

Cambridge University Press is part of Cambridge University Press & Assessment,
a department of the University of Cambridge.

We share the University's mission to contribute to society through the pursuit of
education, learning and research at the highest international levels of excellence.

www.cambridge.org
Information on this title: www.cambridge.org/9781009444828
DOI: 10.1017/9781009444811

© David Shatz 2026

This publication is in copyright. Subject to statutory exception and to the provisions
of relevant collective licensing agreements, no reproduction of any part may take
place without the written permission of Cambridge University Press & Assessment.

When citing this work, please include a reference to the DOI 10.1017/9781009444811

First published 2026

Cover image: Sunny day. Manuel Breva Colmeiro / Moment / Getty Images.

A catalogue record for this publication is available from the British Library

Library of Congress Cataloging-in-Publication Data
NAMES: Shatz, David author
TITLE: Judaism and the philosophy of religion / David Shatz,
Yeshiva University, New York.
DESCRIPTION: 1. | Cambridge, United Kingdom ; New York, NY, USA : Cambridge
University Press, [2026] | Series: Cambridge studies in religion,
philosophy, and society | Includes bibliographical references and index.
IDENTIFIERS: LCCN 2025024741 (print) | LCCN 2025024742 (ebook) |
ISBN 9781009444774 hardback | ISBN 9781009444811 ebook
SUBJECTS: LCSH: Jewish philosophy | Judaism and philosophy | Religion – Philosophy
CLASSIFICATION: LCC B154 .S53 2026 (print) | LCC B154 (ebook) |
DDC 298.01–dc23/eng/20250916
LC record available at https://lccn.loc.gov/2025024741
LC ebook record available at https://lccn.loc.gov/2025024742

ISBN 978-1-009-44477-4 Hardback
ISBN 978-1-009-44482-8 Paperback

Cambridge University Press & Assessment has no responsibility for the persistence
or accuracy of URLs for external or third-party internet websites referred to in this
publication and does not guarantee that any content on such websites is, or will
remain, accurate or appropriate.

For EU product safety concerns, contact us at Calle de José Abascal, 56, 1°, 28003
Madrid, Spain, or email eugpsr@cambridge.org

To Chani
And to our precious children and grandchildren
Meira and Raphael, Gedalyah and Rifky
Daniel and Karina, Shmuel, Aaron, Ariella, Tova, Lilly, and Mia
The lights of our lives

Contents

Preface		*page* ix
Acknowledgments		xi
Stylistic Notes		xiii
	Introduction: The Varieties of Jewish Philosophy	1
	An Overview of the Chapters	21

PART I GOD

1	Is Perfect Being Theology an Imperfect Theology?	27
2	Where in the World Is God? Nature and Divine Action	63
3	The Problem(s) of Evil	84

PART II HUMAN BEINGS

4	Problems of Free Will: The Bible's Near-Silence	117
5	"It Was Not You Who Sent Me Here": Free Will and God's Foreordaining of History	125
6	How Free Is the Will? The Challenge of Scientific Determinism	149
7	Here Today, Here Tomorrow: Death and the Afterlife	172

PART III GOD IN RELATION TO HUMANITY

8	Divine Commands and Human Morality	203
9	One God? Judaism and Religious Diversity	238

PART IV FAITH AND REASON

10	Reason, Faith, and Some Spaces in Between	263

PART V CONCLUDING REFLECTIONS

11 Features of Jewish Philosophy: A Closing Assessment 293

Bibliography 299
Index of Biblical and Rabbinic Sources 329
General Index 337

Preface

This book began with an invitation from Chad Meister and Paul Moser, editors of the series Cambridge Studies in Religion, Philosophy and Society, to contribute a work that would focus on Jewish philosophy. From the outset I knew that, rather than dwell on a single topic, I wanted to write a critical survey of many issues in Jewish philosophy, since I believed that such a project would help fill a need and would bring together many questions I had been pondering through the years. Despite the book's scope, there are numerous topics and much literature that had to go unmined here. Chad and Paul's support (and patience) is deeply appreciated.

Over the years I have been blessed with numerous colleagues here and abroad who have generously provided input to written material. Yitzchak Blau, Cass Fisher, Joshua Golding, Samuel Lebens, Meira Mintz, and Aaron Segal read all, or nearly all, of the draft manuscript, while Jerome Yehuda Gellman, Michael J. Harris, Warren Zev Harvey, Daniel Rynhold, Josef Stern, and Alex Sztuden read individual chapters. To the surprise of absolutely no one who knows them, all these individuals had very many useful queries and comments. Meira Mintz did her characteristically superb job of editing and indexing. David Berger, who commented on some parts when they were published originally, as well as Ephraim Kanarfogel, Charles Manekin, and Marc Shapiro, were outstanding go-to people for queries. In the notes I have expressed thanks to other correspondents on particular points. My colleague Shalom Carmy, with whom I coauthored a part of Chapter 8 for a different volume many years ago, and have discussed many topics, has been an extraordinary presence in Jewish intellectual life for well over five decades. Howard Wettstein has always provided stimulating insights. My students' comments and questions in class discussions have so enriched my thinking that remembering all those I should thank is a hopeless task.

My editor at Cambridge University Press, Beatrice Rehl, gave sage advice and was ever-attentive and supportive. Jeremy Langworthy copyedited the manuscript with great skill. Nicola Maclean and Hemapriya Eswanth shepherded the book through production with professionalism and efficiency. I thank them all.

Yeshiva University has been the ideal home for my work for over four decades. I began my career in analytic philosophy after having had an extensive Jewish education since childhood and attained rabbinic ordination. Yeshiva's ideal is to synthesize Torah with *madda*, or general culture, and with Yeshiva University as my base, I was able to integrate my involvement in analytic philosophy with Jewish philosophy, indeed with Judaism writ large. I am indebted to three individuals who served as presidents of Yeshiva during my teaching career, all outstanding leaders – Rabbi Dr. Norman Lamm, whose dynamic, mesmerizing sermons shaped my interests when I was a teenager; Richard Joel, Esq.; and Rabbi Dr. Ari Berman. I have enjoyed the support of provosts Morton Lowengrub and Selma Botman as well as deans Karen Bacon and Rebecca Cypess. My research has been generously supported by the Ronald P. Stanton Legacy Fund, in the form of the Ronald P. Stanton University Professorship, and I express my gratitude to the Legacy for facilitating many projects. Jane Galland, Executive Director of Administration at Yeshiva University's Stern College for Women, helped facilitate production of the manuscript, while Josephine Isaac, Administrative Assistant at Stern College for Women, handled numerous details of my travel and research requests. Zvi Erenyi of the Mendel Gottesman Library at the university was extremely helpful in providing requested materials.

Academics have a habit of quoting themselves. A quarter century ago, in an earlier book, I had occasion to pay tribute to my wife Chani. Indulging now in self-plagiarism, I repeat what I said there: "Personifying wisdom, understanding and empathy, she is a model of steadfast devotion and love." Since the time those words were written, Chani and I have been privileged, with God's help, to see our family grow in a way that has brought us profound, inexpressible joy. It is to her and all our progeny, and their spouses, that I dedicate this book with love and gratitude – for their very existence.

Acknowledgments

Chapter 1 includes an excerpt from "Can Halakhah Survive Negative Theology?," in *Negative Theology as Jewish Modernity*, ed. Michael Fagenblat (2017). Reprinted by permission of Indiana University Press.

Chapter 2 is a revised and expanded version of "Divine Intervention and Human Sensibilities," in *Divine Intervention and Miracles*, ed. Dan Cohn-Sherbok (1996). Reprinted by permission of Edwin Mellen Press.

Chapter 3 incorporates material from "On Constructing a Jewish Theodicy," in *The Blackwell Companion to the Problem of Evil*, ed. Justin McBrayer and Daniel Howard-Snyder (2013). Reprinted by permission of Wiley-Blackwell.

Chapter 6 is a revised version of "Is Matter All That Matters?: Judaism, Free Will and the Genetic and Neuroscientific Revolutions," in *Judaism, Science and Moral Responsibility*, ed. Yitzhak Berger and David Shatz (2005). Reprinted by permission of Rowman & Littlefield.

Chapter 8 includes an excerpt from "The Bible as a Source of Philosophical Reflection," coauthored with Shalom Carmy, in *The Routledge History of Jewish Philosophy*, ed. Daniel H. Frank and Oliver Leaman. It also includes an excerpt from "Law, Virtue, and Self-Transcendence in Jewish Thought and Practice," in *Self-Transcendence and Virtue: Perspectives from Philosophy, Psychology, and Theology*, ed. Jennifer Frey and Candace Vogler. Both reprinted by permission of Routledge.

Chapter 9 includes material from "A Jewish Perspective on Religious Diversity," in *The Oxford Handbook of Religious Diversity*, ed. Chad Meister. Reprinted by permission of Oxford University Press. It also includes material from "Theology, Morality, and Religious Diversity," in *Jewish Philosophy Past and Present: Contemporary Responses to Classical Sources*, ed. Daniel Frank and Aaron Segal (2016). Reprinted by permission of Routledge.

Stylistic Notes

1. Following a common practice, I use "R." to abbreviate "Rabbi" when it is used as an honorific. In the case of talmudic and midrashic rabbis I keep the "R." throughout all references (such as R. Akiva). For later rabbis, I generally use R. for the first reference in each chapter but only the last name thereafter.
2. When speaking of the ancient rabbis of the Talmud and Midrash, it is common to capitalize "the Rabbis" and "the Sages." The reader will thereby know that the author is referring to a specific group. The terms are treated as proper names of the group. "Rabbinic" when capitalized mid-sentence refers to traits, practices, and so on of that group. When "rabbi" and "rabbis" are used as nouns rather than titles or proper names, the words are not capitalized; and "rabbinic," when not referring to the group I mentioned, is not capitalized. (Although in many contexts it is preferable to name the Sage who makes a statement, here "the Talmud states" or "the Midrash states" is often sufficient.)
3. I capitalize Midrash, Mishnah, and Halakhah (Jewish law) when referring to the corpus as a whole, and present them without italics, but use lower case and italics when referring to individual passages or rulings (e.g., "this *mishnah* is famous," "this *midrash* is difficult," "this *halakhah* is widely observed").
4. In the case of classic medieval and modern works, especially those that have been published many times under different publishers, I usually point the reader to the text by section and chapter numbers rather than page numbers. Page numbers are given only when the reference is to a specific page or pages within the section or

chapter; the page numbers will be those of the edition listed in the bibliography.
5. When a talmudic source is not designated as being from the Babylonian Talmud (Talmud Bavli) or Jerusalem Talmud (Talmud Yerushalmi), it is from the Babylonian Talmud.
6. Sometimes an author's name is spelled differently in a cited work than it would be by my transliteration rules. Example: "Saadia Gaon (1948)" would be spelled Sa'adyah Gaon by the rules, but the cited book uses "Saadia" and another "Saadya." Likewise for Nachmanides/Naḥmanides. When the title of the work is cited, I use the spelling it uses, but otherwise I use the transliteration rules.
7. Years of birth and death are given at the first reference. Names of twentieth- to twenty-first-century philosophers generally are not given with dates.
8. Translations of the Bible are generally taken or adapted from the Jewish Publication Society translation (1999); *Tanach* (Mesorah Publications, 2011); Robert Alter's *The Hebrew Bible: A Translation with Commentary* (W. W. Norton and Company, 2018); and translations on Sefaria.org. Translations of Talmud are those of ArtScroll *Talmud Bavli* (Mesorah Publications) or of R. Adin Steinsaltz, sometimes with modification. The latter is available on Sefaria.org. Translations of midrashic passages are adapted from Sefaria.org.
9. Regarding transliterations: *Sheva na* (*mobile*) is represented by e. The letter ח is represented by ḥ. When the letter ע begins a new syllable in the middle of a word, it is preceded by a reverse apostrophe. When the letter א begins a new syllable in the middle of a word, it is preceded by a forward apostrophe. The other transliteration rules should be evident.

Introduction

The Varieties of Jewish Philosophy

While analytic philosophy of religion is a vibrant field, it generally focuses on generic forms of theism or on Christianity. This book furnishes a critical overview of issues in the philosophy of religion, but it does so by fusing the insights of analytic philosophy with the riches of Jewish tradition. The focus on Judaism makes the volume distinctive. The book is also unlike, however, many works that fall under "Jewish philosophy." For many of those works are primarily historical; and of the ones that are primarily philosophical, few utilize *analytic* philosophy to a significant degree. The book is somewhat of an outlier, then, both *qua* philosophy of religion and *qua* Jewish philosophy.

To be sure, treatments of Judaism using the tools and resources of analytic philosophy are increasing significantly, as are (albeit less so) treatments of analytic philosophy using the tools and resources of Judaism.[1]

---

[1] See esp. the essays in Lebens, Rabinowitz, and Segal (2019a) along with the website of the Association for the Philosophy of Judaism, theapj.com, which they launched. See also Frank and Segal 2016, Sztuden 2018a, and Lebens 2020b. Jerome Gellman, Joshua Golding, Josef Stern, and Howard Wettstein are among the earliest authors to apply analytic methods to Jewish philosophy. A paper by the prominent metaphysician Eli Hirsch (1999) in which he relates theories of identity he locates in the Talmud to philosophical discussions, followed by several other papers by him in the same genre (2006, 2019), served as an inspiration to some of the philosophers now at the vanguard of analytic philosophy of Judaism, even though Hirsch was not addressing theological issues. See also Lewinsohn 2006–2007. Note in addition the special issue of *Faith and Philosophy* (14[4]: 1997) edited by the prominent Christian analytic philosopher Eleonore Stump, who has contributed to Jewish philosophy as well. Books by Jewish philosophers that relate analytic philosophy to the Hebrew Bible include Katzoff 2020; Seeskin 2016; Weiss 2018. Harris 2004 analyzes both biblical and rabbinic texts on divine command theories of morality. Hilary Putnam, who ranked among the most important analytic

And I have benefited immensely from these works. However, the book's scope – the range of topics, arguments, and sources – helps broaden the discussion. For nonspecialists, the chapters attempt in the first instance to furnish accounts of central topics; yet new questions, arguments, and approaches will emerge through critical discussion, and I hope these will engage specialists and contribute to current debates.

Robert Merrihew Adams writes (1994, 5): "Progress in philosophy is more likely to consist in understanding possible alternatives than arriving at settled conclusions." With this caution in mind, I do not end up with a position on every issue I raise nor solve every problem. Rather, on occasion I sort through possibilities. To use a talmudic phrase, we often must "let the matter stand" (*teiku*). In a popular rendition, that single word is an acronym for: "Tishbi [Elijah the prophet] will answer questions and problems" – that is, the issue will be settled only in messianic times. Philosophers who face objections to their views but are not ready to surrender them (thereby making it more likely that the debate will continue to the messianic age!) might be comforted by this Yiddish expression: "No one ever died from a question."

What is distinctive about this book *qua* philosophy of religion – the stress on Judaism – is straightforward; what is distinctive about it *qua* Jewish philosophy requires substantial discussion. To place that part of my endeavor in context, I will (1) characterize the varied methods and styles with which Jewish philosophy has been approached – the diverse forms that it has assumed, particularly in recent times and (2) situate the present work's objective and methods against this background and explain its relevance.[2] While the standard notion that, in the history of the Jewish people, productivity and engagement in Jewish law (Halakhah) dwarfs productivity and engagement in philosophy, may be correct, this book will reinforce the point that, even so, philosophy, broadly defined, has a strong and robust presence in that history.[3]

---

philosophers in the twentieth and early twenty-first century, turned to Jewish philosophy late in life, but he focused on Continental Jewish philosophy, not analytic; see Putnam 2008. Numerous thinkers utilize methods that are analytic and produce creative Jewish philosophy without being called analytic philosophers.

[2] On how the term "Jewish philosophy" was born, see Westerkamp 2008; Frank 2004; Stern 2017, 229–30.

[3] On top of which – though this will not be a persistent theme in my own analyses – Jewish law is itself infused with philosophical ideas, ranging from staples of theology like God and human nature, to staples of analytic philosophy like time, causality, and identity. This thesis in reflected in myriad analyses of particular *halakhot* (laws). Louis Ginzberg (1928, 116–17) goes so far as to say that Halakhah and not Aggadah (= nonlegal rabbinic

STUDYING VERSUS DOING

My starting point is a distinction between studying philosophy and doing philosophy. To study philosophy, as I am using the term, is, first and foremost, to interpret the works of authors. Finding a good construal of a philosophical work or text requires placing it in the context of the author's thought, but it also generally involves – although it does not absolutely require – placing it in a social, historical, or biographical setting. This can mean discovering influences, identifying an author's targets, and limning a work's critical reception by contemporaries and succeeding generations. Studying can also include working on a critical edition of a text.

"Doing" philosophy, by contrast, entails *critically evaluating* ideas and arguments, seeking to determine their truth or plausibility, and often constructing an original viewpoint. Doers of philosophy ask not only "What did Aristotle teach?" but also, with greater emphasis, "Was Aristotle right?" and "Can we build a better theory using these Aristotelian ideas?"

The paradigm of doing philosophy is analytic philosophy. While often called a contemporary *movement* – the name is of twentieth century vintage – analytic philosophy carries on methods and aspirations that date back to the dawn of philosophy and pass through, to some degree, almost any philosopher who ever lived. Analytic philosophy is a culture of argumentation, criticism, and rebuttal, full of complex definitions, distinctions, examples and counterexamples, expressed in a relentless pursuit of rigor and clear thinking and in a highly dialectical dynamic.

Of course, every discipline aims at rigor and clear thinking. Even so, William James described philosophy in particular as "an *unusually stubborn* [my emphasis] attempt to think clearly." The analytic philosopher's sometimes insatiable craving for precision and coverage of even the most far-out-seeming challenges and arguments marks a similarity between

---

material, e.g., narrative, philosophy) is the *main* source for Jewish thought because "[i]t is only in the Halakhah that we find the mind and character of the Jewish people exactly and adequately expressed." Other statements of the Halakhah-theology nexus include R. Joseph B. Soloveitchik 1986, 101–2 and Soloveitchik 2002, 9–10: "it is impossible for one to philosophize about Judaism and speak about its experiential universe without having the Halakhah at his fingertips." See also Lamm 1990, 12: "There is no entry into the world of *halikhot* [by which he means Jewish thought] save through the Judaism of Halakhah." Cf. Lorberbaum 2015, ch. 3. Note 1 mentions samples of finding analytic philosophy in legal positions; cf. Segal 2019b. One case where Jewish law seems at *odds with* Jewish theology is theodicy; see Chapter 3 (the complacency argument).

analytic philosophy and Talmud study that is obvious to anyone who has toiled in both. (As Eli Hirsch writes [1999,76], talmudists are "among the most analytical people on earth.") Comedian Steven Wright quipped that a conclusion is where you are when you are too tired to keep thinking. Analytic philosophers get tired only long after most others have shut the lights. (Their critics think they should have turned in earlier.) Analytic philosophers nowadays see value also in Continental figures like Kierkegaard and Nietzsche, but approach them in an analytic way.

Warren Zev Harvey remarked in an unpublished lecture that history and philosophy are to a certain extent enemies.[4] An example of a decidedly unfriendly attitude is the acerbic comment of analytic philosopher Jonathan Bennett (1984, 16) at the beginning of his book on Spinoza's *Ethics*. Discussing *The Philosophy of Spinoza* by the celebrated historian of philosophy, Harry Wolfson, Bennett writes:

> I am sure to make mistakes because of my inattention to Spinoza's ancestry; but I will pay that price for the benefits which accrue from putting most of one's energies into philosophically interrogating Spinoza's own text. I am encouraged in this by the massive work in which Wolfson places Spinoza in a densely described medieval setting: the labour and learning are awesome, but the philosophical profit is almost nil. Such philosophically interesting readings of Spinoza as are contained in Wolfson's two volumes could all have been arrived at without delving into the medieval background.

For Bennett, even though philosophical value is not the only kind in academic work, the project of "densely describing" historical context ala Wolfson "is subject to a law of diminishing returns."

But while the enterprises of history and philosophy are in some ways antithetical,[5] you can't execute one without the other. The principle of "interpretive charity" dictates that a reader *initially* construe a text in a way that makes an author's argument as plausible and close to truth as the interpreter can make it.[6] To arrive at this determination, the interpreter often must sort through multiple construals of arguments and ask

---

[4] See also Novak 2014, 103. Harvey 2025 surveys the views of eighteen thinkers on how the history of Jewish philosophy should be written. Inter alia, he explores the difference between writing the history as pure history and writing as part of doing. Some famous creative Jewish theologians (Abraham Joshua Heschel and Emil Fackenheim come to mind) made the move from scholarly studies of historical figures to articulations of their own philosophy, while the career of theologian-and-then-historian Alexander Altmann showed the opposite trajectory.

[5] R. M. Adams 1994, 5–6 is a counterpoint to Bennett.

[6] See Davidson 1973. I am hesitant to accept the principle in this form because it often leads to *excessive* charity.

which is best – all of which is *doing* philosophy. Additionally, interpretive charity requires selecting an interpretation that coheres with other positions and arguments of the author under discussion. Gauging coherence, too, is a matter of *doing*. And so, historians of philosophy must *do* philosophy when they *study* it, even if they proceed that way without an explicit proclamation. In fact, it has been said that history of philosophy is one way of *doing* philosophy.[7] To be sure, interpretive charity must be tempered by concerns about anachronism. But sometimes, when one does philosophy *by* doing history of philosophy, the concern with anachronism is reduced, because the philosophical payoff may be what matters.

There is another point that attenuates the studying/doing distinction. The use of history of philosophy in analytic circles has grown tremendously over the past half-century. Powering this practice is the conviction that great historical figures have much to contribute to current "doing" debates, notwithstanding that those earlier philosophers functioned in a markedly different intellectual context. In fact, "Seeing the contextuality of historical voices makes us sensitive to the contextuality of our own voices – and can lead us to otherwise undetected assumptions we are making."[8]

Doers of philosophy accordingly must not consign the history of philosophy to the dustbin; they may weaken their doings if they toil as intellectual Robinson Crusoes. There are other reasons it could be irresponsible to ignore the past. For example, those who seek to move a political or religious tradition forward while genuinely regarding it as a tradition worth carrying on would need to gain accuracy about the views of the past even while being prepared to modify those views.

In sum, trying to "study" without "doing" and trying to "do" without "studying" won't work well. Yet, that said – and I've said a lot by way of qualifiers – we all recognize the difference between a primarily historical project and a primarily philosophical one.

What does all this have to do with Jewish philosophy? I reply with a bit of intellectual history.

---

[7] See Stern 2017, 255–56; R. M. Adams 1994, 5–6; Franks 2006, 395. Bernard Williams is reported to have thought that "history of philosophy is in the first instance philosophy" (Adrian Moore, quoted in P. Williams 2006, ix). Cf. Barnes 2007. In discussing the interpretation of texts to this point, I have implied a conception of meaning that many will think naïve and antiquated: The best interpretation of a text is the one that is most faithful to authorial intent. For reasons I will later explain, this is not the best framework for doing creative Jewish thought, though it is for writing history.

[8] I quote from correspondence with Josef Stern. See also P. Williams 2006, ix (quoting Adrian Moore); R. M. Adams 1994, 6.

OPPOSITE TRAJECTORIES

In academic settings, general and Jewish philosophy have displayed opposite trajectories with regard to the place of the historical. A half-century ago, analytic philosophy was criticized for forgetting its past, for ignoring the greats of its history, for only (in my sense) *doing* philosophy. In contrast, Jewish philosophy was criticized for *only* remembering its past, for only *studying*. Jewish philosophy was often assimilated into Jewish intellectual history, and works were often thin in critical discussion and creative rethinking, if not devoid of these qualities. The way Jewish philosophers were developing and presenting Jewish philosophy was markedly different from the way the Jewish philosophers they were studying themselves developed and presented philosophy.[9]

Then came changes – in both fields. As already noted, philosophers engaged or trained in analytic philosophy became far more rooted in historical texts than before. To be sure, they criticized or, alternatively, appropriated these works in the service of advancing contemporary issues, but still with close attention to textual nuances and often historical context. Even the pre-Socratics have been the subject of many treatments by analytic philosophers!

By contrast, at roughly the same time as analytic philosophers turned to past thinkers, a substantial number of Jewish philosophers headed in the opposite direction. They insisted that Jewish philosophy had to be more than studying past attempts to do Jewish philosophy (and not only because characterizing Jewish philosophy as a history of Jewish philosophy is circular).[10] Rather than merely reconstructing the beliefs and arguments of past thinkers, they aimed at constructing a creative, original Jewish philosophy. It needs emphasizing that creative Jewish philosophers by and large do not *ignore* past philosophers. To lift a phrase from Rabbi Lord Jonathan Sacks (speaking in a different context), "constructive" Jewish thinkers live *with* the past, but not *in* the past.

In the 1980s, Norbert Samuelson was the driving force behind the Academy for Jewish Philosophy, which was created to promote constructive Jewish philosophy among scholars already working in Jewish philosophy. Beginning likewise in the 1980s, R. David Hartman, head of

---

[9] My thanks to Josef Stern for this formulation.
[10] However, I think that historians of Jewish philosophy contributed far more to constructive Jewish philosophy than the standard lament has it, without that being their main agenda.

the Shalom Hartman Institute in Israel, held an annual closed conference about Jewish philosophy – mostly in discussion-group format – that attracted prominent analytic philosophers who at the time were *not* doing Jewish philosophy, and sometimes had little prior exposure to it. Among them were Sidney Morgenbesser, Hilary Putnam, Harry Frankfurt, Saul Kripke, and Amelie Rorty. Putnam later published a book on Jewish philosophy (2008), and Frankfurt eventually came to suggest (2013, 122) that the "intellectual quiescence" of philosophy might be combatted "from the direction of religion." These forums went a long way toward stimulating the "doing" of Jewish philosophy and nurturing the integration of Jewish and analytic philosophy.

The conviction propelling such activities, and now this book, has been expressed pointedly by the editors of a volume of eighteen essays devoted to using analytic philosophy to interpret Jewish texts and construct Jewish philosophy.[11] Citing Stefan Goltzberg (2011), the editors note that in earlier centuries, "Jewish philosophy had two major moments": the Arab moment – that is, the medieval period in which the biblical and rabbinic tradition came under the strong influence of Islamic philosophy (Moses Maimonides [1138–1204] was "the shining luminary" of this period) – and "the German moment," which was shaped by Immanuel Kant and G. W. F. Hegel, with some influence of Henri Bergson and others. "The third moment, should it come to take root," is "when Jewish philosophy finally starts to express itself in the vernacular of analytic philosophy."[12] This latter enterprise would not entail the acceptance of any particular doctrine, but would exemplify a certain style and "engage with a certain canon of texts, and help itself to a smorgasbord of conceptual tools and to a specific technical vocabulary." Here is how the editors assess matters:

> That Jewish philosophy has not substantially engaged with analytic philosophy heretofore has come at a steep cost. For one thing, it explains the dearth of living Jewish thought in the Anglophone academy. Jewish thought is in conversation with an intellectual tradition [different from analytic philosophy – D. S.] that is either fading or, at least, not hugely relevant in Anglophone philosophy. Accordingly, it ends up being taught primarily as intellectual history. Debates rage over interpretation of classical texts while substantial philosophical work is, all too often, placed on the backburner. (Lebens, Rabinowitz, and Segal 2019a, 2–3)

---

[11] See Lebens, Rabinowitz, and Segal 2019a.
[12] Goltzberg, 2011, 3.

A *critic* of the project, Tzvi Novick, sums up the program well before launching his criticisms:

> The study of Jewish thought, including Jewish philosophy, has traditionally occurred within Jewish studies and religious studies departments, and thus in a historicist mode. Jewish analytic philosophy, perhaps precisely because it largely eschews historical contextualization in favor of conceptual analysis, can ... allow the academic study of Judaism to escape the bounds of intellectual history, and produce "living Jewish thought," from theology to ethics. (Novick 2019, 326)[13]

While wary of historicism, Novick goes on to argue, inter alia, that sources have to be contextualized more than the analytic approach typically allows. The editors then defend their project. But regardless, Novick is on target when he articulates the analytic philosopher's aim of moving Jewish philosophy beyond the bounds of intellectual history.

This is obviously not to say that no creative, living work was done in Jewish thought until around 1980. That's quite far from the truth. Most of this powerful and engaging *oeuvre*, however, came from rabbinical schools – Hebrew Union College (Reform; e.g., Eugene Borowitz), Jewish Theological Seminary (Conservative; e.g., Abraham Joshua Heschel), Rabbi Isaac Elchanan Theological Seminary (Orthodox; e.g., Joseph Soloveitchik), Reconstructionist Rabbinical College (e.g., Arthur Green) – and from practicing rabbis, not from universities.[14] Exceptions included Emil Fackenheim, Marvin Fox, Norbert Samuelson, Steven Schwarzchild, Leo Strauss, and Michael Wyschogrod. But certainly *analytic* philosophy was not much visible in the development of Jewish thought, Fox and Samuelson notwithstanding; additionally, analytic philosophy of religion did not welcome theists.

The use of analytic philosophy brings Jewish philosophy into alignment with how contemporary Christian philosophers approach examinations of their religion. Christian analytic philosophy has flourished.[15] Over time, a fairly large cohort of Christian analytic philosophers who had originally made their marks in fields like metaphysics, epistemology, and philosophy of language (such as Robert Merrihew Adams, William Alston, and Peter Van Inwagen) published a great deal in philosophy of religion in defense of some core theistic or distinctively Christian

---

[13] See also Hughes and Wolfson 2010.
[14] Rabbi Isaac Elchanan Theological Seminary is affiliated with Yeshiva University, but its towering thinker, Rabbi Joseph Soloveitchik, was on the seminary faculty and taught Talmud almost exclusively after the mid-1950s.
[15] Cf. Seeskin 1991, 164.

positions. The Society of Christian Philosophers was founded in 1978, and its journal, *Faith and Philosophy*, in 1984.

Jewish philosophy is now moving in a parallel direction. And with the increase in pluralism and diversification in academic circles, many textbooks in philosophy of religion now represent Judaism, Islam, Buddhism, and Hinduism, if not more. As is the case in Christian philosophy, Jewish philosophy's practitioners include numerous philosophers known also, indeed often originally, for work in other areas of philosophy.[16] At least one major figure in Christian analytic philosophy, Eleonore Stump, has contributed also to Jewish philosophy, and Jewish philosophers routinely engage the writings of Christian counterparts. Several Jewish philosophers who have earned their doctorates in philosophy departments have helped move Jewish philosophy into an analytic frame and brought it to a far more conspicuous place in analytic philosophy of religion (and for that matter nonanalytic) than it occupied just a short time ago. Looking beyond analytic philosophy, we find continued contemporary interest in Franz Rosenzweig, Martin Buber, Emil Fackenheim, Emmanuel Levinas, and other Continental Jewish philosophers who dominated discussion in the past.

MODELS FOR JEWISH PHILOSOPHY

The first matter that books on Jewish philosophy tend to undertake (here, it's not the first) is the question, "What *is* Jewish philosophy?" Seeking an "essentialist"-style answer is unwise. It is more useful to talk about different tasks or projects that have been thought to fall under the rubric "Jewish philosophy." Among those that have been or might be proposed are the following:

(1) The Jewish philosopher studies a canon consisting of figures who are more or less universally classified as philosophers or theologians and who focused on the interpretation of Judaism and often its impact on general philosophic issues. These include Philo, Judah Halevi, Solomon Ibn Gabirol, Abraham Ibn Daud, Moses Maimonides, Levi Gersonides, Ḥasdai Crescas, Joseph Albo, Baruch Spinoza, Moses Mendelssohn, Nachman Krochmal, Solomon Maimon, Hermann Cohen, Franz Rosenzweig, Martin Buber, Abraham Joshua Heschel, Emmanuel Levinas, Emil Fackenheim, and Joseph B. Soloveitchik. Surely, we must avoid *defining* the canonical texts

---

[16] A list appears in an interview I gave for Tirosh-Samuelson and Hughes 2016, 214–15.

of Jewish philosophy as "texts by Jewish philosophers," just as we shouldn't define "Jewish philosophy" as "the history of Jewish philosophy"; to reiterate, that would be a circular definition. But at least in universities there is a fair amount of agreement on the canon's composition.

(2) The Jewish philosopher not only explicates, but *critically assesses* arguments and positions in the canonical texts studied. In other words: There is doing in addition to studying.

(3) The Jewish philosopher focuses on an expanded canon: the concepts and claims of Judaism, and often their impact on issues in general philosophy of religion, as found in classic received texts and other artifacts, including biblical, talmudic, midrashic, kabbalistic, liturgical, poetic, homiletical, and artistic materials not generally regarded as works of philosophy. These are explicated using philosophical categories and tools, a project that emulates the thinkers in the canon described in conception (1).

(4) The Jewish philosopher seeks to *assess* the concepts, claims, and artistic messages in such materials.

(5) The Jewish philosopher *builds upon* concepts and claims in classic Jewish texts, not only sharpening and restating the ideas therein, but also developing new ones. As a result of the inquiry, one may end up with a position that is far from where the texts began. Such creativity marks Jewish thought through the ages.[17] Often the aim is to use the Jewish sources in the "doing" of philosophy. David Novak (2014, 97–100) calls this latter goal "philosophizing *out of* Judaism." This, as distinct from developing a "philosophy of" Judaism, though these are related.

(6) The Jewish philosopher investigates resources in Judaism (often Halakhah, Jewish law) in order to engage with discussions of contemporary topics in analytic philosophy not usually related to religious thought, such as identity and action theory.[18]

(7) The Jewish philosopher seeks to address the meaning of Jewish experience in the contemporary world, especially in light of the Holocaust and the State of Israel, and explores the meaning of the contemporary world through the prism of classic Jewish texts.

---

[17] Yonatan Brafman (2018) helpfully distinguishes between (i) using Jewish philosophy to critique some Jewish views, leading to revisions of certain philosophical stances and (ii) using it to justify an ideology. He also has a third conception, Jewish philosophy as "therapy." These categories can be used to amplify mine.

[18] See, respectively, E. Hirsch 1999 and Lewinsohn 2006–2007.

(8) The Jewish philosopher applies the concepts and theses of Judaism to concrete social issues, which involves both exploring and going beyond the literature of Halakhah (Jewish law). Thus, if the issue on the table is gender, cloning, or artificial intelligence, one might cite laws, arguments, narratives, or even aphorisms found in Jewish texts, in order to clarify or adjudicate issues.[19]

Clearly, then, Jewish philosophy is a variegated field, and as Hava Tirosh-Samuelson contends (2018, 11), "inherently pluralistic and necessarily diverse."[20] The series *Library of Contemporary Jewish Philosophers* (published by Brill), which Samuelson coedited, features twenty thinkers, and their styles and areas of interest are remarkably diversified – so much so that, surveying the volumes, Warren Zev Harvey (2018) determines that "versatility" is the field's hallmark today.[21] In theory, the varying conceptions of Jewish philosophy that I presented are not mutually exclusive. They could be viewed in the way that different specializations in any field are – as constituents of a whole, reflective of a division of labor. But in practice, as Cass Fisher observes (2018, 232–35) the philosophers who are featured in the series rarely cite one another;[22] and in the field at large, emphasis on one method or style has at times been accompanied by disparagement of others.

In this volume I work mostly within conceptions (2–5). I turn now to some matters of method: selection of materials, desiderata for grounding a position, and contextualization of sources.

ON SELECTING MATERIALS

All eight conceptions of Jewish philosophy suffer from various problems that resist solution, not the least of which is how to identify "Judaism." The religion has assumed many and varied forms, and theology, literature, rituals, liturgy, music, art, and social norms have changed over time.[23] Thus, for example, neither the Bible nor the Sages characterize God as a necessary and necessarily perfect being (nor even a perfect

---

[19] See Dorff 2018.
[20] It is interesting that certain specialists in medieval Jewish philosophy, e.g. Warren Zev Harvey and Menachem Kellner, also deal with the squarely contemporary projects in (7) and/or (8).
[21] See Harvey 2018a.
[22] As Fisher further notes, this is an impediment to forming a philosophical *community*.
[23] In addition, Judaism could be a culture or nation. See Batnitzky 2011.

being *simpliciter*) in so many words, but later Jewish philosophy does. Likewise, Ḥasidism (which arose in the eighteenth century) clashes with predecessor views over a broad range of issues – metaphysical, epistemological, ethical, halakhic – and indeed aroused much controversy. Do such historical ruptures and diachronic disagreement (often a function of historical circumstance) condemn us to give up on defining Judaism and force us to embrace historicism? How do we identify the "certain texts," the canon to which Jewish philosophy appeals? Is there such a thing as medieval Jewish rationalism *simpliciter*, or kabbalistic thought simpliciter, or Orthodox, Conservative, or Reform Judaism *simpliciter*? (No.) These questions verge on another question mentioned above: Is there an indigenous Jewish philosophy at all? I have to leave these questions hanging. In doing so, I'm in good company. But a few comments are in order as to what sources are pertinent and to what degree. We need to consider what some perceive as divides or gulfs between different schools, thinkers, approaches, and personae that might provide candidates for source material.

Some who work in Jewish philosophy differentiate (as against, say, conception [3]) between philosophers and nonphilosophers such as biblical exegetes, Kabbalists, and rabbinic legal authorities. The latter group comprises figures who are "uncredentialed" – and may not even see themselves as philosophers! Does this difference matter in deciding whether the person's output qualifies as Jewish philosophy? I think not, because, apart from the question of what credentials were available long ago (did Maimonides have a Ph.D?), thinkers untrained in formal philosophy often have insightful ideas that help contemporary philosophers work through certain topics. As was argued by Mark Steiner (2000), a distinguished analytic philosopher, rabbinic figures over the centuries known as *ba'alei maḥashavah* (masters of Jewish thought) devised positions and arguments that later were propounded independently by analytic philosophers, or (so Steiner believes) were even superior to the analytic philosophers' approaches. But they would have declined the mantle "philosopher" due to its associations with alien cultures and heresy.[24] They were philosophers *malgré lui*.[25] A philosopher of science and mathematics and a Wittgenstein scholar, Steiner taught university courses on the

---

[24] To be sure, some may have covertly had exposure to philosophy, as historians have occasionally shown.

[25] However, when a philosopher criticizes ideas that were intended as inspirational homiletics and not philosophical positions, the target's purposes should be borne in mind even while the idea is subjected to critical discussion.

thought of Rabbi Israel Salanter (1810–1883), founder of the Mussar (ethical) movement. Samuel Lebens (2020b) and other analytic philosophers utilize the kabbalistic tradition to fashion their metaphysics. Frequently, philosophical views arise even when rabbis take positions on questions of Jewish *law*.[26]

Admittedly, the corpus of texts about philosophical matters found in the mammoth Talmud and Midrash of the ancient Rabbis, is unsystematic, even scattershot, and at times self-contradictory and fanciful. While the texts serve homiletic and didactic goals admirably, it has therefore been said, these sources cannot be deemed sources of bona fide philosophy. In fact, allegedly the rabbis distanced themselves from philosophy and allegedly did not care about theology.[27] Against these stereotypes, Cass Fisher (2012) has argued at great length that theology plays a central role in rabbinic thinking and that critics miss their mark.[28] Lebens (2020b) makes extensive use of Talmud and Midrash in developing a theology, while engaging with a broad range of analytic philosophers. I hope that my own use of rabbinic materials will, like Fisher's and Lebens's, negate or weaken the stereotypes. Note that some of the same criticisms that were levelled at Talmud and Midrash could be levelled at the fragments of some pre-Socratic philosophers – and yet, with the surge of analytic history of philosophy, those texts have attracted substantial attention. Also, works on biblical theology have yielded much fruit even though the Bible, too, is unsystematic and awash in ostensible contradictions.[29]

Another alleged distinction that should be questioned is that between theology and philosophy. The usual analysis is that theology works from within a given religious system, while philosophy uses universal reason – universal premises and modes of inference – and is open to the possibility of beliefs becoming falsified on the basis of universal reason. So unlike the theologian, the philosopher, in this conception, is open-minded. Analytic philosophers have tended to harbor a disparaging attitude toward theologians, especially if they associate them with Continental philosophy.

---

[26] See nn. 1 and 3.
[27] See the scholars cited in Fisher 2012, ch. 1. Cf. Harvey 1992.
[28] Fisher focuses on a midrashic Exodus commentary known as *Mekhilta de-Rabbi Yishmael*.
[29] While they contrast, Hazony 2012 and Gericke 2012 both advocate for and develop the claim that the Bible is a philosophical book. Gericke places emphasis on synthesizing this aspect with critical scholarship.

There's some truth in this simple characterization of the theology/philosophy distinction, but I think that the analysis is mostly flawed. Especially nowadays, analytic philosophers are much more conscious of their embeddedness (or, if you like, Heideggerian "thrown-ness") than they were previously. Thanks to the sharpened visibility of the analytic/continental divide, analytic philosophers are aware that they represent only one style of doing philosophy, and that their style is not the only show in town. Also, in grappling with the problem of evil, some analytic philosophers argue that theists are entitled to use particularistic premises, drawn from their religion, that will not be acceptable to atheists – that is, are not "universally" accepted.[30] Feeding philosophers' awareness of their own particularism is the knowledge that not all cultures or even individuals in a culture hold the same intuitions as analytic philosophers. (The area called experimental philosophy deals with such matters.) The notion of "universal reason" wobbles when we recognize such variability.

Further, a volume called *Jewish Philosophy for the Twenty-First Century: Personal Reflections* (Tirosh-Samuelson and Hughes 2014) demonstrates that philosophers have a personal narrative that impacts how they approach their enterprise. Note the subtitle. We can't deny our situated selves. There is no view from nowhere, in Thomas Nagel's famous phrase.[31]

Josef Stern makes a related point. The great Jewish philosophers were steeped in both Jewish texts and their philosophic milieu. Much of their work, though, is pure philosophy – language, metaphysics, epistemology – with no Jewish component. Seemingly, we have in Jewish philosophy both the particular and the universal. But it has been said that what is Jewish in Jewish philosophy isn't philosophy, and what is philosophy in Jewish philosophy isn't Jewish.[32] As against this conception, Stern writes cogently:

Compare fifth-century Athenian philosophy to twelfth-century Latin philosophy to nineteenth-century German philosophy to twenty-first-century experimental philosophy. Can any of them be described as moved by "universal concerns"? ...

---

[30] See also Chapter 3. At a certain point, I there note, the move of saying, "I am entitled to my religion's premises" becomes a tad ridiculous, because a theist could have some wild view of the universe, in which case it's not fair to say, "Well, my religion says that and therefore I can use it." You do at a certain point have to question the premises that are being used.

[31] See also Setira 2022 on the personal and the philosophical in Wittgenstein's *Tractatus*.

[32] See Roth 1999b for one expression of this idea.

So, even if Jewish philosophy has a "specific connection to a particular language or nation" ... it is not different from other philosophies propounded at any given time (Stern 2017, 252–53)

Theology has a complex structure, however. A theologian can start from a certain point dictated by the tradition, but then he or she uses what many will call universal reason (even though, based on what I just said, we know it's not *completely* universal), and then the theologian's starting point changes dramatically. For example, you might start with the idea that an *embodied* God exists, as appears from the Bible, and then reason leads you to believe in an *incorporeal* God. By the time you're done with your philosophical reasoning, you have something very different from your initial view of God, even though your view that God exists is unshaken.[33] This principle, that philosophy clarifies and refines traditional beliefs, lies at the heart of medieval Jewish rationalism. Obviously the question arises when and how to close the floodgates, when and how to draw lines, so that not just anything goes as a result of introducing reason into theology.

While it won't do to distinguish philosophy from theology by means of the distinction between universal and particular, there is another way to distinguish them. It involves *authority*. For the theologian, the received text will have authority of some sort. Even a liberal theologian such as Rudolph Bultmann, who looks to demythologize the Bible – which may not look like reinterpretation of the tradition but rather rejection – accepts and promotes the *kerygma* (message) of tradition. By contrast, the philosopher, *qua* philosopher, does not have fidelity to authority but rather fidelity to reason. Yet even that is not wholly accurate. There are certain doctrines and methods that are part of what is passed down to philosophers and carry authority. Not everything is up for grabs.

Let me say more about another alleged divide: analytic vs. Continental. Decades ago, analytic philosophers and Continental philosophers were at war. Analytic philosophers regarded Continentals as hopelessly loose and opaque, lacking in arguments and intelligibility, and themselves as rigorous and clear. Returning the favor, Continental philosophers viewed analytic philosophers as obsessive logic-choppers whose work was arid

---

[33] See Saadia Gaon, 1948, 26–28 ([or 1981, 45–46], Introduction, VI). The English title of this translation from Arabic, viz. *Book of Beliefs and Opinions*, needs explication. *Emunot* (the Hebrew translation of *amānāt*) are beliefs acquired by tradition, while *De'ot* (*i'tiqādāt*) are *reasoned* beliefs that constitute knowledge. Saʿadyah argues that *emunot* can be converted into *de'ot* by exercising reason. See Chapter 10.

and irrelevant, disconnected from the real, existentially charged problems of human life.

Over time, bridges were built. A significant number of philosophers work in both areas, or apply analytic philosophy to the study of Continentals and/or vice-versa.[34] Views often thought to be essential to Continental philosophy – antifoundationalism, antirealism, relativism, rejection of metaphysics, and other stances – are found in analytic philosophy as well.[35] And analytic philosophers have turned to existential questions, including "how do I live the good life?" (in part because of heightened study of the ancients).[36] But although the gap has been recognized to be narrower than previously thought, it has not and maybe cannot be closed entirely. Conception (7) of Jewish philosophy (seeking the meaning of Jewish existence in the contemporary world) has largely been the province of philosophers in the Continental tradition, though there have been exceptions. In my discussions I will introduce certain Continental philosophers, but briefly.

DESIDERATA

What constitutes an ideal or at least desirable position in "constructive Jewish philosophy"? It would seem that the Holy Grail (to borrow an ironic phrase) in constructive Jewish philosophy, as in constructive Christian or Islamic philosophy, is a position that can both be defended with *unassailable* logic and anchored in certain *unambiguous* texts. But creatures such as unambiguous texts and unassailable logic are at best rare, so the desiderata need to be made realistic. The rootedness of one's theory in the texts will sometimes be loose, or may presuppose one of two or more defensible readings of an ambiguous passage based on one's prior philosophical commitments, or may build upon a minority position that by definition is not as tightly tethered to the tradition as the majority view but is more plausible philosophically. So what we have in those (frequent) cases is not truly a firm, unshakable anchoring, but rather weaker, looser forms of connectivity. Furthermore, a Jewish position on an issue might be formed by fusing scattered elements in the tradition

---

[34] Among those who have published in both areas and applied analytic tools to Continental works are Robert Brandom, John Haugeland, Brian Leiter, John McDowell, and Hilary Putnam.
[35] See Trakakis 2008, Rea 2011.
[36] See also Sztuden 2018a, 229–30.

(say, biblical or midrashic texts) into an integrated whole, even when the whole has not been stated in the tradition in so many words.

A certain position might be the best one for a Jewish philosopher to adopt from a purely philosophical standpoint even though it is not as "Jewish" as other positions – and the reverse. Gabriel Citron (2017) has raised the following interesting question, which brings us back to the topic of authority: "If a self-identifyingly Jewish philosopher is grappling with the problem of suffering, do they have any reason – other things being equal – to prefer a theodicy that is part of the Jewish theological tradition over one that is not?"

Citron suggests two grounds one might offer, one "epistemic," the other "cultural." The epistemic answer is that someone committed to a tradition will find rootedness in the tradition to add epistemic value to a belief. The cultural answer is "there are values other than truth which should have some influence over the philosophical positions that one holds."

Both answers face a challenge. The tradition contains conflicting voices, and each may be sufficiently loud to merit equal epistemic and cultural weight. Also, Jewish sources celebrate the fact that a given text is subject to different readings; that's what the exegetical enterprise is about. So isn't selecting one reading *on the grounds that* it's traditional untenable? Clearly one must *privilege* certain texts and certain readings of them, perhaps on the grounds that they best harmonize with theoretical or practical reason.[37] Unless the seemingly warring texts may be harmonized with one another, often creating a new position more subtle than either, privileging is, if not inevitable, a likely necessity.

ON CONTEXTUALIZING SOURCES

As I have explained, although classic texts are cited extensively, I am "doing" Jewish philosophy much more than I am delineating its history. Points about historical influence may surface on occasion, but such background is generally not emphasized. Often a single idea has to be extracted from a large work or corpus, and there will be little and often no attempt to contextualize using biography or cultural history. This sort of self-limitation is typical for philosophers when they are writing on a topic rather than a thinker; they draw on thinkers in

---

[37] Or, when weights are unequal, on the grounds that they better reflect the majority approach.

a largely a-contextual way in order to construct a viewpoint. The big historical picture often isn't feasible to pursue, or even relevant to an author's aims.

Indeed, as Paul Franks argues (2006, 395), concerning philosophers citing earlier philosophers:

> Sometimes – as in [Saul] Kripke's description of himself as discussing "how Wittgenstein struck Kripke" rather than Wittgenstein himself, or in [Franz] Rosenzweig's assertion of an affinity between [Martin] Heidegger and the late [Hermann] Cohen – what may look like a historical claim is not meant historically at all. It is, rather, a move within contemporary philosophy.

When the aim is to do philosophy, getting texts of predecessors right sometimes is less important than having them set off bells and ignite brainstorms, making the texts fruitful.[38] (Obviously, this is not intended as a license for outlandish readings.) You might want to regard this as a reader-response or subjective-construction-of-meaning theory of interpretation. Steven Kepnes, (2021a; 2021b, 6) suggests applying to Jewish theology the hermeneutic theories of Paul Ricoeur and Hans Gadamer, of integrating older texts for the needs of the contemporary situation.

One might argue, however, that contextualization is called for in our case. After all, to the extent one claims to be doing *Jewish* philosophy, mustn't one get the meaning of past Jewish texts right? Isn't knowing what a Jewish text means *in its context* a prerequisite to claiming that its message is "Jewish"? Many Jews are interested in grounding their beliefs in an authority. Faulty reading of past ideas is no way to legitimately claim that person as one's authority.

This objection does not reflect how Jewish philosophers have typically treated antecedent texts of the tradition. Receivers of texts have been, as Aaron Hughes puts it (2012, 224), "neither delegates nor transmitters." This is what makes constructive theologians constructive. Readings are often ideologically driven, by what has been called "the search for a usable past."[39] In the case of Maimonides, the most celebrated and important of all Jewish philosophers, "Maimonides appears to be whatever the interpreter wishes him to be."[40] Interpretive charity

---

[38] Cf. Adams 1994, 5–6, who stresses the need for historical accuracy.
[39] The term, often used in intellectual history, was coined by Brooks 1918.
[40] J. Harris 2007, ix–x. See also Diamond and Hughes 2012. Diamond and Kellner 2019 focus on how rabbinic figures interpreted Maimonides in ways that suited their personal outlooks.

might license this. Notwithstanding, the search for meaning can stifle exegetical or historical accuracy.[41]

A pure historian will be bothered by historical inaccuracies; the philosopher or theologian less so. It is difficult to know what the balance should be, nor do I think there is one right answer. I wrote earlier: "Constructive theologians build their *own* philosophy, or their *own* stance on particular questions, albeit in a way that is rooted in the past." It is no small challenge to specify what "rooted in the past" means. How much fidelity must be shown? How far can constructive thinkers depart from the original on which they lean? How much eclecticism is admissible? What undergirds these questions is the assumption that fidelity matters. It does, for two reasons. First, the desire to have an authority. Second, the need to continue a tradition. But, again, there is also room for independence, and no algorithm is available to strike the right balance. In a tradition, people respond to predecessors and contemporaries, often developing their ideas or criticizing them, and only some of the time do they emerge in full agreement. Of course this is not the same as simple rejection.[42] The overarching point, however, is that Judaism prizes both accurate reception and *ḥiddush* – novelty, creativity. The tradition combines authority with autonomy in a self-conscious, explicitly endorsed way.[43]

Constructive Jewish philosophy, then, should not free itself altogether from authority and contextualization. Ignoring context (influences, contemporaneous movements) may end up misrepresenting Jewish tradition. Thus, I do not want my marginalizing contextualization to be taken as a wholesale rejection or devaluation of a historical approach. Josef Stern suggested the following in correspondence. It is not so much a matter of grounding one's beliefs in an authority as belonging to a community. To be a good citizen, you need to acknowledge others and their place

---

[41] See Diamond and Hughes 2012, esp. 1–3. Samuel Lebens (2022c) argues that what counts in doing Jewish philosophy is not what a work "really" said, but what its reception history is "in the study halls and synagogues ... I'm more interested in ideas and concepts as they have been, and continue to be, received in Jewish tradition." One difficulty with applying this approach is that there is no single way in which ideas and concepts have been received. I suppose a solution is for the philosopher to work simultaneously with the multiple ways in which the ideas and concepts were received. Another problem, though, is that if one wants to, say, make use of Maimonides's philosophy in developing one's own, the fact that the folk reception of Maimonides does not recognize what he "really" teaches in *Guide of the Perplexed*, and is quite distant from it, would – counterintuitively – not stand in the way.

[42] See also Stern 2017, 243–45.

[43] The same is true in Jewish law. See, e.g., Soloveitchik 1983.

in the community. But being a good citizen does not mean obeying or agreeing with whatever others say; one can advocate for a different view. One learns from predecessors and wants to respect them, but may – and should – aspire to grow the community and its beliefs with dynamism and imagination.

* * *

When I began this project, I knew that my initial aim was extremely broad and ambitious, and needed to be delimited. The area of Jewish philosophy has more than enough topics and texts to occupy a work of many volumes. I have chosen topics that lie within general philosophy of religion, rather than topics endemic to Judaism like the doctrine of chosenness and the revelation at Sinai, though those come up. Thus, the chapters focus on God's attributes and actions, evil, free will, the afterlife, divine commands and human morality, religious diversity, and, finally, faith and reason. Were there no considerations of space, more topics and texts would be explored; and in a differently conceived volume, I would focus on concepts distinctive to Judaism and on how Judaism can respond to challenges of the twenty-first century. Because of the scope of the work, I sometimes have to truncate arguments and objections more than in a one-topic book, while providing footnotes that readers may follow up on, especially when I write "cf." to point to a differing perspective or argument.

I hope readers will find that interactions between Judaism and analytic philosophy can yield fine fruit in both domains. But the reach of Jewish philosophy is far longer than any book like this can go.

An Overview of the Chapters

The introduction you have just read explains the various forms that Jewish philosophy has taken, as well as the methods and source materials with which it pursued in this book. Here is a sketch of what is to come.

Chapter 1 examines the concept of God. In particular, it explores what is known as Perfect Being Theology (PBT), the view that God should be conceived as a perfect being. Since the Bible does not give us an exhaustive list of divine attributes and does not clarify each attribute it does invoke, philosophers who accept PBT ascribe attributes to God based on their own conceptions of perfection, drawing on reason or intuition, combined with their interpretations of canonical texts. The chapter assesses several contrasting challenges to what I call "doing" PBT: that disputes over what attributes are perfections should reduce a believer's confidence that God has the characteristics they ascribe; that nothing can be said about God (negative theology); that in the Bible, Talmud, and Midrash, He is *not* portrayed as a perfect being; and that statements about God should be interpreted in a "nonrealist" fashion – that is, not referring to an actual being. I propose rejoinders to each challenge.

Chapter 2 deals with divine actions, homing in on the question "Where in the world is God?" That is, are events in the world caused by divine interventions or by laws of nature? If both, which dominates? While some Jewish thinkers maintain that God is the only cause of anything, and that belief in other causes is a form of paganism or idolatry, others surprisingly endorse some form of naturalism (the idea that all events in the world are brought about by natural causes [hard naturalism] or that divine interventions are very infrequent [soft naturalism]). In the chapter

I explore, through Jewish texts, several reasons that have been used to ground a theistic naturalist position.

Chapter 3 is devoted to the problem of evil – or rather, the problems of evil (plural). After sorting out a half-dozen forms of the challenge, I examine some particularly striking facets of Jewish discussions of evil, such as "protest literature," "afflictions of love," and "antitheodicy" (according to which it is wrong in some way – religious, moral, pragmatic – to engage in theodicy).

Chapter 4 is the first of three devoted to questions about human free will from a Jewish perspective. This first one is introductory. I identify three challenges to belief in free will: divine foreknowledge; divine control of history, especially significant events; and scientific determinism. (Only the second and the third will be addressed.) I then briefly show that the Bible ignores many problems about free will that philosophers obsess over. This serves as a prelude to Chapter 5, which examines a biblical episode that *does* engage one problem that analytic philosophers have addressed.

Chapter 5 illustrates how a biblical text can bring certain philosophical problems to the fore, especially when attention is paid to its literary techniques. Such techniques are used in midrashic interpretations but have been put to extensive use by contemporary biblical scholars like Robert Alter. The story in Genesis of Joseph and his brothers provides a dramatic rendition of a philosophical problem: the seeming opposition between God's control of history and human free will. I show how the problem is expressed through the narrative; discuss how a variety of midrashim and biblical exegeses address the problem; and relate the issue at hand to work by analytic philosophers like Harry Frankfurt, Thomas Flint, and Peter Van Inwagen.

Chapter 6 takes up another aspect of free will, the challenge of scientific determinism. I argue that Jewish tradition contains surprisingly many thinkers who either deny free will or (more commonly) greatly limit its scope, question its value, or embrace compatibilism (the thesis that free will and determinism are compatible). Some of what these thinkers say can be transferred to the challenge of determinism as it exists today, albeit mostly in a qualified, limited way.

Chapter 7 explores various Jewish conceptions of an afterlife: immortality of the soul; resurrection; reincarnation; and the legacy concept – that immortality consists in one's impact on the future. Working through a wide range of reasons for and against each position, I note the variety that exists in the *kinds* of reasons advanced. I then discuss whether an afterlife has value and why there is death.

Chapter 8 deals with the problem of "religion and morality," focusing on interpersonal commandments. Does God prescribe certain actions because they are right, or are they right because God prescribes them? Does God prohibit certain actions because they are wrong, or are they wrong because God prohibits them? Put another way, does Judaism believe in a standard of ethics that is correct independent of God's commands and will? The chapter begins with two biblical episodes, the *akedah* or binding of Isaac (Gen. 22) and the sin in the Garden of Eden (Gen. 3). I argue against Søren Kierkegaard's celebrated reading of the *akedah*, and then argue that Genesis as a whole supports belief in an independent standard. After that, I discuss the role that morality might play in motivation for performing interpersonal commandments and then the role it plays in the Jewish legal system.

Chapter 9 asks: How should people who regard theirs as a (or the) true religion view other religions: their truth, the salvific consequences of believing in them, their role in the world, their eschatology, and more? The chapter explores Jewish sources on these questions and devotes much space to an intriguing feature of Judaism: namely, that, in Jewish tradition, seeking converts is discouraged.

Chapter 10 argues that the distinction between fideism (faith-centered theories of religious epistemology) and rationalism (reason-centered theories) is overdrawn, because there are numerous avenues that lead to hybrid views. Surprisingly, some arguments of medieval rationalists are in fact hybrids. The chapter discusses also a Hasidic thinker and Pascal's Wager, using them to generate hybrids.

Finally, in Chapter 11, I attempt to articulate some *general* features of Jewish philosophy that emerge from our discussion of specific issues.

PART I

GOD

I

Is Perfect Being Theology an Imperfect Theology?

A third-grader is doodling in her classroom.

TEACHER: "What are you drawing?"
PUPIL: "That's God."
TEACHER: "But no one knows what God looks like!"
PUPIL: "Now they do!"

Would that it were so simple.

* * *

What is God like? Philosophical discussions of the divine nature have for millennia been marked, indeed dominated, by an approach called "Perfect Being Theology" (PBT). This view is found already in Plato.[1] Here is PBT in a nutshell:

God is a perfect being; He has all perfections, and has no imperfections.[2]

PBT is often described with the definition used by St. Anselm of Canterbury (1033–1109) when he presented the ontological argument in chapter 2 of his *Proslogion*: God is "the being than whom no greater can be conceived," or, better, "the greatest possible being."[3]

---

[1] *Republic* 380d–381c (albeit that is a polytheistic context).
[2] Among the many noteworthy works on PBT in the past three decades are Morris 1997; Rogers 2002; Wainwright 2009b; Leftow 2011; Nagasawa 2017; Speaks 2018.
[3] Speaks 2018 distinguishes "greatest possible being," "greatest conceivable being," and "greatest actual being." He rightly shows that the last of these is too weak a concept, but while the "greatest conceivable" being may not be the "greatest possible," for my purposes I can bracket his distinction between the first and the second.

Many philosophers characterize perfection using modal concepts (concepts of necessity and possibility). In their accounts, one component of PBT is that God not only has all attributes that we call perfections, but He has them *necessarily*. In other words, He doesn't *happen to have* those attributes – He possesses them by His very nature; in no possible world does He lack them.[4] A being who lacks even a single perfection is not God, and that includes a being who has all (other) perfections but has them merely contingently. For such a being lacks a perfection – the perfection of having those other perfections necessarily.

Setting aside Anselm's highly contested ontological argument, why should theists embrace PBT? Let's begin with the Hebrew Bible. While no biblical verse states outright, "God is a perfect being," numerous verses speak of or at least suggest His being perfect in particular respects, particularly goodness, power, and knowledge.

- The rock whose deeds are perfect, for all His ways are just. (Deut. 32:4)
- The way of God is perfect; the word of the Lord is pure; He is a shield to all who trust in Him. (II Sam. 22:31, Ps. 18:31)
- The teaching of the Lord is perfect, renewing life. (Ps. 19:8)
- Is anything too wondrous for the Lord? (Gen. 18:14)
- Nothing is too wondrous for you. (Jer. 32:17)
- Is anything too wondrous for Me? (Jer. 32:27)
- He turns circumstances with his stratagems, so they will do whatever He commands them. (Job 37:12).
- I know that you can do everything. (Job 42:2)
- You are strength and might, and it is your power to make anyone great and strong. (I Chronicles 29:12)
- The hidden things are for the Lord our God. (Deut. 29:28)
- If a person enters a hiding place, do I not see him? (Jer. 23:24)
- The Lord looks down from Heaven; He sees all humanity, He gazes from His dwelling place on all the earth's inhabitants. (Ps. 33: 13–14)
- Darkness is not dark for you; night is light as day. (Ps. 139:12)
- He sees to the ends of the earth, and observes everything beneath the Heavens. (Job 28:24)
- His eyes are upon a man's ways; He observes his every step. (Job 34:21–22)
- His understanding is perfect. (Job 37:16)

---

[4] I suppose this entails that, necessarily, He has the perfections necessarily.

Thus, numerous biblical texts point *in the direction of* PBT.[5] As one would expect, we do not find a modal formulation in the Bible ("God necessarily exists," or "God necessarily is X"). This element in divine perfection has its origins in philosophical reflection on the notions of perfection and modality. But other perfections, as we just saw, have some biblical support. Some philosophers argue that only a perfect being would be worthy of worship, or that only a perfect being could be a creator.[6]

In this chapter we will engage four objections to PBT through the lens of analytic and Jewish philosophy. I will not highlight the usual suspects – for example, philosophical objections to the existence of a perfect being, such as the problem of evil – but rather objections that challenge the very *project* of *doing* PBT. (I will explain the phrase "doing PBT" later.)[7] Some objections apply even if a perfect being exists, and one challenges PBT from within theistic and Jewish tradition. There are other objections to doing PBT,[8] but I have selected ones that will implicate Jewish sources most saliently.

CHALLENGE I: CAN WE IDENTIFY PERFECTIONS CORRECTLY?

In PBT, each of God's attributes logically flows from one core attribute: perfection. But *which* attributes flow from perfection? PBT supposes that human beings can form correct value judgments about what properties go into perfection and are thus "great-making." The first objection to consider is that, even if some people think they are making correct value judgments, others will have different understandings of "perfect" and think *they* can form correct value judgments. *And, says the objector, we can't know whose value judgments are correct.* Scripture is not sufficient as the basis for ascriptions, because Scripture does not itemize perfections exhaustively, and often uses figures of speech when it does "supply" them. There is a high risk of error and inaccuracy in assigning attributes to God, and one never knows when a completely accurate characterization

---

[5] "Perfect" is the translation of *tamim*. Ramal (2019, 172–73), however, believes that *tamim* is confined to ethical contexts.
[6] See, e.g., Wainwright 2009b, Wierenga 2011, and Gellman 2019.
[7] The problem of evil does come up in the chapter, but I don't simply use the argument "there's evil, so a perfect being doesn't exist" to show PBT false.
[8] See Nagasawa 2017, Speaks 2018.

of the perfect being has been found, or how close one is to the prize. So *doing* PBT will prove fruitless even if a perfect being exists.[9]

At the risk of belaboring a point by presenting a truckload of examples, I will give flesh to this objection by considering, over the next few pages, some common claims about what God is like. I am not attempting to describe each view with precision; rather, my aim is to give a bird's-eye view of controversies that beset efforts to correctly identify attributes of a perfect being. It's a quick, general survey of views and problems. Not all the points are decisive or even optimally formulated. Rather, if the image that readers form of the state of the art is that it's a mess, I will have succeeded.

Disagreements about Attributes

Depictions of a perfect God routinely begin with the three omnis: omnipotent (all-powerful), omniscient (all-knowing), and omnibenevolent (all-good). Most philosophers add to this stock of attributes. Some believe a proposition maintained through much of ancient and medieval philosophy: that God must be immutable (unchanging). This notion is generated by the Greek conception that permanence is a perfection and change an imperfection (prime examples are Plato's Forms and Aristotle's heavens), and it is reinforced among theists by the idea that what is already perfect should not be influenced (made to change) by any events outside of it. From the immutability thesis it is inferred that God must also be impassible – lacking emotion. (A being's emotional states fluctuate.) An ascription of impassibility is reinforced by other arguments, such as the argument that emotions are bodily whereas God has no body. Support is adduced as well from the prophets: "I, the Lord, am unchanging" (Malachi 3:6), and immutability is often read into the biblical verse commonly translated as "I am what I am" (Exod. 3:14).

Many thinkers ascribe what they regard as additional perfection-making properties. Most philosophers hold that God's being perfect entails that God has no beginning or end. In addition, as we noted earlier, theists have the concept of God existing necessarily and of His *necessarily* possessing all perfections. Some philosophers include omnipresence – being everywhere. Says Isaiah: "The entire world is full of

---

[9] An analogous challenge has been raised to virtue ethics: that "virtue" is too elusive a term to yield a robust sense of what character one should form. But then again, even prescriptions for action-focused ethics can be elusive.

Challenge I: Can We Identify Perfections Correctly?

His glory" (Isa. 6:3).[10] In arguments for ascribing particular perfections, verses are cited, but no suggestion should be made that we should form our concept of God based entirely and straightforwardly on Scripture. The biblical material is malleable. Instead, PBT theorists read off what God is from what perfection is – or what they think it is – and interpret biblical material to conform to that conception.

Yet – and here lies the problem I described earlier – there are theologians who quarrel with these added ascriptions, and, moreover, believe that the alleged perfections are in truth *im*perfections. Consider impassibility.[11] Besides replying to the medieval philosophers' objections, contemporary philosophers argue that, to be perfect, a being must experience what we human beings regard as the appropriate response to each situation.[12] So God not only may but must have emotions, ranging over love, anger, compassion, and more. All these emotions are significant players in the Bible and in rabbinic literature through the ages, occurring countless times. Can we really accept a theory that renders it false that God is loving as "loving" as commonly understood? Does He not love Israel, for example (Deut. 7:8)? Isn't an emotionless God incapable of caring?[13] If impassibility falls, so must immutability, assuming that immutability entails impassibility. As for the verse from Malakhi, "For I, the Lord, do not change," in context that can refer to His moral steadfastness.[14] The Exodus verse commonly translated as "I am that I am," proponents of a changing God maintain, should be translated as "I will be what I will be." The suggestion is that God will not always be the same as at previous moments. A school called Process Theology views development, change, and responsiveness as fundamental to understanding God; and Charles Hartshorne (1984) presents God's *perfection* as dipolar, as possessing both of two contrasting attributes – for example, both permanent and changing.

As for omnipresence, it courts pantheism. Pantheism eliminates the distinction between the creator and the created; and it finds dung in God

---

[10] See also *Midrash Tehillim* 24:2.
[11] As Lebens 2022b stresses, the question of impassibility is tied up with the question of whether God is a person.
[12] See Oakes 1990; see also Hasker 2004, 132–34. But cf. Stump 2019.
[13] Abraham Joshua Heschel (1962) insists on God's pathos, which he thinks prophets tap into. Todd Berman (2022) argues that biblical, rabbinic, medieval, kabbalistic, and Ḥasidic literature support Heschel as against his critic Eliezer Berkovits (1964). Heschel maintains that even anger reflects concern, but is uncomfortable with taking anger with complete literalness. See Held 2013, 147–54. Halper 2019 argues there are times that a perfect being *must* get angry.
[14] See Oakes 1990, 133.

(and vice versa) and locates God in a bathroom.¹⁵ To be sure, many Jewish thinkers, saliently Kabbalists, have accepted divine omnipresence by maintaining pan*en*theism, just as Hartshorne does. This is the view that everything is in God, but God transcends "everything" else. So God is both immanent and transcendent.¹⁶ Jewish thinkers, using biblical texts, often portray God dialectically – as both separate and omnipresent, transcendent but also immanent. ("Holy, Holy, Holy is the Lord/His glory fills the entire world" [Isa. 6:3].) Apart from the need to adjudicate between competing senses of "in" (one author catalogues thirteen senses¹⁷) this sort of metaphysics seems at best to solve only the first problem (viz. how to preserve *some* difference between created and creator) and not the second (since in panentheism, dung is in God and God is in bathrooms).¹⁸ Some object that panentheism *collapses into* pantheism. So positing that God is both transcendent and omnipresent does not cast off all objections to omnipresence. The allegedly immanentist verse, "the earth is full of His glory" may be taken as: What we see in the world evinces or manifests God's glory. Yet, some analytic Jewish philosophers (e.g., Samuel Lebens 2020b), support kabbalistic metaphysics, including a form of Ḥasidic idealism: namely, that only one mind exists – God – and the world is an idea in God's mind! This complicates discussion still more.

Even ascriptions of the three omnis have been contested (omnipotent, omniscient, and omnibenevolent). They generate major problems for theism: the problem of evil, for example (how could a being with the three omnis allow evil?), and the problem of how human beings can act freely if God is omniscient and in particular has foreknowledge. Moreover, some philosophers argue that omnibenevolence (construed as maximal benevolence) is not a perfection because it is not even a coherent attribute. For

---

[15] Wurzburger 1962 argues that a distinction crucial to Jewish law, that between sacred and profane, collapses in monistic (including panentheistic) views. An alternative is that categories like "sacred," "holy," and "profane" are best construed not ontologically, as assertions about the existence of certain properties, but as assertions about "institutional status" and what behaviors are proper as regards certain objects, such as the Temple. See Kellner 2006a, chs. 3–4, and Leibowitz 1992, esp. 24–26, 46–47. Panentheism makes it hard to grasp *why* certain behaviors are prescribed or proscribed vis-à-vis certain objects and places – isn't God everywhere?

[16] On classical and contemporary panentheism – including its recent revival – see Meister 2017.

[17] Phillip Clayton, cited by Meister 2017.

[18] On Jewish approaches to the problems that dung poses for theism, see Lebens 2021a. On the concept's significance in Maimonides, see Stern 2013, ch. 9.

Challenge I: Can We Identify Perfections Correctly? 33

benevolence has no upper limit; we cannot say that someone is *maximally* benevolent.[19] As for omnipotence, Peter Geach rejects the notion that God is omnipotent in the sense of "God can do everything," on the grounds that God cannot do certain acts – sin, for example, or commit suicide.[20] Geach *replaces* "omnipotent" with "almighty" – having power over all things. It is difficult to see, in general, why power per se (as in omnipotence) is a perfection all by its lonesome; is being able to lift a valise full of rocks a manifestation of a perfection?

Feminist theology poses the following challenge: The classic attributes – power (omnipotence) being a prime example – appear androcentric.[21] In response, Peter Byrne (1995) and Jerome Gellman (2019, 2021a) argue that omnipotence per se is not a perfection, but if a being – male or female – uses its power for the good, its power is a perfection. Gellman, basing himself on considerations about loving God, argues that God does not have to be omnipotent or omniscient *überhaupt*, but rather must possess whatever power and knowledge are needed to express His good character. Some versions of Process Theism and Open Theism limit God's omnipotence, opting to say He "persuades" rather than controls.[22]

In most cases mentioned so far, the argument against ascribing attributes X, Y, Z to God is that a perfect being would not have X, Y, Z because X, Y, Z entail imperfection. In some cases, though, as I noted earlier, the notion that X, Y, or Z should not be ascribed to God has less to do with judgments about what attributes are part of perfection and more to do with what attributes best cohere with other claims of theism. John Stuart Mill (2009, 127) argued that dropping the attribute of omnipotence rescues theists from the problem of evil; Levi Gersonides (1288–1344) resolves the ostensible conflict between divine foreknowledge and human free will by denying that God has foreknowledge of free human actions. God's perfection in knowledge, maintains Gersonides, does not entail foreknowledge of free human actions – because in those cases there is not yet a truth of the matter to know. Rather, "God is omniscient" entails only "God knows *all that is knowable.*" "Future

---

[19] See, e. g., Rowe 2004 and cf. Hasker 2004, 170–73, 180–81, 202–6.
[20] Geach 1973. The famous question of whether God can create a stone that He cannot lift – if He can He is not omnipotent, and if He can't He's not omnipotent either – is meant to call into question the coherence of the concept of omnipotence. On Jewish views of omnipotence, see Rubin 2016.
[21] See, e.g., P. A. Johnson 1992.
[22] On Process Theology, see Cobb and Griffin 1976; Pinnock 1994; Haught 1995, 60–69; Lubarsky and Griffin 1996; Hasker 2004.

contingents" – future-tensed statements about what free choices someone will make – are neither true nor false, hence not knowable.[23] One author, a nontheist, attempts to show that God, because of His omniscience, cannot forgive sin and therefore is imperfect.[24] So omniscience leads to another untoward theological result. But, of course, in all the cases described, some people have rebutted the relevant arguments.

A somewhat more complex example involves the attribute of being outside of time. In isolation, many people would not think that being "outside of time" is a perfection. Often, however, beginning with Boethius, God's being outside of time has been proposed as a solution to the apparent conflict between divine foreknowledge and human free will, even without stating that being outside of time can be identified as a perfection independently of the free will problem that it is introduced to solve. Even so, if one assumes that every property God has is a perfection (a questionable claim, to be sure[25]), then this added claim would follow from the thesis that God is outside of time. Hence being outside of time may be added to the roster of perfections. Being outside of time anyway seems to be a corollary of being immutable, which for some *is* a perfection, since a being located in time changes.

Here, though, we encounter – here we go again! – an argument that this so-called perfection is in truth an imperfection. For a being who is outside of time is unable to distinguish three categories of events: which events are going on *now*, which events are in the past, and which events *will* transpire. Such ignorance would render God unable to intervene at the right time (because He is not aware of what is happening *now*). This inability is clearly an imperfection. How could He know what is going on now – whether the Jews are in bondage in Egypt or living securely? Praying for one's needs would not make sense, since the pray-er asks God to intervene at a particular time, and God doesn't know what is going on *now*.[26]

---

[23] See Gersonides, 1987, Books 3 and 4, esp. 3:4–6. See also Cahn 1967.
[24] Minas 1975.
[25] The reason is that the claim in question needs to be distinguished from the earlier claim that every attribute God has flows from perfection. As Aaron Segal pointed out in correspondence, it is in fact problematic because trivial properties and disjunctive properties (especially disjunctions of perfections and imperfections) are not perfections. The disjunctive ones flow from perfection.
[26] See Kretzmann 1966; Wolterstorff 1982. A problem that God being outside of time incurs has been put this way: "Can God know what time it is?" (See Kretzmann 1966.) Cf., however, Stump 2016, who tries to reconcile the God of the Bible and the God of the philosophers.

Challenge I: Can We Identify Perfections Correctly?

One attribute that was central and impactful in medieval thought was unity.[27] To say "The Lord is one" means, for many medieval philosophers, not just that there is only one true god, and not just that there is no other being possessing His attributes, but also that He is metaphysically one, possessing no parts.[28] This is how Maimonides understood the verse, "Hear, O Israel, the Lord is our God, the Lord is one" (Deut. 6:4). Unity figured in his arguments against anthropomorphism, the view that God has a body: All bodies are divisible, whereas God, being "one," is not divisible.[29] Because of His unity, God surely could not possess multiple attributes; all His attributes would have to be one attribute. Some theologians prefer to say that God is identical with His attributes (which are all one). Maimonides went further. He inferred from God's being "one" that He cannot possess attributes *at all*, because being composed of attributes – even a mere single attribute – makes God a composite entity.

Why must unity be ascribed to God? One argument is that if God were compound, there would have to be a cause of His composition, but there can't be a cause of His composition, because God is the creator of all. But some thinkers have rejected the ascription (and the argument).[30] In fact, there is an air of self-contradiction here, as God, for Maimonides, purportedly has no attributes, but He has unity. And can He even exist if He has no properties?

Let's see where we are. Identifying God's perfections is a mess. Initially, it seemed that reliance on one's own reason and/or intuitions, and, in particular, one's value judgments, gives good grounds for making certain ascriptions of (perfection-making) attributes and not others. Yet the specter of inaccuracy has reared its head, due to the difficulty of finding one view we can call that of correct reason. Disputes about what attributes are perfections abound. To avoid error, it may seem theologically safest to limit ascriptions to attributes spelled out in the Bible. But, as we have seen, it isn't always clear what the relevant biblical terms mean, so we are left with correct words and a sense of options, which may not be enough. Clearly, then, it is naïve to think that PBT is clean and neat.

---

[27] The common term today is simplicity; medievals spoke of unity. I'm not sure the terms are synonyms, but that isn't significant here. For extensive discussion of simplicity, see Vallicella 2010.

[28] Maimonides, *Mishneh Torah*, Laws of the Foundations of the Torah 1:7.

[29] Some medieval Jews accepted anthropomorphism, but the nature of this anthropomorphism is at least often qualified; e.g., God can make himself embodied, but is not embodied. See Kanarfogel 2008.

[30] Cf. Lebens 2020b, 8–10.

Which attributes to assign to God is no straightforward matter even if we embrace PBT. Throw in that we should exemplify the virtue of humility, and our limitations are even clearer.

Is There a Problem Here?

There's a lot of dispute – so what? Does uncertainty per se generate an *objection*, a reason for not holding to the heart of PBT, the ontological claim that God is perfect? No: It seems to be an objection to *doing* PBT – that is, to working the theory out in detail – not to believing the statement *God is perfect*. Notice, however, that it is not *only* adherents of PBT who have to worry about making a wrong choice of attributes. People who think God is imperfect also must figure out what attributes to assign and probably want to do so in a way that makes God at least a great Being, even if not a perfect one. So why would getting the attributes right be a task exclusively for doing PBT?

Well, maybe it isn't – maybe the challenge or objection indeed applies to Imperfect Being Theology (IBT) as well. Or maybe it does not apply – for the following reason. PBT wields a single criterion for ascribing attributes, and it is uncertainty about how to apply this single criterion that led to uncertainty about which attributes to ascribe. Imperfect-being theology (IBT) needs a criterion for assigning attributes, one other than *attributes that perfect beings would have*. It isn't clear whether that alternative criterion, whatever it is, runs afoul of the objection from uncertainty. If it doesn't, PBT is in a worse position than IBT.

I suspect that IBT *would* be faced by the problem of uncertainty. Saying God is "*almost* perfect" will not cut it as a criterion. If, like John Stuart Mill and R. Harold Kushner (2004), one declares that since evil exists, God is not perfect, how does one choose the respect in which God is not perfect (power, goodness, knowledge)? Might He lack all? Proponents of an imperfect-God thesis are left having to concede that while there is some lack in God, what is lacking is not known.

So, all theologies, whether PBT or IBT, face the challenge of choosing attributes. Notwithstanding, I will frame the ensuing discussion in terms of PBT and explore whether the existence of the "challenging task" turns into an objection to *doing* PBT. The prospect that because of epistemological worries one can't "do" PBT is rather disconcerting. It shuts down the most prominent enterprise in theistic analytic philosophy of religion.

The following rebuttal to the epistemological challenge comes to mind. Lots of philosophical topics, maybe even the overwhelming majority, are

Challenge I: Can We Identify Perfections Correctly? 37

not clean and neat. Disputes abound in metaphysics, ethics, aesthetics, and possibly every other branch of philosophy. *Most*, maybe nearly all, philosophical topics elicit disagreement. (Science displays polarities of opinion too, but over time scientific agreement is easier to achieve than in the case of philosophy.) Why should we worry about the propriety of "doing" PBT just because there are disputes in theology? Why does it *matter* that there are all these controversies about what attributes God possesses? After all, in each case philosophers and theologians will take a position based on what seems right and logical to them, just as in any other disputed philosophical matter. You pay your money and you take your choice.

Well, for one thing, according to a view currently gaining much traction in epistemology, any philosopher who believes a particular philosophical thesis is likely to confront disagreement on the part of other philosophers of equal intelligence and knowledge of arguments. That disagreement generates "higher order evidence" for each opinion-holder that he or she is mistaken.[31] Let's lay this argument aside, though, because, as Pyrrhonian skeptics would note here, skepticism that arises from the fact of disagreement would not put theism and PBT in a worse position than other views in philosophy or any other discipline.

So: *Is* mistake a problem? One argument for the importance of getting things right is that there is an imperative of *imitatio Dei* – emulating God.[32] Without a firm grip on the attributes of God, we cannot fulfill this imperative. But as we try to apply this principle to specific disputes about attributes, it becomes bizarre. Should I be omnipotent or limited in power? Should I be inside of time or outside? Should I be metaphysically one or possess multiplicity? Clearly, these questions are ridiculous. And certainly we can't fulfill "be perfect like God is." It won't do to reconstrue *imitatio Dei* as *striving* to have God's attributes, because even if striving for something that one knows one cannot attain is not irrational, matters get absurd when we think of striving to become immutable, outside of time, and so on.

Clearly, then, a theist is not obliged to apply *imitatio Dei* to *every* attribute. In fact, the Midrash mentions several attributes of God that should *not* be emulated – zealotry, vengefulness, pride and trickery.[33]

---

[31] See the essays in Machuca 2013.
[32] According to Rabbinic interpretations, key biblical sources for this imperative are Deut. 8:6, 10:12, 11:22, 13:5, 20:9 as well as (on one view) Exod. 15:2.
[33] *Midrash ha-Gadol* to Gen. 37:1. In *Guide of the Perplexed* 1:54 (1963, 126–27), however, Maimonides justifies a ruler imitating God's "harsh" traits, which other theories

In illustrating the imperative of *imitatio Dei*, the Rabbis of the Talmud and Midrash cite ethical deeds and ethical characteristics.[34] Getting other attributes wrong does not impede fulfilling the directive. To be sure, there will be disagreement over how to *apply* compassion and graciousness (Exod. 34:6) to concrete situations – when would we be having *excessive* compassion, for example. But the word for the trait may have an agreed-upon meaning. Even thinkers like Maimonides who believe that God has no emotions explicate the seemingly psychological attributes in Exodus 34:6–7 in terms of the actions God performs (His effects in the world), and, for those who adopt that thesis, hopefully there is enough agreement for the practice of *imitatio Dei*.

If making errors in our theology will not render *imitatio Dei* unfulfillable because we can imitate moral attributes, why *would* getting *other* attributes wrong be a problem? Indeed, to refuse to have any theology at all – say, to suspend belief because of fear of error – carries a large cost. Aaron Segal (2012) points out (190):

> It is quite plausible, if not platitudinous, that a religious person will, of necessity, deploy *some* concept of God and possess *some* theological beliefs or stances, even if they are a bit inchoate or largely "negative" [i.e., they say what God is not]. How can one meaningfully pray or repent or accept the yoke of Heaven when reciting *keri'at Shema* [Deut. 6:4–9] if one has absolutely no conception of God? And if one cannot, then adopting no theology, rather than risking acceptance of a wrong one, is simply not possible for a religious person.

Even Maimonides, who introduced thirteen principles of faith, the denial of any of which – and even nonaffirmation of any – constitutes heresy and incurs severe punishment,[35] was willing to let the masses believe *some*

---

of *imitato Dei* say humans should not emulate. He explains that, *in imitation of God*, the ruler must act (notably, administer punishment) without emotion. (In his legal code, however, Maimonides presents *imitatio Dei* as requiring emotions. See *Mishneh Torah*, Laws of Character Traits *(De 'ot)*, ch. 1. See H. Davidson 1973.)

Making exceptions such as "vengeful" threatens to effectively make the proper formulation vacuous: "Imitate those attributes and actions of God that you should imitate." Roth 1999c maintains that *imitatio Dei* is merely an embellishment to ethics, not a genuine ethical principle.

[34] Sotah 14a (on imitating deeds); *Mekhilta de-Rabbi Shimon bar Yohai, Be-shalah* 3 and *Sifrei* to Deut. 11:22 (on imitating character traits). If someone analyzes prima facie attributions of emotion as attributions of actions, as Maimonides does, the distinction collapses. Maimonides (Book of Commandments [#8]) cites the *Sifrei* source and not *Mekhilta* because the former's language does not suggest anthropopathism. Instead, the text says, "Just as the Holy One, Blessed Be He, is *called* compassionate, you too *be* compassionate."

[35] In the introduction to his commentary on the Mishnah in *Sanhedrin* 10:1.

false things about God.³⁶ They need *some* concept, and, per Segal, as human beings they need certain practices, like prayer and repentance, as well as motivation to follow the commandments. The belief in immediate direct divine intervention in response to prayer, and the belief that God literally gets angry, states Maimonides, are "necessary" to produce certain conduct or character though not ipso facto "correct."³⁷ For Maimonides, as we've seen, the very belief that God possesses attributes is wrong! Notwithstanding, Maimonides let the masses live with their mistakes.

Maimonides did expect much correctness, however; more to the point, the desire for correctness may gnaw, nurturing fear of error. To incorrectly understand God's nature strikes us as more consequential than holding incorrect views on the mind–body problem, universals, or the existence of mind-independent moral properties. But again, why? Should one truly eschew reflection on the nature of a perfect being for fear of making a doxastic mistake?³⁸

One may be worried about theological error because the Abrahamic religions are concerned with identifying heresy (a point Segal brings up and was just alluded to). It may be thought that one who has a mistaken concept of God (or no concept) will have no entry to the next world. The off-the-cuff answer to this worry is that (a) not all false beliefs are heretical beliefs and (b) religious authorities come to the rescue here – they inform us about what constitutes heresy. Maimonides and later medieval philosophers created lists of dogmas.³⁹ In R. Solomon Schechter's phrase, "the great dogma of dogmalessness," at times ascribed to Judaism by Moses Mendelssohn, is false.⁴⁰ Having a list of attributes obviates worrying about heresy. Further, a religion could retain the notion of heresy but define the parameters of proper belief broadly within those parameters. Fear of heresy need not restrain one from assigning attributes so long as they fall within a certain range, a range dictated by authority.

---

³⁶ E.g., *Guide of the Perplexed* 1:35. Cf. 1:36.
³⁷ See, e.g., Maimonides 1963, 512–514 (*Guide of the Perplexed* 3:28). "Useful" beliefs, to be sure, might be true, but the masses do not *properly* understand the "useful" true statement that God gets angry.
³⁸ On "the wrong god," see Geach 1994, Halbertal and Margalit 1992, Sullivan 2012.
³⁹ See Jacobs 1964; Kellner 2004; Shapiro 2011. Maimonides's setting down dogmas concerning divine attributes appears at odds with his negative theology, but this fact should not obscure the general point about the usefulness of dogmas with regard to the question at hand.
⁴⁰ See Schechter 1888, 48. Cf. n. 44 below on Mendelssohn. Some did deny that dogmas should be identified. See Shapiro 2011, 30ff. On dogma in medieval Judaism see Kellner 2004, also Kellner 1999, 2006b, passim.

A few other mitigating points should be kept in mind. First, there is a difference between condemning a sin and condemning a sinner. Perhaps *inadvertent* heretical belief (*shogeg*) does not make the holder of the heretical belief a heretic. This was not Maimonides's view, nor that of Isaac Abravanel (1437–1508), but it was held by others who set out principles of faith, such as Shimon ben Tzemaḥ Duran (1361–1444) (*Ohev Mishpat*, 9).[41] Also, one hopes that God understands the difficulties in identifying truths about Him despite misleading texts, as well as the pressures that social circumstances exert on belief, and is lenient in imposing admissions requirements for post-mortem bliss.[42] As Marc Shapiro (2011) shows, for almost all of Maimonides's thirteen principles, there were rabbis before and after who did not believe that principle, and that includes anthropomorphists and those who did not embrace divine unity. It seems discomfiting to grant that all were heretics because of Maimonides's refusal to recognize the excuse of *shogeg*. (Shapiro himself, however, believes in the importance of dogmas [2011, 30–31].)[43]

Mention of heresy invites a more radical question: Why is it important to determine what constitutes heresy? Much of modern thought, animated by the ideals of free thought, tolerance, and pluralism, believes that there is no good answer and therefore relegates questions of heresy to, at best, the sidelines, maybe even regarding heresy-hunting as offensive. Echoing Moses Mendelssohn's alleged position in *Jerusalem* that Judaism has no dogmas,[44] which was the target of Schechter's quip about "the great dogma of dogmalessness," some authors have assailed

---

[41] See Kellner 2004, 207–13; Shapiro 2011, 8–13. Abravanel argued (*Rosh Amanah*, 12) that if inadvertent heresy (Kellner's phrase) does not impede salvation, we get the seemingly absurd result that someone who is inadvertently mistaken about every faith principle could still achieve salvation. On involuntary unbelief, see R. M. Adams 1985.

[42] See also R. Abraham ben David's comment to Repentance 3:7. Given Maimonides's rejection of *shogeg* as a defense, it is somewhat anomalous that he excuses descendants of Karaites because they are like "captured children" influenced by upbringing. (See *Mishneh Torah*, Laws of Rebels 3:3 and discussion in Kellner 1999, 82–86.)

[43] On some views, only a public proclamation of a heretical belief qualifies as heresy, because a *mishnah* that identifies heresies (*Sanhedrin* 10:1), and a Maimonidean text in *Mishneh Torah* (Laws of Repentance 3:7) stipulate only that "one who *says* X" forfeits a share in the World-to-Come, not "one who *believes* X." Based on (a) linguistic grounds, (b) texts that prohibit having certain thoughts, and (c) philosophical grounds, I disagree. See also Shapiro 2011, 13.

The *mishnah* does not speak of understandings of God, but Maimonides does. See Kellner 2006b, 33–38; Shapiro 2011, 29n150.

[44] I say "alleged position" because Mendelssohn held that universal beliefs grounded in reason are mandated beliefs. See Shapiro 2011, 31 (esp. n. 155) and M. Gottlieb 2020.

the notion of mandating Jewish belief, especially but not only when heresy is met with coercion and punishment. Besides considerations about autonomy, there is the fact that morally excellent people might hold heretical beliefs but seem undeserving of condemnation.[45] The attack on the notion of heresy is crystallized in the title of a book by Menachem Kellner (2006b): *Must a Jew Believe Anything?*, which is directed mostly at Orthodox Judaism. But it is hard to see how any denomination of Judaism (or of any religion) can define itself without itemizing principles that demarcate its *central* beliefs. The fear of being deemed a heretic is not so much fear of divine punishment, but, as Kellner indicates, fear of not being a member in good standing in a community of which one wants to be a part; and criteria for *membership* are by their nature limiting. Yet, while beliefs are part of what is needed to form community, a community must distinguish central from peripheral (or relatively peripheral) beliefs, and this reduces concerns over theological error.

Segal notes, however, that, especially for Maimonides (and here I add: despite Maimonides granting the leeway for error described earlier), some misrepresentations are not just inaccuracies – they fall under the prohibition of *avodah zarah*. Though commonly translated "idolatry," *avodah zarah* literally means foreign *worship*, worship of something other than God.[46] The usual association is that the prohibition applies to *behavioral* worship (as in bowing to an idol). But Maimonides (with little precedent) applied the category also to holding certain false *beliefs*. Now, if contemplation of God is part of proper worship, and God has attributes $A_1 \ldots A_n$, but in one's conception of God, God does not have *all* these attributes, and a fortiori if He has *some* of their negations, how can one be worshipping God?[47] (This has been called conceptual idolatry.[48]) In fact, how could one's false beliefs even be *about* Him? After all, *that* God does not exist.[49]

Religious people might be fearful of getting things wrong because they would be "depriving" God of a perfection. (Technically, of course, one can't "deprive" God of anything, hence the scare quotes – what I mean is: They would be failing to understand and appreciate the full scope of His

---

[45] Stump 1999. She defends the notion of heresy while opposing harsh treatment of heretics and coercion.
[46] As stressed by Berger 2010d, 381–82. See further Goldschmidt 2022.
[47] Segal 2012–2013, 191, n. 12. See also Fagenblat 2017b, 8–9.
[48] See W. Wood 2021, part III.
[49] See also M. Steiner 2017, 55–56. Maimonides (*Guide of the Perplexed* 1:50) implies that most people who affirm God's existence don't know what they are talking about.

perfection.) If they suspend judgment about certain attributes, then not only might they incur the problems Segal points out (depending which attributes are in doubt) they may worry because such suspension likewise "deprives" God. In order to turn back the objection to PBT based on unclarity about what perfection entails, a proponent of PBT must insist that one should take a risk, for assigning no attributes to God at all is more risky than believing based on one's own understanding. This means denying the following principle: It is worse to believe in (and worship) the wrong God than to not believe in God at all.[50] This denial may be rooted, as R. Abraham Isaac Kook suggested (1983, 32), in the recognition that false, even idolatrous, religions have *some* good characteristics – they might stir passion about their deity and motivate people to worship that deity. Because of the gravity that Judaism, especially Maimonides, attaches to the sin of conceptual *avodah zarah*, having a theology carries a substantial risk, but for all that, taking the risk makes sense.

There may be another remedy. To wit: The "wrong God" problem arises only if we assume that the referent of "God" for a particular speaker is determined by the properties a speaker attributes to the putative bearer of the name. The name is shorthand for a description. If, by contrast, one adopts the causal theory of proper names made famous by Saul Kripke (1980), the speaker might successfully refer to God as long as the name was passed down by someone who even long ago had an encounter with God and named the entity then encountered, calling that entity "God."[51] However, William Alston (1989b) Jerome Gellman (1993), Meghan Sullivan (2012), and Hugh Burling (2019) have discussed whether a causal theory of God-reference should be accepted, rejected, or integrated with descriptive constraints, given concerns about getting God's attributes right and the possibility of reference drift.[52] It seems at the least odd to declare that the attributes one assigns to God are irrelevant to determining reference. But would "the God worshipped by Abraham, Isaac, and Jacob" suffice for that? What about "the perfect being," or "the being worthy of worship"? How to synthesize causal and descriptive theories of reference in the case of God requires (and is receiving) much scrutiny.[53]

---

[50] Yitzchak Blau pointed me to a passage by R. Tzadok Ha-Kohen (*Tzidkat ha-Tzaddik*, 259) stating that one who worships *avodah zarah* is more likely to come to believe in God than is an atheist.
[51] See also W. Wood, 2021, ch. 7.
[52] See also Fisher 2026, chs. 1, 7.
[53] Johnston 2009 thinks that "God" functions as a description or title and not as a Kripkean proper name.

While in practice, disputes about what God is are settled by religious authorities, they follow *their own* reason and intuitions, and their own reading of Scripture and tradition, or follow their own authorities. The questions I have asked may be asked about all these choices by authorities. Further, the authorities disagree with one another. Must each regard some others as heretics or violaters of the prohibition of *avodah zarah*? And where would this leave the general public, many of whom are theologically illiterate? Yet Maimonides's stature precludes rejecting his view that having certain beliefs of the form "God is P" constitutes foreign worship. It appears, then, that there should be religious anxiety in embracing a particular theology, anxiety occasioned by risk of error. Note that besides the chance of being wrong (here I'll reiterate), one may be assigning an *im*perfection to God and not giving God his due. But to have religious belief and religious practice one must deem the risk worth taking, especially if (a) some mandatory beliefs are codified, relieving adherents of the burden of identifying all attributes correctly and (b) God tolerates human error.[54] If this approach is convincing, then doing PBT survives the objection based on fear of mistake – although maintaining this position may itself induce fear of mistake, the mistake of being too lenient with oneself.

FURTHER CHALLENGES TO DOING PBT

Thus far we have addressed Challenge I to PBT, the challenge of identifying perfections. Challenges II and III come at us from opposite directions.

Challenge II: God is utterly transcendent and indescribable. We can say nothing about Him, or at least nothing beyond that He is transcendent and indescribable. God does not even *have* attributes. So doing PBT is fruitless and pointless.

In contrast to Challenge II is Challenge III:

Challenge III: The Bible, Midrash, and Talmud portray God in the most specific of terms. God is depicted highly concretely: as embodied, emotional, mutable, zealous, and fallible. He regrets doing certain things, regarding them as mistakes. He is even corporeal, on a literal reading. Thus, PBT flies in the face of biblical and rabbinic tradition, and the latter is authoritative. God (according to III) is

---

[54] We will see in Chapter 9 that some theories of religious diversity (e.g., those of John Hick and R. Abraham Isaac Kook) affirm that beliefs will vary because they are historically conditioned responses to the divine.

*im*perfect. For advocates of Challenge III, the philosophers replaced the God of the Bible and the God of the Rabbis with an abstract God of their own making, creating a historical rupture with biblical and rabbinic understandings.

There are manifest differences between these challenges. (a) Most obviously, II views God as transcendent, while III views Him as, to put it loosely, in the world, and as describable in terms we use for everyday objects, including human beings. Furthermore, (b) Challenge II does not in the first instance challenge the "perfection" piece of PBT, but rather the "theology" piece; it denies altogether that we can describe God (and hence might be read as denying that we can describe Him as *either* perfect or imperfect). Challenge III, by contrast, sees the Bible as having a theology and does not object to describing God. What it challenges is the "perfect" piece of PBT, for it denies that perfection characterizes the biblical God. Finally, (c) to speak historically, Challenge II has ancient roots in Neoplatonism and ample medieval endorsement, although it has been revived in the modern period – so much so, that negative theology has been deemed theological orthodoxy in Jewish thought today, "a shibboleth for Jewish thought" (Fagenblat 2017b, 4). Challenge III has primarily a contemporary pedigree.

Finally, there will be a fourth challenge, antirealism:

Challenge IV: PBT falsely assumes that statements that seem to refer to a being (God) are statements asserting the existence of an extramental reality. The statements are rather expressions of certain commitments, attitudes, etc.

Challenge IV is incompatible with Challenge I and Challenge III. Whether it is compatible with Challenge II depends on whether positing *human inability* to assign attributes to God renders the term "God" nonreferential (but not in the same way as Challenge IV). Also, Challenge IV is not so much a direct challenge to PBT as a position that needs to be taken if one does not accept belief in God at all but wants to in some way make religious statements worth preserving.

CHALLENGE II: APOPHATICISM AND NEGATIVE THEOLOGY – CAN WE SPEAK ABOUT GOD AT ALL?

The word "apophatic" is derived from a Greek word meaning "unsaying." Plotinus (205–70), founder of the mystical school Neoplatonism, posited a hierarchy of being in which "the One" occupies the highest rung, and lower rungs emanate from the One. The One cannot be described; it is beyond intellect and beyond being.

Challenge II: Apophaticism and Negative Theology 45

God's statement to Moses, "My face cannot be seen" (Exod. 33:20), has become for Jewish thinkers an iconic expression of God's unknowability. The biblical idea that God appears in a cloud has likewise been construed as an image for unknowability.[55] The statement "No one can see my face and live" (Exod. 33:20) is often taken as referring to the *dangers* of seeking knowledge of God. The quest can be a destructive force.[56]

Apophatic theology and divine ineffability attracted strange bedfellows: The approach reverberated among *both* Maimonideans and Kabbalists. Now, it is one thing to say, as in Challenge I, that we do not know which attributes to assign to God; it is another to say that no descriptions apply to God at all, and that God has no affirmative attributes. To be clear, advocates of apophaticism may not intend to deny the truth of PBT. They may consider being "beyond saying" a perfection. But insofar as apophaticism does not assign perfection to any specific attributes and denies that God's perfection entails having these-or-those attributes, it precludes doing PBT in the robust, attribute-specific way in which it is usually done, just as in the case of challenge I.[57] For that reason I am taking apophaticism as a challenge to doing PBT.

No sooner is this apothatic thesis uttered than a charge of incoherence springs up. By saying that God is indescribable, are we not describing Him?[58] If it will be said that "indescribable" is a purely formal property, that it is about language and does not express a property *of God*, it can be replied that the *reason* given by apophatic theologians for maintaining that God is indescribable is that He is transcendent (or infinite, or ultimate, or what-have-you) – and transcendence is not a formal property. Nor can it be reduced to one; if it were to be so reduced, the stated reason for saying that God is indescribable (viz. He is transcendent) would vanish. So the problem of incoherence remains even if the property of being indescribable does not per se lead to incoherence. And what about

---

[55] See Maimonides, *Guide of the Perplexed* 3:9.
[56] See Seeskin 2017. Elsewhere, however, God is said to speak to Moses "mouth to mouth" and "in a [clear] vision" (Num. 12:8). In Isaiah (40:18), God asks "To whom can you compare me and I am like?" but this need not imply apophatic theology.
[57] Cf. Gellman 2019, 83–84.
[58] See esp. Plantinga 2000, ch. 1. Perplexingly, Sa'adyah Gaon and Maimonides provide reasons for thinking that God cannot be described or that He possesses no properties, and yet say a lot about Him. (See Lebens 2020b, 17–28.) Likewise Martin Buber and Abraham Joshua Heschel declare that God cannot be described, but only encountered, yet then describe Him (e.g., by referring to His emotions). See Fisher 2021, 410–11. Kabbalists display the same sort of inconsistency.

saying, "God exists"? Isn't that description ("exists") acceptable? Again, if we insist that no descriptions apply to Him, including "exists," why isn't this insistence atheism?[59] We can well understand concerns about what William Alston (1995, 53) calls "transcendentitis."

Although apophatic theology is often termed negative theology (*via negativa*) and the terms are treated as equivalent, they are different. According to negative theology, we cannot say what God is, but we *can* say what He is not. But doesn't this entail a positive characterization as well – that God is a being such that we can say only what He is not? And as we say what He is not, aren't we saying something affirmative? We again court incoherence.[60]

As with many other issues, discussion of God-talk in Jewish philosophy revolves around Maimonides. A fierce opponent of anthropomorphism, anthropopathism, and univocal predication (the thesis that terms as applied to God mean the same as when those terms when applied to human beings), Maimonides divides the attributes of God into two groups: attributes of action and attributes of essence. We can describe His actions, but we cannot say anything affirmative about God's essence. Indeed, God has no such affirmative attributes, let alone any that lie within our conceptual repertoire. Importantly, only terms for the attributes of essence are subject to negative theology.[61]

The attributes of action are drawn from the Thirteen Attributes revealed to Moses in Exod. 34:6–7. They strike us as psychological descriptions, such as compassionate, gracious, and vengeful. Maimonides – like Anselm, Aquinas, and others – interprets the attribution of emotions to God as follows (this is not an exact quotation):

> "God is compassionate" means: God does actions such that if a human being were to do those actions we would ascribe to that person the feeling of compassion and call the individual compassionate. God does not actually have that emotion.

Hence, the psychological predicates really refer to divine actions alone, not mental states.[62]

---

[59] See Van Inwagen 2006, 19. Aaron Segal (2021) argues that Maimonides's negative theology is not as austere as most interpreters think, and when it is suitably reconstrued the objections in the last two paragraphs fall away. That rescues Maimonides but not his fellow travelers.

[60] See Plantinga 2000; Lebens 2020b, ch. 1; Segal 2021.

[61] Maimonides, *Guide of the Perplexed* 1:50–60.

[62] When Maimonides speaks of "divine actions," he is referring to the workings of nature, rather than direct interventions. See ibid., 1:54, 3:32 (beginning) and Chapter 2 below.

Challenge II: Apophaticism and Negative Theology   47

Attributes of essence include: knowing, existent, powerful, eternal, one, incorporeal, living, and willing. Maimonides argues that to ascribe all of these, or rather *any* of these, to God in the normal way is to introduce multiplicity into a being who is a metaphysical unity and contravene the verse "The Lord is One." (We discussed this argument earlier, p. 35.)[63]

For Maimonides, to say that God is knowing is to say that He is not not-knowing, and so forth. But – and this is a critical clarification – this negation is to be understood like the negation in the statement, "the wall does not see."[64] The statement, "The wall does not see," is very different from the statement, "John Milton does not see." John Milton is the sort of entity of whom seeing *could* be predicated. What is being negated in the case of the wall is the entire determinable, the general category of sight/blindness. A wall can be neither. So too, what is being negated in the case of "God is not not-knowing" is the determinable knowing/being ignorant. The true upshot of negative theology, then, is that God lies beyond our conceptual repertoire, and "Silence is praise to Thee" (Ps. 65:2).[65]

Gersonides saw grave difficulties in Maimonides's negative theology.[66] First, if the meaning of the attribution of P to God is that the entire category P/not-P does not apply to God, what difference does it make where we start? "God is ignorant" is just as good a starting point as "God is knowing." After all, we can analyze "God is ignorant" as "God is not not-ignorant" = "the category knowledge/ignorance does not apply to God." We then end up in the same place as we did when we started with "God is knowing." Why choose "knowing"?[67] Second, our ability to draw inferences to or from truths about God is vitiated by the equivocity of the terms. We can validly draw these inferences only if we assume that

---

[63] Maimonides's translation of God's psychological attributes into descriptions of the types of actions that God performs often flies under the radar in critical discussion – and gets a pass. It shouldn't. What differentiates action from "mere" causation of a result is that acting requires intention and willing. But in Maimonides's view, God has no inner states, and hence has no intention or will. How, then, can He perform *actions*? True, Maimonides understands willing equivocally (*Guide of the Perplexed* 1:58), but will the equivocal understanding suffice to explain how God performs actions?

[64] Ibid., 136 (*Guide of the Perplexed* 1:58).

[65] Some scholars maintain that Maimonides allows for a mystical, nondiscursive knowledge of God. See S. Jonas 2021. Cf. Valubregue 2017, Goodman 2017, Seeskin 2017.

[66] Gersonides 1987, 2:107–15 (*Milḥamot Hashem* 3:3). Cf. Segal's (2021a, 116) reply.

[67] As Gersonides saw, Maimonides may argue, in response, that the Torah makes its particular choice of adjectives that appear to be assigned to God by using political considerations – the need for the masses to relate to God as having only perfections. See Maimonides, *Guide of the Perplexed* 1:26, 1:46.

"incorporeal" and "exist" means the same when applied to God as when applied to humans. Most striking of all, Maimonides's argument for negative theology – that since God is One, no multiplicity exists in Him – would be invalid given the equivocity of "One." Gersonides therefore interprets predicates ascribed to God differently.

Kabbalists adopt negative theology, but in their own vocabulary. We cannot know what the infinite God (*Ein Sof*) is; but Kabbalists differentiate between God-in-Himself – infinite, incomprehensible, and ineffable – and manifestations or powers of the Godhead known as *sefirot*, which emanate from it.[68] Of course, "God is infinite, incomprehensible and ineffable" seems to qualify as a description of the indescribable.

Negative Theology and Contemporary Jewish Philosophy

Apophaticism and negative theology come to the fore yet again – forcefully – in modern times. Inspired by Immanuel Kant (1724–1804) and Martin Heidegger (1889–1976), many philosophers contend that metaphysics is impossible. (This stands in contrast to many or most theistic analytic philosophers of religion.) Books, Jewish or not, appear with titles like *Religion After Theology*, *Religion After Metaphysics*, and *Negative Theology as Jewish Modernity* (note the word "as" in the latter title). The most vigorous and colorful assaults on metaphysics in Jewish philosophy were launched by the Israeli scientist and philosopher Isaiah Leibowitz (1992). His noncognitivist approach to religious statements sees Judaism as consisting entirely in acts of obedience to Jewish law, acts that should be *motivated* only by pure obedience.

The opposition to metaphysics has repercussions in modern times. It has been invoked to generate at least the following theses:

- The concept of divine revelation is unintelligible.[69]
- We should quash, *ab initio*, inquiries into the purposes of the commandments, since we cannot read God's mind.
- Theodicy is a pointless project.
- Theological readings of the Holocaust, the creation of the Jewish State, and of any event in Jewish history are not legitimate.

---

[68] Kabbalists differed over whether the *sefirot* are the "essence" of God or instead "vessels." The former view clashes with the view that the Infinite is ineffable.
[69] Cf. Statman 2005.

Challenge II: Apophaticism and Negative Theology

In what follows, I argue that while negative theology is an *option* for contemporary Jewish philosophers, it cannot lay claim to being the *only* option. There is no good argument to establish the truth of negative theology. There is also much unclarity about what negative theology *says*. I would have liked to quip that negative theology can be characterized only by saying what it is not, but alas we have all too many ways to say what it is.

Let me lay out four basic ways of formulating negative theology: epistemological, ontological, deontic, and aretaic.

Epistemological Formulations

- Epistemological thesis #1 is the classic Maimonidean teaching described earlier: We cannot know God's attributes of essence, what God is in Himself. With regard to attributes of essence, we can know only what He is not. However, we can know His attributes of action.
- Epistemological thesis #2: We cannot know any of God's attributes, not even attributes of action.
- Epistemological thesis #3: We can know God's attributes – we are not of necessity limited – but in point of fact, we don't know any. The sense of "necessity" used here needs clarification.
- Epistemological thesis #4: We can know some or all of God's attributes, but we cannot know his purposes and intentions: why He created the world, why He chose Abraham and His descendants, why He gave *mitzvot* at all, and why He gave the specific *mitzvot* that He did.
- Epistemological thesis #5: We cannot have metaphysical knowledge at all.

Ontological Formulations

- Ontological thesis #1: God has only attributes of action, but does not have attributes of essence.
- Ontological thesis #2: God has neither attributes of action (He does nothing) nor attributes of essence.
- Ontological thesis #3: There are no facts about God.
- Ontological thesis #4: There are no metaphysical facts at all.

Deontic Formulation

Deontic thesis: It is wrong to explore God's attributes.

Aretaic Formulation

One who explores God's attributes exhibits defects in religious character.

Must We Accept Negative Theology?

I readily concede that negative theology can have salutary effects on human character. Negative theology can induce humility and perhaps create an attitude of tolerance toward other religions and toward groups within one's religion.[70] It leads even to tolerance of atheism, since, as Rabbi Abraham Isaac Kook (1985b, 23–24) put it, if the Deity is unknowable, "there is no difference between formulated religion and heresy." (But of course it's controversial whether all instances of tolerance are good.) Moreover, mystery is an important element in religious life. Keeping negative theology in one's consciousness thus may be beneficial in certain ways. But as a view about whether anything could properly be said of God, or whether we can know anything about God, it is not persuasively argued for, and is deeply problematic.

Concerning the arguments about humility and tolerance, we must ask whether we should adopt certain ontological claims because it's good for our character. It seems like a dubious method for hitting metaphysical truth.[71] Furthermore, religions have managed to produce many humble and tolerant adherents even while sporting a positive theology; and it isn't clear that negative theology has curbed intolerance. (I don't mean we know it hasn't, only that this claim is not established.) There's no reason that someone who ascribes attributes to God cannot approach conceptualization of God with humility and reverence. Indeed, a positive theology can inspire ethical conduct by furnishing specifics for applying *imitatio Dei*.[72] As for mystery, even if mystery is desirable, there are, for

---

[70] See Seeskin 1990; M. Goodman 2015; cf. Kavka 2017, Lebens 2020b, 1–28.

[71] But see pp. 80–82 below. A counterargument noted by Sam Lebens is that humility is truth-conducive; after all, a common theme nowadays in the large literature on epistemic humility is that being humble is likely to result in believing truths and being arrogant is likely to result in believing falsehoods. However, being humble can also lead to a degree of indolence, reducing the chances of acquiring truth.

[72] However, while God's perfections may induce humility, *imitatio Dei* risks inducing arrogance. My thanks to Yitzchak Blau for this point.

Challenge II: Apophaticism and Negative Theology 51

better or for worse, plenty of ways in which God is mysterious without our thinking of Him as totally opaque to human cognition.[73]

We need, too, to ask a fundamental question about how to argue for negative theology. On their face, biblical and rabbinic Judaism do not embrace negative theology. Despite the negative theologian's invocation of "my face shall not be seen," the Bible says way too much about God and about His attributes to make negative theology a preferred or even plausible option within it. The fact that the Bible sets limits to human understanding[74] does not impugn this claim any more than our knowledge that there are limits to what we can know about history implies that we can have no knowledge of history. Strikingly, negative theology takes no prisoners – it does not make room for any knowledge of God's attributes based on revelation, on attributions disclosed by Scripture. Biblical verses saying we come to know God, on particular evidence, then do not make sense.[75] Granted, I can think up arguments trying to show that we don't know what Scriptural terms mean (e.g., clearly some statements about God are conceded to be nonliteral, so maybe all are), but this option (that all are because some are) is only an option.

In turn, these considerations force us to ask whether negative theology is intended as a thesis that makes sense of classical Judaism – a legitimate *interpretive* option – or instead as an approach that scuttles biblical and rabbinic texts and professes little or no allegiance to them. The second route seems less appealing; won't the philosophy be less *Jewish*? Of course, those who endorse negative theology may either uphold their view as traditional (citing especially Maimonides and Kabbalah) or be uninterested in working within classical religion. Fine; but others are not constrained to make the same decision. They may work from biblical and rabbinic texts that they believe impugn negative theology. They are not beholden to Maimonides and Kabbalah.

In addition, religious worship discourages negative theology. Don't we have to know, per Segal, whom – by our lights – we are worshipping and to whom we are praying? If we think we are making it all up, for many people the practice feels inauthentic and people lose interest. (Not everyone, though: interestingly, atheists do pray and engage in acts of worship,

---

[73] Cf. Alston 2005, Wainwright 2009a. Mystery may be more of an element in Christianity than in Judaism.
[74] As in Isaiah 55:8 and the last few chapters of Job.
[75] See Manekin 2017.

as do, of course, advocates of negative theology.) Advocates of negative theology sometimes maintain that assigning attributes constitutes conceptual idolatry because one is *subjecting* God to one's reason. Some Continental philosophers even say that to conceptualize God is to do violence. But it's not clear why these images would be apt, especially if one approaches the task with humility, awe, love, gratitude, and reverence.[76]

Let us turn to "external" (non-Scriptural) arguments for negative theology.

We have already heard Maimonidean arguments based on the doctrine of divine unity and the problem of compositionality.[77] The entire notion that there can be no multiplicity in God is rooted in an outmoded-looking medieval tradition. And even if simplicity/unity is not a problematic concept in itself, it can be questioned whether having properties violates simplicity/unity. Another argument for negative theology, advanced by Sa'adyah Gaon (882–942), is that since God creates everything, and He created properties, He must have existed prior to the creation of properties, and ergo He can't have properties. The difficulty here is that properties, like other abstract objects, aren't created.[78]

Gersonides, as we saw earlier, lodged cogent criticisms of Maimonides and established the need for "affirmative" theology.[79] If Gersonides is right, epistemological theses 1, 2, and 3 will lack support, and so will epistemological thesis 5.

Other arguments may be given for versions of negative theology. Some argue that assigning attributes obliterates or significantly smudges the line between God and humans. But since God is the ultimate ground of being and the cause of all that exists, and since all that exists depends on Him but not the reverse, a rather big difference is present.[80] Again, Kant argued that human beings can have no metaphysical knowledge at all because the conceptual structures needed for us to have any cognition are applicable only to objects of experience, not things-in-themselves. But it is by no means clear that one cannot infer the existence of a non-physical being from objects of experience, and the many philosophers who "do" analytic theology and metaphysics do exactly that. Moreover, if it's Kant we're worried about, we've got a lot more to worry about

---

[76] So too W. Wood 2021, esp. part III.
[77] For an intensive examination of Maimonides's argument, see Stern 2013, ch. 6.
[78] See Lebens 2020b, 8–10. The argument being criticized is in Saadia Gaon 1948, 111–12 (2:8). Cf. W. Wood 2021, 125, n. 3.
[79] See, however, the response in n. 67 to one of Gersonides' objections.
[80] See again W. Wood 2021, part III.

than just not knowing God; we are ignorant of *all* things-in-themselves! We would end up negating ontology, and not just theology. Even if we don't reject Kant, any insinuation that the case of God is special falls by the wayside.[81]

Among other reasons for discrediting metaphysics, there is the old argument that metaphysical claims cannot be verified or falsified. There is also in the negative theology camp the idea that God is *defined as* He who is utterly transcendent and can't be captured in human categories. But these latter arguments are question-begging. Again, we may want to preserve *some* inaccessibility for God, but the claim that He cannot be captured exhaustively in human categories does not entail that He cannot be known at all to human minds or that He does not have properties.

What about the deontic and aretaic formulations? Merold Westphal maintains that it is presumptuous to investigate God: "What we lack [goes the argument] is not so much the power to pull off this project (though, of course, we do) as the right to attempt it."[82] But why would we lack this right? Isn't knowledge of God a worthy ideal? What if God gives us "the right" to study Him?

It has been said, too, that knowledge of God in the Bible is (per Martin Buber and others) knowledge by acquaintance, not by description (propositional knowledge). But the case for a single-model view (acquaintance) needs to be made, and is not easy to construct given the occurrence of rational arguments in the Bible.[83]

A final response to negative theology is that we need to consider but one attribute to refute it: perfection. God (if He exists) is perfect. If that is so, then all we need to know in order to know God's nature is which value judgments are correct. If *God is perfect* is understood (per negative theology) as *God is not perfect in the ordinary sense*, we can ask: Does that mean *He is imperfect*? Is He neither perfect nor imperfect?[84] I don't see why anyone has to surrender PBT because of a view (negative

---

[81] Kant himself may have been more epistemically permissive about belief in God than is commonly thought. See Chignall 2011. For more on Kant and Jewish theology, see Kepnes 2021.

[82] See Westphal 2001, ch. 1, and Rea's discussion of Westphal's critique in Rea 2011. See also Segal 2012–2013.

[83] See the numerous examples in D. Shapiro 1963. I express reservations in Chapter 10 but they are not inconsistent with what I wrote above. See also Barr 1993, Manekin 2017.

[84] Cf. Gellman 2019, 83–84; he argues that Maimonides did not apply negative theology to value terms but only to descriptive terms. At the end of *Guide of the Perplexed* 1:59 (1963, 142–43), Maimonides states that what is a perfection in humans is a deficiency in God.

theology) that purports to force *someone else* to say this in response to an objection.

No one should deny the hold that negative theology has had on Jewish thought historically. Yet the contemporary denial of the possibility of metaphysical knowledge is to my mind a dogma, a trend. The various versions of negative theology arise from assigning reflex-like credence to philosophers like Heidegger, Kant, and Maimonides, a credence whose logical support is weak despite the august stature of the thinkers in question. Negative theology is an option, perhaps, but so is its denial. The problem of negative theology is a problem of the negative theologian's own making.[85]

I should briefly mention a *greatly modified* version of negative theology that emerges from a talmudic passage (*Berakhot* 32b). The Men of the Great Assembly, a group of 120 scribes, prophets, and sages who served as leaders after the destruction of the First Temple, allowed only a few attributes of God to be uttered in prayer ("the great, the mighty, and the awesome"). When a man added to that stock in his prayers, R. Ḥanina asked him sardonically, "Did you complete the praise of your master?" Were it not for the Men of the Great Assembly, he continues, we could not pronounce *any* attributes. "It is as if a mortal king who had millions of gold pieces were praised for possessing silver."

R. Ḥanina can be seen as promoting a modified version of the view that God cannot be described: He *can* be described, but never anywhere near *comprehensively*; so it's better to limit verbalized praises to what has been prescribed. Trying to "top" the licensed praises ends up belittling God, cheapening Him, notwithstanding the pray-er's (or prayer leader's) noble intentions. Apparently, the Men of the Great Assembly allowed use of attributes only as a limited concession to the human need to have some vocabulary by which to relate to God in prayer. This does not entail that the unrecited attributes are completely unknowable. However, Maimonides reads the punchline (gold vs. silver) as an endorsement of his full-blown negative theology: God's attributes are not just quantitatively superior to ours, they are of a different "species."[86]

---

[85] One version of negative theology has been left standing, however – epistemological thesis #4. See Shatz 2017 for a response to that thesis.

[86] Maimonides 1963, *Guide of the Perplexed* 1:59. Maimonides could have also pointed out that the allowed attributes (great, mighty, awesome) can be translated into action and are not attributes of essence. Previously, though (in 1:54), he had limited attributes of action to those in Exod. 34:6–7.

CHALLENGE III: BIBLICAL AND RABBINIC THEOLOGY – IMPERFECT BEING?

The next objection to consider is that biblical and rabbinic theology is decidedly not PBT. The objection has a variety of facets. There is an *exegetical* facet: The Bible's portrayal of God, as well as that of the Talmud and Midrash, suggests that He is imperfect. There is also a *historical* facet that builds on the exegetical – namely, there is a rupture in Jewish theology between biblical and rabbinic times and medieval Jewish philosophy. Finally, there is an *axiological* facet – namely, believing in an imperfect God is better logically than believing in a perfect one.[87]

I begin with two text-based arguments wielded against PBT and in favor of IBT.

The Argument from Biblical Texts

IBT states that God as portrayed in the Bible is not omnipotent, omniscient, perfectly good, immutable, necessarily existent, or simple. Most important here are the first three. In the Bible, God seems limited and imperfect. He makes some decisions that have bad results and He is surprised by those results. He regrets these decisions, such as creating human beings (Gen. 6:7) and making Saul king (I Sam. 15:11). He is not immutable, and He has emotions. Furthermore, even if immutability is not a perfection, and even if having emotions is not per se an imperfection, some of God's emotions are inappropriate. Thus, He becomes angry over sins His people commit, and it takes Moses's arguing with Him to convince God to calm down (Exod. 32:10). God's powers of prognostication, furthermore, are imperfect; He sometimes has to wait to see how people will act. In the case of Sodom, He has to descend to see what is going on (Gen. 18:21). He cannot control human choices, and so people act contrary to His wishes. He ostensibly does immoral things and commands ostensibly immoral acts, such as ordering the utter destruction of the Amalekite people (see Exod. 17:14–16; Deut. 25:19). If we adopt the "divine command" theory that right and wrong are defined by God's will, the last objection falls away; and if we insist that God's conduct determines what perfection is, the others fall away as well. But these responses, while not without some Jewish support, confront a range of objections, some of which are recorded in Chapters 3 and 8.

---

[87] Yoram Hazony (2015, 2019) has been a prominent Jewish critic of PBT on the basis of biblical theology.

The Argument from Theological Conundrums

Reading Scripture as endorsing IBT would solve various problems in philosophical theology – the problem of evil, for example, and the conflict between foreknowledge and free will. By giving up omniscience and/or omnipotence and/or perfect goodness, we can make these problems go away and reconcile Scripture with reason. This argument emerges in what is called "open God" theology.[88] Advocates of open theism indeed appeal to biblical texts to show their consistency with open-God theology even while their theology is mainly driven by philosophical considerations.

Responses to the Objections

How potent are these objections?

The "theological conundrums" rehash hoary controversies in the philosophy of religion. Certainly many philosophers think that philosophical objections to PBT fall away. Assessing the objections will take us far afield, and I shift attention to exegetical matters.[89]

What about textual arguments? As we saw earlier (28–29), some biblical verses describe God's perfect power, perfect understanding, and perfect justice. But proponents of IBT also cite biblical materials that suggest imperfections. What about those? Clearly the weighing of biblical materials requires an exegetical policy.[90]

The evidence adduced by those who find the biblical God imperfect includes His not stopping people from doing things that He doesn't want them to do. Yoram Hazony infers that He is either not omnipotent or not omniscient (because, it is claimed, He doesn't foresee how they will act). But why isn't it equally admissible to view Him as choosing to leave room for human free choice?[91] This commonplace view might be needed anyway as a theodicy, even if God is not perfect, as even a very good but not perfectly good God arguably would not allow as many evils as there are.[92] True, God at times interferes with the execution of people's choices, but does this entail that He *can't* thwart the ones that He

---

[88] See, e.g., Pinnock 1994, Hasker 2004. Process Theists often hold similarly.
[89] Ironically, according to the exegetical claims of IBT, if a philosopher proves there is a perfect being via an ontological argument, this being could not be God!
[90] As Jerome Gellman put it in correspondence.
[91] Hazony 2015, n. 2, and 2019, 9–10, nn. 1–2, notes this and another rejoinder discussed in this paragraph, but I think his reply is unconvincing.
[92] See Lerner 2019, 28.

doesn't thwart? To put it more aggressively, one has the sense that not only do biblical narratives suggest that God *can* do anything He wants to do, but they suggest that He actually *does* do whatever He wants to do. Whenever needed, He performs miracles – lots and lots of them. He also hardens hearts (e.g., Exod. 7:3, Deut. 2:30). The episodes in which He waxes angry and then relents because of Moses's or Abraham's pleading may be in the text to highlight certain moral issues rather than to depict a lamentable divine excitability or whimsicality. (See Chapter 3, on protest literature.) Concerning omnipotence, Jon Levenson (1988) has argued that, in the Bible, God is omnipotent, but God's omnipotence is activated by Israel's conduct.[93]

Consider also omniscience. In the Bible, it would appear from biblical prophecies that God sees very, very far into the future. To make this foreknowledge less impressive, an IBT theorist might understand prophecies as God announcing what He intends to do in the future. Another option for that theorist is to claim that God's foreknowledge is based on probabilities. A third is to understand prophecies as conditional. But as Thomas Flint (2006) shows (100–7), these answers are not plausible. Prophecy is a telling example because Hazony (2019, 26) argues that a perfect God fails to satisfy our sense of reality, "the character of our experience." Does a being *as* powerful and *as* knowing as the biblical God answer to our experience and sense of reality? Even IBT's advocates are buying into a thesis that does not accord with our experience.

Many authors highlight immutability as a parade example of where PBT contradicts Scripture. We have noted already that, in an effort to close that gap, advocates of divine immutability cite biblical verses in which God or a prophet asserts that God does not change.[94] As we saw early in this chapter, however, immutability is *not* essential to a perfect-being conception of God, and biblical verses that ostensibly impute immutability (Malachi 3:6, Exod. 3:14) can be interpreted to fit this philosophical claim.

If the biblical data does contain indications of both perfection and imperfection, though, what should be done? A weighting of sources is needed. The fact God can see the future and read people's minds, and the fact His omnipotence can be activated, moves us toward PBT. So

---

[93] See similarly Sztuden 2019, on the Rabbis' view.
[94] In marshalling verses that (purportedly) imply immutability, theists seem to get themselves into trouble, because God acts one way (He changes) while He describes Himself in the opposite way (as unchanging).

do the numerous verses cited at the beginning of this chapter. A few considerations encourage us to go further: Why worship, and take as a model, an imperfect being, especially one as prone to mistakes as IBT stresses? Another advantage of PBT is that it spares us from accepting a colossal rupture between the Bible and the great philosophers of Jewish tradition.[95] A further consideration is that the biblical material could be interpreted as an instance of what the medieval philosophers described as "the Torah speaks in the language of human beings."[96] The widespread argument that a person cannot relate to the philosopher's God is fine for armchair cogitation but is refuted empirically by the roster of philosophers who have done precisely that – Anselm and Aquinas, for instance, and even, I believe, the negative theologian Maimonides. Put all these points together, and you have a reasonable case for favoring PBT, even if IBT theorists stick to their guns.

With regard to materials from the Talmud and Midrash, we again confront contrasting sources.[97] Some sources suggest that God is imperfect. This will become clearest in Chapter 3, where we will discuss protests against God. Nonetheless, a major scholar of ancient rabbinic literature writes (S. Cohen 2006, 77): "That God is the omnipotent, omniscient creator of the universe, exalted above all his creatures, ruling in majestic splendor, and ultimately beyond human ken, is a common motif in the literature of the Second Temple period." Cass Fisher (2020, 65) contends that "The rabbis are incessant in their claims that God possesses maximal power and knowledge and that God's justice is unimpeachable." Further: "At every stage of the tradition, one can find the idea of divine perfection doing crucial theological work, sometimes explicitly and sometimes implicitly" (ibid., 81). For the rabbis, states Alex Sztuden (2019, 143), God is "incomparable in might, and transcendent" (albeit the title of his article is "Omnipotence is no perfection"). God has power over everything; He has the power to redeem His people; and He exercises his power in the cause of justice.[98] At times, the power may be hidden, and Israel has to, as it were, reenergize God. The

---

[95] Arguably the rupture between the Bible (and the Rabbis) and the later philosophy is more troubling than other ruptures in Jewish history because those sources are fundamental. I suspect that IBT advocates would find the rupture argument question-begging. They are not troubled by the rupture.
[96] See Chapter 5, n. 12 on this originally talmudic phrase.
[97] Howard Wettstein (2012, esp. ch. 6) argues that theology is not central to classical (rabbinic) Judaism. Cf. Fisher 2012, 2026.
[98] See again Gellman 2019.

Rabbis' God is also transcendent, which inches them closer to philosophers, but they embraced immanence as well.[99]

In addition, some Rabbinic materials suggestive of imperfection admit a figurative reading. The regular Rabbinic invocation of the word *kivyakhol* ("as it were") when speaking of God in human terms suggests that the Rabbis consciously exercised poetic license. The biggest difference between the God of the Rabbis and the God of the philosophers is that the God of the Rabbis has emotions in abundance, including suffering and sadness, and is mutable. But the Rabbis did not see possibility as an imperfection, and they were right not to: impassibility entails indifference to suffering. Passibility and relationality are the real perfections.[100] PBT and rabbinic theology are compatible.

Privileging certain exegetical considerations is called for in making an overall judgment. And a plausible case can be made for choosing in favor of PBT.

CHALLENGE IV: ANTIREALIST UNDERSTANDINGS OF GOD-TALK

A final objection to PBT emerges from a sweeping thesis known as antirealism. According to the most common form of antirealism, statements that believers make and that *sound like* they are about an entity (God) are not meant to correspond to "a state of affairs that exists objectively and independently of the ways we might think about it or describe it."[101] Thus Alan Mittleman (2009, 17) writes: "The word God does not make a claim about the furniture of the universe." And Avi Sagi (2009, 27) states: "[R]eligion is a value system that neither relies upon nor reflects metaphysical assumptions or factual data that could be translated into truth claims." Note that PBT is not the only theology that is rebuffed by such views. IBT is as well.[102]

For many antirealists, ostensibly metaphysical and historical statements in truth are used to express a speaker's emotions, attitudes, intentions, and/or commitment to certain actions or a particular way of life.[103] God-talk and stories play the role of useful fictions and fertile images

---

[99] Stzuden 2019, 162.
[100] My thanks to Cass Fisher for stressing this point.
[101] Gellman, 2019. (He is a realist.)
[102] For critical surveys of various nonrealist construals of religious language, see Ross 2013 and Fisher 2021, 2024, 2026.
[103] See Braithwaite 1955.

used to stimulate these attitudes and actions and to organize one's life. Religious discourse, so antirealists claim, needs to be understood as instrumentalist, a term used in philosophy of science.[104]

Insofar as antirealism seems to imply atheism,[105] it doesn't belong in our discussion of *theology*. But because prominent and influential Jewish thinkers today adopt the position,[106] more should be said about its viability for Jewish philosophy.

Antirealism could be construed as a *description* of how those who speak about God think about their utterances; but it could be instead a *recommendation* for how they *should* think about those utterances. On the level of description, it is untenable to maintain that the tradition through the millennia has been nonrealist. As for today, it's true that some people are "orthoprax" – they engage in religious practices (even prayer) without having belief in God. But nonrealists often make their claim in sweeping terms, applying it to *all* people who speak of God. Antirealists who so contend are in effect saying that all Jews who think they believe in an extramental being, God, don't understand what they themselves mean by sentences they utter; the antirealist supposedly understands better. This approach seems implausible (and is likely to give offense).

Having failed as a universal description, the nonrealist's view is better taken as a *recommendation*, a proposal, for rescuing religious language from problems that engulf it if it is meant literally.[107] Perhaps the antirealist's starting point is that belief in the traditional God is at best rationally ungrounded and at worst irrational. As a result, theists face a choice between (i) adopting antirealist understandings (ii) finding a nontraditional *realist* understanding of God-talk. Presumably they should opt for one of these courses rather than self-destruct. Mordecai Kaplan (1958, 1967), founder of Reconstructionist Judaism, adopted strategy (ii). Applying theories of Emile Durkheim (1858–1917) and John Dewey (1859–1952), Kaplan held that the meaning of a religion's terms changes across time, and whereas "God" was once thought to denote a supernatural being, in a scientific age it cannot. Kaplan understood God (for his era) as the sum of forces in nature that make possible the realization

---

[104] See Gellman 1981.
[105] To be sure, one could be a realist about *God exists* but an antirealist about, say, *God's providence over His creatures*. I'm referring to realism about *God exists*.
[106] Fisher's roster of antirealists (Fisher 2026) is remarkable not only in the number of antirealists but in their prominence too.
[107] See also Gellman 1981, 19.

of ethical values. So "God" denotes *something* outside the mind (forces of nature); and to that extent Kaplan's God-talk is realist.[108]

Antirealism is fed, perhaps, by the perception that proper practice matters in Judaism more than correct belief.[109] But this doesn't justify jettisoning belief altogether. In fact, observance of law might be best justified by belief in a commander and authority; and having trust and gratitude seems to imply believing in a recipient of that trust and gratitude.[110]

No less important is this question: when we speak of *recommending* antirealism we must ask: recommend to whom? Philosophers? The general populace? Cass Fisher offers this reflection: "While rhetorical and sociological analyses have much to contribute to contribute to the study of Jewish theology, absent a discourse about God it is difficult to see how Jewish theology can recover its former vitality and assert its relevance in contemporary Jewish religious life."[111]

Whether Fisher is right is an empirical, sociological question, but from my armchair I agree with his assessment that a discourse about God is needed. The question is (1) whether that discourse must be realist and (2) about which audience are we asking the question. Some may think that realism will not make strides on the ground because "been there, done that": antirealism arose precisely because realism failed on the ground. For all that, I believe that realism is the best course if we desire for the general Jewish population the vitality of which Fisher speaks. Of course, the necessity for the general population, or a segment thereof, to have realist discourse is not grounds for thinking that the claims expressed in the discourse are true.

CONCLUSION

In this chapter we have pondered, mostly from the point of view of Jewish materials, four challenges or objections to doing PBT.

The first objection was that, given disputes over which attributes a perfect being would have and the difficulty in resolving those disputes, we cannot do PBT, even if we have adequate reason to believe a perfect

---

[108] Given that, for Kaplan, God makes possible the realization of ethical values, his view runs into its own form of the problem of evil. Steven Kepnes (2013, 24), levels a related criticism at Arthur Green, for whom God is the "single unifying substratum of all that is" and "the inner force of existence itself" (Green, 2010).
[109] See Fisher 2012, 2021, 2026.
[110] On the problem of grounding authority, see Brafman 2019.
[111] Ibid.

being exists. Discussion of this question led us through the concepts of *imitatio Dei*, heresy, *avodah zarah*, and theological risk-taking.

The second objection, from negative theology, is not that we cannot know which attributes God has, but that no attributes apply to Him. The view faces charges of incoherence and objections set out by Gersonides. Standard arguments for negative theology fail to establish it. At best, negative theology is an *option*.

The third objection was in a way the opposite of objections one and two. Objection three says that God has attributes (*pace* objection two) and that we know what attributes God has (*pace* objection one), and that's because we assign the attributes that are in the Bible. But those attributes are not perfections. The proponents of IBT) believe that there is a rupture between biblical and rabbinic conceptions of God on the one hand, and the conceptions put forth by philosophers on the other. This challenge is formidable, but the phenomenon of prophetic predictions and claims like "God knows what is in people's hearts" suggest that God is omniscient, and He appears to be able to do whatever He desires to do. Also, IBT makes it difficult to see why God should be worshipped. Privileging is called for, and PBT is a plausible choice.

The final objection, based on antirealism, is an objection to all theology. I argued that antirealism fails as a *universal* description of how *all* religious language works *for everyone*, so it would be better considered as a recommendation. But the basis for the recommendation needs to be made clear, and following the recommendation could have negative consequences for Jewish society.

The upshot of this chapter is that, with respect to the objections considered here, PBT is a tenable option. But as with any philosophical view, substantial work is needed to develop and defend it. And because intuitions differ about both texts and arguments (e.g., texts get read or weighted differently), no defenses will be, well, perfectly compelling to all.

2

Where in the World Is God?

Nature and Divine Action

That God in some way acts in the "natural" world is generally considered a central tenet of traditional theism.[1] The Bible is so heavily punctuated by stories of direct divine action – miracles – that the number of such actions may exceed the number of biblical events that occur by natural law, at least in the Pentateuch. Tellingly, there is no word for "nature" in the Bible, though the Bible treats the physical world as testimony to God's greatness;[2] only later, in medieval times, does the word *teva* come to denote what we call nature or natural law. Talmudic and midrashic literature continue the motif of divine intervention in the world, offering numerous stories of miracles, many wrought by sages or occurring to them.[3] Miracle stories continue through the ages, including the modern scientific era. God is immanent *in the sense that* He acts in the world, regardless of whether He is immanent in the sense that He is immanent in pantheism and panentheism.

The ascription to God of many direct interventions in the natural order is enormously well-grounded in traditional texts. Miracles glorify God; they celebrate His power, justice, and wisdom. For God not only

---

The title of this chapter (minus the subtitle) is lifted from Gingerich 1993.

[1] "Physical" and "natural" are not equivalent, since mental states, a facet of the natural world, may not be reducible to physical states. See also Sztuden 2016, VIII.

[2] E.g., Ps. 8:2 and 19:2–3, and much of Ps. 104. See Simkins 2022 on different conceptions of nature in the Bible. My thanks to Aaron Koller for the reference.

[3] Gellman (2021a, 34), in showing how the Sages magnified God's greatness, writes that he has "catalogued well over a hundred new or greatly new or grandly embellished miracles in [the collection of *midrashim*] Midrash Rabbah on the Torah." In the Haggadah, read at the Passover Seder, certain rabbis assert that God wrought many plagues in Egypt beyond the ten depicted in the Bible, up to 250.

breaks the laws of nature, He does so in the service of good, just, and wisely pursued results. Traditionally, some interventions convey a sign or message, or supply just deserts. Belief in miracles impacts how human beings experience their lives, both cognitively and emotionally.

To be sure, "direct" may be too strong a word to describe those acts. God may work through intermediary causes; He may set off a chain of events that, via the laws of nature, leads to a result that He desires. Thus, He may not simply strike someone down, but may introduce various events, such as exposure to a lethal food, to secure that result.[4] Even in the iconic cartoon of the deity hurling a lightning bolt at a transgressor, the bolt is an intermediary cause, as are other events. But God is *proximate enough* in such a picture for us to apply the word "directly."

Yet, despite the enormous textual support available to theists who believe in supernatural causation, many Jewish philosophers – most prominently medieval rationalists such as Maimonides, and also many in our age – adopt a different model of how the universe works.[5] Theirs is a "theistic naturalistic" model, in which laws of nature hold sway nearly all of the time and, except for a miracle here and there, God does not directly set off chains of events in the way just described. Transcendence is central, not immanence. (Note that whereas naturalism is usually associated with atheism and denial of the supernatural, in this discussion I am speaking of naturalism within a theistic framework. For the sake of convenience, I will refer to theistic naturalism as naturalism *simpliciter*.)

But if (theistic) naturalism is true, where, in the world, is God? One naturalist response, apart from allowing *some* miracles, is that "divine action" consists in creating the world and the laws of nature, and in endowing created things (water, air, trees, animals, human beings, elementary particles – everything) with certain properties – and then leaving nature more or less to its own operations. God isn't absent, because these are really, in some sense, *His* operations. As Maimonides puts it, "When I speak about the divine actions, I mean the natural actions."[6] If eating grass nourishes an animal, it is ultimately (on this view) God who nourishes the animal, even while nature is doing the direct work.[7]

---

[4] See Naḥmanides's (Nachmanides 1963) introduction to his commentary on the Book of Job, 118–19 (Hebrew; not found in the 1985 English edition).

[5] For a survey of approaches see A. Leibowitz 2014. I omit here certain views, e.g., that providence operates only in the Land of Israel, based on, inter alia, Deut. 11:12 and *Ketubbot* 110b.

[6] Maimonides 1963, 525 (*Guide of the Perplexed* 3:32).

[7] See Alston 1989c, 200–1.

Analogously, a computer or robot's behavior is ultimately an act of the inventor. Although human beings have free choice, God created them that way, and God is the cause of their being able to make a choice.

Is this approach – God creates the world, then leaves it alone (or mostly so) – simply deism, which is so denigrated in theistic circles? Well, sort of, but it is a mistake to claim that in this "sort-of" deism God *must* have no (or little) concern with the world and nothing to do with its operation. Putting aside that He *may* perform some miracles, He designs nature with wisdom; nature is teleological, set up to produce certain valuable ends. And God's decision not to intervene is thought through. This teleological character of nature is called general providence as opposed to individual providence. To be sure, there is a problem of God's responsibility for evil, which challenges teleology, and that will be discussed in Chapter 3. For the moment I am just saying that if theistic naturalism is deism, it's not a deism devoid of divine justice, wisdom, and so on in the designing of the world.

Questions about the scope of God's intervention form key parts of a variety of topics: creation, miracles, revelation, prophecy, the afterlife, redemption, and what we might call "the metaphysics of everyday life." On the practical level, these questions affect the propriety of medical treatment (why not leave it to God?), the pursuit of technology, and political activism, including messianic activism (how will the messianic age arrive – human action or divine miracle?) Naturalists seek, and find to their satisfaction, ways to fit the biblical, talmudic, and midrashic texts into a naturalistic worldview. For Maimonides, to take one example, stories of miracles that are recorded in the Bible are reports of dreams and visions, or else they are descriptions of events that, although unusual, can be explained in terms of natural laws and were programmed into nature at its original creation (admittedly, an obscure idea).[8] Even those who believe in frequent biblical miracles often assert that when miracles occur, they occur in the most natural-looking way

---

[8] On the examples that arise in the coming paragraphs, see *Guide of the Perplexed* 2:29 (miracles); 2:32–48 (prophecy); 3:17–23, 51 (providence). See also Maimonides's commentary to *Avot* 5:6 and *Guide of the Perplexed* 2:29, which cite rabbinic sources for the view that miracles are part of the natural order. For purposes of this essay, which explores the roots of religious naturalism, it would be counterproductive to explore the distinct interpretive possibility, which I accept, that Maimonides's naturalism is less thoroughgoing than many expositions suggest, or became attenuated over time. See Langerman 2004 and Manekin 2007, which argue there was a shift to theological conservatism (on certain issues) in Maimonides's later writings.

possible. Thus, Moses Naḥmanides (1194–1270) suggests that, while Noah's ark was large, it was still too small to accommodate all that it contained. Yet everything fit in by dint of a miracle. Why, then, did Noah need to build the ark even as big as it was? It was to make the miracle look natural ("for the purpose of minimizing it").[9]

Prophecy, in the view of Maimonides and other medieval rationalists, is the outcome of a natural process, one that involves intellect, a faculty called imagination, and moral character. The prophet frames philosophical truths that his intellect has acquired in images and parables, so that the masses can apprehend the truths to some degree.[10] As for rewards and punishments, they are not, on the Maimonidean view, divine incursions into the natural order; rather, they are benefits or adversities that flow *naturally* from human deeds – or, more precisely, from human intellectual and spiritual efforts and achievements.[11] Indeed, Maimonides reduced biblical locutions of the form "God does X" to statements of the form, "within the natural order ordained by God, X occurs."[12] But again, it is, in this formulation, *God* doing X, since God set up natural laws and determined the properties of objects in nature.

The central question of this chapter is: Why do some theists in Jewish tradition insist that God allows nature to operate to a very large extent on its own? Is theistic naturalism, underneath it all, an accommodation

---

While my goal here is not exegesis of Maimonides, it is important to mention an observation by Eliezer Goldman that puts Maimonidean naturalism in perspective, albeit I bracket it in the sequel:

That Maimonides could consider his own conception to be an authentic interpretation of the idea of Providence is due to his cosmology. In his world picture, any event occurring in accordance with natural laws could be regarded as resulting from the divine influence mediated by the heavens (the spheres and the intelligences) ... On the modern cosmic model, the world, even when considered to be created, is construed as self-subsistent ... It follows that, granted the modern world picture, the philosophically concerned religious person confronts a problem of the relation of the wholly transcendent to the created world. (Goldman 1986, 57. See also Sztuden 2016, VII–XLIV)

The laws of nature are a consequence of a constant overflow that functions to sustain the whole system. (Samuel Lebens suggested this formulation.) On the different accounts of miracles in Jewish thought, see Green 2025.

[9] Naḥmanides, commentary to Gen. 6:19. (See Berger 2011, 148, on the significance of this passage.) There is a joke about a Ḥasidic rebbe whose followers lift him on a chair and hold him aloft. Asked why they were doing so, they reply, "So that he can see to the four corners of the earth." Asked why, if the rebbe could see to the four corners of the earth, he needed to be lifted up on a chair, the disciples explain, "It's to make it look natural."

[10] Maimonides follows the Islamic philosopher Al-Farabi (870–951). See the translator's introduction to Maimonides 1963, lxxxvi–xcii.

[11] See Gellman 1991; Shatz 2021, 235–41.

[12] *Guide of the Perplexed* 2:48 (Maimonides 1963, 410).

to a secular worldview? Or can it plausibly be viewed as a faithful representation of biblical and rabbinic teachings concerning God's role in the universe? I will identify and critique various ways to explain the attractions that naturalism proffers to some theists.[13]

One motivation for naturalism is epistemological: there is more evidence for the naturalist view than for its supernaturalist rival. The interventionist position, to its detriment, gives us a "God of the gaps" whose existence is inferred (or, perhaps more accurately, posited) when causal gaps need to be filled in, but who becomes less and less necessary as science proceeds to fill in those gaps by explaining phenomena. The explanations of theistic naturalism that I consider here share a different feature, however. They present not epistemological but rather *religious* motivations for theistic naturalism. (It isn't enough for naturalists to insist that if God is so great He must be transcendent and not immanent, because it is question-begging to claim that immanence is not a great-making property.)

One complicating matter bears mention. Today we know that nature includes random or chance events, notably quantum events and random mutations as described by Darwin. These events are not just epistemologically random (i.e., it's not just that we don't have enough knowledge to predict them), they are ontologically random. Randomness inheres in the universe. How can God exercise providence over a world He ostensibly cannot control, as is the case when some events happen by chance? Randomness in nature complicates the notion of divine intervention in the natural order. The questions are numerous. and have elicited much literature.[14] I will comment briefly when randomness becomes relevant to the discussion.

RELIGIOUS CONSIDERATIONS BEHIND THEISTIC NATURALISM

Consideration 1: The Pitfalls of Occasionalism

It is often assumed that the piety of a position about divine action – how "religious" it is – is directly proportional to the amount of divine intervention it posits. By this logic, the most pious view of all is that God is the only cause of anything. No other entity has any causal powers, active

---

[13] For the Sages, though, the contrast case to miracle is *magic*. See Urbach 1987, 102ff.
[14] See the essays in K. J. Clark and Koperski 2022; note Gellman 2016, ch. 5.

or passive, not even unexercised ones.[15] This position – the very opposite of a full-blown naturalism – was held, inter alia, at least ostensibly, by the Islamic philosopher Alghazali (1056–1111) and the early modern philosophers Nicholas Malebranche (1638–1715) and George Berkeley (1685–1753).[16] It is called occasionalism, because it teaches that what the ordinary person calls "causes" and theistic naturalists call "secondary causes" are really just *occasional* causes – that is, events that are the *occasions* on which God produces a certain effect.[17]

Occasionalism would seem to be simply bad metaphysics, or at the least bad science. It seems so contrary to appearances and common sense! Why, then, would anyone adopt it?

There are two sorts of occasionalist arguments: philosophical and religious. The main philosophical argument draws on the idea that what we ordinarily term causal relationships are contingent, not logically necessary. We do not perceive any logical connection between any two events that we designate as cause and effect; ergo, there are no causal powers in nature. There is no logical relationship between drinking water and quenching thirst, between putting a flame to paper and the paper burning, and so on. By contrast, God's will *is* logically connected to God's achieving what He wills, because, necessarily, anything God wills to occur must occur. So God's will is a genuine cause. Thus argues Malebranche, for example.[18]

The "no necessary connection" argument for occasionalism is presented, via a talmudic text, by R. Eliyahu Dessler (1892–1953). R. Ḥanina ben Dosa's daughter was upset because she had no oil to kindle the Shabbat lights. The rabbi suggested she use vinegar. "Vinegar?," she asked in astonishment. The rabbi explained: "He who told oil to burn

---

[15] Freddoso 1988 arrives at this formulation after noting problems with more moderate forms of occasionalism.

[16] Some scholars moderate this understanding, principally by maintaining that God wills only general laws. For critical discussion of this and numerous other issues as they pertain to Malebranche, see Nadler 2011.

[17] The occasionalist position may seem to be expressed in certain talmudic passages, e. g, "A person does not bruise his finger unless it is decreed from above" (*Ḥullin* 7a), and the proof text from Ps. 37:23. But the passage may be referring only to what happens *to human beings*, who are subject to reward and punishment. Among other Rabbinic statements about the scope of divine activity, however, are "A bird is not caught unless it has been decreed from Heaven – how much more so with a human being" (*Gen. Rabbah* 79:6). Cf. "All is in the hands of Heaven expect for fear of Heaven" (*Berakhot* 33b), which has been variously interpreted.

[18] Malebranche 1992, 94. Malebranche influenced David Hume's theory of cause–effect, but there is a glaring difference, to wit, Malebranche's theistic framework.

can tell vinegar to burn" (*Ta'anit* 25a). Dessler understands this to mean that there is no necessary connection between oil and burning – or any other so-called causes and effects in nature.

However, occasionalists are motivated at the deepest level not by philosophical reflection on the nature of causation, but by a religious sensibility captured by Charles McCracken: "Belief in *nature*, if by that term be meant a realm of entities that produce effects by their own power, is the hallmark of the pagan, and the antithesis of the Christian, view of the world."[19] One author calls this "a remarkably devout theory of causation."[20] Malebranche labels this belief pagan; Dessler declares belief in causal powers outside of God a form of *avodah zarah*, worship of an entity other than God. A striking illustration in Dessler's thought involves "the sin of the spies [or scouts]," which prevented the generation of the desert from entering the promised land (see Num. 13–14 and Deut. 1: 22–45). On the plain reading of the text, the sin was simply that the scouts struck fear in the people by how they described the land's inhabitants. Dessler, however, identifies the sin as the very use of human initiative, the very sending of scouts. The people ought to have abandoned the illusion that they have causal powers and relied on God's might to conquer the land.[21]

But if God causes everything by His will, wouldn't *every* event be a miracle? What would the difference be between the natural and the miraculous? Dessler (1985, 2:240) replies that the difference lies in familiarity: "We call God's act a 'miracle' when He wills an occurrence which is novel and unfamiliar to us ... We call God's acts 'nature' when He wills that certain events should occur in a recognizable pattern with which we become familiar." The obvious follow-up question is why God presents us with the *appearance* of order – when that appearance is likely to mislead many of us. Dessler replies that God wants to test us, to see whether we will recognize that He is the sole cause. "[Nature] is merely an illusion which gives man a choice to exercise his free will: to err, or to choose the truth" (ibid.)

Dessler uses the notion of a test in response to another problem as well. Let's ask ourselves: Why need we labor at all, such as by working to earn a living? Why do we humans take initiative and invest practical effort? Dessler responds: "We have to ... learn to see God's providence even in the world of mundane activity. We have to stand the test and

---

[19] McCracken 1983, 211. See also Loeb 1981, 191–228 (on Malebranche's motivations).
[20] Freddoso 1998, 77.
[21] Dessler 1985, 2:263–82. See Shatz 2010. For a midrashic precedent for opposition to excess initiative, see *Gen. Rabbah* 89:1.

realize that nature has no power" (Dessler 1985, 2:288). "We have to do enough to ensure that the divine bounty which comes down to us from the Lord could possibly be attributed to some other cause" (ibid., 2:264–65). This worldly endeavor must be kept at a minimum, just enough to keep us tempted to attribute success to our own labors. By way of a popular analogy: you may buy one lottery ticket, a minimal effort, but to buy two is a deficiency in *bittaḥon* (trust in God) (ibid., 2:265).

These details invite discomfort. Is it right to tempt ourselves, as we do (according to Dessler) when we labor? Applied to other precepts, that would mean that putting oneself into a position of sexual temptation or the temptation to eat nonkosher food is admissible! Moreover, is it right for God to put us in a position where we may tempt ourselves (since He makes the world appear to proceed naturally)?[22]

A barrage of other objections ensues. In traditional theism, can't I *cause* (or influence) God to do things by praying and by doing good deeds? And what happens to free choice? Aren't we causes of our actions?[23] If free will is labeled an exception (we need the free choice to recognize the truth about causation) – well, *any* exceptions to the principle that God causes everything undercuts the general principle(s) that motivated the occasionalist position.

It is, also, more difficult to justify God's ways in an occasionalist framework than in a nonoccasionalist one. For occasionalists, God, not humans, produces earthquakes and disease; it is God who turns weapons of destruction against Jews throughout history. Producing evil is morally worse than not intervening to stop an evil in progress, so occasionalism exacerbates the problem of evil.[24]

Another difficulty is that, in an occasionalist framework, God throws touchdowns, brews coffee, and fixes leaky faucets. It only *looks like* athletes and baristas and plumbers are doing all that. Does God rig all athletic events? Does He truly care about who gets a particular rebound in a basketball game? When athletes kneel in prayer and ask God for victory, or thank Him after a triumph, can we readily accept that God was really arranging for their team to win?

What's more, the occasionalist axiology views *bittaḥon*, trust in God, as the prime virtue. To be sure, the idea that faith in God can trigger

---

[22] The Talmud interprets Lev. 19:14, "Do not place a stumbling block before the blind," as prohibiting tempting others to sin (*Avodah Zarah* 6a–6b).

[23] See, however, Chapter 6.

[24] See Freddoso 1988, 115–16, and his interesting suggestion that for occasionalists, there may be no intrinsic goods and evils. On Malebranche's theodicy, see Black 1997.

divine protection was emphasized even by medieval rationalists such as Baḥya ibn Pakuda,[25] and it boasts biblical support: "Blessed is the person who trusts in the Lord, and the Lord will be his security" (Jer. 17:7). But the occasionalist's glorification of *bittaḥon* leads to a challenge. If we are aware that all depends on God, and we therefore cut back on practical initiative aiming at *our* benefit, why not also decrease our practical efforts to help *others*?

Dessler's reply to this objection is that we have two desirable traits in tension here, *bittaḥon* (trust) and *ḥesed* (loving-kindness). Trust (in God) is called for when we deal with our own needs, loving-kindness when we deal with those of our fellow human beings (though God is involved in our acts of loving-kindness) (2:280–81).[26] But imagine people who find that repeated acts of *ḥesed* weaken their *bittaḥon* by making them too confident in their own power, too disposed to believe in an autonomous system of nature. Should they risk further attrition of *bittaḥon* in order to help others? Why should *ḥesed* always trump *bittaḥon*? Perhaps the answer is that we need a single rule of exercising *ḥesed*, lest people misassess their traits or adopt *bittaḥon* out of indolence (*bittaḥon* can be the more passive course). But we have the following additional challenge: for an occasionalist, it is not I who am (causally) bringing my neighbor benefit anyway; so if effort on my part is to be at all rational, my responsibility must consist only in my efforts at influencing God to bring about a beneficial result for my neighbor. Which brings us back to the question: isn't influencing God (say, through prayer or good deeds) an instance of our exercising causal power? Furthermore, even if we would receive credit or blame not for our deeds (as we *do* nothing), but only for our intentions, God, not X, would seem to be responsible for the bad or good result.[27]

---

[25] See Baḥya ibn Pakuda 1970, part 4.

[26] Naḥmanides (commentary to Lev. 26:11), who highlights trust (e.g., commentary to Deut. 18:13), suggests a complex justification for administering medical care, one that views it as objectionable in the ideal but justifiable in the concrete. If someone consults a doctor, this itself shows that they are not among the *adat Hashem* (congregation of the Lord) who will enjoy divine protection by dint of trusting in Him; and the doctor therefore need have no compunctions about trying to heal.

[27] The practices of praying for someone's welfare or, say, giving charity so that God will heal another person confront the question: "Ought not God to benefit men according to their needs or merits and not in terms of the rather haphazard and arbitrary condition of being the subject of prayer?" (H. D. Lewis 1959, 251). Why should God make X's fate dependent on whether someone else prays or gives charity on behalf of X?" Cf. Cohn-Sherbok 1989, 3–4, 98–102, 154–56. The question is deepened by the fact that it also matters *who* chooses to pray for the party, the prayers of the righteous being of special efficacy. One response would be that when people pray for others or give charity, they

Naturalism accounts for interpersonal responsibility much more simply. Our actions *genuinely*, without direct divine activity, promote or hinder the welfare of others. Therefore, we cannot thrust responsibility for others' welfare onto (as it were!) God's shoulders. God adopts a policy of nonintervention, in order to promote human responsibility. "Hard" naturalists (as I'll call them) will say that God never violates this policy, while "soft" naturalists will say that He violates it at times. But both types of naturalism greatly reduce divine responsibility for the consequences of human moral indolence and throw it squarely on human shoulders.

I hope I have shown that the religious attraction of occasionalism – its seeming to venerate God by making Him the sole cause of all events – must be balanced against significant *religious* drawbacks involving free choice, evil, temptation, divine concern for trivial events, and interpersonal responsibility. Granted, occasionalists may be willing to pay the price, but they should understand why others will not. Naturalism has the potential to escape all of these problems. We turn now to examine the allegedly positive religious sensibilities it creates.

Consideration 2: Naturalism and Religious Values

What religious values, if any, are promoted by belief in a mostly fixed and unalterable natural order? What should be the theology, anthropology, and self-perception of a person who lives within the natural order?[28] We have already glimpsed naturalism's ability to generate human interpersonal responsibility, an area where occasionalism falters. But there is much more to say about the impact of belief in the natural order on one's religious orientation.

Let's start by elaborating the distinction between hard and soft naturalism. As we've seen, hard naturalism, occasionalism's polar opposite,

---

strengthen community bonds. But to eliminate the petitionary element altogether, and with it the notion that we can influence God, does not seem plausible. The nature and purpose of petitionary prayer needs a wide-ranging formulation. On numerous aspects of petitionary prayer, see Davison 2017.

[28] Since my focus is on how naturalism may promote religious values, not on the rationality of belief in miracles, I will not address the objections of David Hume and John Stuart Mill to belief in miracles. Also, Benedict Spinoza's equation of God with nature – "Deus sive natura," "God or nature" is too distant from traditional theism for purposes of this chapter. Mordecai Kaplan (1881–1983), founder of the movement called Reconstructionism, rejects belief in the supernatural but reinterprets the concept of God to refer to the realm of nature (see Chapter 1). (See Kaplan 1958 and 1967.) My focus is on how those who believe in a supernatural being with certain abilities accommodate or do not accommodate laws of nature.

construes phenomena such as prophecy, providence, and miracles in naturalistic categories, perhaps while maintaining that a supernatural understanding of these phenomena is conveyed for the unsophisticated masses, to keep religion vivid and alive for them. Again, hard naturalists do not deny the metaphysical dependence of the world on God; they will typically insist that He created it and/or that were God not to exist, nothing else would. However, hard naturalists maintain that God does not intervene in the natural order, period. *Could* He? Yes (in one version). *Would* He? No.

Furthermore, according to hard naturalists, it is possible to reinterpret naturalistically not only prophecy, miracles, and providence (as noted earlier), but also practices such as petitionary prayer, which ostensibly make sense only on interventionist assumptions. For example, petitionary prayer helps the believer to introspect, to scrutinize their behavior, to empathize with the community (either because by praying for their needs people become sensitized to others' needs,[29] or because one prays in a communal setting) or to recognize his or her dependence on the natural order God creates. Alternatively, a naturalist could adopt a deontological approach such as that of Isaiah Leibowitz, which regards prayer as a commandment alone, devoid of connection to concrete human interests or indeed any reason.[30]

In contrast to hard naturalism, soft naturalism affirms the existence of a natural order that prevails most of the time, but it insists that some events (which over the course of history add up to very many) can be explained only by reference to direct divine intervention in nature – miracles, that is.[31]

Let us turn now to theistic motivations for *some* form of naturalism – what religious values are reflected in a naturalist metaphysics? To be clear, the authors I'll cite do not espouse the medieval rationalists' accounts of providence and prophecy; but they do give a sense of why the concept of a natural order fits certain religious values.

---

[29] See Soloveitchik 1978b, 65–66. Soloveitchik was not a hard naturalist.
[30] Regarding Jewish naturalist understandings of petitionary prayer, see Cohn-Sherbok 1989, ch. 3; Carmy 1999. On Maimonides's view on prayer, see Fox 1990, ch. 11 and Benor 1995.
[31] There are different categories of intervention: e.g., "violative" interventions that start off new natural causal chains vs. "violative" interventions that bypass the natural order entirely, etc. Likewise there are different senses of miracles and perhaps other conditions that violative interventions must satisfy (e.g., the event must have significance), but these will not figure here.

Value 1: God's Wisdom and Glory

"How manifold are Your works, O Lord, you made them all with wisdom" (Ps. 104:24). Maimonides believed that the universe has a teleological structure that makes the divine wisdom manifest. The laws of nature supply human beings and nonhuman animals with the means to satisfy their needs, and endow human beings with the ability to discern those means;[32] in parallel fashion, the laws of the Torah – the *mitzvot* – benefit human beings as well. Maimonides cites a rabbinic text that suggests that miracles were built into nature when it was created, and thus are not exceptions to natural law but rather manifestations of its workings.[33]

Frequent divine interventions would cast aspersion on God's wisdom. R. Natan Slifkin (2010), in the course of defending the acceptance of the laws of evolution rather than attributing every "new creation" in Genesis 1 to direct divine acts, writes (67):

> Order and structure are part of God's methods and indicative of His greatness. Laws – rational, structured laws – are the greatest expression of His wisdom. This is why the system of natural law is so important and so superior to the miraculous order.

Suppose someone designs a computer program and can repair brilliantly any glitch that comes up. Compare this individual to someone who designed the program so that there would be no glitches in the first place. The second (goes the thinking) is clearly superior. And if the first achieves the repair by means of a miracle, the second is still superior.[34]

R. Joseph B. Soloveitchik (2008, 133) introduces another consideration, divine *glory*:

> In the Jewish view, miracles and wonders occur only when absolutely necessary, when all other means have been exhausted ... Using a short cut in the natural realm [even in this case] does not add any glory to the splendor that shines forth from ordered, law-governed reality. On the contrary, it mars the honor of the Creator. God's natural Providence is the crowning jewel of His management of the world.[35]

---

[32] See, e.g., *Guide of the Perplexed* 3:32, and the texts analyzed in Gellman 1991. Nahmanides, however, views being subject to nature as an absence of protection due to insufficient religiosity (see, e.g., commentary to Lev. 26:11). But see also Maimonides 1963, 624–27 (*Guide of the Perplexed* 3:51) and the analysis in Berger 2011, 142–43.

[33] See n. 8.

[34] Slifkin and I developed this example independently.

[35] See also the comment of Baḥya ben Asher to Exod. 17:13: "Why should the Lord uproot His own handiwork?" Soloveitchik was a giant of Jewish law, and Halakhah's rule-centered character may have influenced him to conceive nature, too, as a set of rules and laws admitting few exceptions. Notwithstanding, Soloveitchik believes in miracles, and denigration of them is not common in his writings.

We should not equate "glory" with wisdom, but the arguments of Slifkin and Soloveitchik are similar.

If miracles reflect lack of wisdom or diminish divine glory, why did God perform so many of them? Doesn't the *frequent* occurrence of miracles mar the creator's glory so much that it can't be restored? And why did God initiate them so quickly, before "all other means had been exhausted"? And yet, there exist *both* texts like Psalms 19:2 that suggest that the order of creation bears testimony to God's greatness, *and* rabbinic sources that accord with Soloveitchik's belittling of miracles.[36]

These arguments from wisdom and glory weaken a bit when we reflect about how random events reflect wisdom or glory. (I refer to ontological randomness, not epistemological randomness, [our ignorance of the true causes].) But randomness does not negate the teleological or glorious features that are present. More important, arguments based on wisdom or glory do not establish hard naturalism over soft. Why would highlighting God's wisdom or glory entail never finding His power and His will? Why not argue that a theory of divine action should reflect *both* God's wisdom and His will, although wisdom gets greater weight? Furthermore, to reiterate, when God breaks the laws of nature, it is in the service of good, just, and wisely pursued results. Thus, miracles manage to display God's power without casting aspersion on divine wisdom or diminishing His glory.

It is not clear why God believes it more important to implement wisdom or manifest glory through laws of nature than to distribute rewards and punishments according to deeds. And the stress on wisdom and glory faces the difficulty posed by the dysteleological, destructive features of nature. Engaging evil is the focus of Chapter 3.

Value 2: Human Responsibility

We saw earlier that, while occasionalism has difficulty accounting for interpersonal responsibility, naturalism fosters such responsibility. But the point is not just that, in a naturalistic framework, humans, and not only

---

[36] In one story congruent with Soloveitchik's approach (*Shabbat* 53b), a man's wife died and he could not pay for a wet-nurse. A miracle occurred and the man grew breasts and nursed the child. R. Joseph declared, "Come and see how great he is that a miracle was wrought for him." But Abbayei responded: "On the contrary, how inferior is this man, that the natural order was changed for him." The commentators seek to explain Abbayei's statement; e.g., R. Shlomo Yitzḥaki (Rashi) maintains that the fact the man needed a miracle, and apparently did not merit earning a living to pay for a nurse, speaks ill of him.

God, can genuinely cause outcomes. It's that responsibility, or responsible choice, requires a natural order. "A world which is to be a moral order," writes F. R. Tennant (1962, 2:199–200), "must be a physical order characterized by law or regularity ... Law-abidingness is an essential condition of the world being a theatre of moral life." Or, as C. S. Lewis (1962) put it (34), "The very conception of a common, and therefore, stable world demands that [miracles] be extremely rare." We cannot make decisions for which we are responsible without knowing the order of nature, and we cannot know the order of nature unless there is such an order.

Religious people, no less than secular individuals, enjoy the benefits of scientific inquiry. Most appreciate the urgency of trying to improve human life through such inquiry. Science has shown palpable, dramatic success in conquering disease, alleviating risk and pain in childbirth, increasing longevity, promoting the welfare of the disabled, harnessing sources of energy, storing information, facilitating travel, detecting potential weather disasters, creating instant communication, aiding trauma victims, treating mental disorders, and improving the overall comfort and quality of life. Technology "has offered power, control, and the prospect of overcoming our helplessness and dependency."[37] Embracing natural means, including scientific research, conflicts with the attitude of dependency and quietism championed, at times, in Jewish tradition.[38] An appreciation of science and technology, therefore, *ostensibly* reflects the values of secularization. So there looms a charge of having surrendered Jewish values by acting through the natural order. Is there an inconsistency between the scientific world's amelioration of the human condition and Jewish tradition?

The tradition encompasses many views, some passivist, but complete reliance on God defies Jewish legal norms. These norms require people to utilize the natural order in such pursuits as medical treatment, economic effort, war and general security. "We do not rely on miracles" is a well-established principle of Halakhah (Jewish law).[39] No doubt, use of the sciences may lead people to arrogance, to the belief that "my strength and power created all this wealth for me" (Deut. 8:17). But as a corrective to this attitude, God states, "remember that it is the Lord your God who gives you *the power* to amass wealth" (Deut. 8:18). Acknowledging

---

[37] Barbour 1990, 1:xiii.
[38] See also Goldman 1986, 53, and Wurzburger 1989, 105–6.
[39] *Pesaḥim* 64b; Jerusalem Talmud, *Shekalim* 6:3; and elsewhere. Though the dictum "We do not rely on miracles" is a subject of dispute in the Talmud, it was codified as binding in later codes. There are also specific imperatives dictating human endeavor in the areas I itemized (medicine, economics, war).

God as the creator of human *capacities* while asserting that humans create success by enlisting such capacities seems to be a good way of integrating the modern secular ethos with belief in God.[40]

Some talmudic texts bear on this point. Philosophers ask the Sages: why does God provide the sun, the moon, and the stars if idolaters will worship them? The answer is: "the world follows its natural course, and the fools who act corruptly will be held to account" (*Avodah Zarah* 54b). People exercise their capacities *within the framework of nature*.

David Hartman writes (1985, 5):

> A basic presupposition of [modern] critiques [of religion] is that in order to reinforce belief in human initiative, it is necessary to uproot commitment to religious outlooks that engender passivity and feelings of self-negation ... Scientific and technological advances in the nineteenth and twentieth centuries confirm the need for a modern conception of the human being that strengthens belief in human adequacy and in the ability to bear responsibility for history.[41]

Soloveitchik (1978a, 33–34)) formulates the need for science in terms of a dual ethic:

> There are ... two moralities: a morality of majesty and a morality of humility. The moral gesture of cosmic man aims at majesty or kingship ... Man, imitating God, quests for kingship, not only over a limited domain, but over the far and distant regions of the cosmos, as well. Man is summoned by God to be ruler, to be king, to be victorious. Victory, as the most important aspect of kingship, is an ethical goal and the human effort to achieve victory is a moral one, provided the means man employs are of a moral nature. To live, and to defy death, is a sublime moral achievement ... Curing, healing the sick, is a divine attribute reflecting an activity in which man ought to engage.
>
> Underlying the ethic of victory is the mystical doctrine that creation is incomplete. God purposely left one aspect of creation unfinished in order to involve man in a creative gesture and to give him the opportunity to become both co-creator and king.

R. Samson Raphael Hirsch (1808–1888) (2018a) also writes in support of utilizing what nature provides (63): "Judaism considers it vitally important for its adherents to become aware that their entire universe is governed by well-defined laws ... only by his own detailed knowledge and regard for these laws can man make nature serve his purposes."

---

[40] See also Gellman 1991 on how Maimonides's writings reflect this perspective.
[41] See also Hartman 1976. The common denominator of the views of Hartman and Isaiah (Yeshayahu) Leibowitz, discussed later in this chapter, is that hard naturalism coheres with other religious sensibilities. But they disagree about (a) the religious desirability of submission and obedience and (b) the religious relevance of human needs and values. (See Hartman 1985, ch. 5.)

Naturalism instills a firm sense of responsibility for taking practical initiative.[42] However, as soft naturalists would point out, an ethic that stresses human responsibility need not exclude divine intervention altogether. In fact, perhaps God will help human beings who are aware that they are responsible for human welfare – God helps those who help themselves, or, in this case, who help themselves and others. Randomness in nature does not negate the ability to make wise practical decisions.

But does an interventionist metaphysics take responsibility out of human hands? On the contrary – doesn't it put our fate squarely in our own hands? Just think of the Bible's stark claim (Lev. 26): "If you walk in my statutes ..." you will be healthy, victorious, secure, and spared all suffering; "If you violate my statutes ..." you will suffer greatly. Potentially, pervasive interventionism can create a stable order, empowering human beings to achieve results that reliance on nature could not achieve! Freud utilized this insight.[43] He saw the origins of theistic religion in the attempt to *control* nature in ways that science could not supply. Still, in the world as we experience it, a person's future cannot be reliably predicted from the person's religious deeds, whereas a person's future often *can* be reliably predicted from the steps that one takes to protect himself within the natural order. In some Jewish texts, it is in the next world that people receive their just deserts.[44] Hence, naturalism gives a person greater control over his or her fate. Of course, no nature-based steps *guarantee* good health and rid us of the unpredictability and randomness we find in the natural order. This last point leads us to consider another motivation for religious naturalism.

Value 3: Explaining Evil

The picture of a tight, invariable correlation between observing the Torah's laws and enjoying health, prosperity, and physical security is often rejected in Jewish tradition. (See Chapter 3.) Consider how the talmudic sage Rava reasoned about certain components of human welfare. Bear in mind, in reading this passage, that *mazzal* (astrological influence) is regarded by talmudic thinkers as based on natural laws:

Rava said: the length of one's life, the number of his children, and the extent of his sustenance depend not on his merit, but on his *mazzal*. For Rabbah and R. Ḥisda were both righteous rabbis; one would pray for rain and rain would

---

[42] See also Gellman 1991.
[43] Freud 1961, esp. ch. 3–4.
[44] See Chapters 3 and 7.

fall, and the other would pray for rain and rain would fall. Yet R. Hisda lived ninety-two years, Rabbah only forty. R. Hisda's household celebrated sixty weddings, Rabbah's suffered sixty bereavements. R. Hisda's household fed bread of fine flour to their dogs and it was not needed; Rabbah's household fed bread of barley flour to people and not enough of it could be found [Moed Katan 28a]

Through stories about Abraham and R. Akiva, the Talmud, echoed by medieval commentators such as the Tosafists, maintains an "override" theory by which exceptionally righteous people, or even just someone who does a good deed, may escape the fate "decreed" (as it were) by astrology, in whose truth the Sages believed).[45] The implication is that without the righteous deeds, nature would prevail. In similar fashion, Nahmanides maintains that, for the large majority of people, "[God] leaves them to the accidents of nature."[46] In contrast, exceptionally righteous people – a very small percentage of humanity – receive reward in this world, and exceptionally bad people receive punishment.

It is hard to reconcile the idea of override with the fact that Rabbah, who was so righteous, lived such a miserable life.[47] The passage above thus leans to a more extreme thesis – viz. *sometimes, even righteousness cannot override the astrological fate (= natural law)*. Further, even if positing theistic naturalism leads us not to expect a distribution of goods and evils that perfectly reflects people's merits, that's not a theodicy. A theodicy would have to *explain* why God chose the setup that He did. Rava, by contrast, merely *describes* the situation of individuals and does not give a *reason* for why God allows the disparity between the lives of Rabbah and R. Hisda. That reason is known only to God.[48]

From this and other sources, to be cited in Chapter 3, we see that Jewish texts at times preclude a heavily interventionist metaphysics, without explaining why God does not intervene more often.

---

[45] *Shabbat* 156a–b and Tosafot on 156a, s.v. *ein*. See also Chapters 3 and 6. Maimonides denied the efficacy of astrology in Laws of Foreign Worship 11:16 and his *Letter on Astrology* (in Lerner and Mahdi 1963, 227–36).
[46] See Nahmanides, commentary to Gen. 18:19 and Lev. 26:11 with Berger 2011; Bahya ben Asher, commentary to Gen. 18:19; Ovadyah Seforno, commentary to Lev. 13:47.
[47] But cf. *Yevamot* 50a, cited by the Tosafists.
[48] One may argue, however, that if God *sometimes* intervenes to override the constellations for an individual of merit, but does not do so for others on the same level, this picture intensifies the problem of evil. For, having committed Himself not to let nature determine all events, God seems arbitrary in allowing overrides for only *some* very righteous people. If you deny intervention altogether, you have a chance at finding a theodicy that reduces arbitrariness. (See Basinger and Basinger 1986, ch. 5.)

Value 4: Guarding against Egocentrism

"Religion is not God serving man; it is man serving God." So goes a pungent paraphrase of the opinion of Isaiah (Yeshayahu) Leibowitz. Interventionism stresses that religion confers benefits; naturalism, that it makes demands. "A utilitarian conception of religion," writes Leibowitz (1992, 63), "depletes religion of all *religious* import."

Interventionism, some argue, encourages preoccupation with self-interest. It creates a deplorable pattern of *mitzvah*-observance based on ulterior motives – *lo lishmah* ("not for its own sake") in rabbinic terminology. Naturalism clears the way for a foundation to religious commitment that is wholly deontological.

Clearly, however, the use of science, such as medical treatment, is likewise geared to benefit individuals materially. True, scientific research aims at enhancing the welfare of *the collective*, including future generations.[49] Think of the protection of the collective afforded by vaccines or technological defense systems.[50] But in interventionist metaphysics, don't religious acts promote the collective welfare as well, now and in the future? Moreover, empirically, throughout history interventionists have been deeply involved in benevolent causes. In the Orthodox Jewish community, it is the primarily interventionist ultra-Orthodox who have been the founders and administrators of social services such as emergency medical services (Hatzalah) and services for hospital patients and their families (Bikkur Cholim.).

Thus, concerns over egocentrism do not constitute a good reason why a religious person should favor naturalism.[51]

FROM MINDSET TO METAPHYSICS

An important question in our context is: Do the advantages of a *sensibility* created by naturalism generate a good argument for the *truth* of naturalism? Consider the concerns about egocentrism and disinterested

---

[49] "What we call civilization is the sum total of a community effort through the millennia" (Soloveitchik 1965, 22).
[50] See also Sztuden 2016, XIV.
[51] Besides entailing that no activity aimed at furthering human ends is truly religious, Leibowitz's position does away with the time-honored project in Jewish tradition of finding a teleology for *mitzvot* and encouraging Jews to reflect on these rationales. The theological price of Leibowitz's theory – the severing of religion from human welfare – is steep and arguably not worth paying.

worship. At best, these create a good argument for not placing divine intervention at the forefront of religious consciousnesses. For a religion might demand that individuals maintain a delicate tension. They might be required to *believe* that God can and will intervene in the natural order (either to satisfy human needs or to execute justice), but at the same time be required not to let this belief motivate them.⁵²

Additionally, when hard naturalists appeal to considerations of egoistic motivation to support their view, they focus on the human point of view and fail to consider God's. A good God will not stay out of human affairs; He will act to better the world and to create a just order by dispensing reward and punishment. Should God withhold good from people just because if He intervenes in things people might then develop a base motivation? It would be better for God to intervene, while demanding that people not let belief in intervention influence their actions. God may wish to limit such intervention, to be sure, for if it is widespread it will make disinterested worship psychologically nigh-impossible. But the crucial responsibility for proper motivation falls on the believer.

To an extent, therefore, arguments for naturalism that are based on the allegedly nonegoistic sensibilities it creates are *non sequiturs*. All that follows is something about the proper religious consciousness and mindset, not something about what metaphysical structure the universe has. We are committed to worshipping God even if God does nothing for us, but it does not follow from this selfless, disinterested commitment that He does nothing for us. Believers can be humble and agnostic with respect to how God relates to the universe, without that uncertainty affecting their commitment. Religious belief can be separated from religious motivation.⁵³

Hard naturalists might object that it is psychologically too demanding to expect people to endorse an interventionist metaphysics while making decisions using a naturalist one. On their view, even though a good God might want to exercise justice and mercy and therefore intervene in

---

⁵² This is a type of tension some have attributed to Kant. Acts done simply to acquire a benefit have no moral worth, but if a desire for benefit does not motivate the act, and instead the motive of duty prevails, the act has moral worth even if the person desires the benefit. See also Chapter 8.

⁵³ To be sure, as Samuel Lebens pointed out to me, one could argue that "the divine plan for the metaphysics of the universe should match the divinely ordained sensibilities of revealed religion." But it isn't clear that this is so, given the "cruelty" attributed to nature.

human affairs, God's ultimate decision would be to refrain from intervening in human affairs *because* He does not want to create an egoistic mindset. But this understanding of God's behavior is problematic. If God makes hard naturalism true in order to prevent belief in interventionism, then He has badly miscalculated. For despite His nonintervention, interventionists are alive and well!

For Isaac Abravanel, as I read him,[54] once belief in intervention loses its vitality and its applicability to decision-making, once its motivational power is suppressed, our acts lose their distinctive religious character and value. Belief in divinely dispensed reward and punishment, he argues, distinguishes the Jewish religious worldview from the views of "the philosophers," and therefore the motivation of self-interest, which is rooted in this belief, is the proper motivation for performing commandments. This motivation gives expression to the belief in God's providence. So we have different sensibilities at work here: one focused on belief in intervention, the other on discouraging self-interested motivation for doing *mitzvot*.

CONCLUSION

There are numerous candidate reasons, all found in Jewish sources, for why traditional theism can and ought to allow itself to take the natural order seriously and to encourage human beings to exploit its workings for beneficial purposes. There are qualified affirmations of the natural order by the Sages. These reasons do not exclude divine intervention altogether, but rather are consistent with both hard and soft naturalism. If, however, we start questioning the connection between sensibilities and metaphysics, we find that an argument from God's justice and goodness weakens both hard and soft forms of naturalism.[55]

The growth of science as both a cognitive endeavor and a practical tool has intensified and complicated the challenge of locating the proper places of natural law and divine intervention in a theistic metaphysics.[56] Like the path from anthropomorphic language to Perfect Being Theology,

---

[54] Abravanel 2013, commenting on *Avot* 1:3. Abravanel restricts this view to ritual commandments as opposed to interpersonal ones.

[55] My catalogue of religious arguments for naturalism should be supplemented by the pool of arguments examined in Sztuden 2016.

[56] Ironically, though, many of the religious sources that we have seen support naturalism are medieval.

the movement from miracles to naturalism is an instance where Judaism displays itself as a tradition whose philosophy is not static. For all that, a theist's conception of where God is in the world will have to be formed on the familiar and heavily trod territory of scientific and philosophical reflection, combined with appeals to traditional texts.

3

The Problem(s) of Evil

No challenge to Perfect Being Theology (PBT) is more familiar – or more existentially gripping – than the problem of evil. If a perfect God truly exists, a being who is omnipotent, omniscient, and omnibenevolent, why is there evil?[1] Some Jewish thinkers who address the problem devise theodicies – explanations of why God allows evil; others maintain that it is wrong for theists even to seek theodicies. Some biblical and rabbinic sources allow human beings to protest against God for allowing evil or specific evils – to remonstrate with Him in forensic fashion, to argue with Him about His ways. Others expect human beings to accept the existence of evil without a whimper. And within each approach there are subdisputes.

In what follows I select six especially striking aspects of Jewish treatments of the problem of evil. They are:

- the rejection of divine command morality
- the prevalence of protests against God
- the rejection of retributivist theodicies
- the endorsement of "afflictions of love"
- Hiding of the Face
- antitheodicy.

In Chapter 7 I will consider another feature – the use of reincarnation as a theodicy.

It bears repeating that the ancient rabbinic sources of Judaism are not philosophical treatises. Theological views often have to be teased out of

[1] As we will see, "Why is there evil?" is just one version of the problem.

stories and anecdotes. Statements in these sources tend to be pithy, aphoristic, ambiguous, cryptic, tantalizing, and contradictory – which makes interpretation immensely challenging and for that reason particularly intriguing.[2]

PRELIMINARIES: STATING THE PROBLEMS

There is no *single* problem of evil. For one thing, we have to distinguish between moral evils (evils that human beings inflict upon other humans, on nonhuman animals, and on the environment) and natural evils (evils such as earthquakes, illnesses, and floods). These categories are not sharply distinct. After all, some natural evils are such that human beings are partially responsible for producing them or not limiting damage (floods, diseases, environmental changes), and moral evils are often created when people utilize harmful means that nature has made available. Thus some evils are hybrids of the categories. Note also that evils do not always involve unpleasant states of mind. Dementia and vegetative coma are generally deemed evils even if they are not accompanied by significant pain or other suffering. Family and friends suffer when a person is in one of the relevant states, but arguably that person is also undergoing an evil, and is in a bad state, although not suffering.[3] Theodicies that work for suffering may or may not work for these other evils.

But supposing we get clear on what kinds of evils we are asking about, we can pose a slew of distinct questions:

(1) Why does God (an omnipotent, omniscient, and omnibenevolent being) allow *any* evil?
(2) Why does God allow *so much* evil?
(3) Why does God allow certain *specific evils* (such as the Holocaust)?
(4) Why does God on occasion fail to fulfill His promise that certain evils will not occur if the Jewish people comply with His commands?

There is also a fifth question, about the distribution of goods and evils:

(5) Why do the righteous suffer and the wicked prosper?

Note that in the Bible and rabbinic literature, the problems of evil are not challenges to belief in the very existence of God, but rather to belief

---

[2] For orientations to the problems of evil, see Meister and Moser 2017, McBrayer and Howard-Snyder 2013, and Meister 2017.
[3] Cf. Stump 2010a, 4, and Ch. 7 below, n. 76.

in His providence, goodness, and fairness; and they express a desire to understand rather than a denial.

Question 5 is dubbed in Jewish sources the problem of "the righteous person who suffers evil, the wicked person who enjoys good" (*tzaddik ve-ra lo, rasha ve-tov lo*). In popular literature, that phrase is often used interchangeably with statements of the general problem of evil. This, however, is a conflation and a mistake.

What I mean is this. Question 5 can arise in two ways.

(A) Suppose we reply to the other questions by endorsing a retributivist theodicy (i.e. the notion that suffering is punishment for sin). Then we may ask question 5 as a follow-up in order to refute the proposed retributivist theodicy. But question 5 is still distinct from the general problem. It is a *rejoinder to a possible reply* to other questions, specifically 1–3, and does not stand on its own.

(B) Even without trying to answer the more general questions, we might believe that the world must exhibit a moral order in which righteous people prosper and wicked people suffer. Question 5 then stands on its own.[4]

To illustrate: The prophet Jonah, on one reading, is so married to the notion of a moral order that he is bothered by divine mercy – he thinks God should not allow someone's repentance to cancel a punishment that the person (in this case, the city of Nineveh) deserves (Jon. 4:2). If we adopt (B), then "the wicked man who enjoys good" is no less a problem than is "the righteous man who suffers evil,"[5] albeit the former receives far less attention than the latter, and bothers people less. Jeremiah (12:1–3) raises the problem of the wicked who prosper ("why does the way of the wicked prosper? Why are the workers of treachery at ease? You have planted them and they have taken root"); and Ecclesiastes (8:11–14) notes, among other depressing features of the world's *havalim* (a word that has been variously translated), that the righteous suffer and the wicked prosper, and that ill comes to the wicked only after a long time. In *Berakhot* 7a, a two-part verse (Exod. 33:19) is explicated by R. Meir as follows: "'I shall be gracious to one to whom I am gracious' – even if he is not deserving; and 'I will have mercy for those for whom I will have mercy' – even if he is not deserving." While in R. Meir's reading the verse

---

[4] The importance of (B) was highlighted in a lecture by Aaron Segal. www.youtube.com/watch?v=PQsSGoB2cuQ

[5] So understood, Jonah goes beyond Abraham's notion that God must not kill the innocent together with the wicked (Gen. 18:25).

could simply be brushing Moses's question aside, possibly, the idea here is that graciousness and mercy are virtues, and God's graciousness and mercy are so great that they spill over to the undeserving. As J. L. Mackie (1977, 188) puts it, in discussing virtues generally, virtues cannot be too finely discriminating. But the result still is that the retributivist's notion of moral order is not instantiated in all cases.[6]

We will see that a retributivist theodicy is not only problematic philosophically; it is rejected in some Jewish texts, at least when they are read a certain way. Notably, Jewish thinkers who reject retributivism often confine that denial to "this world," while affirming that just deserts will be meted out *in the World-to-Come*. In this way the moral order is preserved. But some theodicy is required to explain why punishments are deferred.

One final question should be noted:

(6) Why does God command His people to do acts that appear to us to be evil – for example, to destroy all the Amalekite people?[7] This question will be raised again in Chapter 8.

Besides distinguishing questions 1–6, we need to distinguish deductive and inductive forms of the problem. The deductive form claims (looking at question 1) that the existence of evil logically precludes the existence of a perfect God – renders it impossible – while the inductive form claims that the existence of evil renders the existence of a perfect God (merely) improbable. This distinction has become *de rigeur* in analytic philosophy. Prior to the distinction emerging forcefully in the 1960s, philosophers overwhelmingly utilized the deductive formulation. Failures in the deductive arguments (pointed out perhaps most famously by Plantinga 1967, chs. 5–6) led to a widespread belief that the deductive argument should be retired and that it is the inductive that merits attention. This tide may be turning back, however.[8]

Some philosophers have put forth another distinction, that between presenting a *defense* and presenting a *theodicy*.[9] In a defense, it is argued, one does not claim to read God's mind (that is arrogant and/or futile), but rather suggests a *possible* reason for God to allow evil; in a theodicy, one presents an explanation that one affirms as the *true* explanation of why God allows evil (or evils of a certain amount etc.). Such a distinction would remove the objection that philosophizing about evil is arrogant

---

[6] For further discussion, see Albo 1929, 4:7.
[7] On linking morally problematic laws to the problem of evil, see Stump 2010b.
[8] See Oppy 2017, Sterba 2019.
[9] E.g., Van Inwagen 2006, 7–8.

and/or futile – it may be executed as a defense (a possible explanation) rather than as a theodicy (a true explanation). Although a defense indeed shows more humility than a theodicy, I do not accept the distinction between defense and theodicy in all cases. When you can think of only one explanation for evidence that seems to falsify your belief, and you stick to your belief, that explanation also must furnish the explanation you deem true.[10] My sense is that explanations of evil presented in Jewish texts are meant as theodicies, not defenses.

A further distinction, which I do deem tenable, is between using, in a theodicy, only premises that an atheist would accept, and using premises that are embraced by theists but an atheist does not accept. As Peter Van Inwagen (2006, 6) puts it, "Attempts by theists to account for the evils of the world must take place within the constraints provided by the larger theologies they subscribe to." Or, as Moshe Sokol (2013b, 79) writes, "What counts as problematic for the system depends upon what the system itself teaches." Replies of this sort need limits, though. In particular, theists shouldn't be allowed to invoke wild premises that are part of their belief system and use them to generate theodicies. But while an appeal to claims internal to theism can be abused, such theistic appeals, I believe, are in principle legitimate.[11]

Would viewing God as limited in power, knowledge, or goodness – as something less than (choose one or more!) omnipotent, omniscient, and omnibenevolent – completely defuse the problem of evil?[12] No, as long as we believe that God is at least *very* powerful, *almost* all-knowing, and *almost* all-good. As Berel Dov Lerner (2019, 28) points out, "When a tsunami kills hundreds of innocents, it creates exactly the same problem for belief in a very good God as it does for belief in a perfect God."

A final preliminary. It is commonplace to distinguish between the pastoral and logical dimensions of the problem of evil. Many who have gone through grief and pain have found the often technical solutions proposed by philosophers arid and unsatisfying. Although my concern in this chapter is overwhelmingly the logical dimension, a search for the psychological roots of why people are so deeply affected by the problem of evil is not irrelevant to the logical problem. Cognizance of these roots provides a perspective from which individuals can assess whether, due to self-centered and/or anthropocentric attitudes, they have been

---

[10] See Shatz 2013c, 310–11.
[11] See also M. M. Adams 1999, 210.
[12] See Mill 2009, Kushner 2004. Kabbalah contains the idea that the Godhead is perfected by human actions.

overestimating or underestimating the extent and intensity of evil. They need to ask themselves whether their personal situations affect how they assess the amount of evil in the world, whether what they regard as evils are truly evils or instead only seem so because they are contrary to their interests, whether they are blaming God for evils they caused out of their own free will, and what they can do to better their condition. Maimonides lays blame for a faulty perspective at the feet of the sufferers.[13] Comprehending our psychological condition will (or should) diminish the intensity with which we approach the problem.

But Maimonides's tactic of explaining people's perceptions by pointing to their personal circumstances and mindset cuts both ways. Sometimes people are callous in the way they approach the problem because they "have it good" in life. They may *under*estimate how much evil there is, or be too ready to think that others are complaining beyond what is justified. If they view themselves as responsible for their own moderate tribulations, and believe that they could have done more to help themselves, they might as a result lack empathy for others, ascribing to others responsibility for *their* situations. Weighing the psychological mindset we bring to our assessment of evil and trying to calculate the effects of our personal circumstances surely are important steps toward approaching the problem of evil with proper perspective. But it isn't clear how people can know that they have the right perspective.

I turn now to the six aspects of Jewish thought about evil that I listed earlier.

EVIL AND DIVINE COMMAND MORALITY

In the midst of the Holocaust, in a Rosh Hashanah discourse, the saintly rabbi of the Warsaw ghetto addressed the challenge to belief posed by conditions of life under the Nazis. He told his followers that God's will determines truth (he seems to include *rightness* of action as "truth"), and that therefore the question of how God could allow the horrors they were living through falls away.[14]

---

[13] See Maimonides, *Guide of the Perplexed*, 3:10–12, 3:22–23.

[14] See Rabbi Kalonymus Shapira, cited in Sagi and Statman 1995, 50–51. Sagi and Statman believe that this passage is the only clear affirmation of divine command morality in Jewish sources. Other rabbinic texts, they think, go only so far as asserting that human beings have limited knowledge of an independent standard and therefore need divine commands to, for example, define theft. They note, however (51), that elsewhere Shapira provides theodicies.

The rabbi's insight is vital: that the problem of evil is a problem only if God is held to some independent moral standard. If there is no such standard – if it is true that (paraphrasing Dostoevsky), "If there is no God, everything is permitted" – then there is no problem. What we call evils are God's will; they are automatically justified.

This perspective, even while reflecting enormous piety, faces philosophical difficulties. There are good grounds for holding that Judaism on the whole believes that God complies – and by His nature must comply – with an independent standard of ethics. More to the point, it is *specifically in the context of the problem of evil* that we find evidence for the existence of an independent moral standard. The prophets, the psalmist, and, of course, the book of Job all raise the question of how God can allow evil.[15] If the answer to the problem were simply that God's will determines rightness, how could the prophets be guilty of such confusion?[16] And why would the rabbis toil so mightily to provide theodicies, or declare that God's reasons are hidden (but presumably cogent)?

Perhaps it will be retorted that the prophets are not holding God accountable for violating independent human standards of ethics, but rather for violating *His own* standards – that is, the standards He has commanded human beings to meet. But how can we condemn this putative hypocrisy on God's part (or a failure to abide by Kant's universalizability test) unless we have an independent standard of ethics that tells us that *hypocrisy* or violating universality is wrong? However we slice it, then, the fact the prophets raise the problem of evil cuts against the attempt to neutralize the problem by denying that there is a standard of ethics besides God's will.

PROTEST

Reflecting the rejection of divine command morality, a common motif in Jewish theology, invoked from biblical times through today, is that human beings have permission – perhaps even an obligation? – to confront God and challenge Him about His actions, failures to act, or declared intentions. Thus, when God declares that He will destroy the city of Sodom, Abraham protests that this would entail killing the righteous together with the wicked: "Far be it from you! Shall the judge of all

---

[15] See Jer. 12:1–2; Isa. chs. 62–63; Habakuk; Ps. 13:2; 37; 73; Job.
[16] See Gellman 1977.

the earth not do justice?" (Gen. 18:33). Moses, too, challenges God when God declares He will destroy the sinning Israelites (see Exod. 13:11–14 and Num. 14:13–20). God accedes to his interlocutors, though not completely. Jeremiah (12:1, 15:18), Job (9, 13, 23), and the Psalmist (6, 10, 12, 23, 43, 44, 74, 80, 89) likewise issue protests or challenges. God even articulates His critics' objections (Ezek. 18, 22). In sum, "Biblical religion does not seem to require the man of faith to repress his doubts in silent resignation" (Muffs 2005, 184).[17]

What about the Sages? Dov Weiss (2017) demonstrates that early talmudic figures shared an *anti*-protest consensus.[18] In a later period, though, while such negative sentiments remain, protest became acceptable to a significant number of Sages. According to some opinions, however, protest is allowed only if certain ground rules are observed: the protestor is deferential and nonaccusatory, is intimate with God, and is motivated not by self-interest but by concern for another. Perhaps to soften the protests, the Sages often convey them in particular literary forms – courtroom scenes, prayers, or parables – and they are placed in the mouth of a biblical hero, putting the Sages who describe the scene at a remove (ibid., 103–20). But even with these qualifications and moderating techniques, the words "reprimand," "demand," and "rebuke" fit scenarios that the Sages portray. Indeed, sometimes God agrees with the reasoning and changes His intention. Armed with the pro-protest precedent, many thinkers today teach that those who question God about the Holocaust and other tragedies are not doing anything wrong – and maybe are even doing what God wants.

Weiss suggests that we compare protests in talmudic and midrashic literature concerning evil to rabbinic treatments of laws that the Sages may have regarded as ethically problematic when taken literally. In both cases – problematic laws, and problematic divine behavior or intentions – there appears to operate a standard of ethics outside of God's will.[19] Weiss maintains that in legal matters, the Sages often reinterpreted biblical verses expressing commands because they found the verses morally troubling if taken literally. In like fashion, Weiss suggests, the Sages drew on moral intuitions in nonlegal (aggadic) contexts. However, since the contexts of the protests did not carry practical implications to the same degree as the legal contexts did, the Sages, he suggests, simply raised the

---

[17] Blumenthal 1993 introduces an extreme contemporary post-Holocaust theology of protest.
[18] Weiss also discusses approaches to protest in Christian sources.
[19] Cf. Chapter 8.

moral issues and did not present resolutions, because they didn't have to as the legal authorities did.

Protest presents Jewish PBT with a philosophical problem. Prima facie, only if God is fallible can calling God's attention to His flaws be a correct approach. Thus, legitimizing protest seems to entail a rejection of PBT. Weiss suggests that what made the Sages comfortable with protest is their "humanization" of God, epitomized by the idea that God must observe His own commandments and can be criticized when He does not and instead becomes destructive. But if we adhere to PBT, isn't criticizing God both arrogant and incorrect in substance? What sense does it make for such a God to allow, let alone welcome, protest? Aren't the protestors wrong to question Him?

One answer is simply that a champion of PBT can privilege the earlier, anti-protest views. I suggest, however, that one important element in defending protest against a perfect God – not necessarily what the Sages who allowed protest had in mind – is that not to protest, not to be troubled, means being insensitive or unsympathetic. Consider the following passage:

The Men of the Great Assembly[20] said [to include in prayer]: "The great, powerful and awesome God." ... Moses said, "The great, powerful and awesome God." [Later] Jeremiah came and said: "Strangers are croaking in His Sanctuary. Where are the manifestations of His awesomeness?" He therefore did not say "awesome" [in his prayer in Jer. 32:18]. Then Daniel came and said: "Strangers are enslaving His children! Where are the manifestations of His power?" He therefore did not say "powerful" [in his prayer in Dan. 9:4]. (*Yoma* 69b)

The Men of the Great Assembly explained that God's awesomeness and power are manifested by His restraint and His patience with the wicked.

How could Jeremiah and Daniel reject Moses's words? Aren't they insulting God by deleting certain praises? The Talmud explains their actions by saying that God does not lie and they wanted to be honest, not realizing that "powerful" refers to God's self-restraint. The Rabbis put a premium on religious authenticity, even over theological accuracy.

That they wanted to be honest doesn't dull their audaciousness, however. Perhaps reactions like theirs may be rationalized *in part* because they are so understandable, so natural, so difficult to resist; they come from a place of empathy, devotion to the Temple and the people, and moral sensitivity. Further, if the Sages viewed their scenarios of protest, such as Jeremiah and Daniel's protests, as products of their own homiletic

---

[20] See Chapter 1.

imaginations, as literary conceits, then they didn't think Jeremiah and Daniel were *really* audacious. In any event, the effect (even if not a goal) of allowing protest is to arouse expressions of certain sensitivities. Weiss is utterly on target to call the protests acts of "pious irreverence." The "piety" aspect should not be lost on us.[21]

This reasoning may seem problematic in that it cuts against a prevalent and textually well-supported notion that one must accept God's decree: "The Lord gives and the Lord takes away" (Job 1:21). Is "accepting" a decree compatible with protesting it? If God's interlocutor tries to change God's mind, that is hardly indicative of acceptance. Perhaps, looking at the total picture, we ought to be torn between acceptance and protest, recognizing the claim that each makes upon us.[22]

To summarize, Jewish tradition includes a robust literature of protest. At times, God accedes to the criticisms. Adherents of PBT may maintain that by relating the stories, the Rabbis are inculcating moral sensitivity, compassion for the Jewish people, and concern for the Temple. Those who did not license protests may have upheld God's perfection as well. Alternatively, they may have regarded the protests as correct and reasonable in substance but *ḥutzpah* nonetheless.

REJECTIONS OF THE RETRIBUTIVIST THEODICY

When exploring theodicies in ancient Jewish literature, we confront a strange duality. On the one hand, there is a plethora of sources that make retributivist statements (specifying what misdeeds are punished, and how) or call upon people to examine their deeds when adversity strikes, which in turn will lead to proper repentance and improvement of character. Yet in numerous other texts, the retributivist theodicy, the claim that all suffering and death is punishment for sin, is rejected or ignored as a comprehensive explanation of evil. (The sources that reject retributivism are compatible with the thesis that *some* suffering is punishment for sin.)

Let's take some examples.

---

[21] To be clear, nonacquiescence can reside in a state of mind even if that state of mind is not accompanied by protest. But expressing one's objections may be a better way of cementing, as well as demonstrating, a healthy moral or religious frame of mind.
[22] Surprisingly, as Nichole Marques and Samuel Lebens pointed out, in one respect it can be more presumptuous to defend God than to critique or reprimand Him. In mounting a defense, one presumes to read God's mind. This is not the case in a protest.

The Book of Job

The suffering of the most celebrated sufferer – Job – cannot be explained by his being sinful. On the contrary, whereas Job's friends suggest that to believe in God's justice is to believe that Job must have sinned, the book is clear in the first two chapters that he didn't.[23] In the final chapter, God rebukes Job's friends, because "you [the friends] did not speak properly to me as did my servant Job" (42:7)! How could the friends deserve God's anger for trying to defend God, while Job – the one who rejected their affirmations of divine justice – must pray on their behalf before they can be forgiven? Perhaps the answer is that God is saying to the friends, "Do you folks think I'm crazy? Would I be so unjust as to consider Job wicked?" The retributivist theodicy is here rejected.[24]

The Book of Job may well be far more concerned with the phenomenology of the sufferer than with suffering as a philosophical problem. Yet arguably, the book provides an explanation of Job's suffering. In chapter 2 (verses 1–7), Satan challenges God to a bet. Here's the dispute between them: Will Job, who is well off, remain devoted if adversity strikes him? Satan believes that suffering will corrupt Job; God believes it will improve him. Ultimately, God is proven right: Job achieves a heightened spiritual perception and a heightened sense of interpersonal responsibility. After God speaks to Job out of the whirlwind, Job declares, "I had heard of you by ear, now my eye has seen You" (42:5). This is his heightened spiritual perception. And whereas in the prologue Job brought sacrifices for his family alone, in the end he broadens his concern and prays for his friends.[25] These actions display a heightened sense of interpersonal responsibility. God is proven right. The bet prologue thus suggests that the book wants to show that Job improves both morally and religiously as a result of adversity, which in turn – this is an extra step, not entailed by the preceding claim – can *justify* the adversity. Job in any event is suffering not because he is a sinner, but because he is righteous. Even if, as many scholars believe, the prologue and epilogue are later additions

---

[23] Concerning the view that the prologue and epilogue were added later, see below.

[24] Michael Harris pointed out to me that Job's earlier protestations of his innocence make it appear that he too buys into a retributivist theodicy (why would I be suffering if not for imputed sin?). This fact makes God's commendation of how Job spoke to him (42:7) difficult to understand, given that God criticized the friends for defending retributivism. But God may be referring to Job's speech that immediately precedes His rebuke of the friends (42:1–6). In any case, at the bottom line the book rejects the retributivist theodicy, since Job did not sin except, perhaps, in the tone in which he originally spoke.

[25] Noted by Soloveitchik 1965, 37–38.

to the book, my reading has the advantage of showing how they cohere with the rest of the book.

Ecclesiastes

Ecclesiastes, that most depressing of biblical books, asserts that an identical fate awaits the righteous and the wicked (9:2–3), thereby rejecting the retributivist theodicy.

The Rejection of R. Ammi

There are texts in the Talmud that work with a retributivist theodicy.[26] Strikingly, though, in the place where a sage in the Babylonian Talmud most explicitly advances the retributivist thesis in a sweeping form, the Talmud rejects this view. R. Ammi contends that "There is no death without sin, no suffering without transgression" (*Shabbat* 55a). The Talmud rebuffs R. Ammi by citing a teaching that four people died gratuitously – that is, without sin. Questions have been raised about the scope of this rejection of retributivism, since the "refuting text" states that four people died without sin. Was it *only* those four? Moreover, R. Ammi's proof texts show only that all sin is punished by death or suffering, not that all suffering or death is punishment. And even if death is not always the result of sin, does the Talmud intend to extend the refutation from death to suffering?[27] Whatever its reach, the text certainly repudiates some degree of retributivism, whether as regards both suffering and death, or as regards death alone.[28]

Specific Observed Cases

In other sources, a sage rejects the retributivist view of suffering on the basis of empirical observation. Rava observed that two equally righteous sages endured entirely different material lives – one a life of plenty, the other a life of severe deprivation. From this situation he concludes that "[the number of] one's children, [the length of] one's life, and [the amount of] one's sustenance depend not on merits, but on *mazzal* [the

---

[26] Examples in the Babylonian Talmud: *Shabbat* 32b–33a; *Ta'anit* 7b–8a; *Avodah Zarah* 18b. On the Jerusalem Talmud, see the reference later in this chapter.
[27] See Shatz 2009b, 286–87, nn. 48–49, and the sources cited there.
[28] Note, however, that the Midrash (*Va-Yikra Rabbah* 37:1, *Kohelet Rabbah* 5:4) does not reject R. Ammi's assertion.

constellations]" (*Mo'ed Katan* 28a). (See our discussion in Chapter 2.) Elsewhere R. Jacob states that "the reward for a commandment is not found in this world," but rather in the next (*Kiddushin* 39b). He had witnessed someone fall to his death on his way down after climbing a building in order to perform the two commandments for which the Torah promises long life.[29] R. Jacob therefore concluded that the Torah's promise of reward for performing each of those commandments – "It will be good for you and your days will be lengthy" (Exod. 20:12, Deut. 5:16, 22:7) – must refer to the World-to-Come. More tellingly, in *Ruth Rabbah* (6:4), the same view is expressed by none other than the great Sage R. Akiva in response to the same sort of story (albeit involving a climb down a palm tree and being bitten by a snake).

Unlike Rava, R. Jacob and R. Akiva sought to incorporate just rewards into their scheme and provide a theodicy. (Rava did not discuss whether a worthy person deprived of children, long life, and sustenance is compensated in the next world, nor did he explain why God lets *mazzal* be the decisive factor.) The Tosafists (*Shabbat* 156a, s.v. *ein*) maintain that sometimes righteous actions override the decree of *mazzal*. Note: "Sometimes."[30] It is not explained how one of the Sages of whom Rava spoke (viz., Rabbah) suffered terrible material deprivation with regard to "children, life and sustenance" – and apparently could not override the stars' decree.

Rejection of retribution as the explanation of this-worldly suffering need not result from empirical observations of instances in which the correlation between the quality of one's deeds and the quality of one's circumstances fails to hold. Retributivism is problematic also because it leads to an exercise in blaming the victim. Thus, according to retributivism, Hitler's victims brought it on themselves by wrongdoing (and Hitler was God's instrument). Now, this objection may be accused of begging the question: If we were to believe retributivism, why should we *not* blame the victim? But there is a powerful intuition (disputed by retributivists) that if retributivism is true, we would end up *wrongly* blaming everyone whoever suffered, and that therefore retributivism is false. Further,

---

[29] To wit, the commandment to honor parents (Exod. 20:12, Deut. 5:16) and the commandment to send away the mother bird before taking her fledglings (Deut. 22:6–7). However, the Talmud cites Sages who challenge R. Yaakov's inference. See also *Hullin* 142a. Cf. J. T. *Hagigah* 2:1. In the sources it is suggested that the notorious heretic Elisha ben Avuyah was led astray by an episode of this sort. In popular tellings, the story is of a young boy climbing a ladder.

[30] Cf. *Yevamot* 50a, cited by the Tosafists. See also Tosafot, *Yevamot* 50a, s.v. *mosifin*.

if retributivism is true, why sympathize with those who by suffering are allegedly receiving their just deserts? Why give them aid?

At the same time, any Jewish thinker who rejects retributivism must address the many texts in the Talmud and in countless later sources mandating that those who are afflicted – whether people or communities – "examine their deeds" (e.g., *Berakhot* 5a).[31] If we reject the retributivist theodicy, whence the certainty that one has sinned?

One approach distinguishes the logic of explanation from the logic of response.[32] A person should act *as if* the suffering were punishment, and therefore scrutinize his or her faults and repent. This approach can certainly be challenged.[33] But it is significant that the narrative texts which presuppose that suffering is retribution are, with small exception, instances in which the sufferer, not an outside party, "identifies" the sin, or cases in which the sufferer *asks* a third party to explain the cause of the suffering.[34] Perhaps, calling to mind the Talmud's critique of Job's friends (*Bava Metzi'a* 58b), the reason that third parties do not initiate retributivist explanations of others' suffering to their faces is that it is callous to do so. But, equally, such explanations may simply be incorrect, at least some of the time.

A few caveats are in order. (I'll be slightly repetitive.) First, within classical Judaism, it would be absurd to deny that *some* suffering is punishment for sin. Second, as we have seen, those who reject the retributivist theodicy confine that rejection to *this* world; in the hereafter, all just deserts are meted out. Some, like Sa'adyah Gaon and Naḥmanides, regard the next world as the main locus of punishment.[35] Third, while the standard retributivist theory refers to punishment imposed directly by God, certain adverse consequences flow *naturally* from wrongdoing. Although the slogan learned in childhood, "cheaters never prosper," is palpably false, traits like indolence, timidity, meanness, avarice, and so on often lead to material self-harm, including judicial punishment, social opprobrium, and failure in professional or family life. If we follow Plato and Maimonides, wrongdoers harm themselves by affecting their character for the worse. Sometimes, then, bad deeds are "punished," as Maimonides taught, by the way the world is set up.[36]

---

[31] See also Moses Maimonides, *Mishneh Torah*, Laws of Fasts 1.
[32] See, e.g., Hartman 1985, 196.
[33] See Shatz 2009a, 294–97; Stump 1997.
[34] See, e.g., *Avot de-Rabbi Natan* 2:2. See also H. Cohen 1995.
[35] Saadia Gaon 1948, 210–11, 323–26, 328–29; Nachmanides, 2009, 471–85.
[36] Of course, certain virtues (like selflessness) may cause material harm to an agent as well.

Notice that attributing character flaws, like greed, to other people in order to understand how they messed up their lives sometimes yields useful morals for oneself. A naturalistic account of punishment makes room for finding flaws in others when the purpose is to learn a lesson.

The Abundance of Other Theodicies

The most straightforward evidence that retributivist theodicy is rejected by many Sages is that they offer numerous other theodicies. Yaakov Elman (1999, 192–94) writes:

> The Bavli [Babylonian Talmud] thus provides us with a number of "mechanisms" of divine governance ... These include the astrological sources of the human condition (*Moʻed Katan* 28a), sufferings of love (*Berakhot* 5a–b), *nissayon* [trial], vicarious atonement (*Moʻed Katan* 28a), situations of negligence in the face of hazard (*kevia hezeqa*) (*Kiddushin* 39b), or the workings of a hereditary curse (*Rosh HaShanah* 18a; *Yevamot* 105a) ... the "sliding scale" of judgment applied to persons depending on their righteousness, the judgment of the righteous to a "hair's-breadth" (*Yevamot* 121b), either because of their responsibilities as moral leaders of their generation, to whatever (geographical or social) extent their influence carries (*Shabbat* 33b; *Shevuʻot* 39b), or the inordinately severe punishment meted out for certain sins ... the consequences of being a member of a community or the community of Israel; the danger of the Destroyer (*Bava Kamma* 60a); God's hiding of His face during Israel's exile (*Hagigah* 5a), or the necessities of God's plan for history. (*Taʻanit* 5b)

Elman's list comprises only theodicies found in the Babylonian Talmud and Midrash. As noted by David Kramer (1993) and Elman (1999), the Jerusalem Talmud gives a much greater endorsement to retributivism than the Babylonian.[37] In post-talmudic Jewish philosophy, we find other theodicies, including, for example, the Neoplatonic thesis that evil is a privation (adopted by Maimonides in *Guide of the Perplexed* 3:10–11) and various kabbalistic options: that evil is an illusion, that evil results from divine self-contraction (*tzimtzum*) to make room for the world or represents a rupture in the Godhead ("the breaking of the vessels"), that demonic forces (the "other side," *sitra aḥra*) produce evil, that suffering or death is the result of *gilgul* (transmigration: an evil soul is reincarnated and suffers in one body for sins committed while in another body; see Chapter 7). But the large point here is that the very prevalence of nonretributivist theodicies in the Babylonian Talmud and Midrash

---

[37] Elman says that Jewish sources from ancient Palestine (as in the Jerusalem Talmud) accept only one nonretributivist theodicy, afflictions of love.

suggests that retributivism should not be deemed the sole view, perhaps not even the standard view in Jewish thought, even if introspection and self-criticism is an appropriate response to personal suffering.

While the rejection of retributivism as a theodicy is well attested to, we are left with a problem we noted earlier: preserving the moral order. As I noted, Jewish thinkers who reject retributivism often affirm that just deserts will be meted out in the World-to-Come. In this way the moral order is preserved. Yet, why defer the rewards and punishments? A possible answer is that if the moral order were evident in this world, people would then act only out of impure, self-interested motivation. Or, perhaps some other theodicy, like the soul-making theodicy, will explain why a good person might experience the suffering in this world.

AFFLICTIONS OF LOVE

The longest discussion of theodicy in the Talmud is found in *Berakhot* 5a–b, and a particularly interesting theodicy is posed there: afflictions (or tribulations, or sufferings) of love, *yissurin shel ahavah*. It is not a general theodicy, but rather one that explains specifically the sufferings of the righteous. Let us examine it closely:

Rava (some say R. Ḥisda) said: If a man sees that afflictions come upon him, he should examine his conduct; for it is said, "Let us search and examine our ways, and return to the Lord" (Lam. 3:40). If he examines [them] and finds nothing, he should attribute it to the neglect of Torah study, for it is said: "Happy is the man whom you discipline, O Lord, and teach him from your Law" (Ps. 94:12). If he did attribute [the suffering to this neglect of Torah study] and [on further examination] did not find [neglect], it is certain that these are afflictions of love. For it is said: "He whom the Lord loves – He rebukes, like a father the son whom he loves." (Prov. 3:12)

Rava said in the name of R. Sehorah, who said it in the name of R. Huna: Whomever the Lord desires, He crushes with afflictions.[38]

After citing a proof text, Rava goes on to impose a qualifier: the person who is afflicted must accept the afflictions – that is, must be willing to endure them – in order for the afflictions to continue. If the individual endures them acceptingly, they are rewarded. There follows a lengthy discussion in which various Sages brandish proof texts about afflictions of love and also try to determine which afflictions can be

---

[38] The concept of afflictions of love arises again in *Bava Metzi'a* 85a. For example, Rebbi (Rabbi Judah the Prince) declares "*yissurin* (afflictions) are precious"; and the sufferings of another sage, R. Elazar ben Shimon, "came to him out of love and left out of love."

considered afflictions of love. (Is being deprived of children in this category, for example?)

Then the Talmud relates several stories involving Sages who were suffering. In all, the sufferer expressed a preference to be cured, even though this meant foregoing the reward that they would receive for enduring "afflictions of love." These Sages say about their sufferings: "neither them, nor their reward." Because their preference was to be cured, they were indeed cured, foregoing the reward.[39] In contrast, the sufferer who acquiesces is rewarded.[40]

What exactly is the reward for?[41] An appealing reading is that God afflicts the person so that they will receive reward *for the very enduring of the suffering* – which exemplifies faith and acceptance of God's will – and for not opting out like the Sages who were suffering in the three talmudic stories. The afflictions, in this understanding, are not punishments, but rather *opportunities* to do something (viz., endure the suffering) over and above the worthy deeds one has already done. The thinking here resembles that of the soul-making theodicy, the thesis that God allows evil in order to help human beings build virtues for which evil is a logically necessary condition[42] (e.g., benevolence, sympathy, courage, faith), or actualize virtues that they possess but have not been expressed in action. The virtues that come to mind here are faith, acceptance of God's will, strength of spirit, steadfastness, and loving God. Suffering improves people.[43]

The "afflictions of love" theory differs from the soul-making theodicies constructed by analytic philosophers in a few ways. One element

---

[39] The sharp language "neither them, nor their reward" has been taken as a rejection of – a protest against – the whole concept that suffering can be a reward. But that account is probably overreading.

[40] We may wonder whether the passage implies that it is appropriate for a person to endure suffering *in order to* receive reward.

[41] For sources pertinent to some of the views that follow, see Harris 2016–2017, 67–71. A very helpful source in classical Jewish literature is the fifteenth century work by Albo, *Book of Roots*, 4:13–14.

[42] About the words "logically necessary": Soul-making theodicies need to specify virtues that are *logically* connected to suffering, not ones that are *empirically* connected. If the connection is only empirical, the objection will be raised that God could have created the world in such a way that the virtues could arise without suffering. The classic statement of the soul-making theodicy is Hick 1978 (originally published 1966).

[43] In *Bava Batra* 10a, the wicked Turnus Rufus challenges R. Akiva: If God cares about the poor, why does He not feed them? R. Akiva explained: It is so that we can avoid Gehinnom (Hell). The first impression is that the point is that there is evil so that humans bear responsibility. The sequel in the text suggests a more complex interpretation, however.

that many readings of "afflictions of love" add to classic soul-making theodicy is that the person is rewarded.⁴⁴ From a soul-making perspective, what would be important is not that improved character is assigned an *extrinsic* reward; rather, the improved character is itself a (naturalistically generated) reward. Virtue is its own reward.

Because the response of the sufferers who opted out of suffering was, "neither them, nor their reward," it seems clear that affliction is a reward for something or other. Nonetheless, interpreters sometimes view the afflictions as in the first instance punishment, not reward. In one prevalent approach of this kind, God is punishing the individual in this world for minor sins, so that in the next world the person receives greater reward (and one supposes is thereby comforted).

Remember, though, that the Talmud says that if the sufferer *finds no sins*, the afflictions can be attributed to God's love. "Afflictions of love" is to be invoked only when the person ends the search for sins empty-handed. (This reading seems to me better than construing "finds no sin" as attributing a mistake, an oversight, to the sufferer.) Apparently, attributing afflictions to God's love is proposed as an alternative to the retributivist framework.

Maimonides forcefully rejects the notion that God would bring suffering upon someone in this world who is sinless in order to enhance their reward because this approach ascribes "injustice" to God.⁴⁵ He cites Deuteronomy 32:4, "A God of faithfulness and without iniquity," and then R. Ammi's dictum, considered earlier: "There is no death without sin, and no suffering without transgression." Of course, one response to Maimonides is: No, God *would* afflict such a person. God wants to benefit those whom He loves, to have them grow in the virtue of faith (which they can do even if sinless) or come to express it, and if that means putting them through some painful hoops, that is justified.

---

⁴⁴ Here are some other differences. Contemporary theories seek to justify God's *allowing* suffering; they explain that God to a large extent leaves the world alone. In contrast, "afflictions of love" justifies His *directly inflicting* suffering. Moreover, afflictions of love are for the righteous; soul-making theodicies are universal in application. Finally, the classic Jewish sources do not say much about how afflictions of love improve people other than the sufferer. Contemporary analytic philosophers, in contrast, say much about sympathy and benevolence evoked in others and less about the sufferer's improvements in conduct toward others. Suffering can lead one to care more about others. In the movie *The Doctor*, for example, a crass physician becomes a cancer patient, and by dint of that experience comes to empathize with his patients and treat them kindly. Cf. Harris 2016–2017, 75–76.

⁴⁵ See Maimonides, *Guide of the Perplexed* 3:24 (1963, 497–98; see also 470–71).

In another approach, a variant of the improvement motif, the afflictions are visited upon the person because the person has defects of character, and the afflictions are administered not to punish them but to remove the defects – a purge.[46] The afflictions are means of improving the person by some metaphysical or biological process that purges material desires, just as certain illnesses can diminish appetites. However, the core idea that afflictions can lead to improvement of character and that spiritual and moral improvement is an outcome of affliction may be played out without purging mechanisms. Specifically, as we have said, because the righteous are righteous, God gives them an opportunity – as a privilege, a benefit, a reward – to display further virtue.

Construing "afflictions of love" in terms of improvement of character involves a move we may call the axiological shift. The key principle is that faith, strength of spirit, love of God, and closeness to God are greater goods than material welfare, so the problem of evil dissipates. The sufferer achieves tranquility through adopting this perspective. An axiological shift was employed by Maimonides,[47] and the approach calls to mind the memorable thesis of Epictetus (1983, sect. 5): What upsets people's minds is not events, but rather their *judgments* on events.

A talmudic story provides a vivid example of how axiology affects the response to suffering. On the verge of being executed by the Romans for teaching Torah, the sage R. Akiva is said to have been joyful over the opportunity to fulfill the commandment to "Love the Lord your God with all of your soul" – that is, to love Him even when his soul will be taken (Jerusalem Talmud, *Sotah* 5:5). He saw himself as benefiting from the opportunity to express his love.

The axiological-shift theodicy is both limited and problematic. How can it explain the suffering of children, nonhuman animals, and adults who lack the very capacity to assign value? Clearly, the axiological-shift theodicy cannot be *comprehensive*; it must be supplemented by theodicies that can fill these lacunae, such as a broader soul-making theodicy that includes the soul-making of parties other than the sufferer.

In the talmudic stories concerning afflictions of love, some Sages prefer relief from such tribulations to the rewards they bring. This suggests that an individual's axiology must be respected even if it is less than

---

[46] On variants of this idea in rabbinic sources, see Shatz 2009b, 293, Harris 2016–2017, 72–74.
[47] *Guide of the Perplexed* 3:22–23, on Job. As noted earlier, Maimonides takes human beings' preoccupation with human suffering and death as indicative of an anthropocentric orientation, and he also asserts that humans bring evils upon themselves (ibid. 3:12).

ideal, and that person's suffering accordingly alleviated. But we certainly try to relieve the suffering even of those who *are* accepting their tribulations. Why?

Another challenge to the axiological shift theodicy is that even though R. Akiva viewed his imminent death as a means of maximally fulfilling the commandment to love God, intuitively one should not court or seek out such circumstances. But why not, if love of God is the highest value?[48] One answer is that too many lives would be lost if proactive martyrdom were encouraged;[49] further, not everyone who courts the circumstances will react with love when the moment for martyrdom actually arrives, so courting the circumstances would have been for nought. In addition, an analogous objection could be raised against all soul-making theodicies that include benefits for the sufferer (e.g., why not seek out illness that will call for courage and stimulate others' benevolence?). "Afflictions of love" is not in a special difficulty on this score.

Some reflections in the preceding paragraphs take the "afflictions of love" theodicy as a form of soul-making theodicy. An alternative understanding is advocated by Michael Harris (2016–2017), who construes "afflictions of love" as what Christian philosophers like Laura Ekstrom (2013) have called a theodicy of "divine intimacy." Says the Psalmist: "As for me, the nearness of God, that is the good" (Ps. 73:28). Closeness to God, intimacy with Him, is the highest good, and suffering facilitates closeness. Although prima facie this view of suffering fits best within a Christian context, it can find a place in Judaism as well.

A powerful passage by R. Joseph Soloveitchik (2002, 133–34) illustrates intimacy with the divine. Speaking poignantly of the loneliness he experienced during a potentially fatal illness, he writes:

Gradually this feeling of loneliness pervades one's whole being with ever-increasing predominance; the whole self becomes immersed in solitude and the awareness of being taken away from the community. The man who is bound to others by countless invisible threads is torn loose from his social bearings. He makes his exit from the community because he was singled out.

The night before my operation, when my family said goodbye to me, I understood the words of the psalmist, "When my father and my mother forsake me, the Lord will take me up" (Ps. 27:10). I had never understood this verse. Did a parent ever abandon his child? Of course not! Yet in certain situations, one is cut off even from his parents or his beloved wife and children ... Suddenly one

---

[48] Apparently, it is not enough for love to be possessed only as an *unexercised disposition* to perform certain actions. Cf. Lebens 2020b, 42–45, on "agent worth."

[49] See Stern 2019.

realizes that there is no help which his loved ones are able to extend to him. They are onlookers who watch a drama unfolding itself with unalterable speed. They are not involved in it. I stand before God; no one else is beside me. A lonely being meeting the loneliest Being is a traumatic but also a great experience.

As Diogenes Allen (1980, 99, 201) suggests, intimacy can be achieved either *in* suffering or *through* suffering. That is, either the suffering itself involves moments of intimacy or, alternatively, it leads to moments of intimacy.[50]

The intimacy theodicy initially seems very strange.[51] It posits a God who so much wants people to be intimate with Him that He makes them suffer! The talmudic stories do make clear that the Sages who were suffering were free to reject the "rewards" of suffering (here now equated with intimacy). This autonomy accorded to the sufferer mitigates the objection at hand, since the suffering becomes consensual. But there are other problems. For one thing (and this applies to other versions of afflictions of love), why does God make these sages suffer if presumably He knows in advance that they won't want it, despite whatever rewards are forthcoming? For another, if these sages are rejecting the chance for intimacy (or, for that matter, the development of virtue), doesn't this cast aspersions on them? Harris (2016–2017, 87) is correct that "it is simply acknowledged [in the stories] that the pain being experienced is such that it is legitimate to prefer not to suffer and not reap the rewards of suffering." But a follow-up question is why this attitude should not be viewed as a less-than-ideal response, albeit a legitimate one, that suggests the sufferer is not on the highest level. The intimacy theodicist may respond by biting the bullet – that is, by conceding this to be the case; "refusing" the suffering and losing a chance for divine intimacy is legitimate, but less than ideal.[52]

In concluding our review of afflictions of love, let me reiterate: Whereas in the Talmud these afflictions are brought on by direct divine activity, conventional soul-making theodicy embeds the theodicy in a naturalistic framework – in which God adopts a mostly laissez-faire approach to suffering. So, rather than speak of this or that affliction as one of love, in a soul-making theodicy we would speak about how suffering, even if brought on by nature and not direct divine action, can provide an opportunity for exercising virtue (and/or intimacy). In a naturalistic

---

[50] See also Stump 2010a, Citron 2017.
[51] Cf. Harris 2016–2017, 85–86.
[52] See also Harris 2016–2017. Note that someone whose "soul" is "being made" or is the recipient of such a person's beneficence might not want the suffering.

framework one cannot get rid of the suffering as certain Sages did in the stories – namely, by opting to care more about relief from suffering than getting the rewards.

COLLECTIVE SUFFERING AND *HESTER PANIM* (HIDING OF THE FACE)

Throughout Jewish history, the challenge of explaining the communal or collective suffering of the Jewish people has been unavoidable. The rejections of a sweeping retributivism that we saw earlier applied to evils befalling individuals. Evils befalling the collective are a different matter; Jewish tradition ties collective suffering to punishment in a way that leaves much less room for a theological alternative to retributivism. The liturgical statement "Because of our sins we were exiled" is but one example of a retributivist motif that courses throughout the Bible and rabbinic literature.[53]

The category often used in Jewish thought to describe periods of great communal tragedies and horrendous evils is *Hester Panim* – Hiding of the Face.[54] But what does this mean? If "God is hiding His face" means simply, "God is allowing this evil to befall the community," then *Hester Panim* is no *explanation* of the evil, but rather merely a *redescription* of the phenomenon to be explained. The critical question, then, is *why* God hides His face.[55]

In the Pentateuch, *Hester Panim* is a divine reaction to the Jews' waywardness. In Deuteronomy 31:17–21, God refers to "many evils and troubles" that will befall the Jewish people if they turn to alien gods and

---

[53] Did the Holocaust bring the problem of evil to a new order of magnitude, or generate a new question? Berkovits (1973) argues no; the suffering or death of one innocent child poses just as large a theological problem as the slaughter of many millions. Apparently, Berkovits is thinking of the deductive form of the problem, which has been discredited by Pike and Plantinga. Ostensibly that leaves unsolved the inductive or evidential form of the problem, and, prima facie, the magnitude of the evil in the Holocaust indeed greatly intensifies the problem. (See also Katz 1983, 268–70.) A counter to this thought is that the probability on the theistic hypothesis of a small amount of evil is just as low as that of much evil (as Aaron Segal mentioned to me). In any event, merely discussing the atrocities of the Holocaust and other horrendous evils in detached, mathematical terms may obscure their existential power and horror (see M. Adams 1999).
[54] Existentialist philosophers like Martin Buber and Emil Fackenheim spoke of "the eclipse of God."
[55] Much has been written in analytic philosophy about divine hiddenness (e.g., Howard-Snyder and Moser 2001, Rea 2018). This literature, however, predominantly uses absence of evidence as an argument against God's existence, which is not how hiddenness functions in Jewish thought.

break the covenant. To describe the punishment, the Torah states: "And I shall hide My face on that day" (Deut. 31:18; see also 32:20). Apparently, the punishment of *Hester Panim* is the withdrawal (for a time) of divine protection, as a result of which the people stand exceedingly vulnerable to calamities. The general theme of hiding as punishment is repeated by Isaiah (54:8, 59:2, 64:6). But if *Hester Panim* is a punishment, as these verses indicate, and collective suffering is presumed to be a punishment, we must ask: What could possibly have been the collective sin that warranted the Holocaust?

The answers that were suggested involved finger-pointing: secularization; assimilation; cooperation with secularists in the effort to return to Zion, an effort which was also said to exemplify an unseemly degree of human messianic endeavor. The Sages censured those who tell a sufferer they are suffering because of their sin (*Bava Metzi'a* 58b), and it seems arrogant to read God's mind. But the deeper problem with retributivist explanations is that even if the Jewish people as a whole were sinful, as the Talmud suggests in explaining the destruction of the Temples (*Yoma* 9b), some individuals must have been righteous relative to whatever sin the accuser believes has been committed. So we confront Abraham's question to God about Sodom, "Will you destroy the righteous together with the wicked?" (Gen. 18:23). If someone attributes the Holocaust to secularization and assimilation, how will that individual explain why God let the world of European centers of Torah study be destroyed and great rabbis murdered?[56]

In response to the challenge, R. Eliezer Berkovits (1908–1992) (1973, ch. 4) suggests that there are two types of *Hester Panim*. One is punitive, as the verses I quoted imply. The other amounts to the nonpunitive notion that God withdraws from history in order to allow human beings to exercise their free will – what philosophers call the free will theodicy.[57] God hides His face not as a punishment but so that human beings may exercise responsibility. Man must have freedom because "it is his essence." And yet, for Berkovits the withdrawal is not total:

That man may be, God must absent Himself; that man may not perish in the tragic absurdity of his own making, God must remain present. The God of history must be absent and present concurrently ... Because of the necessity of His absence, there is the "Hiding of the Face" and suffering of the innocent; because

---

[56] Transmigration (among other accounts) has been enlisted as another explanation of the suffering and death in World War II. See Chapter 7.

[57] Berkovits's view very roughly resembles the Kabbalistic notion of *tzimtzum* (God contracts to make room for the world). Berkovits (1973), notes this (173–74, n. 14).

of the necessity of His presence, evil will not ultimately triumph; because of it, there is hope for man. [107]

God is mighty in the renunciation of His might in order to bear with man. Yet He is present in history. He reveals His presence in the survival of His people Israel. [109]

Berkovits cites Isaiah 45:15, "You are a God who hides Himself, O God of Israel, the savior," and also Psalm 44, as examples of nonpunitive *Hester Panim*. (In fact, the Psalmist specifically says that the people were faithful [44: 9, 18-19, 21-22].[58]) He locates his theodicy in the thought of the Sages (1973, 101–7). Now, the Psalmist wonders, "*why* do You hide Your face?" (44:25). If Berkovits's account is correct, it's odd that the Psalmist seems stymied. In any case, as the long quotation shows, what makes Berkovits's free will theodicy distinctive (though not unique) is that in his full account, which I will not develop more here, *Hester Panim* is, paradoxically, compatible with God being present. For He both hides – "absents Himself" – and reveals His presence in the survival of His people and the creation of the Jewish state.

Questions have been raised about the free will theodicy in general, about Berkovits's own dialectical version, and about Berkovits's application of the theodicy to the Holocaust.[59] However, Martin Buber, Emil Fackenheim, Abraham Joshua R. Heschel, Norman R. Lamm, and Jonathan R. Sacks explain Hiding of the Face as follows. Humanity is to be blamed for the hiding because they did not let God in. They became alienated from Him, and the question about the Shoah (Holocaust) is not "where was God?" but "where was man?" God is not hidden but hiding, because people shut Him out.[60]

But is this understanding truly an alternative to retributivism? The deed–fault–punishment motif is there, in different language, and with it comes the problem of collective punishment, since not every Jew shut God out.[61] R. David Wolpe (1997, 51) pointedly characterizes *Hester Panim*, in the approach described, as "a phenomenological image, rather than an ontological assertion ... a description of the condition of the human heart." As Wolpe implies, something more is needed to find a *theodicy*.

---

[58] My thanks to Michael Harris for this point.
[59] See, e.g., Katz 1983.
[60] Kabbalistic authors convey the idea that there is revelation through concealment. To *experience* God as hiding is to acknowledge His existence and relationship with us. R. Israel Ba'al Shem, founder of Ḥasidism, remarked that sometimes people are so alienated from God that even the hiding is hidden. See Lebens 2020a.
[61] See also Peli 1979.

ANTITHEODICY

Despite the abundance of theodicies in the Talmud and Midrash, there are passages in which the Sages discourage and even object to speculating about theodicies. When Moses gazes far into the future, he observes R. Akiva teaching the Torah. At some point he says to God: "Master of the universe, you have shown me his Torah. Now show me his reward." The text continues:

> God said to him: "Turn around." Moses turned around and saw that people were weighing the flesh of Rabbi Akiva in the meat market [after his gruesome death]. Moses said, "Master of the universe – This is Torah and this is its reward?" God said to him: "Be quiet! Thus did I plan things." [*Menaḥot* 29b]

Marvin Fox (2003d) argues that, whenever the Talmud or Midrash sets out a theodicy, it includes as well a counterweight such as this one, an objection to this whole human enterprise.

I will use the word "antitheodicy" to refer to the view of some theists that it is irrational, unethical, inappropriate, or otherwise wrong for theists even to seek theodicies, let alone give them.[62] Antitheodicy has been amplified by philosophers in the Continental existentialist tradition. Perhaps the overwhelming difficulty of explaining the Holocaust has given rise to this line of thought.

Antitheodicy insists that our reaction to evil must not be to *theorize* about it, but rather to *respond to* it: to sympathize with victims, to combat evil, to relieve suffering, and to repair our faults, not to figure out why evil is there. "We do not inquire about the hidden ways of the Almighty, but rather about the path wherein man shall walk when suffering strikes" (Soloveitchik 2002, 156). The fundamental question is not why people suffer, but rather "What obligation does suffering impose upon man?" (Soloveitchik 2000a, 56). In short, "Response, not explanation, is focal" (Lichtenstein 1999).[63]

A number of arguments can be made in favor of theodicizing (we may call them protheodic), in addition to arguments from the abundance of theodicies in rabbinic literature:[64]

---

[62] The term "antitheodicy" has been used in different ways; see, e.g., Braiterman 1998. Hick 1978, 6–11, seems to have coined the term.
[63] See also Carmy 1999.
[64] Arguments that are not textual become necessary if there are conflicting texts and one must decide which to privilege.

(1) Only if armed with a theodicy may one know what is meant by the tradition's assertion, "God is just." Otherwise, one is just mouthing words. Such an argument was used by Moses Naḥmanides, who declared that religious people who object to seeking theodicies are "fools who despise wisdom."[65]
(2) Theodicy yields composure of the mind. Without having a theodicy, one will be tormented. (This argument was likewise used by Naḥmanides.)
(3) Lack of a theodicy renders the universe morally unintelligible for theists. A theodicy renders the universe morally intelligible.

It is not the case that the goals specified in these arguments – knowing what "God is just" means, attaining composure of the mind and moral intelligibility – can be attained only by a *correct* theodicy. An incorrect one can serve as well. But it's worth *questing for* a good theodicy. Argument (3) is strong on this score. After all, we engage in science in an effort to make the universe intelligible, even though our aspiration will not for sure ever be fulfilled; the universe may not be completely intelligible (think quantum physics), and perhaps we will often have a false sense of correctly understanding the universe. But what would life be like if we would avoid pursuing goals because they *may* prove unattainable (or at least unattainable by the individual)? There is value in the process, in the quest. Add to this that we may achieve *some* intelligibility. Unless one knows in advance that the quest is futile – and how could one know in advance without engaging in the quest? – the possibility of not attaining the goal is not a good reason for avoiding theodicizing.

We come, finally, to another protheodic argument:

(4) The default position must be that one must investigate objections, for only that course is intellectually honest.

Argument (4) is not all that strong, since the need to investigate objections is a function of cost-efficiency. There are considerations of time allocation, for example, and considerations of what one might lose by sowing doubt through fixating on theodicy. But it's reasonable to suppose that, up to a point, some sort of norm dictates investigating objections.

Antitheodic arguments can be divided into three groups.

---

[65] See Nachmanides 2009, 2:518–19.

Type one: Moral objections
(1) Theodicizing reflects or produces arrogance and presumptuousness.
(2) Theodicizing produces moral complacency. If we believe that all evil is justified, why lament its existence and why fight it?[66]
(3) Theodicizing reflects or produces a fatalistic outlook (living an existence of *goral*, fate).
(4) Theodicizing necessitates a detached attitude toward anguish and horror.
(5) Theodicizing erodes self-confidence.

Type two: Religious objections (theodicizing contravenes or threatens religious values)
(1) The problems discussed under "moral objections."
(2) We need mystery.
(3) We need to believe on faith.
(4) Seeking a theodicy creates risk of heresy.

Type three: Theodicizing is pointless/futile/superfluous.

I will confine my remarks under this third heading to three arguments: futility, mystery, and (again) complacency. (I have examined most of the other headings critically elsewhere; see Shatz 2019a.)

The theme of futility is found in Jewish sources. For instance, "We cannot explain either the prosperity of the wicked or the suffering of the

---

[66] See Soloveitchik 2002, 86–115. The concern over complacency has been framed by Jonathan Sacks (2005, 222–23) drawing upon a homiletic idea of his teacher R. Nachum Rabinovitch, one focused on Moses's encounter with God at the burning bush.

> "Moses hid his face because he was afraid to look at God" (Exodus 3:6). Why was he afraid? Because if he were fully to understand God he would have no choice but to be reconciled to the slavery and oppression if the world. From the vantage point of eternity, he would see that the bad is a necessary stage on the journey to the good. He would understand God but he would cease to be Moses, the fighter against injustice who intervened whenever he saw wrong being done. "He was afraid" that seeing heaven would desensitize him to earth, that coming close to infinity would mean losing his humanity.

> I am reminded of the adage: "If the world were perfect, it wouldn't be perfect." Soloveitchik (2002), oddly muting theodic parts of the tradition, states (101) that Judaism has an "ethic of suffering" but not a "metaphysic of suffering," because a metaphysic of suffering implants moral complacency. I will argue that such approaches will promise to explain the inconsistency if a soul-making theodicy is adopted.

> The complacency argument reminds me of an exchange that actually took place between two baseball announcers during a game played on Mother's Day. Ralph, known for his malapropisms, asked Tim, "How are you celebrating Mother's Day?" Tim replied, "My mom is looking on from a better place." To which Ralph responded, "Glad to hear that, Tim."

righteous" (*Avot* 4:19).[67] One might choose to privilege such sources over those that express theodicies. However, if the choice as to which sources to privilege is made on philosophical grounds, how may one conclude that no theodicy can work, without examining theodicies that are out there? A further problem with the futility argument is this: If we can't understand God's ways, how can we know how to act? Don't we need His acts as a model?[68]

One reply to this last question is that Judaism has a robust set of moral prescriptions that are given by God or by people He authorizes to issue prescriptions (rabbinic authorities). So there should be no concern that, if we embrace the futility argument, we will be morally at sea.[69] But this reply will not work if, despite being given many directions explicitly, authorities need to trust their moral judgments in order to *interpret* laws – including laws that, if taken literally, the authorities find morally objectionable – or decide cases for which there is no exact precedent. Apparently, God allows legal authorities to use the judgments that *seem* right to them. Admittedly, we must wonder why He allows so much room for error in moral judgment. But He does, and that makes decision-making possible despite the futility argument

Futility and mystery are different: The desire for mystery may arise even if a search for theodicy will not prove futile. Still, the desire some theists have for mystery and opacity is related to futility. Both a conviction that we can never explain evil and a desire for mystery may arise from belief in God's greatness. But given all the complexities about divine attributes, aren't theists already up to their necks in mystery? Why let mysteries procreate without resolution? Where would it end? And why not try to *understand* the divine?[70]

Let's turn to the complacency argument, which I've included under both moral arguments and pointlessness arguments. To begin with, there is vast empirical evidence that people who endorse theodicies *are* kind, charitable, active in the fight against evil (e.g., vigorous in administering social services), and even saintly. So the claim that having a theodicy leads to complacency isn't borne out empirically. And don't *all* Perfect Being theists, *including antitheodicists*, think that there

---

[67] See also *Berakhot* 7a, *Menaḥot* 29b.
[68] There is a resemblance but not identity between the futility argument and the "skeptical theism" position in the analytic literature. On the differences, see Shatz 2019a, 202.
[69] See Schnall 2007.
[70] See also Hick 1978, 6–11. Alston 2005 seeks a balance between mystery and possessing truth.

is some justification or other, even if they don't know it? Yet they are not complacent.

Since the empirical version of the complacency argument fails, we should ask whether as a matter of *logic*, having a theodicy leads to complacency. As a *general* thesis, the charge is false; it depends what the theodicy is. A way to both have a theodicy and engage in moral action is to develop a theodicy in which the reason for evil is one that encourages moral action. A soul-making and a free will theodicy are good candidates. Ironically, then, the complacency objection, far from squelching theodicies, gives us a condition that a theodicy must satisfy, and thereby leads us to particular theodicies that satisfy this condition (soul-making and free will). These theodicies highlight the need for human activity, the view that human beings are "partners in the work of creation" (*Shabbat* 119b), and turn back the complacency objection. A not insignificant gain generated by turning the complacency objection into a theodicy is that it prevents a disconnect between Halakhah and theology – the former counselling action (war against evil), the latter passivity (peace with evil).[71]

CONCLUSION

This chapter has ranged over numerous aspects of the problem of evil that have figured in Jewish treatments of the subject. We have seen that:

(1) The problem of evil presupposes that there is a correct standard of ethics outside of God's will; and the prophets' raising the problem of evil indicates they utilized such a standard.
(2) Jewish sources are divided over the propriety of protesting God's ways and remonstrating with Him, but as time went on, a permissive and even encouraging approach came to dominate. We discussed how such an approach could be justified within PBT.
(3) Significant Jewish sources reject the retributivist theodicy as applied to individuals.
(4) The concept of suffering of love can be understood either as a reference to punishment for minor sins perhaps ending in reward, or as a reference to reward for enduring the suffering, or as the purging of material desires, or as soul-making theodicy, or as a divine intimacy theodicy.

---

[71] See further Shatz 2009b.

(5) Hiding of the Face is a retributive concept in the Pentateuch, but the presence of a nonretributivist Hiding of the Face elsewhere in the Bible opens the possibility of a nonretributivist theodicy such as the free will defense.
(6) There are plausible arguments for theodicizing; but arguments for antitheodicy fail.

The ancient Sages do not present a systematic philosophy in the manner of medieval and modern thinkers. But, especially when viewed in light of later, systematic interpretations by Jewish and non-Jewish thinkers, they provide us with many perspectives on evil that are of great utility in approaching the iconic challenge to Perfect Being Theology.

PART II

HUMAN BEINGS

4

Problems of Free Will

The Bible's Near-Silence

R. Abraham Joshua Heschel (1907–1972) (1955, 412) wrote: "the Bible is God's anthropology, rather than man's theology." In this chapter and Chapters 5 and 6 I want to consider a central issue in any theorizing about *anthropos*, the human being, regardless of whether Heschel is correct. I refer to free will. I will illustrate, however, that with regard to this topic, the Bible and Jewish tradition provide *both* anthropology and theology.[1]

PHILOSOPHICAL CHALLENGES

Of the capacities that are usually attributed to human beings in ordinary discourse, the one that is most widely thought to distinguish human beings from nonhuman animals is free will. But this alleged capacity faces deep logical jeopardy; belief in free will comes under philosophical attack from numerous sides. It is thought to conflict with:

(1) God's foreknowledge (knowledge of the future), which is an aspect of divine providence;
(2) God's foreordaining of history (another aspect of divine providence); and
(3) Modern science, especially neuroscience and genetics.

---

[1] The reader may wonder why three chapters are devoted to free will. This chapter is a preliminary, and I thought I should cover at length at least two of the three deterministic challenges that I lay out. (See chapters 5 and 6.)

Divine foreknowledge, God's foreordaining of history, and scientific laws – these are just different ways in which human choices and actions might be determined. Determination of a particular choice or action ostensibly precludes free choice and/or free action (since the agent can't do otherwise) and therefore precludes responsibility.[2] It also appears to preclude the rationality of "reactive attitudes" – condemnation, guilt, gratitude, forgiveness, approbation, indignation, and the whole "complicated web of attitudes and feelings which form an essential part of the moral life as we know it."[3]

Challenges (1–3) differ with respect to their scope, however. If God knows everything that will occur, the argument that foreknowledge precludes free will extends to *all* human choices and actions. God's foreordaining of history, by contrast, would create a prima facie difficulty only with regard to those events of history that He foreordains. Finally, belief in scientific determinism – the thesis that *all* events are determined by antecedent conditions and by natural laws – is widespread among philosophers. But a scientific determinist with regard to choices and actions does not *have to say* that all events are determined. Some events are not, notably quantum events. Nonetheless, philosophers very often present the determinations of actions and choices (or what seem to be choices) as a fallout from a universal determinism and, for reasons to be explained in Chapter 6, do not think that quantum events salvage free will.

Observe as well that "determined" does not mean "caused," although causation is one form of determination. While in challenges (2) and (3) the determination in question involves *causation* of the choice or action, this is not the case with regard to challenge (1). That is, the argument for an incompatibility between free will and divine foreknowledge does not assume that divine foreknowledge *causes* a person's choices. The claim is that it *determines* the choices (i.e., is a sufficient condition, that is, logically sufficient). When applied differently, the distinction between causation and determination yields a distinction between *backwards* causation and *backwards* determination, and this opens up a controversial response to the foreknowledge–free will problem proffered by Trenton

---

[2] However, responsibility for an act or omission does not require (in our commonsense, "folk" framework) that the act or omission was performed freely. A person who negligently but not deliberately flicks cigarette ash on a patron in the next row of seats in the stadium is not "freely" doing that, because he or she does not will it. Nevertheless, that individual is responsible for the negligence.

[3] The term "reactive attitudes" is salient in Strawson 1962; the quoted phrase is on p. 201.

Merricks (2009, 2011), which resembles one found in Saʻadyah Gaon (Saadia Gaon 1948, 191 [4:4]).[4]

Regarding terminology: There are differences between the terms "free will," "free choice," and "free action." Free will may be thought of as a power or capacity to choose and act freely, or a faculty for free choice and action, however one defines "freely."[5] Free choices and free actions are the *results of* the exercise of free will, or perhaps expressions of free will. Some philosophers believe that, with regard to ascribing responsibility, the focus should be free willings rather than free actions, because, inter alia, whether a will translates into a certain action and a certain result is a matter of luck – that is, of circumstances beyond the agent's control. Typically, however, issues surrounding free choice and free action are referred to as issues of "free will," and that will be my default term though it is loose. On occasion, I will use "freedom."

My point in what follows is that well-known philosophical problems involving free will are strikingly inconspicuous in biblical and Rabbinic material. I will be discussing in this chapter only problems (1) and (2).

PROBLEMS OF DEFINITION

Robert Nozick remarked (1981, 293) that the problems surrounding free will are "the most frustrating and unyielding of philosophical problems." One reason for the persistence of controversy is that no matter where you turn to define free will, eventually you run into a brick wall. If we don't know what free will is, how can we figure out whether we have it in a world in which God has foreknowledge, and/or God controls history, and/or neuroscience and genetics reign in explaining human thought and behavior?

I present – as a starting point only – one utterly conventional necessary condition of what free will is: that possessing free will vis-à-vis particular choices/action requires a two-way power. To have free choice or free will vis-à-vis a particular action, the person must be able to do, *in the very same circumstances*, something other than what he or she in fact does. This thesis is often called the Principle of Alternative Possibilities (PAP)

---

[4] See Brody 2020–2021, 63–65. Cf. Fischer and Todd 2011. Merricks's original suggestion is that both the secular "sea battle" argument examined by Aristotle for the impossibility of free will and the foreknowledge–free will argument can be refuted by allowing backwards determination as opposed to backwards causation. A person's choice would determine God's belief without causing it.

[5] Cf. Ekstrom 2011, 369–70.

or the Forking Paths Principle (borrowing from Jose Luis Borges's story, "The Garden of Forking Paths"). PAP fits the intuition that free will signals *control* – the ability to make things go one way or instead another.

The first issue affecting all forms of the determination versus free will problem, is whether PAP is true. If it is not, then "compatibilism" – the notion that free will is compatible with determination – is true (barring *other* sources of incompatibility[6]). If free will does *not* require alternative possibilities, as many if not most philosophers argue today, then, barring further problems, neither God's foreknowledge nor determination by physical causes will automatically deprive an agent of freedom or responsibility. (Control of history may remain problematic, however, as we will see, when God actually manipulates people's wills.) In Chapter 6, I will offer a more detailed description and assessment of compatibilism.[7]

BIBLICAL SILENCE

How does the Bible think about free will? To a certain extent, it doesn't. Unlike the problem of evil, which is stated front and center in many biblical texts (see Chapter 3), the Bible doesn't seem to care about the problems surrounding free will that philosophers have long obsessed about.

To be sure, the Bible seems very cognizant of a phenomenon we associate with free will: the presence of "thick" motivations. We find thick motivations in Eve's eating from the forbidden tree (Gen. 3:6), Esau's desiring to kill Jacob over Jacob's theft of his blessing (Gen. 27:41), Joseph's brothers weighing options for dealing with him (Gen. 37:18–36), and Pharaoh devising a strategy (viz., affliction) to prevent the Israelites from dominating Egypt (Exod. 1). In all these biblical cases, and many others, an agent develops a strategy or plan that is driven by a clear motivation (though, as we will see in Chapter 5, Joseph's brothers' thick motivations may not reflect free will). Nonetheless, a variety of problems concerning free will are passed over in silence.

---

[6] One putative "other source" is that determination rules out free will because we do not "own" our determined actions. But this new claim draws on the obscure concept of ownership, which *may* reduce to the absence of determination.

[7] Classical compatibilism – the version of compatibilism developed by David Hume, John Stuart Mill, and other British philosophers – did not reject the Forking Paths Principle so much as reinterpret it. They insisted that people act freely provided that (a) they do what they do because they desire to; (b) if they were to desire not to do the action, they would not do it. Problems with this view will emerge in Chapter 6.

Foreknowledge versus Free Will

Challenge (1) (If God always knew what I will do at time *t*, how can I act freely at *t*?) pervades theological writing. But it goes unmentioned in the Bible. The solutions that philosophers propose to preserve free will do not boast strong textual support and some philosophers and biblical interpreters believe, that if we follow the texts alone, God *lacks* foreknowledge, *pace* Perfect Being Theology.[8] This "solution" would explain why the problem is never articulated or implied in the Bible: there is no problem to solve. (In Chapter 1 we discussed the attribution of foreknowledge to God.)

Coercive Incentives

Sa'adyah Gaon (Saadia Gaon 1948, 189 [4:4]) argues that, without our having the capacity to choose between alternatives, rewards and punishments would make no sense, and God would then be unjust in distributing benefits and adversities in response to human conduct. But when the Bible states that the decision whether to observe the commandments is a choice between life and death (Deut. 30:19), we are placed under pressure from coercive incentives! If so, how can our choice to perform or not perform the commandments be free? The Bible seems satisfied with securing compliance and apparently does not require that the compliance be free. A variety of solutions are available – for example, the view of Thomas Hobbes (*Leviathan* ch. 14) and Bernard Williams (1986) that coerced behavior is free because *all* free choices take place within the context of incentives.[9] Yet the Bible does not raise the concern about free will, let alone address it.

Hardening of Hearts

God hardens the heart of Pharaoh so that he will not release the enslaved Israelites when certain plagues strike (Exod. 7:3, 9:12, 10:1, 20, 11:10, 12:9). Likewise, he hardens the heart of the Moabite King Siḥon in order that he should fight the Israelites and then lose (Deut. 2:30), and of the Canaanite army so they will wage battle against Joshua's troops (Josh. 11:20). These hardenings pose problems on multiple fronts: God's

---

[8] This is an important claim throughout Katzoff 2020. Cf. my discussion of "Imperfect Being Theology" in Chapter 1.

[9] Cf. *Bava Batra* 47b–48a, where a *sale* made under coercion is deemed valid, whereas a *gift* given under coercion is not.

intervention prevents the exercise of free will; it eliminates an agent's chance for repentance; and, in the Pharaoh case, it extends the period of suffering for both Israelites and Egyptians, by dint of Pharaoh's keeping them enslaved. To the extent the Bible *does* think that hardening requires a justification, its rationale is that the hardening is executed for the sake of God's greater glory and so that Egyptians and Jews will know God (e.g., Exod. 10:1). For many, that will not be a satisfying justification. All that suffering and loss of life so that God can flex His glory? Various answers have been proposed,[10] but with little textual support, and the Bible's silence is for that very reason deafening.[11]

Divine Interventions

The literary approach to biblical narrative (which the Midrash uses often) works with a variety of techniques, such as *leitwort* (key word), intertextuality, type scenes, and more. When Laban said to Jacob, who had fled to Laban after stealing the blessing intended (at least on the standard reading) for his older twin Esau, "we don't give [in marriage] *the younger before the elder*" (Gen. 29:26), was it a deliberate dig at Jacob? Was it God controlling Laban's speech? Was the Bible formulating whatever he did say in a way that would bring out irony? Consider also repetitions of stories, in which descendants get into the same situations as their ancestors. Commentators (taking their cue from Midrash) say about these repetitions, "the deeds of the fathers are a sign for the sons."[12] There is a fatalistic tenor to this phrase, a sense of predetermination. Granted, the later personality may reverse an earlier pattern, suggesting free will is operative. Yet where does the Bible so much as raise such questions?

Unrationalized, Seemingly Whimsical Actions

Notwithstanding the presence of thick motivations in many narratives, we also find unrationalized acts and failures to act. Why (in Gen. 40) did Pharaoh execute Joseph's other cellmate, the baker, but not the wine steward? (Eventually these decisions contribute to Joseph attaining a high position in Egypt.) Why did Queen Vashti refuse King Ahasuerus's

---

[10] See Shatz 1997a, 1997b, 1997c.
[11] However, in I Kings 18:37, Elijah tells God "You have turned [the Israelites'] hearts backward," and apparently that they should therefore be excused.
[12] See Naḥmanides, commentary to Gen. 12:6, paraphrasing *Midrash Tanḥuma*, Lekh Lekha 9; commentary to Gen. 12:10, quoting *Gen. Rabbah* 40:6.

invitation to a party in chapter 1 of the Book of Esther, paving the road to Esther's being chosen as queen and eventually rescuing the Jews from Haman's malevolent designs? Unrationalized motivations make us wonder whether perhaps divine actions are determining characters' decisions, undercutting free will. But the problem is not laid out for us.

A likely reaction to these examples is, "Look, the Bible is simply not the place for complex ironing out of philosophical issues." But that's precisely the point: At the bottom line, it is not the place to find the questions, let alone their resolutions.

The Rabbis were interested in the relationship between providence and human free will,[13] but it is questionable whether *foreknowledge* versus free will worried them. One talmudic source commonly thought to present the problem of reconciling foreknowledge and free will is R. Akiva's statement in a *mishnah* in Tractate *Avot* (3:15): "All is *tzafuy* and permission is given." *Tzafuy* is usually translated as "foreseen," which would mean that the *mishnah* is raising problem (1) – that is to say, God foreknows, but permission to act (read: free will or free choice) is nevertheless granted. This would not be a solution, of course – just a presentation of the problem. However, some scholars think the passage should be translated, "All is seen [not: *fore*seen] and permission is given." This means merely that humans have free choice but God knows what they are doing at the *present* time. Thus, R. Akiva is not stating a contradiction, but rather affirming an incontestable truism: Since God knows what you are doing (as opposed to what you will do), you should exercise your free choice responsibly. No philosophical *problem* is presented.[14] If so, biblical and talmudic/midrashic sources say almost nothing about problem (1). Tzvi Novick (2014) and others defend the conventional reading by marshalling other rabbinic texts. But even if the conventional reading of the *mishnah* is correct, we can say that *the Bible* is unconcerned with the foreknowledge–free will problem.

DO THE PHILOSOPHICAL PROBLEMS MATTER?

Curiously, while problems (1) and (2) present formidable – and popular – brain-teasers, for many people they have little existential impact. As a rule, so far as I can tell, people do not bring any emotional

---

[13] See Urbach 1987, ch. 11.
[14] See R. Ovadayah mi-Bartenura, commentary to *Avot* 3:15; Urbach 1987, 257–58; Manekin 1997a, 8–11.

investment to discussions of these two conundrums. Agnostics and atheists often endorse free will without worrying, "Oh no! What if God exists!? Then He knows everything I will do and my choices aren't free!" By contrast, the threat of scientific determinism posed by neurophysiological and genetic theories (problem [3]) genuinely worries people.[15] In fact, the theory of scientific determinism was often presented by philosophers merely as a "what if" possibility; the very *possibility* of its truth was thought to be scary. In sharp contrast, no one I know thinks that the very possibility that God exists is scary because of the problems that His existence would pose for free will.[16]

How can we explain the discrepancy between people's indifference to challenges posed by divine knowledge/divine causation and their often weighty concern regarding scientific determinism? Perhaps the explanation is as follows. In the worst-case scenario, if we are deprived of free will because we affirm that God has a plan for history or that God knows what I will do, we are sacrificing belief in free will to affirm another religious principle – namely, divine providence (in some form). To give up one religious principle in the face of pressure from another religious principle – and in particular, divine providence – is understandable from a religious perspective, and it reflects pious motives. By contrast, to embrace scientific determinism and to then surrender free will is to surrender a religious doctrine because of an external body of knowledge – namely, science. This step is one that religious people are less prepared to take. In support of this account, consider that religious people *would* be worried if a supercomputer (rather than God) were to know their action in advance.[17]

In any event, I bring this chapter to a close with the following contention. If we read very carefully, *there is one* philosophical problem that the Bible does seem to care about: whether God's foreordaining history diminishes or precludes free will. It is this problem that will occupy us in Chapter 5.

---

[15] Fischer (1994) implies that the two problems should be equally worrisome. (Note that although the problems are parallel, a proposed solution to one may not work for the other.)

[16] Some may think, however, that since they believe in free will, they must believe there's no God, and *this* scares them because they would have no source of help and support. (My thanks to Meira Mintz for painting this scenario.) These people are either ignorant of philosophical solutions to the foreknowledge problem or reject them.

[17] As was pointed out to me by Aaron Segal.

5

"It Was Not You Who Sent Me Here"

Free Will and God's Foreordaining of History

In recent decades, many analytic philosophers have argued that the Bible can serve as a significant source for reflection on philosophical problems.[1] This recognition – of which we already have seen examples – is part of a larger appreciation by analytic philosophers of the philosophical value of literature and narrative.[2]

In this chapter, I take up the question: Does God's foreordaining of history diminish human free will?[3] I proceed by studying one particular biblical narrative, the story of Joseph and his brothers (Gen. 37–50), using techniques drawn from what is called the "literary" approach to biblical narrative – used by both Midrash and academicians – and incorporating the insights and questions raised in Jewish and analytic philosophy. Before embarking on the analysis, I want to position the discussion in the context of various ways in which philosophy and biblical material can interact.[4]

READING THE BIBLE PHILOSOPHICALLY

There is an old tradition in the Abrahamic religions – exemplified in ancient Jewish thought by Philo but associated especially with medieval

---

[1] Examples include Gellman 1994, Carmy and Shatz 1997, Shatz 1997a, Manekin and Eisen 2008, Stump 2010a, Hazony 2012, Wettstein 2012, Seeskin 2016, Weiss 2018, Katzoff 2020. Johnson 2021 sees the Bible as presenting a distinctive kind of philosophy. Cf. Gericke 2012.
[2] Perhaps the seminal statement of the value of literature for philosophy is Nussbaum 1986.
[3] See Hasker 2004 and Flint 2006 for extensive treatment of the philosophical issue.
[4] I confine myself to the Hebrew Bible, with which I am most familiar.

rationalism – of interpreting the Bible in light of prevailing philosophical and scientific theories. A prominent aim of the rationalists is to harmonize the Bible and philosophy. The medieval bond between the Bible and philosophy is manifest in the facts that two major Jewish philosophers of the period, Sa'adyah Gaon and Levi Gersonides, authored biblical commentaries, and many other philosophers interwove philosophy and exegesis to differing degrees: Solomon ibn Gabirol, Abraham ibn Daud, Moses Maimonides, Joseph ibn Kaspi, and Joseph Albo. Also, although Maimonides's *Guide of the Perplexed* is not a biblical commentary, its *stated* goal is the exegesis of philosophically problematic terms and stories in the Bible.[5] Biblical exegetes who were not primarily philosophers incorporated elements of philosophy or Kabbalah (which arguably qualifies as a philosophy as Neoplatonism does) into their commentaries. These exegetes include Rabbis David Kimḥi (Radak), Moses Naḥmanides, and Isaac Abravanel.

In part, the enterprise of interpreting the Bible to accord with one's general worldview may be defended by the principle of interpretive charity, mentioned in the introduction: initially construe a text in a way that makes an author's argument as plausible and as close to truth as you, the interpreter, can make it.[6] Your reading should match philosophical, scientific, or other theories you endorse on extrabiblical grounds. For those who believe in the divinity and inerrancy of Scripture, far more than *ordinary* interpretive charity is involved. The text is infallible; only its interpreters err.[7] So, faced with challenges to the Bible's truth, religionists ought to harmonize biblical texts with background theories.

However, this bare formula needs nuancing so as to capture different methods of achieving harmonization. The most familiar one is figurative interpretation, which was at work in our chapter on attributes (think of anthropomorphic expressions). But we can distinguish a figurative interpretation that is logically forced upon the interpreter by a philosophical or textual difficulty from a figurative interpretation that has a near-optional quality. That is, even when a biblical text does not

---

[5] See esp. Maimonides 1963, 5–6 (beginning of the introduction to part one of the *Guide of the Perplexed*) and the "lexicographical chapters" found among chs. 1–45 of part 1 of the *Guide*. In truth, though, the book has additional aims.

[6] See D. Davidson 1973.

[7] See Galileo's letters to Castelli and Grand Duchess Christina concerning the ostensible clash between heliocentrism and Josh. 10:12–13 (Finocchiaro 1989, 49–54 and 87–118, respectively).

conflict with philosophy or science, the interpreter may spot and seize an opportunity to read the text figuratively as a locus of philosophical/scientific wisdom.[8] In some other cases, a seeming conflict between the Bible and philosophy is resolved by reference to the Bible's aims. An example is an approach used centuries after the medieval rationalists in response to the seeming conflict between Genesis 1 and evolution: to wit, the Bible is not a science textbook; its aims are moral and spiritual.[9] Galileo is thought to have said, "The Bible teaches the way to go to heaven, not the way the heavens go."[10] Might a degree of inaccurate *philosophy* in the Bible to be expected as well, even without reconstruing particular verses?[11]

Controversy arose over efforts at harmonization via figurative readings, due in large measure to three factors: (a) The philosophy that was implied by a nonliteral reading seemed religiously radical (e.g., there are no or few miracles; see Chapter 2). (b) The Bible seems otiose if the truth lies in philosophy. Finally, (c) Rationalists incurred resentment because they projected elitism. After all, they saw the Bible as a two-layered text, with the exoteric, outer layer geared to the multitude while the hidden, esoteric level is geared to philosophers; and the task of the philosophical exegete is to pierce through the inferior layer, penetrate to the rich and philosophically pristine esoteric truths, and perhaps keep them hidden from the masses. The outer layer is there only because "The Torah speaks in the language of human beings."[12] This may be taken to denigrate the masses, even though one phrase used to characterize the exoteric/esoteric distinction – "apples of gold in settings of silver" (Prov. 25:11) – accords some value to exoteric readings (silver) in at least some cases.[13]

---

[8] Gersonides's commentary on Song of Songs is one example.
[9] Shatz 2008, 217–27.
[10] This statement appears to be a remark by Cardinal Baronius. See also the texts cited in n. 7.
[11] See Shatz 2008.
[12] In its original talmudic context, this idiom (found at *Yevamot* 71a, *Sanhedrin* 64b, *Sifrei Numbers* 112) has nothing to do with interpreting anthropomorphic, anthropopathic, and other philosophically problematic texts. It is concerned with when a law should be derived from a particular feature of the biblical wording (a doubled noun or verb). Moreover, in its original context, the phrase is used by a school of legal exegesis that seeks to *limit* novel interpretations, rather than one that calls for new interpretations (as is the case in medieval philosophy). See Stern 1987, 549–50 and Golding 2001, 41. The medieval authorities known as the Geonim (*c.* sixth–eleventh century) seem to use the phrase as an expression that captures their view about interpretation, without imputing that meaning to the Talmud.
[13] See Maimonides 1963, 11–12 (introduction to part one).

5 "It Was Not You Who Sent Me Here"

Even today, when analytic philosophers confront the charge that philosophers have long Hellenized the Bible – when there is a growing sense of discontinuity between philosophical traditions and biblical texts with regard to such topics as divine impassibility, immutability, simplicity, and timelessness – some analytic philosophers seek to explain individual verses and larger narratives, and to solve various conundrums, in terms of some favored, cutting-edge philosophical theory held by the explainer. Often, to reiterate, the explanation will enjoy no support from biblical evidence, because the texts at hand will be general and open-ended, so that a variety of philosophical accounts will fit them.

Formidable questions arise. Should there be a presumption of literalism in interpretation? Why or why not? If one allows figurative interpretation, how does one set limits? Joshua Golding (2001) suggests answers to these questions from an Orthodox Jewish perspective. My aim here, though, is to examine a case (the Joseph narrative) in which the Bible shows interest in a problem about free will and responsibility that is discussed by philosophers. Philosophical discussions will play a role in exegesis, and vice versa.

THE PROBLEM

The influential twentieth-century biblical commentator Nehama Leibowitz (1981) writes about biblical narrative (1981, 394):

> Interwoven into the account of mortal doings is the unseen hand of Divine Providence. On the surface, the actors in the story make their own way in life, set in motion their own plans, succeed or fail, start again, all on their own initiative. That is the immediate superficial impression. In fact, however, it transpires that it is Divine Providence which is carrying out, through mankind, its own providential plan.

Leibowitz seems to suggest that in the biblical stories, the real actor is God. However, Robert Alter, one of the academic founders of the Bible-as-literature approach, argues (1981, 33–35) that the use of a narrative genre serves to *preserve the tension* between providence and human choice. Writes Alter (1981, 38):

> If one may presume at all to reduce great achievements to a common denominator, it might be possible to say that the depth with which human nature is imagined in the Bible is a function of its being conceived as caught in the powerful interplay of this double dialectic.

The famous historian of biblical religion Yehezkel Kaufmann (1958, 128) points to a feature of biblical writing called "dual causality": Biblical

The Problem

events occur "through both natural causes [including free choice] and divine guidance, which determines a purpose for the event."[14]

In narrative, unlike analytic philosophy, one can simply set out contradictions and not resolve them. In the tension-laden episodes, the Bible may have no interest in resolving the tension but only in calling attention to it and having us experience our reality in a dialectical or antinomic fashion. The latter is Alter's way of approaching the text.[15]

Prima facie, the prospects for resolving the tension are dim. Claiming compatibility between God's foreordaining history and human free will makes a stronger assertion than does general compatibilism (the thesis that free will and determinism are compatible). Unlike the situation in which natural laws and initial conditions determine an action, God's intervening to bring about certain events prima facie involves direct interference in one human agent's will *by another agent*; and nontheistic compatibilists usually agree that *this* sort of interference, as in hypnotism and brainwashing, deprives an agent of freedom.[16]

Against this backdrop, I turn to the Joseph narrative. In Genesis 15:13–15, God informs Abraham (then called Abram) about the future that awaits his descendants:

> Know well that your progeny will be strangers in a land that is not theirs; and they will be enslaved and oppressed for four hundred years. But I will judge the nation that they will serve, and thereafter they will leave with great wealth.

The oppressor is not identified, but, unmistakably, the reference is to the Egyptian enslavement of the Israelites, as described at the beginning of the book of Exodus.

Question: Is God merely making a *prediction* – disclosing that certain events will occur – or is God *decreeing* that the depicted bondage will happen? If the latter, then the bondage is part of God's plan for history. If, by contrast, all we have here is a prediction, the bondage in Egypt and the events leading up to it are entirely contingent upon the choices

---

[14] Others use the term "double agency." See the anthologies Thomas 1983; Hebblethwaite and Henderson 1990. The double agency I am interested in here involves God's hand and human choices. Sometimes, though, double agency involves the theme of God's hand vs. natural law. See Gen. 30:14–21; 30: 31–43 and 31: 4–13. In those episodes, is the cause nature, or God? (I believe that in both cases the text's answer is: God.)
[15] Charlotte Katzoff (2020) shows that the tension pervades the book of Genesis; she does not leave the tension unresolved, however. Instead, she generally sides with free choice.
[16] Going further, William Alston (1989c) argues that God could not be even a "second agent" of free human actions, and that dual causality (or double *agency*) is not a persuasive approach in the case of freely willed actions.

that human beings make. There is little or nothing stage-managed, predestined, or inevitable about them (except for whatever inevitability is implied by divine foreknowledge, but that is a different matter). On the "mere prediction" reading of God's words to the patriarch, there is no problem of dual causality because half of the causal duo is missing; there is no *divine* causality.

However, Jewish commentators generally assume that God, whether for knowable or instead inscrutable reasons, *decrees* the entry into the foreign land and the bondage; He is not merely providing Abraham with a prediction. This understanding is encouraged by the string of seemingly coincidental events surrounding Joseph that leads up to the Egyptian bondage – events suggestive of a divine plan.

The story begins in Genesis 37. Joseph's brothers, jealous of the love he receives from his father and resentful of his dreams of ruling over them, plot against the youngster and throw him into a pit. The encounter was made possible by the fact Joseph had sought to meet up with them at the behest of his father, but he learned their whereabouts only because, while "wandering about in the field," he received information from an anonymous man he encountered. He is sold[17] as a servant to the Egyptian Potiphar. After great initial success, which the Bible explicitly attributes to God, Joseph lands in prison as a result of a trumped-up sexual accusation by Potiphar's wife. He interprets correctly the dreams of two cellmates, who were servants of Pharaoh. Two years later, Pharaoh has a dream. His wine steward – Joseph's erstwhile cellmate, whom Joseph had twice asked to remember him unto Pharaoh, but who had forgotten – recounts for the king Joseph's prowess.[18] The king summons Joseph to interpret, and the king is so impressed by the explanation that Joseph is elevated from dungeon to palace. He is appointed as the king's viceroy, with special responsibility for dealing with an impending famine that he has predicted to the king based on the ruler's dreams. When famine strikes Canaan, the elderly Jacob, Joseph's father, sends his sons to procure food in Egypt – all except for the youngest, Benjamin. The brothers must request relief from Joseph – whom they do not recognize. Joseph recognizes them and gives them a hard time. He accuses them of spying, imprisons them, keeps one brother in prison after releasing the rest, and

---

[17] On who sold him, see the analysis of classical commentaries in N. Leibowitz 1981, 400–9.
[18] The other cellmate, the baker, was executed – as Joseph had predicted from the man's dream.

eventually manipulates events to get them to return to Canaan to bring Benjamin. Jacob consents with great reluctance and fear.

After the brothers bring Benjamin to Egypt, Joseph pulls another ruse; he plants a precious goblet in Benjamin's sack, leading to Benjamin's arrest. Judah pleads for Benjamin's life, and Joseph eventually breaks down and reveals his true identity. The brothers then bring Jacob to Egypt (God must allay his fear of going), where Joseph enables the family to settle and prosper. Slowly, however, Joseph's prominence erodes, and the next Pharaoh (whom we meet at the beginning of Exodus), a king who "knew not Joseph" (Exod. 1:8), introduces harsh decrees against the Israelites. They are oppressed and enslaved.

To many readers, including the Rabbis, at least parts of the sequence seem too coincidental; the events seem orchestrated to fulfill the prediction to Abraham.[19] Joseph's two dreams themselves, suggesting that he will be a powerful ruler to whom his family will bow – dreams that kick off the story – contribute to our sense of inevitability. While God is not *explicitly* implicated in the events that bring Joseph to Egypt, nevertheless, as Charlotte Katzoff (2020) stresses, certain linguistic clues suggest that divine activity is operating. Early in the narrative, as we noted, Joseph is dispatched by Jacob to find his brothers, and an anonymous character – "the man" – points the way (Gen. 37:15–17). (It just so happened (!) he had overheard them saying they would go to Dothan.) Sensitive to the man's emergence, the Rabbis identify him with an angel, a messenger of God; in fact, the word "man" appears three times, suggesting, says a *midrash* (*Gen. Rabbah* 84:14), *three* angels – thus indicating divine intervention. How convenient, too, that a caravan chances by and Joseph is sold. And how convenient is the exact combination of motives and characters that drive the story. Various other literary features point to divine causality as well. Thus, in the story of Joseph, we are led to see God operating through a natural-seeming series of events.

Returning to our question of whether God was making a prediction to Abraham or issuing a decree: If God were merely letting Abraham know where human choices will lead, without God intervening, why would God have to plant "the man" (or men) and exercise all the other manipulations of circumstances? Evidently, the future events divulged to Abraham are at least in part a result of God's orchestration.

---

[19] Commenting on the language used in Gen. 37:14 when Jacob sends Joseph to find his brothers, a *midrash* (*Gen. Rabbah* 84:13) suggests that the entire narrative to follow was a playing out of the prediction to Abraham.

5 "It Was Not You Who Sent Me Here"

ASSIGNING RESPONSIBILITY: JOSEPH'S AND THE BROTHERS' PERSPECTIVES

As viceroy of Egypt, Joseph confounds and threatens his brothers while hiding his true identity. They cast blame upon themselves and refer to their actions as sinful: "Surely we are being punished because of our brother" (Gen. 42:21).

After Joseph reveals his identity, he expresses a different understanding in the matter of allocating blame:

Do not be distressed nor angry with yourselves for having sold me here, for it was to sustain lives that God sent me ahead of you ... God sent me ahead of you to ensure your survival in the midst of the land, and to sustain you for a great deliverance. And so, it was not you who sent me here, but God; He has made me father to Pharaoh and ruler throughout the land of Egypt. [Ibid. 45:5, 7–8]

Later, after Jacob dies, the brothers fear that, with their father gone, Joseph might take revenge. They make up a story: that Jacob had commanded the brothers to tell Joseph to forgive them (50:15–17). We next read:

Joseph said to them, "Fear not, for am I in lieu of God? Although you intended me harm, God intended it for good – in order to accomplish at this time that many people shall be kept alive." [Ibid. 50:19–20]

Joseph sees himself as God's instrument (despite what he says in 50:19), but his outlook differs from the brothers' in three respects:

(1) He does not see himself as an instrument for their *punishment*. On the contrary, he is an instrument for their *benefit*, as he will provide them with sustenance.
(2) He does not say that which the brothers think: that God is responsible for the choices that he, Joseph, made about how to treat them when they arrived. Joseph is evidently secure in his choices,[20] and – ironically – he doesn't ask himself whether his being part of a divine plan renders *him* unfree with regard to the way he treats them.
(3) He mitigates the brothers' blame.

In this attempt to mitigate, he makes at least four distinct claims (I paraphrase):

---

[20] Or ostensible choices. (God may be manipulating him.)

- You sold me (45:4,5) but ...
- (He continues) Don't be upset. All's well that ends well. God put me here to save you, and I did (45:5).
- You didn't send me here; God did (45:7–8).
- You had a bad intention, but God made matters end well (50: 20). (There is irony in the fact that while Joseph is a great seer, his lens does not extend far enough. He does not realize that God's goal is not famine relief, but rather the gathering in Egypt is the beginning of a long and bitter sojourn there.)

The first approach above tells the brothers they are responsible for the sale (and exercised free choice); but the second, following on its heels, asserts that the sale produced a very good consequence and so they must not agonize over having made that choice. This isn't equivalent to saying that the end *justifies* their choice; it tells them only what they should feel (or rather not feel). The third statement arguably relieves the brothers of responsibility – totally. The fourth holds them responsible, but mentions only responsibility for their intent.

Joseph seems to have no uniform position. He vacillates, even to the point of contradicting himself. He appears ensnared in a theological thicket, and his ostensible vacillations, together with the differences between his and his brothers' perspectives, underscore how difficult it is to interpret events and assess responsibility. This supports Alter's view that the narrator accentuates the tension between human action and the workings of providence.

One more feature of the text bears notice, and that is a surprising pattern concerning the role of God. God is said to cause Joseph's successes in Potiphar's house (39:2–5) and his being in the good graces of the warden (39:23). Afterwards, though, God is not named as the cause of any event until after Joseph's "big reveal." God tells Jacob not to fear going down to Egypt (46:2–4). The *characters* attribute various actions to God, yet the narration does not.

Two explanations for the absence of God's name suggest themselves. One is that the absence spotlights for us that human beings, Joseph in particular, bear responsibility for what transpires (e.g., his rough treatment of the brothers and perhaps his not communicating with his father). A second explanation is the opposite: the absence of God's name is meant ironically – as an omission that suggests His presence. Likewise, in the Book of Esther, which resembles the Joseph narrative in many respects, God's name is not mentioned; but the plot – as traditionally understood – unfolds through a series of seeming coincidences that should be taken, via irony, as the work of God's hand.[21]

There is an additional piece to the puzzle. What about the Egyptians, who eventually oppress and enslave the Israelites, per the revelation to Abraham? Did God bring their deeds about? If so, shouldn't they have been absolved of responsibility?

ASSIGNING RESPONSIBILITY: SOME TRADITIONAL APPROACHES

Let's turn to some traditional sources that address the responsibility of agents in the narrative. We are not primarily putting characters on trial to determine guilt or innocence. We are looking for perspectives on the substantive philosophical question of whether (and if so, when) God's having a plan for history renders certain human actions unfree and relieves the agents of responsibility. The narrative scenario is just the context in which the question is being considered. Philosophers are forever constructing imaginary cases, often wild and weird, in order to tease out intuitions. But Eleonore Stump writes (2009, 253):

> When analytic philosophers need to think about human interactions, they tend not to turn to complex cases drawn from real life *or from the world's great literature*; rather, they make up short, thin stories of their own, involving the philosophical crash-dummies Smith and Jones. [My emphasis]

Choosing a classic biblical narrative does not seem inferior to choosing a tale about Jones and Smith, or a lawyerly or sci-fi hypothetical.

In my introduction, I mentioned, in the spirit of a remark Robert Merrihew Adams made about philosophy, that "I do not end up with a position on every issue I raise nor solve every problem. Rather, on occasion I sort through possibilities." Much of this chapter illustrates such an approach.

Approach 1: No Responsibility

Based on an imaginative reading of a verse in Psalms (66:5), the Sages suggested that God uses strategies or ruses (*alilot*) to produce results

---

[21] The name Esther is related to the Hebrew word for "hidden," and, plausibly, the point of the book is that at least in certain times and places, God's providence operates in hidden fashion through a series of what appear to be natural causes, including human choices. See Simon 1997. 23. Cf. M. V. Fox 1991, 244–47.

that He wants. Reflecting this understanding, one midrashic view is that "When You wanted, You implanted love in their hearts [Jacob's], and when You wanted, You implanted hatred in their hearts [the brothers']."[22] Although this text does not overtly address the question of responsibility, such divine intervention should ostensibly absolve the brothers of responsibility. God appears to be interfering with the brothers' free will in order to advance His goals. The Midrash maximizes the deterministic character of the process. Y. Zvi Langermann argues (2020–2021, 100–6), in a different context, that Maimonides believes (astoundingly) that God at times causes people to sin for the sake of actualizing His plan.[23]

If the actions of Pharaoh and the Egyptians are the result of a divine ruse and God manipulates *their* feelings, too, it seems that they, like the brothers, cannot be held responsible for their actions. But whereas the biblical text is unclear whether the brothers were morally responsible, the Egyptian oppressors are certainly held responsible in the Bible, as they are punished significantly. They are smitten by ten plagues, and later drown at sea when pursuing the fleeing Israelites. The drowning, one assumes, is (as noted earlier) punishment for their having drowned Jewish children (Exod. 1). How could divine implantation of motive be consistent with such responsibility?

One option here, obviously, is to argue that God "messed" only with the *brothers'* motivational states, not those of the Egyptians. However, a more interesting response is to adapt (but, I stress, *with alteration*) a view of Nahmanides (in his commentary to Gen. 15:14): namely, that although the Egyptians' choice to enslave and afflict the Jews was determined, they nonetheless had a degree of free choice and responsibility. For they were punished only for the *extent* to which they afflicted the Jews. God's prediction did not require more than enslavement and affliction; in particular, it did not refer to the drowning of Jewish children or the level of oppression that the Egyptians reached, described in Exodus 1:13–14. The idea that punishment was inflicted on the Egyptians only for going to excess gains support from the way the punishment of other nations who harm Israel is expressed in the Bible.

---

[22] Midrash *Tanhuma*, as cited by Rabbi Shmuel Bornztain, *Shem mi-Shemuel*. I have not been able to locate this exact text in the Tanhuma, but *Tanhuma Va-Yeshev* 4 comes close, and the core idea in the Bornztain version is noteworthy. Further, *Midrash ha-Gadol* (Gen. 37:1) speaks of God creating jealousy between Joseph and his brothers.

[23] See Maimonides's commentary to Mishnah *Berakhot* 9:5. Maimonides maintains, says Langermann, that God may punish someone even if He causes their actions. The divine justice is inscrutable.

I am angry at those nations that are at ease, for I was angry only a little, but they overdid the adversity. [Zech. 1:15]

I was angry at my people, I defiled my heritage; I placed them in your hands, but you showed them no mercy. You made your yoke exceedingly heavy. [Isa. 47:6][24]

However, one might argue that, if the punishments administered to the Egyptians are directed only at the *differential* created by the enslavers going to excess, then the extensive punishments that Egypt received are unjust. Since God is just and would not punish them out of proportion to their offense, it follows that they are in fact being held responsible for even the basic level of enslavement and affliction – even though God implanted their desires. If we deem the Egyptians responsible, we are back to our question of how the decree can be reconciled with human responsibility. The same question confronts the other biblical verses which suggest that oppressors sent by God were punished only for going too far.

Let's return to Joseph's brothers. Although the biblical text does not indicate that the brothers were punished, elements of Jewish tradition suggest that the harm done to Joseph is regarded as a great sin. In a part of the Yom Kippur liturgy, ten great Sages of Israel (who in reality lived at different times) are powerfully depicted as being taunted by the Romans about the brothers' sin, and then killed in gruesome fashion. The murder of those Sages seems to be vicarious punishment. To be faithful to this aspect of post-biblical Jewish tradition demands a way of preserving the responsibility of the brothers.[25]

In fact, Joseph does not exonerate the brothers totally. Earlier I said that Joseph seems to have no consistent position. We can, however, somewhat harmonize his utterances. He does not quite say that God caused him to be *sold*. Rather, the brothers *sold* him, whereas God, not they, "*sent*" him to provide sustenance (compare Gen. 45:5 with 45:7–8).[26] In Joseph's mind, God's activity lies primarily in "sending me here," which can be construed as "elevating me to power," not as "*selling* me." On this reading, he does not argue that God got him down to Egypt – he

---

[24] Here is how I just altered Naḥmanides: when Naḥmanides makes the claim that the Egyptians went to excess, he is not concerned with the question of divine determinism but rather with a different question: Weren't the Egyptians fulfilling God's will? (See the last section of this chapter.) A second claim he makes, that the Egyptians did not act out of a desire to fulfill the divine will, is not germane to the question of determinism.

[25] *Pirkei de-Rabbi Eliezer* (38:11) interprets Amos 2:6 as referring to the sin of the brothers in selling Joseph. However, many commentators do not read the verse this way.

[26] Even if the brothers did not themselves make the sale (see N. Leibowitz 1981, 400–9), Joseph thought they did. And their actions and inactions did to a degree cause the sale even if they didn't know it was happening.

believes that the brothers did that – but rather he maintains that God turned their awful choice into a good one. All's well that ends well (by utilitarian standards)! He also blames the brothers for nefarious *intentions* (Gen. 50:20), so the brothers are not lacking in responsibility even according to Joseph; and he tells them not to be upset, not that they aren't responsible for their bad intentions.

When pushed far, ascribing events to divine activity makes God bear responsibility for bringing about Joseph's astonishing failure to communicate with his father for twenty-two years. We therefore might look for a solution that mitigates God's responsibility while preserving human responsibility.

The Stoic philosopher Epictetus (1983, sect. 17) states, "Remember that you are an actor in a play, which is as the playwright wants it to be ... What is yours is to play the assigned part well. But to choose it belongs to someone else." Relative to the sources we have seen, this is not an accurate portrayal of the actions of Joseph's brothers or those of the Egyptians. The protagonists do not even know their part, and they are neither agreeing to play it nor refusing to play it.

Approach 2: Preserving Human Responsibility – God Arranges Only Circumstances

Another opinion in Jewish tradition is that God set up circumstances that would *evoke* (or provoke, to use Katzoff's [2020, 161] word) love or hatred – something very different from *implanting* love and hatred directly. He sent the "man" who showed Joseph where his brothers had gone. He set up circumstances in the context of which the brothers would freely choose to harm Joseph, as well as circumstances in which the Egyptians would freely choose to oppress the Israelites. He *always knew* how they would *freely act* in *any specific circumstance*. It is worth noting, however, that God's sending the man seems morally troubling: It sets a trap for Joseph, and seems to be in legal terms entrapment of the brothers.

Approach 3: Affirming Responsibility – the General and the Particular

R. Isaac Arama (1420–1494) writes:

God's intention does not necessitate the particulars of human actions. Rather, each person goes his way innocently and does what he wants. If these or those individuals do not perform the actions [that will lead to the fulfillment of God's decree], this will not prevent the realization of the objective by others.[27]

Maimonides had already observed that the oppressor of the Jews is not identified in the prediction to Abraham.[28] All the divine plan requires – and all that the prediction says – is that they will be enslaved by *some* nation (unnamed) for 400 years. Is it crucial to the plan that it be the Egyptians? We can't tell, and various explanations of God's reason for decreeing the bondage (e.g., to purify the Israelites) would work equally well if other nations were the oppressors. So perhaps it is not inevitable that the Egyptians be the ones to enslave the Israelites.

In this approach, the general result – oppression – was foreordained; it would happen no matter how people acted. Had the brothers freely refrained from causing Joseph to end up in Egypt or had the Egyptians freely refrained from oppressing them, the Israelites would have ended up in Egypt some other way or some other nation would have oppressed them.[29] "The man" leads Joseph to his brothers, but Joseph could have met up with them some other way.[30]

Approaches 2 and 3 maintain, if only by implication, that regarding some events for which God has a plan, He allows and even prefers that this plan be carried out through human choices. He therefore exercises intervention selectively, creating circumstances to evoke the choices, while not implanting volitions (Approach 2); or, ordaining only the general result, not the means (Approach 3).

A comparison to a school of thought termed Molinism is pertinent here. Named after the Spanish theologian Luis de Molina (1535–1600), Molinism attempts to reconcile the divine plan with human free will by endorsing the thesis that God has "middle knowledge." This term refers to knowledge of how creatures would *freely* choose to act in various *counterfactual* circumstances. The human conduct contributes to the plan, and God chose the actors, but the choices are free. Molinism is not put forth by Jewish thinkers in its classical form,[31] but some Jewish sources do accept that God's plans are implemented through free human choices. And that is what the "God arranges only circumstances" and

---

[27] Arama, *Akedat Yitzhak* 28:1. A version of the general/particular distinction is found in Gellman 2016, ch. 5, esp. 109–11.
[28] *Mishneh Torah*, Laws of Repentance 6:5.
[29] Ibid. 6:6.
[30] See also the general discussion of "top-down" causation in Gellman 2016, ch. 5.
[31] Charles Manekin informed me that there were no Jewish Molinists. Cf. B. Lerner 2009.

"general versus particular" approaches are arguing. However, whereas in Molinism, God chooses His agents, creating certain people because of the free choices they would make, the general/particular approach denies this in that there are "backup" agents. A vexing problem for Molinism is whether middle knowledge is possible – whether God can know how creatures would *freely* choose to act in various *counterfactual* circumstances.[32]

But how can the general be realized without the particulars? The answer emerges if we connect the general/particular account with the notion that "God has many messengers." This approach comes to mind in reading the Book of Esther, which bears numerous linguistic, characterological, and thematic connections to the Joseph story.[33] Both narratives are marked by what appear to be a series of "coincidences." Mordecai urges Queen Esther to plead before the king to nullify Haman's decree that the Jews be killed, sending her the following message: "For if you keep silent at this time, relief and deliverance will come to the Jews from somewhere else, while you and your father's house will perish." (Esther 4:13–14)[34]

This approach of "God has other [or many] messengers" suffers from vagueness. We are told that if the brothers or the Egyptians were to choose differently, the result would come in some other way. "Some other way" – like what? Another human action? How plausible is it that there are other humanly chosen ways that would bring the same result if the Joseph route fails? *Might* there have to be coercive divine intervention if there are no backup messengers? Apparently so.

Setting that aside, the absence of explicit descriptions of God bringing about the events of the brothers' descent to Egypt may be an attempt to convey that divine intervention, though present, is in the larger picture muted and limited. As I noted earlier, after Joseph is jailed, the narrator does not attribute any particular event to divine causality, albeit the characters do. "The man" does nothing more than tell Joseph, "They went that-away." While God plays a causal role in the sale, as indicated, there is not *enough* divine intervention to exonerate the brothers.[35]

---

[32] On Molinism, see Hasker 2004 (con), Flint 2006 (pro).
[33] See G. Cohen 1973, 12–14. Noting the parallels has become commonplace.
[34] To be clear, there is no explicit statement in the Joseph story akin to this one by Mordecai.
[35] Joseph's argument attributing his rise to power to God's intervention is the opposite of what the narration's silence about divine activity seems to imply. Interestingly, though, Joseph seeks to help his own cause along by asking the wine steward to remember him

W. Lee Humphreys writes in this spirit (1988, 129):

We do not suddenly discover at the end that we have been an audience in some grand puppet show staged by a divine puppeteer ... Jacob did not have to favor Joseph with such overt tokens as the cloak. Joseph need not have carried tales, boasted of his dreams, let alone toyed with his brothers later when they in turn fall into his hands. Nor need the brothers have acted as they did. All act upon choices freely made.

Charlotte Katzoff argues (2020, 153–54), similarly, that we should not be inclined to absolve the brothers:

Their intense jealousy and resentment towards Joseph is so convincingly motivated by Jacob's favoritism and Joseph's conceit, the former represented so vividly by the coat of many colors, the latter by the dreams, that we cannot fail to see the heroes a agents rather than puppets.[36]

THE INEVITABILITY ARGUMENT

The Causation Version

Even if we do not worry that there are divine actions in the Joseph story that interfere with free will, we must engage with another challenge to the brothers' and the Egyptians' responsibility: the outcome was inevitable. There are two varieties of this argument. One is based on a condition for causation, while the other is based on a condition for free will.

The driving principle of the causation version of the inevitability argument is that no one incurs moral responsibility for bringing about an inevitable result, *because a person cannot "cause" an inevitable result.* Event X can *cause* event Y only if X's occurring is a necessary condition for Y's occurring. When a result Y is inevitable, this condition is not satisfied.[37] Since the enslavement and affliction of the Israelites in Egypt is part of the divine decree, it is inevitable. So is a prerequisite – the arrival

---

unto Pharaoh (Gen. 40:14), which later the steward indeed does (Gen. 41:9–13). The Sages criticize Joseph for twice making the request rather than trusting in God, stating that he was punished by two additional years of incarceration; see *Gen. Rabbah* 89:2.

[36] Katzoff's argument that well-motivated behavior can be attributed to free choice raises the possibility that poorly motivated choices in Esther are not free as God sometimes manipulates minds and wills. There is, for instance, Queen Vashti's unexplained, seemingly unmotivated refusal to appear at the king's banquet, which ultimately creates the vacancy that Esther fills.

[37] See the articles by Frankfurt, Heinaman, Rowe, and Fischer and Ravizza in Fischer and Ravizza 1993a. See also Fischer and Ravizza 1998, chs. 4–5. For simplicity's sake, I gloss over such distinctions as causation by acts vs. causation by omissions.

of the Israelites in Egypt.[38] So the brothers and the Egyptians cannot be assigned responsibility for their actions.

The first thing that should be said against this argument is that its driving principle is vulnerable to a counterexample. If no one can cause an inevitable result (and therefore no one can be responsible for the inevitable), then no one can cause and be responsible for another person's death, even in the case of a gruesome murder. After all, the person will eventually die anyway! Someone can cause and be held responsible for the death occurring at a particular time and place and in a particular way, but not for the death itself. Thus, the causation version of the inevitability argument rests on a seemingly plausible principle that in truth is implausible, or at least sorely in need of a refinement.

Highly significant for our discussion is William Rowe's examination of the scope of the inevitability principle. Rowe (1993, 13) believes that in certain cases, a person causes an inevitable result. Namely:

If you do something that is sufficient in the circumstances for E, and your doing it *prevents the actualization of other potential generators of* E, then you cause E by doing that thing.

This condition readily handles the fact that killers cause other people's deaths even though the death of any given victim is inevitable. A killer's shooting someone to death precludes anyone else from doing that, so that person's act is identified as the cause.[39]

How would Rowe's principle apply to Joseph's brothers? I'll give just a quick sketch. (a) If the actions of Joseph's brothers are "sufficient in the circumstances" for his being thrown into the pit *and* prevent the actualization of other potential generators of that event, the brothers cause those events according to Rowe's account, even if God has many messengers.[40] (b) The brothers' actions are not "sufficient in the circumstances" for the arrival of the Israelites in Egypt. Many other agents and events were necessary, and since those agents and events come later, it is odd to take them as included under "in the circumstances."[41] Cases of this type abound – cases in which much else has to happen for a certain

---

[38] Although we have noted that the information given to Abraham does not mention Egypt, let's just assume here that God's plan is about Egypt in particular.
[39] Van Inwagen (1978) presents a different treatment of the killing example.
[40] I hedge here because their actions do not exclude the possibility of someone else pulling Joseph out of the pit and then throwing him in it.
[41] The brothers could not have *foreseen* the events either, but foreseeability affects responsibility rather than causation.

result of a given act to be actualized – and in those cases we nevertheless ascribe causation and responsibility. It's difficult to define a cutoff, either for how many other potential contributors to the result there are or how far into the future the results reach; but to say that because they bear responsibility for throwing Joseph in the pit, the brothers cause the family's later arrival in Egypt and the centuries of Egyptian bondage – that seems a stretch. (c) The actions of *the Egyptians* were sufficient in the circumstances to fulfill the decree conveyed to Abraham, and once they occurred they prevented other means of actualizing God's prediction. So the Egyptians satisfy Rowe's sufficient condition.[42]

Much more could be said about applying Rowe's view, but the preceding sketch (and its mixed results) suffices in our context.

The Free Will Version

The second form of the inevitability argument deals not with whether one can cause the inevitable, but with whether the inevitability of an event leads us to consider the actions that led up to it "unfree." According to the Principle of Alternative Possibilities (PAP), to have free choice or free will vis-à-vis a particular action, the person must be able to do, *in the very same circumstances*, something other than what they in fact do. But in dealing with the Joseph narrative, Charlotte Katzoff (2020, 161–65) suggests a model for understanding how free will and responsibility can coexist with the inevitability of the result. She rejects PAP using an approach to moral responsibility developed by Harry Frankfurt (1969).

Frankfurt presents a type of case in which, to use an example,[43] (i) Jones is voting for an elected office (ii) if Jones were to show signs of voting for Green, a powerful intervener would cause Jones to vote for Bradley, but (iii) so long as Jones chooses to vote for Bradley on Jones's own, the intervener lets that choice be carried out. In this setting, our intuition is that Jones freely votes for Bradley, even though Jones's voting for Bradley is inevitable. The reason that the inevitability does not render Jones's choice unfree is that Jones has deliberated, and the factor that renders his act inevitable (viz., the intervener) is causally inert. Had the

---

[42] That the brothers descended to Egypt because of the famine does not render their prior misdeeds superfluous as causes of their coming to that land. For had they not harmed Joseph as they did, he would not have been in Egypt to advise Pharaoh about how to amass food, and possibly there would have been no point in the brothers traveling to Egypt for food.

[43] This example is a variant of one devised by John Martin Fischer (1982).

potential intervener not been present, Jones would have voted for Bradley anyway. So PAP is false. Frankfurt maintains that Jones acts unfreely only if he votes for Bradley *only* because it is inevitable that he do so.[44]

The brothers' ending up in Egypt is inevitable; had they, exercising their free choice, showed signs of acting differently toward Joseph, the same result would have occurred as their actual choices yielded. Nevertheless, the brothers would bear responsibility, if one finds Frankfurt's example persuasive.[45]

There has been so much debate about Frankfurt's examples and other arguments for the denial of PAP that it is folly to review them here. Nevertheless, regarding the applicability of discussions of PAP in our context, the following points seem noteworthy:

(A) Denying PAP comes at a cost to some theists, as it makes an otherwise attractive theodicy difficult to execute. To wit, the free will theodicy is based on the theory that God allows people to do moral evils because He must give them alternative possibilities.[46]

(B) Alternative possibilities seem to matter for the Bible; it is because people make meaningful choices between alternatives that they are either rewarded or punished (e.g., Deut. 11:13–21, 12:26–28).[47]

(C) Points (A) and (B) do not dispel Frankfurt's argument; they suggest only that a believer in God and in the inerrancy of the Bible has motivation to *seek* a response to the examples. However, a defender of PAP may argue that Frankfurt's cases do not have

---

[44] Often overlooked are Frankfurt's qualifications of his view in Frankfurt 2008.

[45] Similarly in Esther: Mordecai says (as we saw) that if Esther does nothing, the same inevitable result – the salvation of the Jews – will come about. But this does not remove Esther's moral credit for in fact summoning the courage to go the king and ultimately rescuing her people.

[46] See also Fischer 1994, 182–83.

[47] Admittedly, this blunts my earlier point (in Chapter 4) that in these verses coercive incentives are at work. But the commandments were often disobeyed, suggesting that the incentives to obey did not remove alternative possibilities. Earlier I was merely noting that there is a prima facie problem of coercion that the Bible does not consider; in the text, I suggest a response – that the incentives did not coerce.

In *Shabbat* 88a, God is said to have held a mountain over the Israelites to ensure they would accept the Torah. One sage objects that this scenario could become a grounds for people to deny their obligation to obey, claiming that they accepted under coercion. The mountain poised overhead did coerce them to accept the Torah, unlike the promises and threats in the Bible. Rava suggests, based on a reading of a verse in Esther, that the Jews accepted the Torah voluntarily later in history. (It could be argued that the fact that people disobeyed after Sinai suggests that the Israelites had free will once the threat of being crushed by the mountain was lifted.)

their desired effect when it comes to decisions and volitions. Jones has alternative possibilities for his *decisions* and *volitions*, and *these* are not vulnerable to Frankfurt-style objections.[48]

(D) Frankfurt's intervener must wait and see how Jones is tending to vote before deciding to intervene. By contrast, if God is omniscient, He need not wait to see what the brothers will do. Katzoff's bold reply to this disanalogy, which she grounds in other biblical narratives as well, is precisely that the biblical narrative does not subscribe to the doctrine of God's foreknowledge and omniscience.[49] But since there is in the Bible the phenomenon of prophecy, it may be argued that God never has to wait and see how things develop. He never has to fashion a horde of contingency plans and prepare to execute them depending on how things turn out. An important question here is whether in prophecies God is in truth only announcing His intentions, speaking conditionally, or using probabilities, as opposed to seeing the future.[50]

But if an appeal to Frankfurt does not remove the argument that the brothers and Egyptians should not be held responsible for the inevitable, is there any argument for holding them responsible? These are some key issues surrounding the claim that if a result is inevitable, a person cannot *freely* bring it about.

NAHMANIDES AND FULFILLING GOD'S WISHES

In the preceding pages, we have been occupied with the problem of reconciling ascriptions of free will and responsibility with the existence of a divine decree whose fulfillment is inevitable. There is a second problem to consider, however, one identified by Nahmanides. This second problem is not concerned with inevitability. Rather, Nahmanides argues that if God *desires* a certain result, one *ought* to try to bring it about. While one cannot cogently argue, "Joe will inevitably die; therefore I should

---

[48] Fischer 1994 dubs this the "Flicker of Freedom" approach and rejects it; for discussion, see Widerker 1995, and cf. Katzoff 2020, 161–65. (Ironically in light of this analytic debate, Joseph blamed the brothers for their *intentions* [Gen. 50:19–20].)

Even were God playing only the role of Frankfurt's counterfactual intervener, though, we might be troubled by the claim that God would intervene if He saw the brothers backing off their evil designs.

[49] This approach fits an "open God" model. See Pinnock 1994, and Fredosso 1998's reply to an earlier presentation of Hasker 2004.

[50] See Katzoff 2020, 11–12. Cf. Flint 2006, 12, 101–7, and Chapter 1.

Nahmanides and Fulfilling God's Wishes

kill Joe," prophecies and dreams are reflections of what God *wants* to happen.[51] So, Nahmanides asks, how can people (here, the Egyptians) justly be held culpable for trying to bring about the realization of what God wants to happen?

Morality, not modality, is Nahmanides's theme. He is not arguing that because a result is inevitable, that creates an obligation to bring the result about. He is arguing that if a result is desired by God, that creates an obligation to bring the result about. He explains that the Egyptians were punished only because they went too far (a contention I critiqued earlier) and because they did not *intend* to fulfill God's will.

Most likely, the idea that knowledge of God's desire creates permission to violate laws is to many disturbing and dangerous. A talmudic passage concerning King Hezekiah and the prophet Isaiah cuts against the idea. God had brought afflictions upon Hezekiah:

King Hezekiah asked Isaiah: "What is all this [punishment]?" Isaiah told him: "Because you did not engage in procreation." Hezekiah replied: "But that was because I saw through divine inspiration that children who are not good will issue from me." Isaiah replied: "Why do you concern yourself with the hidden matters of the Merciful One? What you are commanded to – you must do. And what is found to be good by the Holy One, Blessed Be He – He will do." [*Berakhot* 10a]

Hezekiah should have procreated as commanded. As Walter Wurzburger (1969) comments:

The intrinsic worthwhileness of an act does not depend upon the net effect of its consequences, but solely upon its conformity to the standards of normative precepts ... Our standards of evaluation must be geared not to an ultimate historic destiny but to the immediate situation at hand.

But how did Nahmanides get from the desirability (for God) of the ends to the rightness of the means? His position could be viewed as an

---

[51] In the comment under discussion, Nahmanides restricts his thesis to one who hears a prophet's prediction and tries to fulfill it. Absent this restriction, one might reason ridiculously: God ordained that all humans are mortal; therefore, a human death reflects God's desire; so why can't I kill people? (Even with prophecy, though, the person's ordained time and manner of death may not be known.)

The case of Joseph suggests that for Nahmanides, a dream can serve the function of a prophet with regard to the call for action. Nahmanides justifies Joseph's rough treatment of his brothers in his commentary to Gen. 42:6, using the idea that Joseph manipulated his brothers to retrieve his youngest brother Benjamin and thereby bring it about that his dream of all his brothers bowing down to him (that is the obvious interpretation of the dreams in Gen. 37) would be fulfilled.

outgrowth of models that we articulated above (which isn't to say this is how Naḥmanides would defend his position – in fact I don't think he would do it this way). According to Molinism, God's plans are realized through human actions. Our free choices contribute to the ends contained in God's plan. Yes, God gives norms to follow, but we know that some people may contribute to the advancement of the divine plan while at the same time violating a norm that is usually applicable. In particular, even evil choices, such as Egypt's choice to enslave the Israelites and the brothers' choice to harm Joseph, contribute to God's plan, if not constitute it in some cases. Given this fact, if an individual sees that a certain normally bad means will bring about God's ends, they need not take the usual nefariousness of the means as reason for ruling them out. God will not bring about the result unless human choices fail to do that; He prefers that human beings be the agents and implementers of His plan. If everyone were to say, "I won't do this, but no matter – someone else will if I won't," God ultimately would have to bring about the end Himself, which we were told is not the preferred way. The end will occur whether I act or not, but I *should* act, because God *wants* to remain a counterfactual, not actual, intervener. From this perspective, R. Isaac Arama's objection to Naḥmanides's argument – that Joseph should "leave it to God" – is flawed.[52] God's plans are preferably realized through human choices.[53] There is nothing wrong (on this view!) with playing God when you know what He wants.

Why would God deem human choices the preferred option? One answer would be that He desires to preserve free choice and thus limit His interference in human choices.[54] Or, instead, a theologian might say that God must be distanced from evil – making Him a permitter of evil, as opposed to a doer. The former rationale seems the more logical, since (a) none of the views portray full divine distancing from evil and (b) if there is a problem with evil, then even a little evil done by God creates a problem, even when His causal activity is due only to the lack of others to do the job.

That said, a problem with God's preferring that humans advance the plan is the role that *humans* are called on to play in the production of evil when God desires the result that the evil will bring about. Is it

---

[52] Arama, *Akedat Yitzḥak* 28:1.
[53] However, Joseph's justification of his brothers on the grounds that the end is divinely ordained applies the reasoning even to unintended consequences.
[54] This answer is not readily available to Naḥmanides, because, as we shall see in Chapter 6, he does not deem free will an ideal. But I am trying to ground the *position* he takes.

plausible that an agent ought to abandon ordinary moral principles in such situations? One would need a version of divine command theory in which God's desire is a source of obligation that can override moral considerations.

These are some of the ins and outs of a Naḥmanides-type position, though Naḥmanides did not develop and defend the position in the way I have devised.

CONCLUSION

In this chapter we have explored a variety of interconnected themes.

(1) Although, per Chapter 4, the Bible deems indifferent to philosophical problems about free will, one problem is treated: The seeming incompatibility between divine control of history and human choice.
(2) The literary approach to biblical narrative sharpens our perception of the tension between divine control and human choice in the Joseph story.
(3) The Midrash and later commentators devise a variety of responses. The most attractive of these, albeit it is imperfect, is that only the whole is determined, not the parts, and that "God has many messengers." A corollary is that God prefers that His plan be advanced by human beings.
(4) In two ways, the inevitability of a result in a given context threatens the possibility of being responsible in that context, but there are ways to make room for responsibility in the circumstances.
(5) Naḥmanides raises a fresh issue: How can someone be held culpable for a result if that person does what God wants? I sought to explain and assess the framework in which Naḥmanides's view emerges.

Besides attempting to shed light on the biblical treatment of free will, I have illustrated how philosophical awareness can sensitize us to literary dimensions of a text and how literary analysis can bring out philosophically interesting interpretations and positions.

Whereas philosophers and exegetes try to resolve logical problems about free will and divine planning, the Bible perhaps wants primarily to impress upon us how deep the problems run. Perhaps it aims not at a solution, but, as Alter's approach suggests, at our experiencing and internalizing the conflicting pulls that constitute the problem, the tension between free will and divine decree. Both pulls must be part of religious experience. Joseph's multiple perspectives on his brother's actions, and the contrast between his brothers' understanding of his role and his own perspective, bring home profound ambiguities in the attempt to be free, responsible agents in a world governed by a God who plans and shapes history. Even when great minds resolve the ambiguities and conundrums, theists must on occasion park resolutions at the door and return to the original, elemental text, so as to remind themselves of the dual reality in which, from a theistic perspective, humans function, and through which they must navigate.

6

How Free Is the Will?

The Challenge of Scientific Determinism

In our discussion of the seeming conflict between divine planning and human free will as it appears in the Bible, we explored what Alan Mittleman (2015) has described as "the awareness of being caught up in the play of larger forces that we can scarcely understand, let alone control" (123). Besides being weakened by beliefs about divine activity, our experience of ourselves as free agents – choosing within a set of alternatives – appears to clash with the notion that our actions and thoughts are produced entirely by biological causes. It is the threat that scientific materialism (or physicalism) poses to free will that will occupy us in this chapter.[1]

Francis Crick, codiscoverer of the double-helix formation of DNA, famously articulated what he called "The Astonishing Hypothesis": "[T]hat 'you,' your joys and sorrows, your memories and your ambitions, your sense of identity and free will, are in fact no more than the behavior of a vast assembly of nerve cells and their associated molecules." (Crick 1994, 3)

This notion that all reality is composed of matter – materialism – has a long pedigree, extending back to pre-Socratic philosophy. But in our time materialism has matured from an essentially speculative assertion, or one that was defended on a priori grounds, into a well-developed, empirically

---

[1] While it is common to use "physicalism" and "materialism" interchangeably, some differentiate between the two "isms" when discussing the mind-body problem. As Olson and Segal 2023 explain, materialism is a thesis about human beings (that human beings are made entirely of matter), while physicalism is a claim about the world as a whole (that all properties are physical properties). That said, it will be easier here to use "materialism" to cover both theses.

grounded scientific theory. It may justly be called a central image, a model, a sovereign approach – in Thomas Kuhn's (1962) famous phrase, a scientific paradigm.

The current materialist revolution has altered how many of us conceive of mind and personality. Neuroscientists seem to be successfully mapping a gamut of mental phenomena onto states of the brain – from higher-level cognitive functions, to emotions and personality traits; to raw experiences of color, taste, and sound; to moral judgment, economic choices, religious experience, and religious beliefs. Simultaneously, geneticists have explained how neural pathways are set, and they identify genetic causes of character traits, personality disorders, and the like.

At grassroots level, materialism gains credibility by means of the dramatic applications of science in daily life. In contemporary medical ethics, you are your brain – alive if it lives, dead if it's dead. And society's extensive use of mood-altering drugs has altered people's conceptions of themselves; often, they view themselves as purely biological beings.[2]

It is commonplace to argue that materialism reflects scientism, which combines two claims: (i) a methodological principle that only science is a source of knowledge and (ii) an ontological view that there are no nonmaterial entities. But materialism does not entail scientism. For, what if the champion of materialism maintains only that, *as a scientist (e.g., neuroscientist), bound by certain procedures of the discipline*, one must not consider any other source of knowledge and must not posit immaterial entities? This approach surely is not full-blown scientism – and arguably not scientism at all – since it leaves alive the possibility that immaterial entities exist and can be known to exist by some way other than the application of scientific method. Or is the materialist claim that, if alleged nonmaterial entities or processes cannot be accommodated in an account that meets the constraints of science, immaterial entities don't exist, period? A "yes" is full-blown scientism (or scientism *simpliciter*). Similarly, would materialists concede that the best *scientific* explanation of a phenomenon need not be the best *overall* explanation? In any event, numerous philosophers believe that materialism cannot fully explain consciousness.[3] Yet the sense that something true and important has

---

[2] See Kramer 1993.
[3] Many embrace some form of property-dualism. "Property dualists" deny that there are nonphysical substances but maintain that there are nonphysical properties, such as the redness of a mental image or the sharpness of a pain. Most famous, perhaps, is Chalmers 1996. Nevertheless, substance dualism – which accepts an immaterial self – is not lacking in support among philosophers. See Loose et al. 2018; Koons and Bealer 2010; Audi

been discovered about human beings is credible and widespread. Theists ignore it at the cost of an inadequate anthropology and an inadequate understanding of what it could mean for human beings to be created in the image of God.

For the sake of discussion, let's start with the assumptions that materialism entails determinism[4] and that determinism precludes free will. (In Chapters 4 and 5 we had occasion to probe the second assumption.) Some libertarians – philosophers who believe that (i) free will is not compatible with determinism *and* that (ii) we do have free will – maintain that free will involves an "agent" or "will" or "self" that controls the physical body. Agent-causation, selves, and wills are often thought to be incompatible with a materialist ontology, and if free will is understood by way of agent-causation, then materialism's challenge to free will would become all the greater.[5]

The challenges that the absence of free will would pose are obvious and widely known. As explained in Chapter 4, if free will is absent, there goes (apparently) moral responsibility. Gone too (apparently) are "reactive attitudes" – feelings like blame, resentment, condemnation, guilt, gratitude, forgiveness, approbation, indignation, and the whole "complicated web of attitudes and feelings which form an essential part of the moral life as we know it."[6] For a materialist, it would seem, to keep these attitudes is to *hold* people responsible even when they are not responsible from a moral point of view. Free will, according to many, is also related to human dignity, and without free will, dignity dissipates.

Faced with this materialist challenge, a religious person may seek precedents in which religious thinkers confronted deterministic explanations of human thought and behavior – and found a way to either salvage free will in the face of the challenge or to overcome a sense of loss. These

---

1996; Foster 1991; Hart 1988; Swinburne 1997; Plantinga 2011; Segal's contributions in Olson and Segal 2023. A view that the problem of consciousness is not just unsolved but is insoluble by our minds is often called mysterianism. Some philosophers today gravitate towards panpsychism to explain consciousness

For coverage of a wide swath of issues in philosophy of mind, see the anthology Chalmers 2021. Among the best-known critics of materialism today are Nagel (2012) and Plantinga (2011). Nagel is an atheist, Plantinga a theist. Dissenting neuroscientists and philosophers voice their view in Libet et al. 1999. See also Schwartz and Begley 2002, Mele 2014.

[4] Bracketing the problem of randomness in nature until later in this chapter.
[5] On whether agent-causation *is* compatible with materialism, however, see Cover and O'Leary-Hawthorne 1996; Clarke 2003; Turner 2009.
[6] Strawson 1962, 201.

precedents fall under three headings: restrictivism, devaluation, and compatibilism. None of these approaches serve fully, but they either diminish the significance of our lacking free will, or, by contrast, make the case for free will more promising.

It must be noted that there were Jewish rabbinic determinists. Among medieval determinists were Ḥasdai Crescas (some implausibly regard him as a compatibilist[7]); and some Ḥasidic thinkers denied all or almost all human free will. Without diving into specifics of Ḥasidic thinkers, we may say that their stance was adopted because, to blend different but related themes: God controls everything, an extreme form of divine providence; God is immanent, and there is no ontological separateness from God;[8] God is the only existent (Deut. 4:35: "there is none other than He" [acosmism]); there is no will other than His.[9] In fact, human will is nothing more than God's will.[10] The point is not so much that there is no free action, but that there is no human agency or action at all. (And, not to put too fine a point on it, no human beings at all separate from God.).

The views presented below do not deny free will but instead restrict it, devalue it, or think it compatible with determinism. Two more points before we proceed. First, Jewish philosophers often developed their views in the context of challenges from divine foreknowledge and foreordaining, not challenges from physical determinism. Second, as noted

---

[7] See Crescas 2018, 188–205 (2:5). Crescas, like numerous others, was influenced by the apostate Abner of Burgos (1260–1347). The basic question about Crescas's determinism is how to explain responsibility for performing *mitzvot*. See Segal 2023.

[8] As Hefter 2013 points out, this view can germinate either philosophically or phenomenologically.

[9] Much attention has been devoted to the deterministic outlook of "the Izbicer" (R. Mordecai Joseph Leiner [1800–1854]) and his disciples – his son Jacob and R. Tzadok ha-Kohen of Lublin (1823–1900). Gellman 1997 shows that although R. Mordechai Leiner and R. Tzadok denied free action, they affirmed freedom as regards intention and devotion. I don't put them in my "restrictivist" category, because the restrictivist theories I have in mind allow that there are some free actions. However, some passages in Leiner's writing suggest we have free will even with respect to action. For treatments of this and other perplexities in Leiner's thought, see Gellman 1997; Hefter 2013; Lebens 2015; Brown 2019. I thank Zvi Leshem for helpful correspondence.

[10] R. Shneur Zalman of Lyadi (1745–1812), in his classic *Tanya*, claimed that the separate existence of created things is illusory. The doctrine of *tzimtzum* (divine contraction) was understood by R. Shneur Zalman epistemologically rather than ontologically. That is: it *appears* to us that the Infinite (*Ein Sof*) has withdrawn from the world, but the truth is that He is in everything; hence, the creaturely consciousness of separated-ness is only an appearance. In actuality, we have *bittul ha-yesh*, the eradication of any existence but the *Ein Sof*. So the problem for him is not just how there can be free action, but how there can be human action, period.

by Charles Manekin (2025), no Jewish philosopher before Isaac Arama (fifteenth century) used the term "free choice" or "free will" (*beḥirah ḥofshit* and *ratzon ḥofshi*). The term entered philosophical Hebrew from Latin (*liberum arbitrium*), and means something different from what is commonly understood. But the earlier medieval sources, which have a different conception of free will, will prove serviceable.

RESTRICTIVISM

"Restrictivism" refers to the thesis that there is free will but it is limited.[11] This position can marshal a surprising degree of support in Jewish tradition.

Determinism and Medieval Astrology

The talmudic rabbis thought that the day or perhaps hour of a person's birth determines much about them, not only their material success or failure but their character traits and deeds: anger, kindness, promiscuity, wisdom, assiduousness, thievery, spiller of blood, a tendency to either extreme goodness or extreme badness (*Shabbat* 156a).[12] Most medieval Jewish philosophers and scientists, including the greatest scientist among them, Levi Gersonides, likewise believed in the truth of astrology – that all terrestrial events are caused by the movements of heavenly bodies.[13] Even though the Talmud favors the view that "there is no *mazzal* for Israel" – that is, Israel is not subject to astrological determination (*Shabbat* 156a) – it is clear from the talmudic stories that are adduced to corroborate this view that "there is no *mazzal* for Israel" does *not* mean that astrology does not affect Jews. Rather, astrology does affect the Jews, but righteous people can override the *mazzal* by their conduct. So, Abraham looked at his horoscope and expressed the worry he would not have a biological heir. In response, God said to him: "Leave your astrology! The astrological configurations do not affect Israel. What do

---

[11] See Campbell 1951, Van Inwagen 1989.
[12] In this last case it may be that *which* extreme a person goes to (goodness or badness) is a matter of choice, and perhaps when the Talmud indicates that a blood-spiller could be a slaughterer or *mohel*, that too is a matter of choice. But this isn't clear. Cf. Novick 2014.
[13] See Schwartz 1999. Even Maimonides, who was almost alone in attacking astrology, accepted that the stars affect terrestrial events; human choices were an exception. See the letter in Lerner and Mahdi 1963, 227–36. See also the text mentioned in Chapters 2 and 3 above, where Rava declares: "Length of life, children, and sustenance depend not on merits but on *mazzala*" (*Mo'ed Katan* 28a).

you assume – that Jupiter [under which you were born] is in the West [causing your infertility]? I will move it to the East" (*Shabbat* 156a). God here shifted the location of Jupiter, altering the astrological conditions. From then on Abraham is subject to new natural conditions.

The Talmud goes on to relate that R. Akiva was told by astrologers: your daughter will be bitten by a snake in her bridal chambers and die. That night she took a brooch and stuck it in the wall, and it happened that it killed a snake. Her father inquired: What have you done to merit escape? She told him that she had helped a poor man. Here, too, the astrological determination was overridden.

Illustrating this concept is a passage by the medieval figure Rabbi Abraham ben David (Rabad, 1125–1198) who asserts, "And it is well known that all of man's deeds, great or small, were given by God to the power of the *mazzal* (*be-koah ha-mazzal*). God also gave man the intelligence (*sekhel*) to elude the hand of Fortune, and this is the power given man for good or evil."[14] The Tosafists maintain, however, that the *mazzal* will not always be overridden by virtuous conduct; sometimes even a righteous person's welfare is determined by constellations and not choice.[15]

Charles Manekin (1997a, 180, n. 36) tells us about Gersonides: "Nowhere does Gersonides say that one freely chooses to be drawn after one's temperament. Rather, he says that one's choice itself is 'drawn' after temperament." Free will is located only in the power of reason to override temperament.

Astrology as embraced by medieval figures was the functional equivalent of contemporary genetics. The stars set your character and natural tendencies (dispositions), just as genes plus environment are understood to do in modern times, though astrology went far beyond explanations of traits. Thus, in a certain respect, a Jewish thinker might feel about genetics and neuroscience, "been there, done that." We had a deterministic theory in earlier times, and the clash with free will was "solved" through the concept of override. The overall theory restricts the scope of free will.[16]

---

[14] See Rabad's comments (*Hassagot ha-Rabad*) on Maimonides, *Mishneh Torah*, Book of Repentance, 5:5.
[15] Tosafot, *Shabbat* 156a, s.v. *ein*.
[16] It is questionable whether, when the agent does not exercise the override, this situation should be described as one of exercising free will. The person could have (in the medieval theory) chosen to act in a way that would have overridden the "natural" (astrological) causes of action. But it isn't clear that the astrologically caused acts were ipso facto free.

The notion of overriding a causal process that leads to certain actions is reminiscent of a famous experiment performed by Benjamin Libet in the 1980s. To make this long story short, Libet found that brain activity indicative of a decision to, say, flex one's right wrist, precedes the subject's awareness of making the decision. The implication, loosely put, is that the brain determined the decision before the person became aware of it. However, Libet also maintained that the subject can "veto" the decision at the last moment – this is called "free won't." Although this freedom doesn't depend on righteousness (!), there is a rough resemblance between Libet's view and the override views we are exploring. (Libet was severely criticized on a number of grounds. See Libet et al. 1999.)

The analogy between medieval astrology and modern genetics is imperfect. Medieval thinkers assumed that whether or not a person would try to quell natural tendencies would be up to that individual, and not predetermined by anything physical. To be truly analogous to astrology, the genetic/neuroscientific view would have to say that the choice to override biological dispositions itself is not determined by biology – and the view certainly doesn't say that. In addition, in the Talmud, righteousness overrides the constellations only by dint of divine intervention. Hence the override theory does not provide a full precedent. Even so, the fact that according to much of the Jewish tradition astrology causes human dispositions is significant in that it allows great scope to a deterministic scientific theory (albeit today astrology would not be that theory).

The Physical Roots of Sin

Medieval thinkers also believed that wrong, sinful acts can be traced to the body, but people can overcome natural tendencies of their material nature. Responsibility flows from one's ability to battle and conquer such inclinations. We may call this, too, an "override" theory. The notion that spirit or intellect can override matter is isomorphic to the notion that good deeds can override astrology.[17]

Maimonides states, "All man's acts of disobedience and sins are consequent upon his matter and not upon his form [viz. the intellect], whereas all his virtues are consequent upon his form."[18] Maimonides nevertheless holds that (through following the intellect) one may override the

---

[17] I will bracket the metaphysical question of how override works.
[18] Maimonides 1963, 431, 433 (*Guide of the Perplexed* 3:8).

influence of matter.[19] As is common in Maimonides, however, there are contradictory strains. He writes also, "There are, moreover, many people who have received from their first natural disposition a complexion of temperament with which perfection is in no way compatible." For example, some people are prone to anger or rashness, and "perfection can never be perceived in such people."[20]

However one resolves the contradictions in Maimonides about matter, the key point is that Maimonides, like Jewish believers in astrology, views vice as the outgrowth of physical causes, and he views virtuous action, where it does take place, as the overriding of matter through the discipline of Torah. Likewise, Gersonides, who as we saw believes that character traits are caused by astral phenomena but that a person's reason can override astrological causation, concedes by the very statement of this thesis that an act not based on reason is determined by the person's physical makeup.[21] Indeed, Jewish literature often represents the *yetzer ha-ra* (evil inclination) as a biological urge.[22] It is true that the spirit (or, for Maimonides, form, which denotes intellect) is said to be able to control matter, suggesting that spirit's delinquency is complicit in matter's sin. But the causal antecedents of wrong are still biological. (It seems to me that "spirit's" failure to control the body is like a person's failure to douse a fire with water – the failure isn't a cause of the fire, although the person is responsible for not dousing it.)

R. Joseph Soloveitchik points out cogently that chapter 1 of Genesis describes "the unity and continuity of organic life, considered an indispensable postulate in all biological sciences ... Man and beast share equally in the same biology, physiology and pathology."[23] Needless to say, from a religious perspective, this acceptance of physicality, of "man-natura," must not eradicate what Soloveitchik calls "man-persona," the

---

[19] In *Eight Chapters* Maimonides writes that training can change one's natural disposition to a virtue or vice. See the passage in Weiss and Butterworth 1975, 83–84.

[20] Maimonides 1963, 77 (*Guide of the Perplexed* 1:34). But cf. ibid., 433 (*Guide* 3:8). See Sokol 2013d.

[21] See Manekin 1997a. Note esp. Manekin's statement (177):

> The power possessed by humans to make opposing choices follows, according to Gersonides, from two facts about their condition: they possess intellect, which motivates them to choose according to reason, and they are corporeal creatures whose material faculties (sense, imagination, etc.) motivate them to choose in opposition to intellect.

Also see ibid., 180.

[22] Cf., however, R. Samson Raphael Hirsch's reading of *yetzer mahshevot libbo* in Gen. 6:5 (in his commentary to the Bible) as referring not to instinct or impulse, but rather to that formed by one who creates – namely, the *yotzer*. See also H. Cohen 1995, 181–82.

[23] Soloveitchik 2000a, 6; see also Soloveitchik 2005, esp. 3–82.

spiritual being in Genesis 2, who stands apart from and above the rest of nature and upon whose behavior the redemption of physicality depends (2000b, 4–26). But in essence, half the materialist thesis – the idea that what we call "the bad" is biological – is consistent with a prominent theme in traditional thought. And even when it comes to the good, a talmudic model (embraced by Soloveitchik) counsels finding creative, healthy outlets for destructive drives of the *yetzer ha-ra*, rather than eradicating them.[24] Biology is redirected, not exterminated. Responsibility for biologically induced action may be traced to the power of override.

"The Small Point of Freedom"

R. Eliyahu Dessler argues that the vast majority of a person's actions are determined either by environment or by a character shaped by previous choices. A person retains only a *nekuddat ha-behirah*, a point or small area of free will, at which moral struggle takes place.[25] Dessler stresses the role of environment in molding character, while contemporary scientists highlight the role of biology, but this does not affect my point. Dessler's willingness to restrict free will suggests that free will is more limited in Judaism than the ordinary person supposes.

In an instructive article, Solomon Schimmel catalogues evidence that "Although Maimonides and most other Jewish philosophers vigorously defend the doctrine of free will ... in practical terms, the doctrine is never carried to its logical conclusions and is considerably circumscribed in several ways" (Schimmel 1977, 42). (Schimmel mentions, among other evidence, the educational system, which works, at least in part, by reducing choice.) The examples of astrology, matter as the cause of sin, and Dessler's "point of choice" suggests that Schimmel has a point. But as a response to materialism, each of these restrictivist approaches falls short because insofar as they leave some room for free will and human choices, they would need some nonmaterialist account of those.

DEVALUATION

A second response to the challenge of scientific determinism is to minimize the value of free will, suggesting that the loss determinism generates is of small importance.

---

[24] See, e.g., *Gen. Rabbah* 9:7.
[25] For similar views in the secular literature, see Campbell 1951; Van Inwagen 1989. For further exploration of Dessler's views, see Carmy 2006, 126–30.

The Question of Arrogance

Attempts to place humans above nature, and in particular to preserve a human will that is above physical causation, assert human superiority and distinctiveness. Such attempts could be viewed as arrogant, religiously objectionable efforts to shift power away from an almighty deity into human hands and to confer upon human beings supranatural control in the form of free will. Indeed, many explications of free will view the essence of free will to be control over the world – the ability to make the world conform to what we want.[26] It is religiously healthier, one may argue, to have a worldview that encourages humility, shame, and insignificance.[27] Some psychological studies – but not others – suggest that people with humility experience less angst over skepticism concerning free will.[28]

Naḥmanides and Dessler

According to Naḥmanides, prior to the sin in the Garden of Eden, Adam and Eve automatically did what was right, just as they automatically breathed and digested. After the sin, they lost this automatic connection to the right and the good; doing good became instead a matter of choice. When, upon eating of the fruit of the tree,[29] they became *yode'ei tov va-ra* (knowers of good and evil) (Gen. 3:22), they acquired the capacity to choose between two alternatives in a situation – the good and the evil.[30] The loss of innocence, the acquisition of free choice, is a step backward. In messianic times, when God "circumcises your heart and that of your seed" (Deut. 30:6) – when the Jewish people repent – they will return, says Naḥmanides, to a situation of automatic conformity.[31] For Naḥmanides, then, free choice, moral struggle, is not

---

[26] The subtitle of John Fischer's 1994 book, *The Metaphysics of Free Will: An Essay on Control*, is indicative.
[27] In Chapter 2, I questioned the move from mindset to metaphysics, but it is still worth raising the issue of how belief in free will relates to humility and arrogance.
[28] See Nadelhoffer and Wright 2018.
[29] Or before eating. See the next note.
[30] Nachmanides 2010, commentary to Gen. 2:9. Actually, it seems more accurate to say that eating was a *symptom* of free will, rather than a cause. The sin, freely committed, occurred before eating. See also Chapter 8.
[31] Michael Harris noted in correspondence that Naḥmanides does assign free will a positive function in the rest of his comment to Deut. 30:6. Still, in the ideal scheme of things, as I read Naḥmanides, conforming to the good is more important.

a good; conformity to the good is better, even without choice.³² Hence, believers can live with determinism if conformity to the good results therefrom.

A number of considerations support Nahmanides's devaluation of free choice. Jewish law permits coercion in the case of certain types of behavior,³³ and the Bible seems untroubled when it relates episodes of God's "hardening of hearts" (e.g., that of Pharaoh and Sihon).³⁴ The very fact that God uses promises of rewards and threats of punishments to influence behavior likewise suggests (this subject came up in Chapters 4 and 5) that conformity to the right sometimes or often counts more than free choice; and our educational techniques contain at least a measure of deterministic influence. In addition, Jews pray each day to "Force our wills to be subjugated to you."

Dessler takes a position superficially resembling that of Nahmanides. Dessler believes that to be unfree but to automatically do the good is greater than being free and choosing to do the good: "The ultimate good of all our service is to transform himself from one who chooses (*boher*) to one [whose actions are] necessitated (*mukhrah*)."³⁵ However, in Dessler's thought, unlike that of Nahmanides, it is not that being coerced by the good (*mukhrah*) is per se good. Rather, what is good is *turning oneself* into a *mukhrah* by using free choice. Notwithstanding this distinction, the idea that Nahmanides and Dessler have in common – that, abstracted from its connection to the good, free will is not something of value – might lead people to make peace with the loss of free will preached by modern science.

Robert Nozick (1981, 327) coins the term "tracking bestness" to refer to the process of doing the right thing without free choice:

---

³² The value of struggle is upheld by, inter alia, R. Mosheh Hayyim Luzzatto (Ramchal, 1707–1746) in *Mesillat Yesharim* (*Path of the Righteous*). See also Soloveitchik 1983, 139–43 (n. 4).

³³ See, e.g., Mishnah *Arakhin* 5:6; Maimonides, *Mishneh Torah*, Laws of Divorce 2:20 (see the discussion later in this chapter) and Laws of Murder 11:5. But see Korn 1991. Cf. Korn 1991.

³⁴ See Shatz 1997c, abridged in Frank, Leaman, and Manekin 2000, 51–57.

³⁵ Dessler 1988, 2:62 (in my own translation). Actually Dessler has a still higher stage beyond *mukhrah*. At this stage, there is no subjective feeling of compulsion at all, but rather *avodah me-ahavah*, service out of love. "At this point the human being becomes truly free, finding no resistance within him to the good which he loves." R. Isaac Hutner writes: "Removal of choice that results from strengthening the use of choice is nothing other than revelation of the capacity for choice" (Hutner 1991, 71). My thanks to Yitzchak Blau for this reference.

Let us ask which you would choose for yourself: tracking bestness (without the process) or the process of free will (without tracking bestness). Our difficulty simply in choosing the second indicates the value of the first, of tracking bestness.[36]

Biological factors that predispose a person to altruism or appreciation of the good could be viewed as "automatically" instilling the good in us. To that extent, the deterministic situation might be viewed as good, even if not as good as the pre-sin situation in the Garden of Eden.

COMPATIBILISM

Until now, we have reasoned, or assumed, that if science shows that thought and behavior are determined, whether by environmental influences or biological ones, then we don't have free will or moral responsibility. However, many philosophers dispute the move from "determinism is true" to "there is no free will," "there is no moral responsibility," and "reactive attitudes are not justified." The popular assumption that free will, responsibility, and reactive attitudes are incompatible with determinism is merely one view, known as incompatibilism. Other philosophers embrace compatibilism, according to which determinism is compatible with free will, moral responsibility, and justified reactive attitudes. Some Jewish philosophers were compatibilists, which opens another option for dealing with the materialist challenge to free will.

Compatibilist accounts in contemporary analytic philosophy can usually be broken down into three subtheses, albeit not every compatibilist accepts all three claims and some compatibilists use additional ones.

Subthesis (A): Indeterminism Excludes Free Will

Libertarianism affirms that there is free will and that free will requires rejection of determinism. Libertarians often welcome quantum physics as having shown that determinism is false – thereby, they say, salvaging free will. But suppose that someone robs a bank because of a random neuron misfiring in that person's brain. There is no fully deterministic pedigree for the person's act, but the individual is hardly exercising free will, and anyone who holds the person responsible for the act

---

[36] Cf. Shatz 1988. According to the view that free will all by itself is valuable, regardless of the moral character of the act – a view accepted by the free will theodicy – a horrific but free act has *some* value. The approach that devalues free will might deny this, or at least not assign much value to the "free" part.

is simply wrong. The person's behavior in this example is not something the person *does*; it is something that *happens* to the individual. Undetermined neural events do not imply that there is free will, but rather that there isn't.

For compatibilists, undetermined choices are "arbitrary," "capricious," "random," "uncontrolled," "irrational," "inexplicable," or "matters of pure luck or chance." "Undetermined events in the brain or body ... would occur spontaneously and would be more of a nuisance ... than an enhancement of freedom or responsibility."[37]

Subthesis (B):Utilitarian Considerations Suffice for Responsibility and Reactive Attitudes

Incompatibilists argue that if actions are determined, it is impossible to justify punishment. Compatibilists respond that punishment is, in fact, not based on retribution for failure to exercise moral responsibility, but instead on social utility – society's need for protection. If this is correct, people can properly be punished for actions even in a deterministic world. Judaism is not short on utilitarian approaches to punishment.[38]

Reactive attitudes may likewise be justified by their utility. Praise and blame function causally to encourage or discourage certain sorts of behavior. Further, we praise and blame people for their intelligence, good looks, and native athletic ability, even though these qualities are genetic and the bearers of those qualities often deserve no praise for having them.[39] In similar fashion, we often praise people as "good people" without having the foggiest idea of how much of their goodness is self-initiated and how much is due to genes or upbringing alone. The same applies to blame. Some compatibilists might ask: How many of us, when blaming perpetrators of atrocities, really think that it is relevant for blame whether an individual mass murderer was the product of environment, lacking exposure to other value systems? For such compatibilists, our judgments are not dependent on whether the actions are determined, nor do they believe that they must be.[40]

---

[37] Kane 1999, 10. Kane, a libertarian, seeks to address this problem. See also Kane 1996.

[38] See, e.g., Maimonides, *Guide of the Perplexed* 3:41. For a lengthy listing of harsh punishments meted out by rabbinic authorities, see Schreiber 1979, 375–424.

[39] See, e.g., Pereboom 2001, 139–40; Schlossberger 1992, 4–7, 79, 101, 112, 117–18.

[40] Of course, some people are not blamed when we learn the causes of their actions. But since I will be arguing against compatibilism anyway, I'll let this point pass.

Subthesis (C): Free Will Does Not Require Alternative Possibilities

The canonical argument that determinism excludes free will, moral responsibility, and reactive attitudes supposes the Principle of Alternative Possibilities (PAP) (known also, we saw in Chapter 4, as the Forking Paths Principle). In order for a person to act freely in a given situation and/or be responsible and/or deserve the reactive attitudes, the person must possess a two-way power. He or she must be able to do, in the very same circumstances, something other than what they in fact do. If PAP is false – if freedom does not require alternative possibilities – then, barring further problems, neither God's foreknowledge nor determination by physical causes will deprive an agent of freedom or responsibility. The issue at hand, then, is whether PAP is true; if not, compatibilism is viable.[41]

As we saw in Chapter 4, Harry Frankfurt and other philosophers have produced examples that appear to show that PAP is false.[42] For Frankfurt, someone can indeed be responsible for an action even when she cannot do otherwise. But there is a second type of counterexample. Many of the everyday actions that we regard as free, and for which we assign responsibility, are determined by people's character and psychological nature. Consider this passage from David Hume's essay, "Of Liberty and Necessity" (*Enquiry Concerning Human Understanding*, VIII):

> Were a man, whom I know to be honest and opulent, and with whom I live in intimate friendship, to come into my house, where I am surrounded with my servants, I rest assured, that he is not to stab me before he leaves it, in order to rob me of my silver standish; and I no more suspect this event, than the falling of the house itself which is new, and solidly built and founded.

Hume's point is that in real life, we treat people as if their acts are determined. "A prisoner … discovers the impossibility of his escape, as well when he considers the obstinacy of the jailer, as the walls and bars, with which he is surrounded." In Hume's view, we may talk like

---

[41] As I mentioned earlier, however, compatibilists do not always reject PAP but rather reinterpret it. Another problem that determinism poses to free will is that if our thought and actions are determined, we do not own them. See Chapter 4, n. 7.

[42] See Locke, *Essay Concerning Human Understanding* 2:21:10 (a man chooses to remain a room, but the door is locked anyway so he is not able to get out); Van Inwagen 1978 (a person witnesses a mugging and decides not to call the police, but couldn't have reached the police anyway because the phone lines are down).
Locke applies the Forking Paths Principle to actions, while Frankfurt applies it to decisions. As mentioned in Chapter 5, David Widerker (1995) has argued that Frankfurt's examples cannot be effective in the case of decisions because those examples presuppose conditions about the scenario that a libertarian defender of PAP would not accept.

libertarians when we delve into philosophy, but in everyday life we think like determinists.

Soloveitchik puts it this way (Peli 1984, 1972):

Free choice does not mean a state of chaotic anarchy, with sudden and frequent changes of mind that have no rational explanation ... We usually expect a certain display of consistency in a man's thought and actions; we expect him to embody a certain way of life with its own consistency of character. The law of cause and effect, action and consequence, does prevail in a man's life ... The question now is: Where does "free choice" come in?[43]

Some deeds are psychologically impossible – unthinkable[44] – for us or for people we deal with. If you attend a lecture by a renowned rabbinic scholar, you know very well that the speaker will not pull out a machine gun or tell scatological jokes; and if he did, you would not attribute it to free will. If you are offered $5 to torture an innocent child, you will not and cannot comply. You cannot now spread a vicious rumor that your colleague, who you know is morally upright, is a child molester. When we say of people, "They cannot hurt a fly," we are not saying they lack free will. When Martin Luther stated, "Here I stand; I can do no other," he did not mean that he is not freely standing up to the Catholic Church and that he bears no responsibility. If George Washington cannot tell a lie, this hardly means he lacks free will and gets no credit for confessing to chopping down the cherry tree.[45] To take this point further, there might even be people who have powerful urges to do things and think they are refraining from doing them as an act of will, when in fact they simply could not go through with the act. Be that as it may, the moral of the Luther, Washington, and other cases seems to be: To act/refrain freely or decide freely, one need not be able to do otherwise, decide otherwise, or desire otherwise.

I call such examples character cases. In these cases, it is folly to look for alternative possibilities (i.e., other actions that the person *could* have done). After all, what are we looking for? Basically, we want to find a real possibility that the agent would do something that is contrary to all of their values and reasoning. But if this is the desired "alternative," the

---

[43] Peli 1984, 172.
[44] See Frankfurt 1988. Cf. Michael Zimmerman 1996.
[45] Mark Twain thus reportedly quipped: "I am a greater person than George Washington. George Washington can't tell a lie. I can – but I won't." This paragraph amalgamates cases found in Dennett 1984, 131–52; Van Inwagen 1989; and Wolf 1990. Of course, we can *picture* the person doing the act, but that's not the same as saying the person is *able* to perform it. See Shatz 1988, 1997b, and 1997c.

demand for an alternative possibility amounts to the demand that the person be able to do something insane, like Dostoevsky's Underground Man, who believes that to be truly free is to be able to act against all logic and all his interests. To insist that being able to act insanely is a condition for free will is strange, quite apart from the utter lack of evidence that the people in my examples are able to act insanely.[46]

Libertarianism versus Compatibilism

Can a defender of PAP account for the freedom of the agents who lack alternative possibilities in these character cases? One strategy for retaining the principle is that of Aristotle, who maintains that, although people with a fixed character who act in character seem to have no real choice in the matter, in fact people choose their characters and are therefore responsible for actions that flow from the characters they have chosen (*Nicomachean Ethics* 3:5).[47]

But this principle is false. Do we truly choose our characters? Educational institutions and home environments use rewards and punishments to mold the character of young children. As Schimmel (1977, 425) puts it:

Rather than cultivating and encouraging the exercise of free-will as some internal operating factor, these [educational] techniques tend to preempt freedom by substituting determinants of behavior whose locus is the social environment rather than the individual's will or reason.

Selecting teachers who can be role models is an instance of trying to influence behavior through means that one presumes can be effective. When a teacher is not providing a good enough role model, we seek a better role model. Our educational and social practices thus belie the idea that character must be the result of choice. R. Shlomo Wolbe (1986) goes so far as to state as "a fundamental principle in the education of others and of ourselves," that "one should relate to every person as if he had no *beḥirah* [free choice], and as if he is 'compelled' by his 'nature,' education, habits and emotional needs" (1:156). It is true that people could later in life reflect on their acquired values and retain or reshape their personality as a result of that evaluation. But our intuition that people act freely when they act in character does not depend on whether this evaluation has taken place.

---

[46] See Wolf 1990.
[47] See also Kane 2000.

I maintain also that the fact that a person once chose a certain character does not entail that every choice made thereafter as a result of that choice is a free one.[48] Suppose an addict is overwhelmed by irresistible cravings for drugs, but brought on those cravings by continually failing to resist earlier desires for drugs. I do not think that the addict now shoots up freely just because of this causal connection. A more accurate description would be that right now the person acts unfreely due to earlier free choices. Similarly, suppose you choose to travel through a dangerous area in which muggings are frequent. While there, you are coerced into handing over valuables. Shall we say that you freely surrendered the valuables just because you made a choice that enabled the later situation to arise? Clearly not.[49] It is not true that an act will be considered free now, when there are no alternative possibilities, simply because they resulted from earlier choices that were made when alternatives were genuine. One can freely sell oneself into bondage, but bondage is bondage.

What seems more plausible is that when one makes choices in the context of alternative possibilities, and those earlier choices cause the individual to do certain later actions without entertaining alternative possibilities – as in the example of the addict or the mugging victim – the person bears a degree of responsibility for the later act even though it is not free. A bus driver whose bus crashes due to a seizure, when they should have foreseen this possibility, is not *as* responsible as if they had crashed the bus deliberately. But the driver is nonetheless responsible.

My own view is that the best strategy for a libertarian to adopt in the face of character cases is that of Dessler. That is, one could argue that free will is restricted and that the agents in question do not have it, but then find a theory of responsibility that explains why agents in those cases are responsible for what they do. Elsewhere (Shatz 1997b, 63–73), I have tried to do precisely this, arguing that a libertarian may coherently assign responsibility even in cases of fixed character. It is important to consider, however, why developing a compatibilist alternative to libertarianism will

---

[48] For general criticism of the Aristotelian position that we choose our characters, see Dressler 1987, 695–96; Moore 1997, ch. 13.

[49] Maimonides (Laws of the Foundation of the Torah 5:4) states that if a person can escape a hostile ruler and does not, and as a result is coerced into worshipping idols, the person is not considered as acting under duress but instead is an *oved avodah zarah be-mezid* (i.e., is deliberately committing the sin of idolatry). I believe that this ruling is best understood as a ruling about the person's responsibility, not the person's freedom. For further scrutiny of such situations, see Responsa Tashbetz (Shimon ben Tzemaḥ Duran) #63. (I thank R. Dov Linzer for the latter reference.)

be difficult. What, after all, is the compatibilist's alternative to libertarianism? If free will does not entail alternative possibilities, shall we say that acting or deciding freely is just a matter of doing what you want to do? No, for if that were all that is involved, we may as well assign responsibility to cats and dogs. Furthermore, intuitively we do not regard compulsive behavior (e.g., of kleptomaniacs), the behavior of people who have become addicts through no choice of their own, or the actions of people suffering from phobias as free, responsible behavior. Why so, if free action is a matter of acting on desire? Contrary to the classical compatibilist view, people don't have to be in chains – that is, unable to satisfy their desires – in order to act unfreely. What, according to compatibilists, is the difference between free and unfree acting or willing?

Many contemporary philosophers who reject PAP propose the following theory. Freedom of the will is a matter of conforming the will to the judgments of either (a) reason or intellect or (b) one's "deep self" (in Hebrew, the *ratzon elyon* as opposed to *ratzon tahton*, the "higher" will as opposed to the "lower").[50] The notion that free will lies in conformity with reason has deep roots in Plato, Aquinas, Spinoza, Kant, and others in general Western thought, and is found as well in Maimonides, Rabad (Rabbi Abraham ben David), Gersonides, and others on the Jewish side.

Josef Stern (1997) and Moshe Sokol (2013d) regard Maimonides as a compatibilist.[51] On this view, Maimonides is indifferent to determinism versus indeterminism because his view on free will is consonant with either position.[52] This is a common stance in medieval Jewish philosophy, since, as we noted earlier, the terms "free choice" or "free will" did not enter Hebrew (from Latin) until the fifteenth century. Jewish philosophers in the Middle Ages tended to see reason, not liberty, as the main component of freedom, and only later in history did the requirement of being able to do otherwise become important. In other words, a person with free will is someone who conforms his or her desires to reasoned value judgments – period. No ability to act evilly or insanely is demanded.[53]

---

[50] Philosophers who adopt (a) often rationalize that endorsement in terms of (b), invoking the Platonic-Kantian idea that the true self is the rational self. While I question the thesis, I will work with a version of (a) that accepts this rationale.

[51] In particular, Sokol reads Maimonides as endorsing the type of "sane deep self view" expounded by contemporary philosopher Wolf 1990. Charles Manekin sees an affinity between Gersonides's and Wolf's views; see Manekin 1997b.

[52] See also Stern 1997, 232, n. 25.

[53] There is a distinction, however, between doing right and doing what the agent regards as right.

In one place, Maimonides seems to develop a notion of a "deep rational self," combining the notions of the centrality of the intellect in freedom with the notion of freedom as conforming to one's true, inner self. In *Laws of Divorce* 2:20, Maimonides discusses the case of a man who refuses to give a *get* (writ of divorce) when Jewish law require him to do so. A valid *get* requires the desire of the husband to effect the divorce; and yet a Jewish court can legally coerce him until he says, "I want to give her the *get*." There are various ways in which this law could be explained, but Maimonides proposes that insofar as this man is violating a precept of the Halakhah, he has been attacked and coerced by his evil inclination. By beating the man, the court weakens the impulse and allows the true self, the self that represents what the person most values – and is the objectively right thing – to be expressed.[54]

This "true self" conception of freedom runs into a number of major difficulties:[55]

Selfhood
Why is the self identified with intellect, while desires are deemed external to the self? Can we simply dismiss Humean and Freudian views of the self, for example?

The First-Person Perspective
In his defense of a conception of free will that does not include a condition that the agent be able to act otherwise, John Martin Fischer makes the following intriguing concession:

> Moral responsibility is surely only one aspect of a complete understanding of agency. Another dimension of agency pertains to our view of ourselves as practical reasoners. That is, we deliberate about the future ... And in this deliberation and practical reasoning, we typically take ourselves to have genuine alternative possibilities ... [I]t is not a straightforward task to give a picture of deliberation and practical reasoning according to which we may not have alternative possibilities. [Fischer 1994, 206]

Fischer is acknowledging that his own denial of PAP fits a third-person perspective (onlookers ascribe responsibility and freedom even in the

---

[54] One approach to the hardening of Pharaoh's heart, which can be plausibly read into Maimonides Laws of Repentance 6:3, is that Pharaoh's deep self was restored through hardening; God allowed the true self to have its way. See N. Leibowitz 1981, 110–17. Cf. Shatz 1997a.

[55] My criticisms of compatibilism are explained most fully in Shatz 1985, 1988, 1997a, 1997b, 1997c.

absence of forking paths) but not a first-person perspective. Determinists still speak of decision, choice, self-control, effort, etc. Indeed, as Schimmel (1977, 427) points out, just as Jewish thinkers who affirmed free will circumscribed it in practice, psychologists who espouse determinism, including the behaviorist B. F. Skinner, invoke concepts like rational-emotive control of behavior, phenomenological freedom, and delaying gratification when they are, as it were, off duty.

Akrasia versus Compulsion
The thesis that freedom of the will is a matter of conforming will and behavior to value judgments does a nice job of explaining why people who act from inner compulsion or who have phobias are unfree; in many cases their behavior does not conform to their value judgments. But human beings are notoriously prone to acting against their better judgment even in cases where intuitively their behavior is free and they are responsible for it. Acting against better judgment out of weakness of will – akrasia – is very different from compulsion. Intuitively, the difference is this: The *akrates* is able to act differently, to do the right thing; the compulsive is not. But to say this is to reinstate a version of the very Forking Paths Principle that the "reason view" of free will was meant to supplant.[56]

Evildoers
A particularly difficult corollary of the notion that free will is a matter of conforming to judgments of the intellect is that only right-doers, not wrongdoers, are classified as free. No evil acts are free. To cope with this strange result, some philosophers have suggested – along lines sketched earlier – that freedom involves being *able to act rightly*; when people act rightly, we declare them free even when they are not able to act otherwise. They are, after all, able to act rightly, since they do act rightly. But when they act wrongly and were not able to act rightly, we do not hold them responsible and free.[57] To require that they be able to act rightly, however, is to reintroduce PAP in modified form, with all the problems that that entails in a deterministic world.

Brainwashing
For one to have free will, it is not enough that one's actions conform to one's values; we must ask how the person acquired those values. If they

---

[56] See Watson 1977.
[57] See Wolf 1990; A. Wood 1984. I refer to what *is* right, not what the agent deems right.

were implanted by brainwashing, hypnosis, and the like, the person did not act freely. The "reason" view does not explain why this is so.

Coercion

If freedom is a matter of acting in accordance with reason, then the paradigm of free action is coerced action! In coercion, you have just one rational choice. Intuitively, though, coerced acts should be classified as unfree (notwithstanding views of Thomas Hobbes and Bernard Williams, mentioned in Chapter 4).

Clearly, the smoothest way to deal with these objections is to reintroduce PAP and thereby vindicate incompatibilists. But as we saw, incompatibilism has its own problems. Here, then, is the real problem: No matter where you turn to explain what free will is, eventually you run into a brick wall. We don't know what free will is. It is this "frustrating and unyielding" character (Nozick 1981, 293) that leaves us unsure of what direction to take in responding to the challenge of genetics and neuropsychology.

A HISTORICAL REFLECTION

Major revolutions in the physical sciences in the past five centuries – the Copernican, the Darwinian, and now the neuroscientific – have in one way or another dethroned human beings from a special place in the universe. Similarly, David Hume brought to the fore the instinctual, nonrational, and even irrational side of human thought. Even Immanuel Kant, who elevated human beings because, inter alia, they can arrive at the moral law, highlighted the limitations of human knowledge. Sigmund Freud, one who noted science's dethronement of humans, made the instinctual side of human beings a central motif in the explanation of human behavior, though he made certain odd behaviors rationalizable by probing what takes place at the subconscious level. Today's enthronement of biology and the denial of free will by many materialists seem to further reduce human power and standing.

R. Abraham Isaac Kook (1865–1935) sought providential readings of history, and viewed history dialectically. For a follower of Kook, the development of contemporary neuroscience might be viewed as a needed ethical corrective for the world, a large dose of humility, a dialectical counter to Enlightenment hubris. In this perspective, the same human beings who dared to replace God now seem to have reduced themselves to glorified beasts. Ascribing a curious glee to some scientists and philosophers who advocate this self-conception, Norman Lamm (2006c, 113) remarks, "Never before have so many been so enthusiastic about being so trivial." Determinism can lead to despair, something that concerned Maimonides greatly in his letter on astrology.[58] The narrative of the past few centuries might be attributed to God's guiding history in a more "humbling" direction than it took in the Enlightenment. From a theological point of view, understanding materialism as part of a divinely ordained story creates a measure of comfort with materialism.

Or does it? Viewed from another angle, the materialist thesis is not humbling, but rather expands human power. If everything is matter and nothing is disembodied spirit, then with sufficient scientific knowledge and technological advancement, humans can control a very broad range of events.[59] If scientific method is the only way of knowing about the world, then, as John Haught (1995, 83) states, science projects an "apparent sense of intellectual dominion." Earlier, I mentioned the view that belief in free will places humanity above nature and may reflect arrogance, while disbelief reflects humility. But if the disbelief arises from that sense of intellectual dominion, perhaps the disbelief isn't so humble after all.

To call these reflections on providence speculative is a gargantuan understatement. Even religious people are often wary of providential readings of history, especially when contradictory narratives can be constructed – which is often. Can we know God's intentions? Still, Kook seems correct that it is important to indulge in assessing not only the truth of theories but their spiritual and moral impact on human life.

CONCLUSION

Judaism affirms free choice, but modern science suggests that free will is at best limited and in a strictly deterministic framework nonexistent. We have seen that Maimonides, Rabbi Abraham ben David, Naḥmanides, and Eliyahu Dessler, along with some Ḥasidic thinkers, adopted views that go against simplistic conceptions driving affirmations of free will. Medieval and modern rabbinic Jewish thought contains a surprising willingness to accept biological and deterministic explanations of human

---

[58] In Lerner and Mahdi 1963, 227–36.
[59] On these themes, see also Haught 1995, 83–84, 93. Freud (1961, esp. chs. 3–4), however, as noted earlier, offers a theory of religion predicated on the idea that whereas humans are unable to control nature by natural means, religion claims to give them the ability to control nature by influencing the divine through supplication and other methods.

actions even while affirming free will. In fact, certain medieval figures also adumbrated elements of the compatibilist approach to free will found in philosophical literature today.

If no Darwinist had ever lived, religious intellectual life would now be easier; but it would not ipso facto be richer, nor closer to the truth. Likewise, if the world had never discovered the complex causes of disease and natural disasters, theology would be much simpler – but people not only would have less capacity to heal and alleviate suffering, they would also harbor a skewed picture of how God operates in the world. The world has had to "adjust its priors" – change its paradigms of how God relates to the world. Here as elsewhere, for contemporary Jewish philosophers, the challenge is to situate themselves within both Jewish tradition and contemporary science and philosophy. This chapter has suggested options rooted in Jewish tradition, options that engage with some suggested in analytic philosophy.

7

Here Today, Here Tomorrow

Death and the Afterlife

In an age dominated by materialist metaphysics, it is easy to understand why many people do not believe in a soul or an afterlife. Still, many Jews have at least a vague sense from Jewish mourning practices and the prayer of remembrances of the dead recited on holidays (Yizkor) that *Judaism* believes in an afterlife. And they may know that this afterlife is according to tradition a consequence of how one acts in their this-worldly sojourn. Yet they often, if not generally, harbor simplistic images, and probably do not realize the extent to which the topic of an afterlife is a vexed one in Jewish thought. Jewish tradition is brimming with conflicting conceptions of the hereafter, and competing evaluations of the concept's importance.

So, is there life after death? If so, what kind? Will souls live on instead without a body, perhaps eternally? Will the bodies of the dead be resurrected at some point in history, perhaps collectively? Alternatively, will a person's soul "body-hop," moving from human body 1 to human body 2 after body 1 dies, and then possibly to body 3 once body 2 dies, then possibly to body 4, and so on – or even to an animal, vegetable, or mineral? These three versions of belief in the afterlife are called, respectively:

- (Disembodied) immortality of the soul.[1] The term *olam ha-ba* ("World-to-Come") generally is associated with this idea, thanks largely to Maimonides's using the phrase in that way.[2]
- Resurrection of the dead (*teḥiyyat ha-metim*).
- Transmigration of souls/reincarnation (*gilgul neshamot*).

---

[1] Or at least postmortem continuity of a disembodied soul, even without immortality. On some views, disembodied souls of the wicked are destroyed after being punished.
[2] *Mishneh Torah*, Laws of Repentance, ch. 8, esp. 8:8.

In general, *tehiyyat ha-metim* is conceived of as a communal resurrection, whereas immortality and reincarnation apply principally to individuals.

All three models appear in prominent Jewish sources, and which should be the right model, and even whether there is an afterlife, has been the subject of great debates: Sadducees versus Pharisees in ancient times, Maimonideans versus anti-Maimonideans in the medieval period, and Reform versus Orthodox Jews in the modern. The reasons for the debates will be explained later, but in brief they have to do with both philosophical cogency and textual interpretation. Beliefs about the nature of the afterlife are also a function of one's beliefs about a variety of topics – the scope of divine intervention in the natural order; religious epistemology (faith or texts vs. reason); literalism; one's theory of what a person is; one's value judgments about what sort of existence is most worthy; and more. In other words, which position one adopts implicates at various points large questions about religious and philosophical orientation. In modern times, as in the thought of Hermann Cohen (1842–1918), we also find a fourth vision of the afterlife, one we might call the "legacy" (also called "social") conception (Cohen 1995, 296–337). In this model, the individual lives on figuratively – by exerting impact on the future.

There can be (and have been) hybrids of the approaches outlined. For example, if we assume mind–body dualism, then even in a model that stresses resurrection, the soul will probably be said to exist independently post-mortem until the resurrection, and probably to endure eternally thereafter in the body.[3] Likewise, reincarnation works well with immortality of the soul, and in fact the aim of body-hopping is often held to be purification of the soul, which can be coupled with its ultimate release from any body. Reincarnation is also compatible with the resurrection of a previous host body.[4] The legacy concept is obviously compatible with immortality, resurrection, and reincarnation; people make an impact on the future by what they do *before* a literal afterlife. Notwithstanding these and other hybrid options, those who espouse immortality have often denied resurrection or belittled it, and those who advocate for the resurrection model at times claim that living eternally as a disembodied soul is unappealing or conceptually impossible. Thus,

---

[3] Maimonides 1985 (*Essay on Resurrection*) rejected eternal endurance of resurrected bodies, claiming that those resurrected will die again. (See later in this chapter.)

[4] On one view, the last body the soul occupied is the one resurrected. But Kabbalists developed a doctrine of "soul sparks" in which the resurrection of one body affects all souls that had inhabited it. See Gillman 1997, 182–86.

advocates of a particular one of the four views do not always incorporate the other views in their models.

In this chapter, we begin with a sketch of key texts and then move on to explain and assess the primary reasons for and against each of these four views. It is important to distinguish different considerations that support or undermine particular claims concerning the afterlife:

(i) scriptural or rabbinic support
(ii) metaphysical arguments
(iii) "fit" with other religious claims and with Jewish practices.
(iv) symbolic power
(v) value (of having a specific kind of afterlife)
(vi) psychological effects

We will see these considerations at work. We will also address those who question the value of an afterlife altogether. Finally, we will reflect on theodicy – on why there is death.

KEY TEXTS

In the Bible, rewards and punishments for obedience (including both bodily behavior and faith or trust) take place in the physical world, not a future existence. Still, the Bible says more about the afterlife than commonly alleged.[5]

Although God banished Adam and Eve to prevent their living forever (Gen. 3:22–24), Scripture refers frequently to a person descending to *she'ol*, which has been called a kind of netherworld, a "bleak and forlorn subterranean realm."[6] Often *she'ol* appears devoid of retribution, but sometimes it is a venue for punishment.

Certain figures (the Patriarchs, Ishmael, Moses, Aaron), were "gathered unto" their kin.[7] We also read of the practice of necromancy (Deut. 18:11), and of a sorceress who "raises up" the prophet Samuel "from the earth" (I Sam. 28:13) after his death, "disturbing" him (28:15). Hannah (Samuel's mother) says of God that He "deals death and gives

---

[5] Kugel 1999, 210, says that the claim the Bible has no concept of an afterlife "will not withstand scrutiny." See also Levenson 2008, Angel 2017.

[6] Raphael 2009, 59. See Deut. 32:22; I Sam. 2:6; I Kings 2:6, 9; Isa. 14:9, 11, 15. On the complexities of Sheol (e.g., who goes there), see Levenson 2008, 35–81 and R. Steiner 2015, ch. 11.

[7] Gen. 25:8, 25:17, 32:50, 35:29, 49:33, Num. 20:24, 27:13, Deut. 32:50. "Gathered" is the conventional translation; cf. R. Steiner 2015, ch. 10.

life, casts down into She'ol, and raises up" (I Sam. 2:6). The prophets Elijah and Elisha each revive a boy who has died (I Kings 17:17–24; II Kings 4: 18–37). Elijah goes to heaven (II Kings 2:11) but will return to herald the messianic age (Mal. 3: 23–24). Ezekiel 37:1-8, 10 could be read as affirming a future resurrection, but should more likely be read as referring to the revival of the nation Israel. Better evidence of resurrection, though still susceptible to a figurative reading, is Isaiah 26:19: "Your dead shall live, my dead bodies shall arise; awake and sing, you who dwell in the dust." In a fleeting reference in Job (19:25–26), the protagonist appears to speak about immortality. Psalms 16:11 suggests an eternal afterlife. But little flesh (pardon the phrase) is given to that belief.

The most significant reference to resurrection appears in the late biblical book Daniel: "And many of those who dwell in dust will awaken, some to eternal life and some to shame and everlasting contempt" (12:2-3). Resurrection, of course, manifests God's power, but what is pronounced in Daniel is the doctrine's role in providing justice and a partial theodicy. The righteous and the wicked at last receive their just deserts.[8]

A word about biblical ontology. According to a modern scholarly orthodoxy, a view that to be sure is not unprecedented,[9] the Bible does not believe in disembodied souls; its ontology is not dualist, and when it speaks of humans possessing a *nefesh*, this means only that humans are living beings (*nefesh* = life). As Richard Steiner (2015, 1) describes matters before arguing for his contrary view, "For over a century the Israelite [*nefesh*] has fought a losing battle for the hearts and minds of biblical scholars, seeking to retain its traditional status as an entity separate from the body and capable of existing outside it." Indeed, in the standard view, belief in disembodied souls was inconceivable in the Ancient Near East. Steiner robustly contests the scholarly orthodoxy. After concentrating

---

[8] Cf. Jer. 51:39, Job 4:20 and the interpretation of Daniel in Saadia Gaon 1948, 271. Numerous explanations have been suggested for the perceived lateness of an explicit biblical assertion of a literal resurrection. But Jon Levenson (2008) argues that earlier parts of the Bible, pre-Daniel, had a concept of resurrection, albeit the biblical material is not totally consistent or systematic and resurrection is embedded in the context of a national collective. Maimonides, in his *Essay on Resurrection*, relies on Daniel, but he also notes (1985, 225-28) some verses that seem to contradict belief in resurrection. He maintains that these refer to the course of nature and are therefore compatible with the belief in a miraculous resurrection. See also the verses noted by Segal 2016, 158, n. 2. Some scholars think, though, that the letter is meant for the masses and does not express Maimonides's real view.

[9] Thomas Hobbes, for example, held the view. See R. Steiner 2015, 3.

on a verse in a prophecy of Ezekiel (13:18), he marshals a broad and variegated array of evidence that the biblical terms *nefesh* and *ruah* refer to disembodied souls, or souls that could exist disembodied (e.g., verses that distinguish body and *nefesh*) and that, further, belief in disembodied souls was widespread in the Ancient Near East.[10] Steiner also argues that the Bible refers to a disembodied afterlife when it speaks of being "brought in" to one's people.[11] The impact of this ontology on how the Bible understands the afterlife is profound.

Clear affirmations of an afterlife are found in the Apocrypha (200 BCE–200 CE). Jubilees affirms immortality (23:31); Maccabees II affirms resurrection (2:6–7). Much more germane to this volume, however, are teachings of the Rabbis of the Talmud and Midrash.

The Sages of the Talmud and Midrash utilized two terms that came to form the basis of later discussion. One is *olam ha-ba* (the World-to-Come). We are told that "all of Israel" have a portion in this World-to-Come except for three categories of heretics (Mishnah *Sanhedrin* 10:1). The other term used by the Sages is *tehiyyat ha-metim* (resurrection of the dead). This resurrection takes place either shortly after the coming of the Messiah or following a substantial messianic age. Not only must one believe in resurrection to enter *olam ha-ba* according to the Mishnah (*Sanhedrin* 10:1), but one who does not believe that *the doctrine of resurrection appears in the Torah* does not have a share in the World-to-Come – even if that individual believes the doctrine itself on some other ground.[12]

The Sadducees denied the existence of an afterlife; the Essenes affirmed immortality; and according to Ephraim Urbach (1987, 235) the Pharisees spoke only of resurrection, not immortality. The phrase "World-to-Come" refers to a certain period in history during or after which resurrection occurs.[13] Indicating the belief's status in post-biblical Judaism, the opening of the core prayer known as the *Amidah*, recited in every service, refers to God a half-dozen times as the one who resurrects the dead. (The stress is on God's power, not, as in Daniel, His justice, albeit

---

[10] See also Pleijel 2019.
[11] In chs. 10–11, Steiner argues for a complex interpretation of the biblical afterlife.
[12] To corroborate that belief in resurrection is found in the Torah, the Talmud (*Sanhedrin* 90a–b) presents textual arguments of the "derash" kind, i.e., divorced from the plain meaning. For discussion, see Levenson 2008, ch. 2.
[13] See Nachmanides 2009, 2:518–51 (*Gate of Reward* [*Sha'ar ha-Gemul*]). Another term, *le-atid lavo* ("in the future to come"), seems close in import to *olam ha-ba* when the latter is construed as referring to a point in history.

His "great compassion" and "faithfulness" are invoked as well.[14]) The Rabbis also speak about the habitats of those who have an afterlife: *Gan Eden* (a paradise) and *Gehinnom* (hell or purgatory). Some texts about *Gehinnom* affirm eternal torment for some of the wicked; others, limited torment; others, annihilation of their soul, either immediately or after a period of suffering.[15]

In medieval times, Sa'adyah Gaon's view of the afterlife highlights resurrection; he sees the human being as a composite of body and soul, and so the afterlife must include the body. Resurrection is for Sa'adyah the only model that allows for the person in the afterlife to be the same as the one who lived previously, and absent a body, the individual does not truly exist *in whole* between death and resurrection. (To be sure, the soul exists while stored up during that time, and there is some degree of punishment.) Sa'adyah maintained that there would be two resurrections. The first is for virtuous Jews, who will be rewarded with an embodied existence consisting of enjoyable physical activities; the second is for everyone, both those who are rewarded and those who are punished, but, in accord with a rabbinic teaching we will discuss later, without bodily activities. This, according to Sa'adyah, is the Rabbis' World-to-Come.[16]

A crucial component of the history of Jewish belief in an afterlife – a turning point – is (no surprise here) the perspective of Maimonides. In certain of his writings, Maimonides describes the afterlife without reference to the body. Indeed, in his *Mishneh Torah* he explicitly denies that the body is present in the type of existence that he calls "the good stored up for the righteous."[17] Already much earlier, in Maimonides's introduction to his commentary on chapter 10 of tractate *Sanhedrin*,[18] there are oddities that might suggest to some readers that, contrary to appearances, his conception of the afterlife is of a bodyless existence.

---

[14] Noting Ps. 146:5–9, however, Gillman (1997, 126) suggests that, while the explicit message is power, retribution is a "subtext" here.

[15] See Brody 2016–2017.

[16] Saadia Gaon 1948, 264–86 (Treatise 7); 336–56 (9:5–11). Sa'adyah introduces the notion of *Gan Eden* and *Gehinnom* as reward and punishment (1948, 340 [9:5], 423 [a variant of Treatise 7] only in a limited way, as noted by Brody (2016–2017, 99–100).

[17] *Mishneh Torah*, Laws of Repentance 8:1–2. Actually Maimonides distinguishes two kinds of souls, "nefesh" and "neshamah." Only the former can exist disembodied. (See *Mishneh Torah*, Laws of the Foundations of the Torah 4:8–9.)

[18] The chapter is called "Perek Ḥelek" (the chapter "Ḥelek") because it begins with the words "Kol Yisra'el yesh lahem ḥelek le-Olam Ha-Ba," "all of Israel has a share in the World-to-Come [except for three categories]."

For example, when Maimonides lists the thirteen principles of faith, belief in which is necessary in order to attain the World-to-Come, he provides detailed, lengthy explanations of each principle, until he reaches the last – resurrection. This final principle is formulated as "The principle of the resurrection of the dead, as we have explained." The trouble is that what "we have explained" leading up to the thirteen principles is that the World-to-Come is an *incorporeal* existence! Is Maimonides taking "resurrection of the dead" figuratively, symbolizing that the righteous live on even after physical death? Or does he believe in resurrection despite his describing only immortality?

Maimonides was attacked for his ostensible denial of *teḥiyyat ha-metim* yet also was quoted by some as authoritative support for such a denial. Reacting to these events, he composed a missive (*The Essay on Resurrection*) in which he complained that he had been misunderstood. Yet, even while there affirming resurrection on the basis of Daniel,[19] rebuffing the charges against him as a canard, repudiating attempts to invoke his words (or his silence) as support for a denial, and explaining why his stress on immortality should not be read as a denial of resurrection,[20] Maimonides was philosophically – and perhaps viscerally – unable to deem a bodily existence as an *ultimate value*. In all likelihood this is the main reason he declared that *the resurrected dead will die again*.[21] In the *Essay on Resurrection* he also affirms strongly that miracles occur, an affirmation that contrasts with Maimonidean texts discussed in Chapter 2.[22] Not only would bringing the dead back to life be a miracle, but the resurrected beings' living forever would compound the miracle – indeed, it would constitute a logical impossibility, since material bodies by their nature must be subject to corruption.[23] So immortality would be the ultimate state.

---

[19] Maimonides seems to shun support other than Daniel, including the Talmud's exegeses in *Sanhedrin*.

[20] He writes (Maimonides 1985, 225) that because resurrection is a miraculous event whose nature is "easily grasped," he chose rather (in his other writings) to elaborate on immortality, which is a "hidden matter."

[21] Cf. Abraham Ibn Ezra's commentary to Daniel 12:2 and Albo 1929, 4:30–31.

[22] In *Mishneh Torah*, Laws of Kings 12:1, Maimonides writes, "Do not think that in messanic times some element of the natural course of things will be abolished." (See also 11:3.) In actuality, as David Berger pointed out to me, what he says is that in messianic times nature won't change, not that natural laws will not be violated. Maimonides in Laws of Kings 12:3 describes the messiah identifying lineages, notably priests and Levites (without DNA!), an achievement whose occurrence is hard to explain without a miracle.

[23] See Maimonides, *Guide of the Perplexed* 3:8, 3: 15.

Maimonides also invested the term "World-to-Come" with a meaning different from that intended by the ancient Sages. For him, it is not a period in eschatological history; instead, it's where the individual's soul "goes" after death.[24] For this definition and more, he was taken to task by Naḥmanides.[25] (Ultimately, for Maimonides, *olam ha-ba* may have been a state of mind, an orientation, that one can achieve even while embodied.[26])

Notwithstanding his defense of himself, Maimonides's emphasis on a noncorporeal afterlife stirred great opposition.[27] Among philosophers, Ḥasdai Crescas (1340–1410) held that resurrection was the most appropriate afterlife for a human being, whose body and soul had been bound together and participated in activities together. Crescas denied, however, that the so-called resurrected body is the same as the one that died. Crescas also rejected Maimonides's evaluation of intellectual achievement as the path to immortality; for Crescas, love of God and true service played the crucial role.[28]

The Middle Ages also saw widespread belief in transmigration, promulgated by Kabbalists. The view had already been opposed by Sa'adyah Gaon and later would be rejected by Joseph Albo.[29]

Skipping now several centuries to the flowering of the Enlightenment – the age of reason – we find that Jewish thinkers of that time highlighted immortality of the soul. In the *Phaedon*, Moses Mendelssohn offered proofs of immortality, emulating Plato's *Phaedo*. The Reform movement, scientifically oriented, rejected belief in resurrection because resurrection required a miracle. Many Conservative Jews likewise rejected belief in a literal resurrection.[30] These denominations' prayerbooks either changed the Hebrew text to drop or alter references to resurrection, or offered novel English translations of liturgical expressions. Hebrew phrases that literally mean "you resurrect the dead," "who resurrects the dead," and

---

[24] See *Mishneh Torah*, Laws of Repentance 8:8.
[25] Nachmanides 2009, 2: 518–51. On medieval views of resurrection and immortality, see Schwartz 2017.
[26] See Hartman 1976.
[27] See Septimus 1982, ch. 3. Maimonides's view that immortality essentially consists of partial conjunction with the Active Intellect (which seems to consist [obscurely] of a collection of truths), seems to eliminate personal immortality while affirming collective immortality. I will adopt a simpler account.
[28] See Crescas 2018, 205–40, 287–300 (2:6:1, 3:1:3).
[29] Saadia Gaon 1948, 259–63 (6:8); Albo 1929, 4:29.
[30] For an innovative politically-centered account of the shift to immortality, see Batnitzky 2009.

the like, were rendered instead, "You implant immortal life within us," "You give life to all," "You are master of life and death," "who calls the dead to life everlasting."[31] Orthodox prayerbooks translate the text literally to connote reviving the dead.

With this historical sketch in place (it truly is only a sketch), I turn to the reasons for and against the different positions. I will say little about *Gan Eden* and *Gehinnom*, despite the enormous attention that many traditional thinkers devoted to these concepts, and despite the fact that no treatment of Jewish views of the afterlife can be *complete* without reference to them.[32] Instead I will focus on the typology of models with which this chapter began: immortality, resurrection, reincarnation, and legacy. These lend themselves much more to philosophical and theological analysis.

ARGUMENTS VS. REASONS

A thinker's choice of which afterlife scenario to regard as primary or exclusive, is not whimsical. Cultural context is one factor, but this does not preclude having reasons that could back one's beliefs, beyond the evidence of traditional texts. Indeed, a variety of *arguments* are given by Jewish philosophers in favor of each conception. But we can also identify *reasons* that fall short of, and perhaps are not intended as, arguments in the usual sense.

What I mean is that often a thinker's choice of a position on a religious issue is not grounded – perhaps cannot be grounded – in a set of premises from which a certain conclusion is alleged to deductively or probabilistically follow. Indeed, some of the arguments concerning the afterlife fail in obvious ways if we demand such support relations between premises and conclusion. But in theology, a choice of position is often a matter of finding the best fit with certain doctrines of one's religion, rather than deriving some beliefs from other beliefs in a deductive or probabilistic fashion.

How should we understand "fit"? One way is what I call the Amazon books way: People who buy belief X also buy belief Y, because one or both enhances the *psychological* appeal of the other. Both appeal to a certain sensibility, a cast of mind. But fit may be conceived as normative as well as descriptive: People who buy belief X *should* buy belief Y. Why? Because teachings of the religion should interrelate and display

---

[31] See Gillman 1997, 193–211. Some prayerbooks provide options. See also Levenson 2008, ch. 1

[32] On their role, however, see Brody 2016–2017; Wiederblank 2018, 281–477; Raphael 2009, passim.

coherence; religion should cultivate systemic interconnections. There might be a certain methodology, or ultimate explanation, or underlying principle,[33] that leads to holding several views as a package, even if none logically implies the other or even makes the other more probable. Examples to come will clarify the idea.

We should also consider that certain terms (such as immortality and resurrection) might be interpreted by a thinker symbolically. Particular versions of belief in the afterlife might be assessed by their power to symbolically convey certain ideas, even if the symbolic meaning was not the original intent behind usages of the terms. Some considerations we will examine are psychological, taking into account what impact certain doctrines will have on a believer's consciousness. Some look at the values certain ideas promote. Others, of course, adduce textual support from biblical and rabbinic sources. Although some considered theology a "science," manifesting logically airtight connections,[34] the reality is that the philosophy of particular religions does not always proceed that way. I'll indeed cite here varied sorts of support for certain models. This is not to say that theologians and philosophers always are conscious of the relevant distinctions.

REASONS FOR THE IMMORTALITY CONCEPTION

Both immortality and resurrection have a theodic implication: that the "next world," whether it involves a disembodied existence or a resurrection, is where deserts are conferred. But here are some historically significant grounds proposed for favoring the immortality model.

Plato's Legacy

In the Platonic tradition, carried on by Maimonides, the ideal life for human beings is a life of the intellect, and the body interferes with both the pursuit and the attainment of that goal. It is a prison from which the soul yearns to escape, to use Plato's image in the *Phaedo*. Bodily appetites distract people from seeking knowledge; and bodies can cognize only other bodies, not that which is not physical. Plato's anticorporeal axiology, his denigration of matter and the body, has limited appeal for contemporary readers, but we have already seen that historically it

---

[33] This phrasing was suggested by Aaron Segal.
[34] Cf. Aquinas, *Summa Theologiae* 1:1:2–7. To be clear, Aquinas held that some religious truths are not demonstrable and must be based on faith.

was a driving force in thought concerning the afterlife. Moreover, even today, the notion that the soul's activities are "higher" than the body's has hardly been abandoned. (Notably, antimaterialism has been quite visible in contemporary philosophy of mind.[35])

Selfhood

Immortality is supposed to be immortality *of a person* – and the soul, it is said, *is* the person. The body is merely the soul's temporary and incidental dwelling place. At the end of the *Phaedo*, Socrates maintained that those who point to his grave and say, "There lies Socrates" are mistaken; only his *body* "there lies." Resurrection of the body thus does not bring the person "back"; he or she has always existed – as a soul – and exists throughout after the body dies.

Indeed, what would resurrection accomplish if a person is the soul? (In Sa'adyah, recall, the person is a composite, so resurrection is appropriate.) One answer is that since the body participated in the person's activities, it should be resurrected when the day of judgment comes.[36] An ostensible difficulty here is that while the body participated in sin, it is not an agent such that it could be held culpable.[37] Naḥmanides, in an effort to explain the why of resurrection, assigns mystical significance to the body.[38]

One may question (as John Locke did) whether the person is the soul and thus whether personal identity across time is a matter of a soul's persistence.[39] A problem for medievals was how to individuate souls, since Aristotle taught that matter is the principle of individuation. If for this or any other reason, souls cannot be individuated, there could be no individual immortality, only at best collective immortality – a doctrine some medieval philosophers taught or implied. But whatever its complexities, the notion that the person is a soul is a prevalent basis for highlighting the immortality model of the afterlife.

---

[35] See Koons and Bealer 2010; Loose et al. 2018; Van Inwagen and Zimmerman 2007; Olson and Segal 2023 (Segal's contribution is antimaterialist).

[36] See also R. Meir Abulafia, *Yad Ramah*, *Sanhedrin* 90b; Crescas 2018, 287–97.

[37] Nachmanides 2009, 2:535. In truth, *any* corporal punishment involves punishing the body even when it is not regarded as an agent.

Naḥmanides identifies an earlier period of reward and punishment just for the soul, right after death, and then another, for both body and soul, in messianic times. See Brody 2016–2017, 116ff.

[38] Nachmanides 2009, 535.

[39] See Locke, *Essay Concerning Human Understanding* 2:27:11–31 (passim). It isn't clear whether Locke's objection is ontological or epistemological.

Naturalism

Philosophers who were in large measure naturalists sought to keep God's miracles to a minimum, if not deny their occurrence. Resurrection would be a miracle; immortality occurs naturally. For Maimonides, in order to continue to exist after death of the body, the soul must engage in intellection and the acquisition of truths, and if it acquires the right truths, immortality follows. It's plausible that Maimonides holds as well that the soul's going out of existence – what the Bible calls *karet*, being cut off – is likewise a natural process.[40] The affirmations of miracles in *The Essay on Resurrection* do not have to affect these particular processes. (As we have seen, denial of miracles was prominent in the Reform movement's argumentation for the immortality model.)

Epistemology

As in Plato's *Phaedo*, immortality of the soul was taken by some, including Reform theologians, as provable. The future resurrection, by contrast, because it is a miracle, could be established only on the basis of biblical and rabbinic sources. These carried little probative weight for some theologians.

Rav's Depiction

For Maimonides, the primary *textual* argument in favor of an incorporeal model of the afterlife is a statement of the talmudic sage Rav:

In the World-to-Come, there is no eating, drinking or procreation [and other activities]. Rather, the righteous sit with their crowns on their heads and bask in the splendor of the *Shekhinah* [divine presence]. [Berakhot 17a][41]

On Maimonides's reading, since Rav denies the existence of *corporeal activities* in the World-to-Come (Maimonides cites only eating and drinking), he denies the existence of *bodies* in the World-to-Come. The rest of the quotation ("the righteous sit with their crowns on their heads

---

[40] *Mishneh Torah*, Laws of Repentance 8:1. The intellectualist/naturalist thrust of this chapter is not explicit, but correlating it with such texts as *Guide of the Perplexed* 3:51 and 3:54 leads to that understanding. Stern 2024 views Maimonides as a skeptic about the possibility of metaphysical knowledge, and adjusts his formulation of the "AfterDeath" (as he terms it) accordingly.

[41] *Mishneh Torah*, Laws of Repentance 8:2.

and bask in the splendor of God's presence") is construed figuratively by Maimonides, to denote the righteous having the crown of knowledge.

As Rabad (R. Abraham ben David) urged in his gloss to the quoted passage, Maimonides's argument is fallacious. Even if there are no bodily activities in the afterlife, there may be bodies of a special kind – bodies that do not require physical sustenance. Indeed, says Rabad, Moses and Elijah managed to fast for forty days and forty nights because their bodies were of a special kind. Thus, Rav's statement is compatible with the existence of bodies in the afterlife, and the "crowns" are, on Rabad's reading, literal.

In the *Essay on Resurrection*, Maimonides explains his wholly incorporealist reading of Rav using the assertion that God does not create things that lack a function. If there is no eating, drinking, or intercourse, argues Maimonides, the bodily parts used in such activities serve no function. Hence, there is no reason for them to exist in the afterlife – to the contrary, there is reason for them not to exist. This argument would seem to apply no less to special bodies than ordinary ones. A critic could reply that the body parts would be present in the afterlife because they are essential for personhood, not because they will be needed for existence. Nahmanides offers a mystical response to Maimonides's "no need for the body" argument, as noted earlier. (Once Maimonides affirms temporary resurrection, he ascribes ordinary physical activities to the resurrected until they die again.)

The Same Body

A final argument for favoring the immortality model is that a resurrected body needs to be the same as the one that died. Since bodies decompose, how can this identity hold? Among responses to this objection are: God gives the resurrected person a new body (Crescas's theory), or else (this is an approach in contemporary philosophy) the theorist adopts a "gappy" conception of the body, whereby the body goes out of existence for a while and then comes back, but is still the same body.[42] These answers may fail to persuade. True, the problems with reidentifying a *soul* across time are themselves formidable; but in the case of the body, we seemingly know that the earlier body has decomposed and prima facie is here no longer, whereas we know no parallel truth about a soul.

---

[42] See Brody 2016–2017, 119; Dougherty 2014, 166–78. Other solutions include that in D. Zimmerman 2010; cf. Hasker 2011.

REASONS FOR THE RESURRECTION CONCEPTION

Individuation

A proponent of resurrection may favor this view because he or she denies the existence of the soul. A proponent operating within traditional theism is more likely to maintain that, while souls separated from bodies post-mortem exist, they cannot be individuated. Individuation is possible only with resurrection of a body. Two problems arise. First, as already discussed, how can the body be the same body? If it is not, in what sense is the person being resurrected? Second, if, as the pro-resurrection view under consideration maintains, the souls cannot be individuated, then talk of "the soul" returning to the body is hard to understand even if the premortem and resurrected body are the same.

Selfhood

The body is essential to one's sense of self, no less than an enduring soul.

Proper Compensation

In one's lifetime, body and soul acted together as a unity; hence in the hereafter they should be compensated together.[43]

Miracles

Immortality leaves God out of the picture, since it occurs naturally. Isaiah (25:8) states that "He will swallow up death forever" – that is, it is God who defeats death. Resurrection, a miracle, gives expression to God's being death's conqueror.

Fit and Systematicity

Another sort of argument involves fit and systematicity. To clarify, consider the following argument:

(1) God has the power to perform miracles.
(2) Resurrection of bodies is a miracle.

---

[43] Cf. *Lev. Rabbah* 41:6.

(3) Disembodied immortality is not a miracle. It follows from the soul's nature.
(4) Therefore, God will bring about resurrection.

This argument is patently invalid. Although God has the power to perform miracles, that does not entail that He will perform every conceivable miracle. We must therefore revise the argument. Consider this:

(1) The most important events in the history of the Jewish People take place through miracles.
(2) Resurrection is (or would be if it occurs) one of the most important events in the history of the Jewish People.
(3) Therefore, resurrection will occur by a miracle.
(4) Disembodied immortality and reincarnations are not events in the history of the Jewish people, but rather in the life of an individual. Furthermore, immortality is not a miracle, and perhaps reincarnation isn't either.
(5) Therefore, the afterlife consists of resurrection and not immortality.

From a formal point of view, this is hardly an impressive argument either. Crucially, premise (1) begs the question against someone who thinks that collective resurrection (which would be a miracle) will not occur and that the afterlife consists of disembodied immortality.

Similar strictures apply to the argument that the ultimate good of the afterlife must be a communal affair, and since resurrection of bodies allows social interaction and community, while immortality does not, resurrection is the right model for the afterlife. To say that the afterlife must be communal begs the question.[44]

If the pro-resurrection arguments based on miracles and community are one and all faulty, why don't those thinkers who advanced them realize the problems we've noted and desist from producing the reasons they do? The answer, to reiterate, is that their reasoning is of a specific kind. Many are seeking not entailments or certain probabilistic relations between premises and conclusion, but rather *fit*. In choosing between propositions p and q, a theologian chooses the one that connects with and best fits other theological propositions. Resurrection *fits with* teachings about God's ability to perform miracles and His presence in major public events, such as the Exodus, and with teachings about Jewish

---

[44] These arguments anyway do not rule out a hybrid concept: Perhaps a part of the afterlife at the end of days consists of disembodied immortality, and another part consists of resurrection.

community and peoplehood, so it is preferred. Immortality leaves God and community out of the picture, so it doesn't fit well. Theology, in this approach, should aim for systematicity: Its component parts should ideally interrelate maximally.

The fewer the components, the easier it is for the parts to interrelate. If my components are Franz Rosenzweig's triad of "Creation, Revelation, and Redemption," it won't be hard to connect them. As my belief system grows more complex and wide-ranging, maximal fit becomes a pipedream. But we should do our best. So, if by choosing a particular model of the afterlife I can relate belief in an afterlife to other beliefs like divine sovereignty, miracles, and community, I should do so. This, at least, is the approach of theologians who invoke notions like miracles, power, and community in giving reasons for a particular model of the afterlife. It is, I think, quite reasonable.

Symbolism

A widespread practice in contemporary theology, most closely associated with Paul Tillich (1960), is to understand some, many, most, or all religious statements as symbols and metaphors that *point to* various truths (e.g., ontological, moral) that are not expressed literally. The import of a symbol may depend on time and place.[45] Advocates of a symbolic approach may claim that they are mining the original intended meaning of the statements. Alternatively, they may deny that the messages they extract were *intended* by the authors of the sources (those authors meant what they said literally), but hold that it is hopeless to affirm the statements as literal truth. Only a symbolic reading will make the statements worthy of being preserved. In this approach, the adherents cling to the statements, symbolically construed, lest they be forced to abandon them altogether. The symbolic approach, in this account, is born of practical necessity.

Applied to resurrection, the symbolic approach might convey messages such as the following,[46] even if there will be no literal resurrection:

- God "imposes death and gives life" (Deut. 32:39).
- God is present in our lives.
- The human being is a psychosomatic unity – mind and body.
- Our lives as individual, embodied persons are significant.

---

[45] Although metaphors are not identical with symbols, we will refer to this as the symbolic approach.
[46] See Gillman 1997, 219–45, who locates these messages in various thinkers.

- God's salvation is collective.
- People's destiny is not in their hands, but in God's.
- God's power is unlimited.[47]
- "The death of death marks the final step in the triumph of the monotheistic God."[48]

Notably, the doctrine of immortality can likewise be construed as carrying salutary symbolism; for instance, it symbolizes that our lives are significant.

It is evident that a great deal of subjectivity enters into the choice of message. Another rich symbolic reading of belief in the afterlife, applicable to both resurrection and immortality, is the legacy view to be considered later.

Psychological Impact

Another category of reasons operates in models of the afterlife: psychological impact. Consider this line of thought:

(1) If there would be a resurrection, it would demonstrate God's power and sovereignty.
(2) Believing in resurrection would impress upon us the power and sovereignty of God.
(3) Therefore, it is beneficial religiously to believe in resurrection.
(4) Therefore, resurrection occurs.

Here we have a different criterion for choice of a metaphysical view. We go from mindset to metaphysics. But the argument is invalid because we can't get from (3) to (4) without an additional premise, viz. that psychological benefit is sufficient for truth. That premise is, if taken as a universal statement, false. Also, it's not clear how X's belief can be formed by psychological impact alone when X knows that the belief does not rest on evidence but only on psychological impact. Perhaps the answer is that images make a doxastic impression, as in literary and other artistic depictions. These reflections conjure up the topic of how pragmatic reasons figure in religious belief, a topic to be broached in Chapter 10.

* * *

---

[47] This message faces a challenge: If resurrection is a *mere* symbol, doesn't this suggest that God's power is *not* unlimited?
[48] Gillman 1997, 263.

In sum, the model of resurrection draws largely from considerations of fit, symbolism, and psychological impact, in addition to textual arguments. Denial of resurrection will come largely from those skeptical of miracles and those who find the problem of continuity of the person's body insurmountable.

REASONS FOR THE REINCARNATION CONCEPTION

In reincarnation or transmigration, "subjects undergo cycles of life and death, living as one form and dying and then living again in another form any number of times."[49] An adult human being might be reborn as an infant, nonhuman animal, insect, or even as a vegetable or mineral. Reincarnation dates back at least to the Pythagoreans and is widespread in Eastern religions. Famously, Pythagoras is said to have chided a man who was beating a dog that the dog could be the man's grandmother.

Beginning with the Middle Ages, reincarnation (called in Hebrew *gilgul*, transmigration) has a fairly large home in Judaism, particularly in mystical circles including *Sefer ha-Bahir* and *Zohar*.[50] Nahmanides views it as the key to the Book of Job.[51] Further "proof" of reincarnation comes from the biblical commandment of *yibbum* (levirate marriage).[52] If a man dies without children, his brother is obligated to marry the deceased's wife, and we are told that a child born to this couple "shall be established [or: accounted for[53]] on the name of his dead brother" (Deut. 25:6). Although literally, the verse means only that the deceased's *name* is perpetuated, a kabbalistic explanation has it that the child born to the new couple would be the deceased coming back to embodied life. The deceased's brother has the best chance of siring such a child. That is why the widow and the brother must marry.[54]

---

[49] Goldschmidt and Seacord 2013, 393.
[50] The Hebrew term *gilgul* focuses on the movement of the soul, while the term "reincarnation" focuses on the product of that process. A particularly fertile Jewish source on reincarnation is *Sha'ar ha-Gilgulim* by the kabbalist R. Hayyim Vital (1543–1620), reflecting teachings of R. Isaac Lurias (*Arizal*) (1534–1572). Some thinkers regard *gilgul* as a dogma of Judaism.
[51] See Nahmanides's cryptic comments on Job 33:30 and at p. 23 of his introduction to the book in Nachmanides 1963, vol. 1. See also Bahya ben Asher's reference to Job in his commentary to Deut. 25:9.
[52] See, e.g., Nahmanides, commentary to Gen. 38:28.
[53] These are the respective translations of the word by Robert Alter and the Jewish Publication Society.
[54] The Bible spells out a procedure (called *halitzah*) through which the deceased's wife and brother do not have to marry.

This biblical support aside, why else might a theologian opt for the doctrine of *gilgul*? For many, the principal consideration is that belief in this doctrine has great theodic value. It doesn't explain the existence of evil per se,[55] but with regard to the old problem of moral order or distribution of evil – "Why do the righteous suffer and the wicked prosper?" – reincarnation provides an answer: In a previous life the individuals did lots of good or, instead, lots of evil, and they are now being rewarded or punished for that conduct. (The cycle doesn't have to go on forever.) Since subjects might be reincarnated as infants and nonhuman animals, reincarnation, unlike several other theodicies, would explain the suffering of those beings. A substantial number of sources use reincarnation to explain the suffering of animals.[56]

Theodicy is not the sole reason for belief in reincarnation. Reincarnation also makes possible growth and soul-making. Jerome Yehuda Gellman (2019, ch. 9) develops a novel version of reincarnation and a theodicy involving the multiverse that turns on the possibility of soul-making. The multiverse, Gellman believes, greatly increases the possibilities for improvement. Although I will stress the theodic usage of reincarnation, this soul-making feature is significant too.

Not only does the doctrine of reincarnation resuscitate the retributivist theodicy that was discredited in our chapter on evil, but Tyron Goldschmidt and Beth Seacord (2013) argue that it provides a more comprehensive theodicy than others. That's because the latter dwell mostly if not exclusively on why the righteous suffer, while a reincarnationist theodicy also explains why the wicked prosper. Goldschmidt and Seacord reply to a variety of objections. For example, subjects who are supposedly reincarnated do not recall their past wrongs, and they are thus not experiencing their adversities as punishments for past wrongdoing. Goldschmidt and Seacord respond that we would punish a war criminal even if, suffering from Alzheimer's, he did not recall his wrongdoing. Also, Goldschmidt and Seacord suggest that believers in *gilgul* may use a reincarnationist theodicy as a *supplement* to others, thus solving problems that the other theodicies face while also freeing them from having to give a reincarnationist theodicy for every evil.[57]

---

[55] See Goldschmidt and Seacord 2013, 395.
[56] See Sears 2003, ch. 5. Dougherty (2014), a Christian, invokes reincarnation for this purpose.
[57] Crescas 2018, 347 (4:7), raises an objection to *gilgul*, but then adds: "Yet since the sect that affirms transmigration has a foundation in the tradition, the doors of investigation are locked in this matter. If it is a received tradition, we shall receive it favorably. Let this suffice for [this] issue."

Some years ago, a prominent rabbi explained the Holocaust as retribution for sins committed by the victims in a previous existence – essentially turning the victims into perpetrators. Similarly, I heard a speaker declare at a funeral that the deceased, who seemed to be a wonderful, pious person, suffered for several years before death because her soul had migrated from another body, a body in which that soul had sinned. Although it is difficult to show that such claims are false:

(a) Some theists will argue there is a significant chance that there is a better explanation.
(b) Reincarnationist theodicies may be maligning innocent individuals and ought to be shunned as possibly false accusations.
(c) If the person is righteous now, shouldn't that work more in their favor, insofar as they have repented and grown?
(d) Imputations of (previous) sin may diminish sympathy for the victims, dull the sense that the deaths being explained were tragedies, and perhaps even give people justification for harming others. Proclaiming reincarnation as a theodicy thus risks being callous toward the righteous.
(e) *Ḥeshbon ha-nefesh* – self-examination, scrutiny of one's deeds – will not make sense if one does not recall sins of one's previous life.

The concept of *gilgul* has often been assessed independent of its strength or weakness as a theodicy. Many of the considerations are psychological. In favor of *gilgul*, some argue that belief in *gilgul* enables people to gain the confidence that their goals will eventually be achieved; there will be more time to complete the work. Some people would be disheartened by the prospect of *gilgul* and will put in greater effort to get things right in the here and now. Belief in *gilgul* could thus serve as an incentive to act rightly.[58] R. Moshe Ḥayyim Luzzatto (1707–1746) (1997, 124–26), cited by Goldschmidt and Segal (2017), explains that reincarnation maximizes our chances of becoming virtuous: "One ... would be able to rectify at one time that which it ruined [by sinning] at another time, or perfect that which it did not perfect." Living a second time gives a person a second chance. In Chapter 2, I questioned whether psychological arguments can support metaphysical views. But citing only psychological impact short-changes the argument. The point is that God, being all-good, would design the world in a way that would maximize our chances for achieving our goals. We are not looking only

---

[58] These and other arguments are cited by Blau 2001, 6–10.

at psychology; we are looking at God's goodness. While we should not assume that God would do everything for us that we want, perhaps He would do for us what we *should* want.

There are also psychological arguments *against* belief in *gilgul*.[59] One is that people who adopt this notion may feel that their current efforts are futile, since they might still suffer from sins committed in a previous life.[60] Alternatively, someone might feel that it is pointless to work hard now, since he or she will have plenty of opportunities to "get it right."

A final point about *gilgul*. We should bear in mind that if memory is necessary for personal identity, a person lacking *any* memories of a previous existence would seem to be discontinuous with any person who existed earlier. Belief in *gilgul* thus does not work well with the memory conception, and proponents of *gilgul* indeed highlight the reincarnated person's lack of memory – that's their point. *Gilgul* identifies a person with a soul, regardless of the person's memory. And yet perhaps, on this conception, eventually all the memories of our past lives will be restored to us.

REASONS FOR THE LEGACY CONCEPTION

Some people live, while others live on.[61] According to the legacy conception, surviving death is attained in part naturalistically: People live on through others to whom they gave birth, or whom they taught or influenced. Some scholars, such as Jon Levenson (2008), find the legacy conception (without calling it that) to be a crucial part of biblical thinking about the afterlife. Among the view's proponents in the modern period is Hermann Cohen.[62]

Cohen writes, in an ontologically deflationary mode:

> The fathers are immortal because their merit lives on in their effects ... And since their merit benefits their descendants, the latter also become immortal, because they participate in the merits of the fathers. It is merit that makes men immortal. It is merit that constitutes the soul. Merit lies in history, not in man. [Cohen 1995, 335–36]

---

[59] See the six arguments summarized by Blau 2001, 10–12.
[60] R. Yedayah Bedersi, *Iggeret Hitnatzelut*, cited in *Responsa Rashba* 1:418.
[61] See Lamm 2015.
[62] Johnston 2010, writing in a non-Jewish framework, develops a similar idea. R. Mordecai Kaplan used a legacy conception as well, as noted by Gillman 1997, 214.

The legacy conception doesn't have to be ontologically deflationary. Joseph B. Soloveitchik, who was influenced by Cohen here as elsewhere, states:

> The first concept of immortality as coined by Judaism[63] is the continuation of a historical existence throughout the ages. It differs from transcendental immortality insofar as the deceased person does not lead an isolated, separate existence in a transcendental world ... It asserts itself in the consciousness of the many, who trace their roots to the one ... [T]he founder continues his existence through the history of his group. [Soloveitchik 2005, 176–77]

The legacy approach may be fortified by an argument advanced, albeit not in a religious context, by Samuel Scheffler (2013). Scheffler asks us to contemplate a Doomsday scenario in which we learn that the world will go out of existence thirty days after we die. This knowledge, Scheffler argues, will cause us to cease many of our projects. Why? Because we engage in those projects for future generations, not for ourselves. Scheffler calls the impact of our projects an "afterlife," albeit not the sort commonly associated with religious belief. His affirmation of an afterlife calls to mind the legacy conception. (Scheffler admits that some projects might continue even with knowledge of the impending disaster.)

The legacy conception draws power as well from considerations of fit (the importance in Judaism of passing down a tradition) and symbolism (having a legacy is symbolized by statements about an afterlife, even if there is also a metaphysical afterlife). Neil Gillman (1997, 249) objects to the approach, though, on the grounds that "I do not remain a totally distinct and individualized human being." R. Louis Jacobs (1973, 318) objects as well: "To say that Shakespeare is immortal in the sense that his plays will always be read is not really to speak about the man Shakespeare at all but about his ideas."

Regarding Gillman's challenge, it's not clear why "I do not remain a totally distinct and individualized human being" just because I am not leading an isolated existence; and Gillman ignores the fact that many of us find relationships, social roles, fiduciary obligations, and so on, crucial to our identity. We are social selves. As for Jacobs's objection, his claim seems false. I *am* talking about a person when I speak of his or her achievements and influence. Should we say that obituaries of famous people's contributions to society are not about *them* but only about the contributions? If so, why do we praise the people and not merely the achievements?

---

[63] Soloveitchik's view is not ontologically deflationary, because legacy is only the "first concept." See Sztuden 2012. See further Zuckier 2023.

Two other objections may be raised to the legacy conception, both of which illustrate its inability to serve certain functions served by other conceptions. One objection is that all too often the legacy model provides little solace. Many people live in obscurity and exercise little influence. Many produce children, and have disciples, but as generations go on, memories of the ancestors disappear from their progeny and their impact ceases. Even people who will leave an impact may not *realize* that they will, and they may not be consoled about death unless they believe that they will acquire an afterlife in the literal sense. In the case of abusive parents, the legacy is harm.

Additionally, the legacy conception forfeits the theodic value that other versions of the afterlife possess. Hitler had tremendous impact; a pious childless couple living in solitude may have none. So on the legacy conception, Hitler has an afterlife, the couple does not. Could it be that many of the wicked have a more fecund afterlife than the righteous?[64] Of course, proponents of the legacy conception could respond, "That's not an objection to my view. That *is* my view." But the consequence is counterintuitive.

In sum, if we introduce "fit" and psychological impact as criteria, the legacy conception will prove very appealing in certain respects, even while faring less well in others.[65]

THE VALUE OF AN AFTERLIFE

While belief in an afterlife pervades Jewish sources, some Jewish thinkers minimize its importance and even desirability.[66] The primary grounds for devaluation is that Judaism requires action in *this* world, an arena in which it is possible to perform the commandments, many of which require bodily action. Even "negative" commandments (i.e., prohibitions – "Do not do X") can't be fulfilled meaningfully unless there is a real possibility of violating them by bodily actions. Thus, Soloveitchik (1983, 30–33) writes,

---

[64] Genghis Khan's DNA, it is estimated, is found in 16 million men. He has the "largest" afterlife of all. It's not the sort of afterlife the legacy view has in mind. Legacy theorists are speaking about meritorious people. It isn't clear, however, how merit is necessary for leaving a legacy.

[65] Samuel Lebens referred me to the teaching of the Disney movie *Coco*: that the dead survive in heaven as long as they are remembered here on earth.

[66] See Segal 2017. Jantzen 1984 questions the value of an afterlife in Christian terms.

Judaism abhors death, organic decay, and dissolution ... It is this world which constitutes the stage for the Halakhah, the setting for halakhic man's life ... The task of the religious individual is bound up with the performance of commandments, and this performance is confined to this world.

He notes the Psalmist's words, "The dead cannot praise God" (Ps. 115:17). Contact with the dead, furthermore, produces *tum'ah* (ritual defilement).[67] These devaluations of the afterlife are directed in the first instance at immortality, which, as we defined it, entails the absence of a body. But since resurrection would transpire only far into the future, loss of bodily *mitzvot* would mark the very long period between death and bodily resurrection.[68]

Some people – such as those who live in misery and those who expect much reward in the hereafter – may prefer an incorporeal afterlife of spiritual bliss to an embodied life of *mitzvot*. But that's beside the point. The argument against highlighting a disembodied afterlife is not that, empirically, people prefer *mitzvot* over such bliss, but rather normative: that, in the Jewish value system, they *ought* to. The value of *mitzvah* activities as a means of connecting to God is (on the view under discussion) not conditioned by people's *reactions* to losing the ability to perform them. Furthermore, people who won't feel loss by not being able to perform rituals in the afterlife may react another way when they recognize the impossibility of performing *interpersonal mitzvot* there, such as giving charity or helping the sick. After death, people may want to do good deeds, but in a "community" of disembodied souls they can't implement those desires. Even "love your neighbor" and "be compassionate" may require certain *behaviors* if they are to be meaningful. Consider also that Jewish law contains a strong mandate to save embodied lives, even when doing so involves violation of the Sabbath laws.

We should obviously not argue that, due to the foregoing considerations, Judaism does not value an afterlife at all. But the following position seems reasonable. That people die is a given. It's a hard, inexorable fact. As long as a disembodied afterlife would have the good features the tradition touts, it is rational to be happy that there is one, rather than no postmortem existence at all. So, however much one values doing *mitzvot*, that should not be taken so far as to say living is worthless without

---

[67] Soloveitchik 1983, 31.
[68] That some *mitzvot* require performance of *pleasurable* bodily activities (eating, drinking, sexual relations) augments the this-worldly perspective. On the place of pleasurable activities in Judaism, see Sokol 2013c, Hecker 2005.

mitzvah-performance. It's a question of what's best and what's second-best. We can rank this-worldly existence higher because *mitzvot* can be performed only in this world. But death is inevitable.[69]

The argument that Judaism requires performance of *mitzvot* and is therefore this-worldly is subject to other rejoinders, as noted by Aaron Segal and Tyron Goldschmidt (2017). For one thing, the argument presupposes that performing the *mitzvot* is valued for its own sake, rather than for some further end. Perhaps there is such a further end – and that end is enjoying spiritual bliss.[70] Such bliss can be attained in this world, but it is heightened in the next. And even though many people die without the *mitzvot* having attained their goal, death would not foreclose the possibility of spiritual bliss in the afterlife. Further, one view in rabbinic literature maintains that commandments will be abolished "in the future that is to come" (*le-atid lavo*, a period in messianic times) (*Niddah* 61b). This suggests that performing *mitzvot* is not an eternal aspect of Jewish existence. (But this is just one view.)

In addition, one of the driving forces behind belief in the afterlife is theodicy and belief in God's justice. When a soul-making theodicy is combined with belief in an afterlife where God metes out rewards and punishments, a theorist can get (quite literally) the best of both worlds: the benefits of both soul-making (moral and spiritual growth through *mitzvot*) and of just deserts in the afterlife.

Aaron Segal has emphasized that the afterlife involves being with God, arguably a greater good than anything in this world. Moreover, reciprocally, God will want to have the righteous with Him in the afterlife.[71] The ultimate impact of these important considerations depends on how much of being with God a person can attain in the afterlife and how much can be achieved in this world; how such companionship should be balanced against the grief that death brings to loved ones; and whether God's wanting the righteous to be with Him is self-interested on His part. Some who grieve might be troubled that their grief results from God's

---

[69] See also Segal 2019a, 325–26. The prohibition against suicide that exists in Jewish law does not entail that this world is *better*, any more than the prohibition against killing other people does.

[70] Even Maimonides, who rails repeatedly against religious obedience that is motivated by self-interest, seems to regard a desire for spiritual bliss as suitable motivation. (I refer to the Introduction to Ḥelek. Contrast that, however, with *Mishneh Torah*, Laws of Repentance 10:1.)

[71] See Segal 2014, 2016, 2017, 2019. This consideration explains why even someone who attained a complete life in this world would need to be with God in the next.

wanting the deceased to be with Him. Although it is common to say, in offering condolences, that the deceased is now with God, perhaps loved ones will not as a rule truly gain comfort from this thought.

The tension between the value of an afterlife, on the one hand, and ambivalence regarding its centrality, on the other, is evident in apparently contradictory statements of a talmudic Sage. R. Ya'akov taught: "This world is like an anteroom before the World-to-Come. Prepare yourself in the anteroom that you may enter the banquet hall" (*Avot* 4:21). Yet he is next quoted as follows:

> One hour of good deeds and repentance in this world is better than the whole of the life of the World-to-Come. One hour of spiritual bliss in the World-to-Come is better than the whole life of this world. [Avot 4:22]

Interpreters seek to dissolve the blatant contradictions between these statements. Perhaps we do well if we step away briefly from logical resolutions and use the contradiction to internalize the conflicting pulls of two perspectives.[72]

WHY IS THERE DEATH?

For thinkers like R. Moshe Ḥayyim Luzzatto (in *Path of the Just*) – who deem life in this world merely a means to a better existence – the question "Why is there death?" seems simple to answer. But Jewish sources proffer numerous other approaches.[73]

In Genesis 3:22, God imposes death as a punishment, and expresses concern that Adam, having already eaten from the tree of knowledge, will also eat from the "tree of life." Human immortality would blur the line between humans and God, upsetting the hierarchical order of Genesis 1. Here, death is good not for those who pass from the world, but for the *world order*. We also have R. Meir's declaration in the Midrash that when the Bible says that the created world was "very good" (*tov me'od*) (Gen. 1:31) it refers to death being good (*tov mavet*) (*Gen. Rabbah* 9:5).[74]

In the Talmud, however, when the ministering angels put to God the question, "Why did you impose death on Adam?" (*Shabbat* 55b), God

---

[72] See, however, the explanations assessed by Goldschmidt and Segal 2017, 116–21.
[73] In this section I am indebted at points to Segal 2014 (audio).
[74] The wording of the *midrash* implies that R. Meir's Torah Scroll actually was written this way. But Maimonides maintains that "death is good" is only an interpretation R. Meir offered of Gen. 1:31 (Maimonides 1963, 440; *Guide of the Perplexed* 3:10). Cf. Shapiro 2011, 96–97.

gives no explanation.[75] Rather, He replies that death is a decree. In one meaning, this passage is saying that death is bad but God decreed it anyway, arbitrarily; in another meaning, the text means only that God has hidden reasons for having death in His world, reasons that render death good.

At many Jewish funerals, the eulogies conclude by invoking Isaiah's prophecy that, in the future, "He will swallow up death forever" (Isa. 25:8). Why hope for that, if death is good? Further, the gravity of murder is most easily explained if death is an evil. The laws of mourning furnish further evidence of the badness of death.

If we are to preserve God's perfection, we need a theodicy for death.[76] That death returns a "borrowed" object (life) to its owner (God) affirms God's property rights, but does not explain *why* He wants our lives back.

At this juncture theologians face a dilemma. On the one hand, if they find no theodicy for why God allows death, they will be left with a challenge to God's perfection. On the other hand, if they devise a theodicy for why God allows death, they will have to explain why Isaiah looks forward to a day when death will be abolished. This dilemma parallels a general dilemma about evil: Theodicies explain why it is good to have evil in the world, yet we want evil to be abolished, and evil is certainly not the target of eschatological hopes.

Here, though, are a few accounts of why death exists (besides the notion that the afterlife is better):

(1) As already stated, there must be a difference between God and humans as regards mortality.
(2) Humans are made out of matter. Per Plato and Aristotle, all material things perish. This does not mean that death is a good thing, just that it is inevitable. The natural next theodic question is why humans are made of matter. Perhaps that can be explained in terms of ideas like the Great Chain of Being and Principle of Plenitude.[77] The basic idea of these principles is that the world contains many diverse sorts of entities, and this variety contributes to its goodness. Matter is part of a robust universe.

---

[75] The question is also raised in the continuation of *Bereshit Rabbah* 9:5 (after R. Meir's statement).

[76] Followers of Epicurus and Lucretius will argue that death isn't bad because (a) in death there is no sentience and no pain; (b) if X is dead, X cannot be the subject of any predicates and cannot be undergoing an evil. These arguments have been the subject of many a discussion, e.g., Kagan 2012, 205–33. But they have not been salient in Jewish philosophy.

[77] Maimonides 1963, 504, 506 (*Guide of the Perplexed* 3:25).

(3) Maimonides also argues that the perishing of material things is necessary for propagation of the species.[78]
(4) Death is a punishment for Adam's sin, inflicted on his descendants. (In a passage we cited earlier, the angels question why the punishment was inflicted.)
(5) If human beings were to live forever, courage and seriousness of purpose would be lost, indolence would set in, and we could not achieve self-sacrifice.[79] The possibility of martyrdom, of giving one's life for the highest values, depends on death's being a reality.
(6) There is the problem of boredom – in Bernard Williams's (1973a) memorable phrase, "the tedium of immortality." Williams argues that if one lives very long, one loses the desires that constituted one's identity.[80]
(7) Awareness of mortality punctures arrogance.[81]
(8) Soloveitchik advances two further arguments. One is that we must distinguish between the value of death for the individual and its value for the community. "Death … is an evil experience if viewed from the perspective of individual existence. However if seen under the aspect of the total destiny of man as such, the elimination of the old and obsolete or the departure of people who belong mentally to a different age is the greatest of blessings" (Soloveitchik 2002, 126–27).[82] Gerald Blidstein (2012, 143–44) pointedly summarizes Soloveitchik's reasoning: "[D]eath is the price of renewal and enrichment … Mental attachment to the past [on the part of an older generation] demands their replacement by others who are more appropriate for the present." Different times require, for example, different sorts of leaders. For death to disappear altogether would leave a *vastly* counterutilitarian result – the stifling of potential change.[83]

---

[78] See ibid., 440 (3:10). Cf. the problems raised in Shatz 2021, 230–35.
[79] See Kass 2001. Kass has argued for curbing antiaging scientific endeavors. Cf. Linden 2022.
[80] See also Kagan 2012, ch. 10. Cf. Fischer 2011.
[81] Soloveitchik 2002, 131.
[82] See also Blidstein 2012, 139–51. Soloveitchik's rationale is (unknowingly) echoed by the late famed American entrepreneur Steven Jobs: "Death is very likely the single best invention of life. It's life's change agent. It clears out the old to make way for the new." See also Nuland 1995.
[83] Notably, Soloveitchik elsewhere argued, as we have seen, that Judaism values life and "abhors death."

(9) Soloveitchik's second argument is tied to the legacy (or "social") conception of immortality:

> Death gives man the opportunity ... to build even though he knows that he will not live to enjoy the sight of the magnificent edifice in whose construction he is engaged... to enrich – not himself, but coming generations. Death teaches man to transcend his physical self and to identify with the timeless covenantal community ... It enhances his role as a historic being and sensitizes his moral consciousness. [Soloveitchik 2002, 4]

One must learn self-sacrifice; one must identify with the future community and understand one's significance in bringing it about. Every person must leave room for others to later fulfill *their* potential. "It is not your obligation to finish the work, but you are not so free as to neglect it" (*Avot* 2:16). Death provides human beings with heroic opportunities. It is appropriate to label this approach a soul-making theodicy for death. Scheffler (2013), in his secular perspective, makes the point that not only are future people dependent on us, but we are dependent on them if we are to lead successful lives.

CONCLUSION

The Bible refers to an afterlife, and the Rabbis of the talmudic period speak extensively of resurrection of the dead. Post-Talmud, while Sa'adyah highlighted resurrection, Maimonides highlighted immortality, generating much controversy. Mystics opted for a model of reincarnation.

The choice of an outlook is not always defended by texts or straightforwardly philosophical arguments, though those are of course very important. Considerations of fit, symbolism, and psychological impact may be applied as well. Finally, Jewish tradition reflects the conflicting pulls of, on the one hand, the great value of a life of *mitzvot* and the concomitant notion that death is an evil – and, on the other hand, the faith that God will provide us, posthumously, if we merit it, something better than we have here.

PART III

GOD IN RELATION TO HUMANITY

8

Divine Commands and Human Morality

What is the relationship between religion and morality? We have here not one question but many.

The question that most quickly springs to mind is the following loose variant of an issue posed by Plato in the *Euthyphro* (10a):

Is an action right because God commands it, or does God command it because it is right? Similarly, is an action wrong because God prohibits it, or does God prohibit it because it is wrong? In short, is "divine command morality" a correct theory of morality?[1]

This query has been or can be worded in a variety of other ways:

- Is there a correct standard of ethics that is independent of God's command?
- Is there a correct standard of ethics that is independent of God's will?[2]

---

[1] I call these "loose variants" of Plato's question because Plato speaks of "pious," not "right"; "pious" is a religiously charged term. Also, Plato speaks of the gods, not God; and of what the gods *love*, not of what they *command*. Lebens 2023a, 136–39, usefully suggests that Plato's question be formulated as whether God's command is "explanatorily prior" to an action's rightness or wrongness, or instead the reverse. Usually, by contrast, the formulation of Plato's question is in terms of the *meaning* of ethical terms. Lebens also notes that even if an act is right or wrong independent of God's command, God's command may be the only way to create ethical *obligation*. This position resembles that of Berkovits 2002, 14–17. In cases where God has not explicitly commanded that we do or refrain from X, the approach excludes the possibility of a moral obligation to do X even when doing X is right or refraining from doing X is wrong on nontheistic grounds. Yet Jewish law, as we will see, sometimes incorporates moral judgments *and* obligations that are not the subject of a divine command. A way out here is to posit that God commands us to incorporate all moral rights and wrongs into the scope of our legal obligation, an option considered later.

[2] The difference between divine command and divine will be explained later.

- Is it the case that, in the words attributed (imprecisely) to Dostoevsky's character Ivan Karamazov, "If there is no God, everything is permitted"? Or are there ethical truths that would hold even if there were no God?
- Is a purely secular account of "right" and "wrong" possible?

The question we just posed in different forms may be termed ontological; it concerns the *existence* of an independent ethical standard (independent of God's commands). This is not to say that ethical standards might exist in the concrete, perceptible, and tangible way that doughnuts and airplanes do, but only that the question has the form of an inquiry into an existence claim.

Let us label the ontological question as Question 1. We may pose other questions in addition:

Question 2: If there *is* a standard of ethics independent of God's will, can human beings *know it* without revelation? This is an epistemic question.[3]

Question 3: If there is a standard of ethics independent of God's will and human beings can know it without revelation, should they nonetheless be *motivated* to practice God's prescribed ethics out of obedience to His will, and not because it reflects a correct independent standard? Or, should they be motivated instead by independent moral reasoning? Or perhaps by natural feelings, such as compassion and love for one's neighbor?

Question 4: If there is a correct standard of ethics independent of God's will and human beings can know it without revelation, may the (rabbinic) authorities who decide Jewish law utilize that standard (or what they believe to be that standard) in making their decisions? Or must they follow only expressly formulated rules of Jewish law? This is a jurisprudential question.

Question 5: If there is a correct standard of ethics independent of God's will, what is its content in Jewish sources? Utilitarian? Deontological? Virtue ethics? Ethics of care? Some combination of these?

---

[3] The word "standard" here is a catch-all for the elements of an ethical system, including, inter alia, intuitions and judgments about individual cases and intuitions and judgments about rules. The term "natural law" is often used as a synonym for "a correct standard of ethics knowable through reason," but it has other associations (such as a teleological picture of the world) and is used in a different sense later in this chapter, so I mostly avoid it in my formulations.

Let's consider these issues. For ease of discussion, I will bracket the question of whether there may be *more than one* correct standard.

QUESTIONS 1–2: IS THERE AN INDEPENDENT STANDARD OF ETHICS? IS IT KNOWABLE?

As explained in the introduction to this book, an ideal "Jewish" theory would be both philosophically cogent and rooted in classic texts. But this ideal is sometimes not attainable, because often no account satisfies both requirements. Moreover, it is sometimes difficult even to find a single unambiguous classic text as support for one's view. In an extensive study, R. Michael Harris (2003) has formulated no fewer than fifteen claims that are variants either of divine command morality or of its negation. Some of his formulations are ontological, others epistemological. Moreover, Harris carefully and critically analyzes numerous biblical and rabbinic texts that have been enlisted by religious thinkers to determine whether there is a correct ethical standard that is independent of God, and whether that standard is knowable. His approach to the texts proceeds with these fifteen distinctions in mind. His conclusion (2003, 154): "All attempts to present such a monochromatic view [on these questions] are flawed."

Harris's treatment demonstrates the multifarious ambiguities and nuances in biblical and rabbinic texts; many texts that initially appear clearcut are open to conflicting readings. Read one way, a text seems to support divine command theory; read another way, it denies the theory or is compatible with several variants of it. Important for Harris in locating ambiguities is the distinction between the explicit, revealed divine command and the non-explicit, unrevealed divine will.[4] For example, even if we cannot have knowledge of right and wrong (in general or in specific circumstances) by means of a divine *command*, we might be able to acquire that knowledge of right and wrong in the absence of a command by tapping into the divine *will*. Thus, when God holds Cain responsible for killing his brother (Gen. 4), Harris suggests, the text is compatible both with the claim that he should have known on his own, autonomously, not to kill, *and* with the claim that he is blamed because, even in the absence of command, he should have grasped God's *will*. It is clear, Harris believes, that some texts reject some important versions

---

[4] See also Murphy 1998.

of the divine command theory, but they are often compatible with both an independent standard theory and a divine will theory. In this way he objects to several prominent thinkers who paint a monolithic picture (Louis Jacobs, Isaiah Leibowitz, Aharon Lichtenstein, Marvin Fox, and Avi Sagi). The possibility that one can fulfill God's commands without fulfilling God's will, and fulfill His will while violating His command, is found in Ḥasidic thought,[5] and the notion that one can *grasp* God's will without a specific command for one's circumstances is central for some recent Jewish thinkers.[6] So, too, is the notion that God implants intuitions in us that enable us to discern His will without having a command.

While respectful of Harris's wise caveats about ambiguity, I nonetheless venture to raise some arguments for or against particular readings of biblical and rabbinic texts.

Biblical Materials

The Akedah *(Binding of Isaac)*

It is impossible to discuss all of the relevant texts pertaining to biblical morality. One in particular, however, has utterly dominated discussion of the topic: the *akedah* or binding of Isaac (Gen. 22).[7] In Genesis 22, God commands Abraham to take "your son, your only son, the one you love, Isaac" – and make him a sacrificial offering.[8] In *Fear and Trembling*, the Danish philosopher Søren Kierkegaard (1813–1855) characterizes Abraham as the "knight of faith," whose greatness consists in obeying God even while he remains conscious of the moral imperative and its Kantian force. He did the absurd: Abraham was prepared to commit an act whose religious description is "sacrifice," even while its ethical description is "murder." The *akedah* demands a "teleological suspension of the ethical" (suspension for a higher purpose).

Contrary to a prevalent perception, Kierkegaard is not advocating a "divine command morality"; he is not saying that an act is right only because God commands or permits it, and wrong only because God

---

[5] See, e.g., the interesting analyses in Gellman 1994 and 2019, 94–96.
[6] E.g., Wurzburger 1994.
[7] This section and the next (on *Gan Eden*) are revised versions of an article originally coauthored with Shalom Carmy.
[8] On another reading of the Hebrew, possibly motivated by ethical discomfort with the plain reading of the text, God's command is only that Abraham bring Isaac up the mountain to place him on the altar, so that technically Abraham wasn't commanded to sacrifice Isaac. But see Harris 2003, 129–33.

prohibits it. On the contrary: It is precisely because morality *has* independent value, and Abraham would and should *ordinarily* cling to it – when there is no conflicting divine command – that Abraham's choice is so significant. The *akedah* narrative in a Kierkegaardian framework *supports* the existence and knowability of an independent ethical standard *along with* the possibility of God commanding an immoral act.[9] (Were the standard not knowable, Abraham's choice would be unconflicted.)

Kierkegaard gave *arguments* for a religious person having to embrace the absurd. For example, to be religious (for Kierkegaard), Abraham must override all else that is valuable in his life. For a religious commitment requires passion; and just as in the case of a man's love for a woman, passion is measured by how much a person is willing to risk and give up for her, so, too, your passion for God is measured by how much you are willing to give up for Him. *Part of the required price is the possibility of surrender of intellect and moral sense and the willingness to act against all odds and all evidence.* There is nothing *religious* about rational or moral considerations, Kierkegaard maintains, albeit they do have value of another, secular kind.[10]

This understanding of religion should be rejected, I believe; basically, it says that the crazier a religion is (intellectually or morally), the more religious it is. So, as Louis Pojman remarked (1979, 168–69), the irrationalist approach makes Charles Manson's cult more religious than Roman Catholicism. The implication of Kierkegaard's perspective is that true religion requires being fanatical – impervious to rational, moral, and even pragmatic considerations. Rejecting this allure of the absurd means rejecting the argument of the fanatical person of faith, who massacres innocent people and claims that faith requires suspension of the ethical.[11]

But suppose that Kierkegaard's view of religion is highly problematic. This just compounds the challenge – for doesn't the biblical text affirm this objectionable Kierkegaardian thesis, thereby creating moral alarm about the *akedah*'s whole religious orientation? No. For all its power and popularity, Kierkegaard's interpretation of the narrative as depicting a clash between divine command and Abraham's sense of morality, and as identifying religious heroism with the suspension of morality for a higher purpose, is neither the best literary fit to the text nor the view of

---

[9] Harris 2003, 120–23, cites a number of scholars who err on this point.
[10] Isaiah (Yeshayahu) Leibowitz (1992) advocated at least this minimal position.
[11] See also Koller 2020, 96. Adams 1977 assesses two other arguments Kierkegaard gives against using rational arguments in religion.

the ancient Sages.¹² First of all, aside from the fact that child sacrifice was part of Abraham's milieu – so that a command to sacrifice a child would appear morally unexceptionable – the command to sacrifice a child, especially an only child, could be said to make sense. To live a committed life in the presence of God is to be prepared to part with one's most precious possessions. Abraham, on this view, would not have seen such a sacrifice as immoral, not just because others were sacrificing their children, but because – this will sound egregiously crude – a case can be made for the value and importance of the practice.

Instead of viewing God's command as in conflict with morality, the Midrash and liturgy depict Abraham as called upon to suppress fatherly love for the son in whom he had invested all hopes, this for the sake of serving God properly.¹³ Of Abraham, the daily Jewish liturgy and the *musaf* prayer on Rosh Hashanah state: "He conquered his *raḥamim* [compassion], so as to do your will wholeheartedly."¹⁴ So, whereas Kierkegaard views the *akedah* as a clash between morality and God's command, it is at least equally compelling, if not more compelling, to leave out the theme of divine command vs. human morality and instead view Abraham's plight as a clash between parental love/compassion and God's command.¹⁵ Note that if the message were one about morality, the command could just as well have been to sacrifice some stranger.

But can we really shake the conviction that God's command is immoral? At this point it must be emphasized that, at the bottom line, Abraham never kills Isaac. An angel of God comes down and enjoins him from going ahead. "Do not lay your hand upon the child; do nothing to him" (Gen. 22:12). Thus, Abraham expresses his passion for God by bringing Isaac up to the site of the altar, but ultimately the angel of God forbids sacrifice of a child. Although such sacrifice makes *religious* sense, it is at the end of the day *objectionable to God*, as God *will shape His own demands according to the value of human life*. As Aaron Koller (2020, 140) writes, "God wants child sacrifice, as an expression of love and commitment. But God *more* [my emphasis] does not want it, as a reflection of a higher value," viz. human life. The ultimate upshot of the

---

¹² On the points that follow, see also Green 1988, 77–102; Korn 1997, 23–25; Levinas 1996, 76; Levenson 1998; Koller 2020; Weiss 2018, 27–31. Cf. Wettstein 2020.

¹³ He had been led to believe that Isaac would be his heir; see Gen. 21:12.

¹⁴ In some of the prayers known as *seliḥot*, recited in the High Holiday season, Abraham and Isaac complied without conflict or ambivalence, even joyously.

¹⁵ Baḥya ben Asher, in his commentary, views the clash as between love of his child and love of God. (My thanks to Michael Harris for noting this.)

episode, if not its point, is to *prohibit* child sacrifice, even while the beginning of the narrative implicitly acknowledges its logic. Had Kierkegaard assigned the ending of the narrative due weight, he could not have sustained his thesis that in Genesis 22 religion is contrary to everyday morality. The lesson we draw from the end of the episode is the opposite of Kierkegaard's: It's that "murder is never a legitimate way to worship the God of Israel."[16] Religious passion per se is good; but fittingly, R. Abraham Isaac Kook understands the *akedah* as extolling "passion without fanaticism."[17] Religious acts must be controlled by sanity, morality, and compassion. We must not conflate *akedah* and al Qaeda.[18]

Perhaps the most widely cited evidence that the Bible endorses a knowable independent ethical standard lies where Abraham remonstrates with God not to destroy the city of Sodom: "Will you destroy the righteous with the wicked? Far be it from you! Will the judge of all the earth not do justice?" (Gen. 18:25). If God's will alone determined right and wrong, Abraham's plea and perhaps also God's ceding the point would be senseless. Now, Abraham could be protesting that, in destroying the righteous with the wicked, God would be violating His *own* standards, not some independent standard. But this retort still implies there is an independent ethics. For what would be wrong with violating one's own standards, if there is no valid independent ethic that dictates its wrongness?

The difference between Abraham's acquiescence at the *akedah* and his protest that it would be unjust of God to destroy the righteous of Sodom together with its wicked requires explanation. We have one in hand: Child sacrifice was not something Abraham initially viewed as immoral; and as Jon Levenson (1998, 272) observes, there's a difference between an unjust execution (Sodom) and sacrificial worship.

The Garden of Eden

Obscured by the attention lavished on the *akedah* is the much earlier *Gan Eden* (Garden of Eden) narrative and the ensuing chapters

---

[16] Korn 1997, 24. See also Harris 2003, 126–29.
[17] As paraphrased by Carmy 1997, 473–78. See Kook 1986, 158–60, (1985c 2:#379), and also Gellman 1994, 104–16 and Koller 2020. Unfortunately, one pernicious effect of Kierkegaard's influence is that modern thinkers portray Abraham simply as a child abuser, someone who took the wrong horn of the dilemma Kierkegaard sets out between morality and religion. For examples, see Levenson 1998 and Koller 2020, passim. For a classic study of *midrashim* concerning the *akedah*, see Spiegel 1979.
[18] Cf. Harris 2003, 128.

in Genesis. Adam and Eve are driven out of the garden because they violated the first divine command, "And from the tree of knowledge of good and evil, do not eat" (Gen. 2:17). The text suggests that the reason for the injunction was pinpointed by the serpent: "For God knows that on the day you eat from [the tree] your eyes will be opened and you will be like gods, knowing good and evil" (3:5). While we may be inclined to see the serpent's explanation as part of his duplicitous scheme for inducing Eve to sin – it tries to put the command in a bad light – the serpent's account is vindicated later in the story: "And the Lord God said, 'now that man *has become like one of us, knowing the difference between good and evil*, perhaps now he will stretch out his hand, eat also from the tree of life, and will live forever'" (3:22). So Adam and Eve are banished.

If "knowledge of good and evil" is the capacity to make moral discriminations, why would God begrudge this knowledge to human beings? In response, classical construals of "knowers of good and evil" demote its status to a *lower* rung: knowers of sexual passion, knowers of sensual temptation, and knowers of conventional moral judgments as distinct from knowers of theoretical truths.[19] These readings are problematic because they place God – who we are told "knows good and evil" (3:22) – at whatever lower level the interpreters claim Adam and Eve have sunk to by becoming "knowers."

Michael Wyschogrod (2004) offers a way out, a proposal that accounts for 3:22. According to Wyschogrod, "knowers of good and evil" means: beings who make autonomous judgments of good and evil grounded in their own criteria of right and wrong. The turning point in human history was:

And the woman saw that the tree was good for eating and that it was attractive to the eyes and desirable as a source of wisdom. She took from its fruit and ate; and she also gave it to her man with her and he ate. (Gen. 3:6)

The literary allusion is unmistakable: This marks the first time that anyone other than God "saw that [it] was good" (a phrase oft used in Gen. 1) – that is, made value judgments. God made another judgment in chapter 2: "It is not good for the man to be alone" (Gen. 2:18) The point is not so much that the woman made a *wrong* decision, but that the fact God had prohibited the fruit had *no motivational impact* on

---

[19] See Nahmanides, commentary to Gen. 2:9; Maimonides, *Guide of the Perplexed* 1:2; and other sources quoted in N. Leibowitz 1981, 17–27.

her; her decision to eat or not to eat was based upon her own criteria and reasons.[20] The woman had become an autonomous judger. The lack of a stated (or logical) rationale in God's original directive alerts us to its heteronomous character.

Two perhaps unexpected consequences emerge from this reading. First, what if Eve had decided to refrain from eating but only because she found the fruit unattractive? This, too, would have been wrong; for she would have been as unresponsive to God's command as she was when she decided to eat. Second, it isn't that by eating from the tree of knowledge one becomes an autonomous judger. Rather, eating from the tree *shows that* one has made an autonomous judgment. Eating is a symptom, not a cause.

No wonder that later, when Adam explains to God that he hid because he was naked, God scolds him: "Who told you that you are naked? Did you eat from the tree from which I commanded you not to eat?" (Gen. 3:11). If Adam judged that nakedness is shameful, he has judged autonomously.[21]

Wyschogrod's explanation of the sin dovetails with a general motif in Genesis 1, the drawing and preserving of boundaries. Once humans sinned by producing their own judgments, God feared that they will now strive to become immortal as well, usurping another prerogative of the divine (Gen. 3:22). So He banishes them. As for the serpent's charge that God just wants to keep His turf, the hierarchical structure is how things ought to be.

Wyschogrod stops here, and his account thus far is compelling. But when we go further in Genesis, to a sequel he overlooked, we get a much more complex understanding and need to write a large addendum to his analysis. True enough, in chapter 3, God does not want humans to make autonomous judgments. But in chapter 4, Cain kills Abel; as in the case of Adam and Eve, God seeks out and confronts the sinner, and the words by which He does – to Adam, "*ayyekah*" ("where are you?"), to Cain, "*ai Hevel aḥikha*" ("where is your brother Hevel?") – suggests that we are to link the episodes. This time, as well, he holds the sinner accountable (Gen. 4:10ff.). But this time the sinner is not accused of disobeying a command – indeed, the text mentions no explicit

---

[20] This is not to deny that the introduction of sensuality into her thinking is also a critical part of the verse.
[21] See Wyschogrod 2004, 57. Wyschogrod does not directly explain *why* they were now embarrassed by nakedness; precisely at this point, his approach may be combined with the exegesis that relates the "knowledge of good and evil" to sexual arousal.

prohibition of murder.[22] And whereas Adam became a knower (*yodea*), Cain is held accountable for *not* knowing, for evading the responsibility of applying his judgment correctly: "I do not know [*lo yadati*]! Am I my brother's keeper?" To which God retorts, "What have you done? Your brother's blood cries out to me from the earth!" (Gen. 4:10). Here is some sort of rational argument (to be sure a cryptic one). Post-Eden, God expects humans to make moral judgments of their own; concomitantly, they cannot avoid accountability for the judgments they make.

As against the independent standard view, Harris maintains that Cain should have tapped into the divine will even in the absence of a command, of legislation. And that is God's rebuke of him. But this sort of penetration of God's will itself requires a large measure of autonomous judgment.[23] Further, the command/will distinction is absent in the text, and it is too important for the Torah to have left out if it meant to implement it.

Several generations later, the world is destroyed by the flood because of human violence. Naḥmanides maintains (in his commentary to Gen. 6:2) that the sinfulness of social corruption can be grasped independent of revealed divine injunction – and the text indeed mentions no injunction.[24] The transfer of power to human beings continues in augmented form after the deluge. When the world is recreated by the family of Noah after the flood,[25] human beings are given even more prerogatives. They may now eat animals and may now apply capital punishment for the sin of murder (Gen. 9:6).[26] God had in effect legislated against anyone killing Cain, by placing a mark upon him, so the permission in Genesis 9:6 to judge and to kill murderers takes on added significance.

True to this expanding autonomy and responsibility, characters in Genesis apply independent moral reflection. Twice Abraham lies to a

---

[22] Using their distinctive hermeneutics, the Rabbis (in *Sanhedrin* 56a) inferred a prohibition against murder from God's instruction to Adam in 2:17 concerning the trees in the garden. But putting aside general perplexities about such inferences (known as *midreshei Halakhah*), which stray very far from the plain meanings of verses, the biblical text makes no reference to any command, so even if there was one, it was irrelevant in God's rebuke of Cain.

[23] See also Sztuden 2018b, 44.

[24] Harris's distinction between God's commands and God's will may be brought into play – here, more persuasively – because one way of portraying the prediluvian sin is as violence, and Cain had already been punished for violence, which indicates for us the divine will.

[25] On the theme of re-creation, see Fishbane 1979, 3–39.

[26] For further development, see Steinmetz 1994.

king, saying that Sarah (his wife) is his sister in order to save himself from attack by men who want to have relations with Sarah (Gen. 10:12–20, 20:1–18). The sons of Jacob kill the Shekhemites because those people, they say, have turned their sister Dinah into a harlot; the text cites a brief debate between them and their father over the propriety of their deed (Gen. 34:30–31), but renders no judgment. Covenants are made and kept, reflecting the judgment that they are binding. Personalities quarrel and make ethical arguments. Societies in Genesis are built not on prescriptions imposed from without but on moral thinking. Sometimes it is ambiguous whether characters did the right thing; this highlights individual responsibility. Here again, one might suggest that, even though these characters did not receive a divine command, perhaps they were expected to discern the divine *will*. But it is not clear on what basis they could be expected to know that will, or how autonomous reason could fail to infuse their judgment.

Samuel Lebens (2020b, 205) writes: "this God [in Genesis] will punish evil, and promote justice, but he also wants people to work out things for themselves. He's not a *legislator*." Now, God *in effect* legislates by punishing Cain and imposing a penalty on anyone who kills him during his punitive wanderings; moreover, he explicitly legislates by his prescriptions to Noah after the flood about what can and cannot be eaten ("flesh in its lifeblood" cannot be) and about the death penalty (Gen. 9:6). In addition, individual divine instructions may reflect some larger moral principle. But even if He is to some extent a legislator, certainly the rightness or wrongness of much conduct is left ambiguous and does not fall under any legislation.

Only at Sinai does God issue a lengthy set of commands (Exod. 19), and questions about how to act will no longer typically be answered by giving human beings autonomy to judge morality – only legality. Yet even after Sinai, God responds to moral give-and-take. When, for example, the daughters of Tzelofḥad argue that their father's estate ought not to pass from the family simply because he left no sons, God ratifies their claim (and likely their moral arguments – "the daughters of Tzelofḥad speak correctly") and stipulates that daughters inherit in such circumstances (Num. 27:1–11).[27]

---

[27] Uncertainty about what to do arises also in Num. 16:32–36 (the man who chopped wood on the Sabbath). In this and the case of Tzelofḥad's daughters, Moses inquires of God what to do, and a clear divine legislation ensues, but, again, God responds to moral reasons in the latter case.

In sum, before the sin of Adam and Eve, human beings are expected to hearken to God's command and not initiate autonomous moral reflection. That expectation is altered after the sin and as a result of the sin. Sinai represents the restoration of heteronomous commands. But even after Sinai, God is responsive to moral dialectic and acts with justice. We have in these reflections affirmations of both an ontological and an epistemic claim: the existence of an independent ethical standard and our ability to access it. David Novak (2008) argues that, before there can be a revelation at Sinai, there must be a society grounded in natural law (a rationally discoverable ethical standard and code).[28]

Gratitude and Moral Judgment

The existence and cognitive accessibility of an independent standard can be illustrated by means of a single verse: "Give thanks to the Lord because He is good, His lovingkindness is forever [*hodu la-Shem ki tov ki le-olam ḥasdo*]" (Ps. 18:1, 136:1). It appears that "We should thank the Lord" is thought by the psalmist to follow logically from "The Lord has done good for us." But how can this inference hold unless we endorse the *moral principle*, "One should thank a benefactor"?[29] Additionally, we thank God for good things He has done and also praise Him for His actions. Isn't this based on *our* appraisal of what is good? To adapt a point made by Gottfried von Wilhelm Leibniz (1989, 7) about *praising* God: Why thank Him *for* what He has done, if you would thank Him even had He done the contrary?

Hear too this vigorous statement by John Stuart Mill (1996, 10:53):

> Why should I obey my maker? From gratitude? Then gratitude is itself obligatory, independently of my maker's will. From reverence and love? But why is he a proper object of love and reverence? ... Is it because he is just, righteous and merciful? Then these attributes are in themselves good, independently of his pleasures.

Other religious gestures and attitudes make no sense if there is no independent ethical standard. Think of the problem of evil, which is so central to religious thinking and pervades biblical and rabbinic thought. As discussed in Chapter 3, anyone who is troubled by the existence of

---

[28] Albeit Novak's theory of natural law is more complex – he requires that natural law be articulated in traditions.
[29] Some medieval Jewish thinkers saw gratitude as the basis for the obligation to obey divine commands. See, e.g., Baḥya 1970, parts 2–3.

evil, anyone who asks how God could allow the Temples' destruction or the Holocaust, for example, is imposing some external standard of morality on God. Since the prophets wondered how these-or-those evil events can happen, they must be endorsing such a standard. If it will be said that their objection is that God is violating *His own* norms, they are still applying a human standard – one that says beings must act in accordance with their own standards.[30]

Once we look at our actual reactions and judgments in various contexts, we see how central trust in such judgments is in religious life. The most basic religious attitudes and practices – praise, worship, calling God good, feeling gratitude to Him, wondering how He allows evil – depend upon that trust, on having standards that allow religious people to affirm with surety, "God is worthy of worship," "We ought to praise Him for the good He has done," "We ought to thank Him," and so on. And we utilize our moral sense when we raise the problem of evil. While human moral intuition may on occasion mislead, large-scale distrust in it would destroy the basis for many proper attitudes and practices.

Numerous examples have been given by rabbinic writers to substantiate the role of moral reason, and/or moral intuition, and/or natural feelings of disgust. Why were oaths binding in the biblical narratives, before Sinai? Why is the Israelites' oath to accept the Torah binding, unless oaths are binding independent of Torah law?[31] Why are public nudity and cannibalism wrong, even though there is no technical law prohibiting them?[32]

This is not to deny the undeniable – that divine laws sometimes clash with human moral sensibilities, as in the case of the commandment to destroy the Amalekite people. We will address this later in this chapter. But at this point I turn to talmudic and midrashic thought about morality and divine command. The sources combine ontological and epistemic questions.

The Epistemic Question in Talmud and Midrash

In Leviticus 18:4, the Bible states: "You shall observe *ḥukkotai* and perform *mishpatai*, by whose performance one lives – I am the Lord." Now,

---

[30] Cf. Harris's (2003, 64) principle (M).
[31] Avraham Bornsztayn, *Avnei Nezer, Yoreh De'ah* 2:#306. See also Hutner 1974, 123.
[32] Glazner 1977, introduction, and commentary to *Hullin* 89b.

both *hukkotai* (from *hok*) and *mishpatai* (from *mishpat*) mean, "my laws," "my ordinances," or "my statutes." Why, then, does the verse use both words, rather than one?

The Sages characteristically explain ostensible redundancy by means of distinctions. Here they replied by distinguishing two kinds of *mitzvot* (commandments): *mishpatim* (singular: *mishpat*) and *hukkim* (singular: *hok*).

> "You should perform *mishpatai* [my *mishpatim*]" – These refer to matters [here, laws] such that, had they not been written, they should have been written [or, logic dictates that they be written]. These are the prohibitions against *avodah zarah* ["foreign worship" – worship of a being other than God, as in idolatry], adultery, murder, robbery, and blasphemy. "You shall observe *hukkotai* [my *hukkim*]" – these are matters [laws] that the Satan challenges. These are: the prohibitions against eating pork and wearing *sha'atnez* [clothing with a mixture of wool and linen], [and the ritual of] *halitzat yevamah* [see Deut. 25:5–10], purifying a leper [see Lev. 14], and the service of the scapegoat [see Lev. 16]. Lest you say that these are empty acts, the Torah states, "I am the Lord" – I decreed it, and you have no permission to question it. [*Yoma* 67b][33]

The Talmud, then, depicts *mishpatim* as laws such that, "had they not been written, they should have been written." These laws are not binding only because of revelation; for they are worthy of being followed even were there no revelation. Contrary to "If there is no God, everything is permitted," the talmudic passage at hand maintains that certain prohibitions are binding independent of revelation. Perhaps some unstated ones qualify as well.

This talmudic passage appears to *reject* "divine-command theories" of ethics. The Sages' notion that certain commandments ought to have been written even if they weren't in Scripture seems to imply that not only do some of God's commands match independent (call them secular) notions of right and wrong, but God commands them *because* they are right or wrong independent of His command. To be sure, the Sages' phrase "had they not been written, they should have been written" may be construed as saying only that these laws promote social utility. However, social utility is itself an ethical obligation (when it does not conflict with other obligations) and, moreover, one that may be rationally grounded.[34]

---

[33] The wording of this passage differs a bit from the wording of parallel passages in the Midrash, with respect to the examples given and the identity of the challengers.

[34] Even the great positivist H. L. A. Hart (1961, 193–99) concedes that achieving social order, which law aims at, is a moral goal. Cf. Fox 2003d, 185.

At the same time, the text does not imply that this ethic is *knowable* without the divine command. Perhaps the expression "had they not been written, they should have been written," means that while we could not have *figured out* the ethical truth on our own, we can appreciate it once it is explicitly commanded. We might not be able to figure out the proof of a given mathematical proposition or theory in physics on our own; but we (or specialists) can nevertheless appreciate the truth of the proposition or theory once it is presented. So too, perhaps we can appreciate the rightness of a given ethical command *only* once it has been commanded through revelation.

Alternatively, "had they not been written, they should have been written," could be affirming not only the existence of an independent ethic, but also our epistemic ability to discover the truth on our own, without ever being presented with ethical truths by revelation. Both readings are admissible, but, on the first, if a situation arises that is not explicitly addressed in the revelation, how could we trust our moral judgments?

Also relevant here is the topic of Noahide laws. The Talmud teaches that non-Jews (Noahides) are commanded to observe seven *mitzvot*:

> Seven *mitzvot* were commanded to Noahides [gentiles]: the prohibitions against illicit sexual relations, murder, theft, blasphemy, *avodah zarah*, and eating the limb of a living animal, and the duty to establish a court system. [Sanhedrin 56a]

It is commonplace to view the Noahide laws as reflecting a knowable, universal independent standard of ethics, what is often called natural law. But the case of Noahide laws underscores Harris's point about ambiguity, because the talmudic discussion does not fit the commonplace perception. The text describes Noahide laws as *commanded* (*nitztavvu benei Noah* – gentiles were commanded) and does not mention independent accessibility; also, none of the various derivations of the laws in the Talmud appeal to reason;[35] finally, additional candidates proposed for Noahide laws (such as prohibitions against sorcery and castration) do not fit the mold.[36] In later times, the laws were nevertheless considered to be derivable from reason, and it may be that, as scholars have suggested in other instances, ethical reflection lurks unexpressed behind the rabbinic textual derivations in the talmudic discussion. Another reason to attribute to the Sages belief in an independent standard is that they are

---

[35] But cf. Sztuden 2018b, 45–46.
[36] See also Fox 2003c, 65–66.

troubled by the existence of certain laws that seem immoral, a topic we will discuss later.[37]

At this point, we need to ponder more the significance of certain laws being derivable *in principle* without revelation. Set aside the deep and important skepticism many philosophers have about our ability to *actually* derive ethics from reason.[38] Let's assume, however controversially, that we can trust ethical intuition and argument. It is one thing to say that a certain general principle ("taking another's property without permission is wrong," "killing is wrong"[39]) can be derived by reason without revelation or can be comprehended as rational once it has been issued. It is another to say that reason can determine the correct ruling for every situation. And finding *detailed* rulings is what matters for Jewish practice. Some examples used by Sa'adyah Gaon (Saadia Gaon 1948) in a different context are helpful here (145–47 [3:3]). Reason can derive the principle that theft is wrong, but a definition of theft requires a definition of property, and there are many ways to specify when an object becomes someone's property. Likewise, reason can derive the principle that adultery is wrong, but a definition of adultery requires a definition of marriage, and there are many ways to specify how a marriage is effected. So too for punishment – crimes must be punished, but what is the right punishment for each crime, and should punishment vary from person to person? Likewise for expressing gratitude, and likewise for prayer. To affix the specifics, the community may often come to details by means of *sevarah* (logical

---

[37] Sagi and Statman (1995) believe that only one rabbinic source expresses a clear affirmation of divine command morality – namely, the passage by R. Shapira we encountered in Chapter 3. Other rabbinic texts, they think, only go so far as asserting that human beings have limited knowledge of an independent standard and therefore need divine commands – e.g., to define theft. Sagi and Statman cite R. Ovadyah Bartenura, commentary to Mishnah *Avot* 1:1; R. Moses Isserles, *Torat ha-Olah* 3:71; and Ḥazon Ish (Karelitz 1997, 27). A sample from Ḥazon Ish illustrates where they see ambiguity: "The definitions of robbery and violence are not interpreted according to human opinion, but only by the Torah's laws. Any act opposed to these laws is robbery, even if people do not agree. And any act that adheres to *din* [law] constitutes justice even if this runs contrary to human opinion." Isserles wrote: "There are things that are good or evil from the standpoint of *nimmus* [humanly made law], but are not from the standpoint of the Torah." My own sense is that these are divine command theories of some sort and not pointers to epistemic limitations. But this is hard to prove, which is Sagi and Statman's point.

[38] Attributing this skepticism to the Sages is anomalous: it would seem that the Sages had to make the derivation themselves in order to *know* that the *mishpatim* could be thus derived, whether before revelation or after. It can be countered that they know the derivation could be made solely on linguistic grounds, because of the need to find a distinction between *ḥok* and *mishpat*.

[39] These are meant as prima facie principles.

argument), but often *sevarah* is not powerful enough and we must turn to religious authorities. (Saʿadyah says we need "prophets," but it is the Rabbis who answer the legal questions.) If reason cannot arrive at the answers, though, is there *any* reason to choose one definition of property (for example) over the others? If not, doesn't that imply that there could have been a different body of law that would be equally good? At one point Saʿadyah (Saadia Gaon 1948, 147) writes that "if we were to defer in these matters to our own opinions, our views would differ and we would not agree on anything." Does this mean that the choice between candidates for definitions of property and marriage is like the choice a society must make between driving on the left side of the road and driving on the right side – a neutral, arbitrary choice that must be followed by all for society's sake? Is it thus a matter of picking, not choosing,[40] and then achieving uniformity? Or are there reasons to select one option over the other? Saʿadyah is unclear. There do seem to be worse and better normative views about many situations, less rational and more rational. Indeed, specifics might be derived from *sevarah* (logical argument), even when the general law isn't. Even so, as Saʿadyah says, divine or rabbinic directives are likely to be needed for many specifics of decision-making. The power given to certain people to determine law can apply even when the detail of the law is picked rather than chosen.[41]

We have just noted one instance of the need for submission to authority in Jewish law. I'll provide others in the coming sections.

QUESTION 3: RELIGIOUS MOTIVATION

Submission to God vs. Reason

Our third question was: If there is a standard of ethics independent of God's will, and human beings can know it without revelation, should human beings nonetheless be motivated to practice God's prescribed ethics out of obedience to His will? Or should they be motivated by independent moral reasons (what we might call "secular" reasons)? Or, perhaps, should they be motivated by natural feelings? (I'll pose a fourth option a bit later.)

---

[40] On this distinction, see Morgenbesser and Ullman-Margalit 1977. I am not addressing ritual here, but the picking-choosing issue arises there forcefully. Cf. Goodman 1996, ch. 6.
[41] Soloveitchik 1979 assigns a *ḥok* aspect to *mishpat*, but has strong views about what details should be included.

Let's begin with the obedience option. Here is a classic support: "Antigonus Ish Sokho in the name of Simon the Righteous said: Do not be like servants who serve the master to receive reward; be like servants who serve the master not in order to receive reward" (*Avot* 1:3). The key note here is submission. However, it isn't clear whether Antigonus is speaking of ritual laws or ethical laws. (Isaac Abravanel [2013] argues he is speaking only of ritual.[42]) And in any event R. Judah the Prince appears to contradict Antigonus by actually encouraging people to think in terms of reward and punishment when they act (*Avot* 2:1). Later thinkers are divided on whether submission/obedience is the ideal motivation.

One argument for favoring the obedience option is that unless an individual performs acts because of a divine command, there is nothing *religious* in his or her observance of positive and negative interpersonal *mitzvot*. Such observance lacks special features that make it a religious act. (We can readily modify this argument to reflect the command–will distinction: The act must be motivated *either* out of obedience to a divine *command* or out of obedience to a divine *will*.) But a historically impactful objection derives from Immanuel Kant. For Kant, actions have moral worth only if they are performed autonomously (i.e., self-legislated). Actions that are performed heteronomously – out of obedience to another's command, as the Bible requires – have no moral worth, however much they benefit society and should be encouraged. For Kant, being motivated by obedience requires vacating one's status as a moral agent, which must not be done.[43]

In the nineteenth and twentieth centuries, Kant's position on heteronomy generated a critique of halakhic (i.e., Halakhah-based) Judaism by the school called liberal Judaism, which prized autonomy. Furthermore, for Kant, acting "autonomously" does not refer, as it often does today, to following the agent's desire, but rather to following reason. Acting out of desire, such as acting because of incentives the Torah puts forth, involves heteronomous motivation. So Jewish ethics is heteronomous twice over: It demands obedience, and it uses material incentives.[44]

Can this clash between Kantian autonomy and the heteronomous stance of Judaism be removed? Some thinkers respond that although the practicing Jew originally received the commandment by revelation, that individual later appropriates it by reason, and this renders their judgment

---

[42] *Naḥalat Avot* to *Avot* 1:3.
[43] See also Rachels 1971.
[44] For Kant, a *faulty* use of reason cannot result in an autonomous choice.

autonomous.⁴⁵ The acceptance of the law thus has a dual grounding: It is first imposed by God, but later it becomes accessible to reason. Stage one is heteronomous; stage two is autonomous. But while this approach may capture the phenomenology of the Jew who observes commandments, it's problematic as a logical solution to the conflict with Kant. Once the law must be appropriated by reason, isn't its being commanded by God superfluous as a motivation?

During the past half-century or so, views have emerged that reject Kant's core theses. His project of deriving ethics from reason has been rejected, and replaced with a view of ethics that is focused on virtue and tradition, most famously by Alasdair MacIntyre in his influential *After Virtue* (1981). Two decades earlier, Elizabeth Anscombe (1958), had maintained that "ought" has its origins in the context of law, of commander–commanded relationships, and that makes heteronomous obligation the true "ought." Kant, on this view, has a wrong conception of moral agency. Robert Merrihew Adams (1987) convincingly rebuts the thesis that submission to another's will means vacating moral agency. A Nazi following orders is a moral agent, responsible for his actions, despite his heteronomous motivation of obeying his commanders. To which I add that the very demand that people not act heteronomously assumes that they have a *responsibility* not to so act. They must therefore be moral agents.

To sum up the anti-Kantian position: If a person is motivated by a desire to conform to a divine command, this does not entail that the person's act has no moral worth. But we still confront the question of whether, in Judaism, it is *better* to act from submission, or better to act from independent moral motivation – or from some other factor.

Like what? One candidate is spontaneous emotion, such as sympathy for the poor. Thus far, then, we have three candidate motivations for those actions that are agreed to be obligatory: submission to divine command, rational argument, and spontaneous feeling.

But we aren't done. One might use rational arguments drawn not from a secular standpoint, but from a religious one. The Bible teaches that human beings are created in the image of God, a fact that is said to bestow upon them a special moral worth and affect our obligations (as in Gen. 9:6). In addition to this motif of image of God, there are other religious motivations, such as *imitatio Dei* – imitating or emulating God. Religious people therefore have special reasons to act morally that are

---

⁴⁵ See Soloveitchik 1983, 65–66, albeit Alex Sztuden suggested in conversation that Soloveitchik's view is less vulnerable than other versions of this strategy.

not available to secularists. So, we have *four* possible motivations for actions that are agreed to be obligatory: submission to divine command, rational argument devoid of religious premises, rational argument using some distinctively religious premises, and spontaneous feeling.

We should recall another argument in favor of obedience: Even if reason can determine the general contours of ethics, it cannot always determine the details. With regard to at least some details, only submission is appropriate. At least this is a possible position. In the next section I will give other reasons for requiring the motive of submission.

Submission to God vs. Feeling

Among the most notorious figures in moral philosophy are Kant's warmhearted and cold-hearted philanthropists. His analysis falls squarely into place with the Kantian views about moral worth that I described. If a person benefits others only out of feelings of sympathy, Kant (1997, 11–12) writes, his sympathetic deeds deserve "praise and encouragement, but not esteem." For the act "has no true moral worth but is on the same moral footing with other inclinations, for example, the inclination to honor." When benevolent actions flow from natural inclination, the agent acts *in accordance with* duty, but not *from* duty. (We might ask: Isn't a choice to follow reason itself reflective of a desire?)

By contrast, says Kant, consider the coldhearted philanthropist, someone who is "clouded over by his own grief, which extinguished all sympathy with the fate of others," yet "he nevertheless tears himself out of this deadly insensibility and does the action without any inclination, simply from duty; then the action first has its genuine moral worth." A misanthrope who does what duty requires solely from the motive of duty – this person has done something that bears moral worth and is superior morally to one who acts out of sympathy for the plight of others. For Kant, nice guys finish morally last.

Kant's appraisal has been widely mocked. Perhaps the most trenchant and oft-cited parody came from Ferdinand Schiller:

SCRUPLES OF CONSCIENCE: "Gladly do I serve my friends, but alas I do it with pleasure. Hence I am plagued by doubts that I am not a virtuous person."
DECISION [RESPONDING]: "Sure, your only resource is to despise them entirely, and with aversion to do what your duty requires."[46]

---

[46] Schiller, *Xenia*, cited in Henson 1979. As noted earlier, some interpreters of Kant soften and thereby defend his position. (a) They understand him as agreeing that acting from

Maimonides, we might say, was a semi-Kantian. He presents a contrast between two personality types.[47] One is (in the Hebrew translation from the Arabic) the ḥasid ha-me'uleh – supremely pious person; the other is the continent man, the kovesh et yitzro, the one who conquers urges. The ḥasid[48] "follows in his action what his desire and the state of his soul arouse him to do; he does good things while craving and strongly desiring them." In other words, the ḥasid's actions and omissions (i.e., what he refrains from doing) are motivated by a desire to, for example, help others – independently of a divine command to do so. By contrast, the kovesh et yitzro has cravings and desires to do bad actions – but he "opposes by his action what his [appetitive] power, his desire and the state of his soul arouse him to do."[49]

Maimonides asks which of these types ranks higher. He writes that the philosophers, along with King Solomon, rank the ḥasid higher than the continent man, while the Sages appear to rank the continent man higher. Maimonides cites some rabbinic texts:

- Let not a man say "I do not want to eat meat with milk, I do not want to wear sha'atnez [prohibited mixtures of wool and linen], I do not want to have illicit sexual relations," but [let him say], "I want to, but what shall I do – my Father in heaven has forbidden me." [Sifra to Leviticus 20:26 (Kedoshim 9:12)][50]
- Whoever is greater than his friend has a greater [evil] impulse than he. [Sukkah 52a]
- According to the pain is the reward. [Mishnah Avot 5:3]

---

duty in a way that accords with "inclination" (e.g., natural sympathy or desire for reward) is fine as long as this inclination is causally inert when one acts. (b) Going further, one could allow multiple motives and not require the causal inertness of inclination as long as the motive of duty is strong enough to prevail should the other motives oppose it. See Henson 1979, Herman 1981, Baron 1984, and Schoenecker and Wood 2015.

Other nuances: Schonecker and Wood 2015 explain that Kant believes that people should cultivate love and sympathy. Also, Kant is not against virtue ethics. He regards strength of will as a virtue and recognizes others. See Cureton and Hill 2015.

[47] See his introduction to his commentary on the tractate Avot (known as Eight Chapters), ch. 6. Translations of Maimonides's discussion will be from Weiss and Butterworth 1975, 78–80.
[48] This is not related to the Ḥasidic movement that began in the eighteenth century.
[49] Maimonides's distinction corresponds to that between "full virtue" and "continence" in some virtue ethics literature.
[50] Maimonides misidentifies the sage who made the statement. It was R. Elazar ben Azaryah, not R. Shimon ben Gamliel. Also, other versions of the text have "pork" instead of "meat and milk."

These texts, for Maimonides, affirm the value of struggling against impulse, as opposed to doing the right thing without struggle or contrary desire.[51]

Maimonides seeks to reconcile the respective views of the philosophers and the Sages. He maintains that the two groups "are not in disagreement" because the philosophers are referring to "things which all people regard as evils, such as bloodshed, theft, robbery, fraud, injury to one who has done no harm, ingratitude, contempt for parents, and the like." The Sages, however, are referring to "ceremonial prohibitions" (such as those against eating meat with milk or wearing *sha'atnez*). In these cases, "were it not for the law, they would not at all be considered transgressions." Maimonides operates roughly with the Talmud's distinction between *mishpatim* and *hukkim*. Unlike acts and refrainings denoted by *mishpatim*, acts and refrainings denoted by *hukkim* would not be wrong were it not for divine commands.

We can readily understand Maimonides's claim that the continent person is inferior as regards ethical conduct. If you're sitting on a bus and the passenger next to you informs you, "I have this great temptation to murder you, but I am overcoming it," you would, aside from running off the bus, have no thought whatsoever that such a person is great because they overcame desire. Consider as well an example given by Michael Stocker (1976) in the secular philosophical literature, to which I will give a Jewish twist: A person visits a friend who is in the hospital. The patient thanks the visitor for coming and expresses appreciation for the latter's friendship, to which the visitor replies: "Well, *bikkur holim* [visiting the sick] is a *mitzvah* [commandment]." The response is clearly alienating and less than ideal. It's not just the visitor's *saying* this that is objectionable. So is the visitor's thinking/feeling that way: Submission to the law "visit the sick" seems not to be the ideal *motivation* for visiting the sick.

It may be a surprise to many, but some rabbinic thinkers believe that it's best to give charity out of feeling and *not* out of a sense of obligation. (Perhaps we can extend this to *bikkur holim*.) One major twentieth-century rabbinic figure, R. Jehiel Jacob Weinberg, wrote: "It is better that a person give of his own free will, out of a feeling of love … If he gives only because God so commanded, he diminishes the nature of love."[52]

---

[51] Another relevant saying is: "One who is commanded and performs [*mitzvot*] is greater than one who is not commanded but performs" (*Bava Kamma* 38b).

[52] Weinberg 1977, 1:#61. (The translation is from Lewinsohn 2016, 254, n. 17.) For additional references supporting Weinberg's position, see Blau 2000, 29–34.

Question 3: Religious Motivation

Soloveitchik (1975, 8–9) seems to takes a similar position. "When people visit the sick, they must join in their pain; when people comfort mourners, they must mourn with them in the heart; when people give charity, they must bear the recipient's burden and empathize with their pain."[53] The opinion of Weinberg and Soloveitchik seems to work well with that of Maimonides.

To be sure, as Soloveitchik stresses, even generous acts that are egoistically motivated qualify as fulfilling the imperative of *tzedakah*. The Sages say: "Someone who says, 'This *sela* coin [will be donated to charity] so my son can live' – he is a complete *tzaddik*" (*Pesaḥim* 8b).[54] The common practice in Jewish and general society of naming buildings, schools, centers, programs, and the like after donors and seemingly enticing potential donors with offers of such recognition reveals that society as a whole accepts acts that *might be* (but certainly not always are) partially motivated in this way. Indeed, I find that very few people find the practice problematic: The honorees deserve the honor and we should bestow it; also, they want to do good and there is nothing ignoble about creating a legacy. Doing so, in fact, accords with a concept of the afterlife explored in Chapter 7.

Soloveitchik's (2017) as view is highly qualified. He goes so far (at 146–47, 155) as to praise a coldhearted philanthropist for conquering his inclination – an echo of Kant. Bottom line: The person with feeling ranks highest, and affectless behavior falls short of the ideal, but the obligation can be fulfilled without the sentiments. In an intriguing twist, Soloveitchik maintains (154–58) that if the lack of sympathy translates into lack of action, then, albeit only then, does God hold the lack of feeling against the miser.

One potential piece of support for the primacy of feeling as a motivator is that although a blessing is recited when someone performs a ritual *mitzvah* – for instance, "Blessed Art Thou, O Lord our God, King of the universe, who has sanctified us with His commandments and commanded us to kindle the Ḥanukkah lights" – the blessing is not recited in the case of interpersonal *mitzvot*, such as charity. A widespread explanation is that since ethical deeds (or refrainings) are incumbent on everyone, Jew or non-Jew, referring to God's relationship to Israel ("who has sanctified us")

---

[53] As translated by Blau 2000.
[54] The words "he is a complete *tzaddik*" in the cited text may be hyperbolic, or perhaps, as some texts indeed have it, the intent is that the *act* qualifies as "complete charity." (Otherwise, how could one act establish that a person is a complete *tzaddik*? Doesn't his other conduct matter?)

is inappropriate. However, another explanation, one relevant to the present discussion, is that one who performs a deed that benefits another should do it out of natural feeling, not because of a commandment as implied by the blessing.[55]

Further evidence that one should act benevolently not because of a command but because of natural feeling is that, although there is a talmudic debate about whether one must have the intention to fulfill a commandment in order to properly fulfill it, that debate is never applied to interpersonal, ethical *mitzvot*.[56] Additionally, if a goal of Judaism's ethical code is to create feelings of friendship and good feeling, it is best – and perhaps necessary – that people not act because they have been commanded. This is precisely the opposite of Isaiah Leibowitz's position. Leibowitz (1992, 19) notes that the words following "love your neighbor as yourself" are "I am the Lord" – connoting a command.

Some later rabbinic figures disagreed with Maimonides about motivation for interpersonal deeds, arguing that one who conquers his desires is greater even in the case of ethical commandments.[57] But my sense is that most agreed with Maimonides about motivation for interpersonal *mitzvot*. Arama (*Akedat Yitzhak* 100:7–8) distinguishes between reward and standing. Those who struggle may get greater reward because they struggle, but the ideal is not to need a struggle, and so the one who struggles does not rank higher. (Regarding Mark Twain's quip to the effect that "I am greater than George Washington. He can't tell a lie; I can, but I won't" – for Maimonides, Washington prevails.)

Notwithstanding, Maimonides's sharp distinction between the respective motivations for "ethical" and ritual *mitzvot* is problematic. As Jed Lewinsohn (2016) points out in discussing our text, people can act or refrain from acting from *multiple* motives. Weinberg's statement quoted earlier seems to have kept this in mind ("if he gives *only* because God so commanded ..."), and Rabbi Soloveitchik's statement does not rule out the motivation of following God as an *additional* motivation. It would therefore seem, first of all, that even if someone performs a certain commanded act or refrains from a prohibited one for reasons other than obedience to God's command – that is, because of the act or omission's *nonreligious* value – this is no reason to preclude obedience to God's

---

[55] For sources see Blau 2000.
[56] Ibid., 31.
[57] See the commentary of R. Jacob Emden to Maimonides's discussion in *Eight Chapters*, ch. 6.

command as *one* of the (additional) motives. In fact, the performance or omission would seem to lack any *religious* significance if unaccompanied by the motive of obedience. One could even require that the motive of obedience be strongest,[58] because that gives priority to the religious significance of certain conduct. Allowing for multiple motives handles the case of the hospital visitor: The ideal, from within a religious framework, would be to both act from obedience *and* act out of feelings of friendship. This approach undercuts Maimonides.

However, Lewinsohn (2016, 250–51) argues that there is a difference between a negative commandment and a positive commandment, between refraining from a prohibition and performing a prescribed action, and that this difference makes sense of the cited *midrash*'s requirement that in the cases of the ritual commandments, the agent should have a contrary motivation – a desire, say, to eat milk and meat together. In the case of positive duties, one can act from duty even if one has other reasons for doing what is mandated. By contrast, "one cannot be said to refrain from doing X for any reason, including the motive of obedience, unless one sees something desirable in X-ing … [I]t is only with respect to the negative commandments that an independent desire for the transgressive state of affairs is, in general, needed to comply from the motive of obedience" (Lewinsohn 2016, 250–51).

There emerges the following question, then: What could justify sidelining the motive of obedience in the case of *interpersonal* laws, as Maimonides does when he follows "the philosophers"? Allowing motives in addition to obedience – such as recognizing the independent rightness or wrongness of an act, or having sympathy – should not force out the motive of obedience. I can pay taxes both out of a desire to obey the law and out of a desire to aid the less fortunate.[59] It is obedience that will keep the act a *religious* one.

Which brings me to another reason to affirm the motive of submission even in the case of *mishpatim*. It involves what I call the "ineluctability of heteronomy." Even if the proper motivation is natural feeling, *it is God or the rabbinic authorities who are requiring that motivation.* Hence, *ultimately*, that motivation is heteronomous.

We can sum up our discussion. In some sources we find that, surprisingly, submission to rules is not the "favored" motive in Jewish interpersonal ethics. Nor is rational argument. Rather, pride of place – in *certain*

---

[58] *Mutatis mutandis*, a parallel point about multiple motives was made earlier about Kant.
[59] Lewinsohn (2016) gives this example (253–54, n. 18).

of those sources – is given to motivation supplied by the virtues of (natural) benevolence, love, and compassion. Kant's coldhearted philanthropist is hardly the ideal for Maimonides, even though Maimonides is a sort of Kantian as regards ritual. Yet obedience could be *one* motive among several in interpersonal ethics; and preserving that motive cements the religious character of the act. Finally, since the imperative to act from feeling is *mandated* or *imposed*, heteronomy is in that respect ineluctable.

QUESTION 4: IF THERE IS A CORRECT STANDARD OF ETHICS INDEPENDENT OF GOD'S WILL, DOES IT PLAY A ROLE IN HALAKHIC DECISION-MAKING?

On to question 4, the jurisprudential question: "If there is a correct standard of ethics independent of God's will and human beings can know it without revelation, may the (rabbinic) authorities who decide Jewish law utilize that standard (or what they believe to be that standard) in making their decisions? Or must they follow only formulated rules of Jewish law?"

Probably the best way of approaching this topic is to cast it in the light of the great divide in philosophy of law, that between natural law and positivist theories.[60] Natural law theories maintain that there is an essential (i.e., conceptually necessary) connection between law and morality, while positivist theories deny this.

There are at least three versions of natural law theory. (These are compatible to a degree.) In one version, laws by definition must be moral (i.e., consistent with morality – not immoral); so an immoral rule is by definition not a law.[61] The obvious problem is that this seems like a recipe for anarchy, since everyone forms their own judgment as to what rules are moral and worthy of obedience as truly "law."

As against this version of natural law, positivists typically maintain that immoral rules can be laws. In a classic formulation, there is a difference between "law as it is" and "law as it ought to be." The status of a rule as law is determined not by its moral content but by its pedigree – how it was brought into being (by what procedure). A rule with the right pedigree is "posited," that is, put in position, regardless of

---

[60] Like many great divides, this one narrows as each position adjusts itself to meet objections.
[61] This version is most closely associated with Thomas Aquinas.

Question 4: Ethics and Halakhic Decision-Making

its moral quality. H. L. A. Hart (1961), the most famous positivist of the twentieth century, characterizes law as a system of primary and secondary rules (79–99). Primary rules prescribe how to act; secondary rules are rules about rules – rules that state (i) which rules are valid law, (ii) how laws may be changed, and (iii) how conflicts are adjudicated (e.g., by a court system). A major challenge for positivism is grounding the *authority* of law in rules.

In a second version of natural law theory, advocated by Lon Fuller (1969), "immoral law" is not a contradiction in terms, so *individual laws* may be immoral yet binding. Nevertheless, a *legal system* must conform to certain ethical requirements (eight in all). For example, laws must be made public, the system must not contain inconsistencies, and legislation must not be retroactive.

The third version of natural law theory is hermeneutic: It states that in interpreting laws, jurists must bring moral reflection to bear. Positivism in this context would deny that judges *must* incorporate moral reflection or even deny that they *may*.

One way to think about the hermeneutic version is this. Every system of law runs up against two challenges. One is indeterminacy. Often a legal case cannot easily be decided because a crucial term in a rule is not defined or its application is vague (a classic case: "cruel and unusual punishment" in the Eighth Amendment of the US Constitution), or rules conflict. Additionally, sometimes the rules of the system ostensibly "run out"; they do not address the precise situation the judges are considering, so there is no clear precedent by which to rule on the case. How should judges proceed in cases of indeterminacy?

The second challenge to legal systems is the problem of untoward results (or, if you will, yucky results). Sometimes applying the rules yields a result that is (at least arguably) immoral.[62] Should we comfortably declare, "law is law, morality is morality, and some legal results may be immoral, so just follow the law as written"? Or should judges seek consciously to avoid untoward results? In a classic example, *Riggs* v. *Palmer* (1888), a man killed his grandfather in order to inherit his fortune. He was convicted, but argued that he is the rightful heir – which technically it seemed he was. The court rejected his claim because of a principle that no one should profit from their wrongdoing. In an early article, the hermeneutic natural law theorist Ronald Dworkin (1967) adduced this and other cases to show that legal decision-making is not *only* a matter

---

[62] Immorality is not the only untoward result possible; utter impracticability is another.

of applying "rules," but of applying legal "principles." These principles are inferred from the total body of law; and it is the task of the judge to seek the best explanation of the laws by means of discovering these principles. But "best explanation" includes "most morally justified." Dworkin argued, therefore, against a positivist legal hermeneutics, that the abolitionist judges who ruled to apply the Fugitive Slave Act in cases before them (the Act required that a slave from a Southern state who fled to a Northern state had to be returned to their owner) could have justified a ruling in favor of the slave by using moral principles inferred from the Constitution. The judges did not have to feel conflicted as they did, Dworkin argues. Judges choose between competing principles in the body of law and do not simply apply rules – moral judgment does and should licitly contribute to their choice. (I have presented only the "early" Dworkin.)

Scholars of Jewish jurisprudence have seen parallels between Dworkin's position and some juridic approaches found in certain Jewish texts and exemplified in the actual practice of Jewish jurists. (Rabbinic authorities who decide cases are called in Hebrew *posekim* or in English "decisors.") Examples are often cited in which rabbis are said to have explicitly or implicitly utilized their moral reason or moral intuitions – values like justice, fairness, compassion, mercy, human dignity (and divine image), and peace[63] – in deciding cases that, from a rules standpoint, are indeterminate.[64] Moreover, they at times decided against the technical law because applying it would have yielded a yucky result. Naḥmanides understands the command "Be holy" as a command not to live by the technical law alone but to follow the path of holiness (commentary to Lev. 19:2.). A person who, in indulging appetites, does certain acts Jewish law technically does not prohibit (such as gluttony or foul language) is a "disgusting person with the permission of the Torah."[65] Regarding interpersonal morality, we are told (*Bava Metzi'a* 30b) that Jerusalem was destroyed because the judges followed only strict *din* (the law) and did not go *lifnim*

---

[63] As Korn (2021, 46) and others have noted, these values must be held in dialectical balance. This would explain why different authorities committed to the same values come to different decisions: they weigh the values differently and prioritize them differently when they conflict. (See also Halbertal 1993.) Sources for some of these of values include Jer. 9:22–23; Zech. 7:8–9; Mic. 6:8.

[64] See Naḥmanides's approach to interpersonal cases where the rules run out, found in his commentary to Deut. 6:18.

[65] Although Naḥmanides believed in an independent ethical standard (see his commentary to Gen. 6:2), in the passage at hand he finds the "disgusting person" violating an *internal* ethic that limits eating, drinking, and sexual activity.

mi-shurat ha-din (roughly, beyond the requirements of the law[66]). In addition, there are times when an individual must act not in accord with the technical law but in accord with considerations of virtue.[67] Eugene Korn writes (2021, 44): "Halakhic norms do not exhaust moral obligations." And Walter Wurzburger (1994, 32) quotes R. Joseph Soloveitchik as saying, "Halakhah is not a ceiling, but a floor."[68]

Generally speaking, the different denominations of Judaism (Orthodox, Conservative, Reform, Reconstructionist) and their subvarieties (e.g., ultra-Orthodox, Modern Orthodox) appraise the weight of moral reflection in decision-making in differing ways, and likewise view historical examples differently.[69] Such examples range from the rabbis' interpretation of "an eye for an eye" and other harsh punishments as (mere) monetary compensation (*Bava Kamma* 83b–84a); the declaration by R. Akiva and R. Tarfon in the Mishnah that had they been serving on the Sanhedrin (High Court), no one would have been executed, for (according to the talmudic discussion) they would have interpreted the imperative to interrogate witnesses in such a way that a conviction could not result (*Makkot* 7a); Hillel's enabling the collecting of debts during the Sabbatical year, which the Torah disallows, because he saw that people won't lend once they know the debt would be cancelled, thus violating a biblical law (*Gittin* 36a);[70] the ban on polygamy imposed by R. Gershom ben Yehuda (Rabbeinu Gershom) (960–1040), allegedly because of the influence of the monogamous practice found in

---

[66] This translation is *very* rough and captures only the colloquial meaning of the phrase. For scholarly analyses that bring out its complexity, see, inter alia, Lichtenstein 1975; Saul Berman 1975 and 1977; Shilo 1978; Newman 1989; Barer 2018; Lichtenstein 2023, 217–75.

[67] Consider, e.g., the concept of "we compel one who acts in the manner of Sodom" (*kofin al middat Sedom*). If (i) Y is not technically required to do act A for X; (ii) X would benefit from Y doing A; (iii) doing act A would result in no loss for Y; and (iv) Y refuses to do A, then he can be coerced to do A despite its not being required by a law. (Think of Y refusing to back up a few inches to make room for X as X tries to park their car.) Possibly, the coercion is directed to promoting the virtue of the agent as opposed to the interests of the beneficiary. See Lichtenstein 2023, 277–317.

[68] A modified version of positivism called "inclusive" positivism includes a rule, "apply morality in deciding law." This version incurs problems, but for present purposes what matters is whether morality is used to interpret law, not whether there is a rule allowing or mandating that method. Cf. Brafman 2019. However, my view of "the ineluctability of heteronomy" is very similar to inclusive positivism.

[69] See the essays in Dorff and Crane 2013, esp. chs. 11–14. Samuel Fleischacker (2011, 2015) defends revealed religion, but argues that revelation must be integrated with secular morality or else fanaticism results.

[70] Hillel used a legal mechanism, *prozbul*, that transferred the creditor's claim to the court.

Christian society;[71] rabbis opposing slavery despite its existence in the Bible and rabbinic legal traditions;[72] rabbis endorsing approaches to triage that greatly restrict the application of a hierarchical scheme found in a *mishnah*;[73] women eventually becoming halakhically allowed to vote, despite earlier resistance by rabbis when women's suffrage was first being granted in countries like the United States;[74] an increased rabbinic emphasis on not harming civilians during wartime;[75] and an increased emphasis on the equality of all people.

The main question to consider about these examples is whether whatever values may have infused these decisions were *external* to the laws or rather were *derived internally from laws and the* aggadic *(nonlegal, e.g., homiletic or philosophical) tradition*. On this understanding, R. Akiva and R. Tarfon were influenced not by a personal moral system or external system of ethics but rather by a perception that, in the Jewish value system, any taking of life, even a justified homicide such as capital punishment administered by a court or a killing of an enemy combatant in war, carries a taint.[76] Hillel's innovation is another obvious case of an internal principle at work, since Hillel was motivated by the Torah's command to open one's hand for the poor (Deut. 15:7–8).

On a modified model, though, rather than hone in directly on an internal value, such as the value of life, an authority might be influenced by *external* ethics to appreciate and give weight to certain *internal* values of the tradition rather than others.[77] This model resembles Dworkin's approach of identifying internal principles using moral judgment.[78] When the tradition has room for both of two views but truly seems weighted in one direction, and a rabbinic authority adopts a clearly minority position, external moral beliefs might have directed which texts and internal

---

[71] An alternative to this explanation of R. Gershom's ban is given by Grossman 2004, 22–34. Rabbinic authorities suggested reasons for banning polygamy, but the historian's question is why it was instituted at a particular time.

[72] See Shmalo 2011–2012.

[73] See Sokol 2013e.

[74] On the early twentieth century rabbinic debate about suffrage, see Korn 2001.

[75] See Schiffman and Wolowelsky 2007.

[76] See Blidstein 1965. R. Shimon ben Gamliel disagrees, however, as he is concerned about the loss of deterrence: "They too increase the number of murderers among Israel."

[77] This possibility was raised by David Berger.

[78] Halbertal 1993 argues that the presence of disputes about what texts to privilege *shows that* the weighing of contrasting texts is influenced by morality. In Shatz 2013a, 247–50, I question this inference, since the disputes at hand might be explained the way nonethically charged halakhic disputes are, viz. by different intuitions about weighing precedents and understanding texts.

values the authority privileged. (It is not clear that this process, if real, is always conscious.)[79]

The history of interpretation of the command to destroy the Amalekite people (Deut. 20:16–17, 25:17–19; see also Exod. 17:14–16 and I Sam. 15), a law that seems to extend to all times, exemplifies the difficulties in determining the extent that external morality played a role in rabbinic reflections on laws. Commentators developed a variety of approaches to the law, instead of the simple technique of endorsing divine command morality. They argued either that the law is morally justified, or that its primary relevance is symbolic, or that the law does not apply in all circumstances, or that we cannot identify who is from Amalek because the nations have been commingled.[80] The thrust of these approaches is to place the commandment to eradicate Amalek within what we find to be a morally more satisfying framework, albeit some moral qualms may remain. However, as Harris (2003, 134–50) argues, there is no decisive evidence that an *external* morality was at work, given the many laws in the Torah and texts of the Rabbis that reflect the high value of human life and the notion of individual responsibility ("each person shall die for their own sin," Deut. 24:16).

One response to morally problematic laws as a bloc is to posit "progressive revelation."[81] The idea is that changing perceptions of (for example) slavery or the status of women, are themselves part of an ongoing revelation and justify changes. Societies evolve, and, on this view, the law evolves with them – with a divine imprimatur. God licensed humans to give weight to evolved moral beliefs and sensibilities. The evolved sensibilities, on this view, are a part of revelation. In one variant, these changes help to bring the Earthly Torah closer to the Heavenly Torah, to what God intended way back when at Sinai.[82]

---

[79] In some cases, the Rabbis expressed moral reservations but did not see a way to reinterpret the law or render it inapplicable. Consider the law about a *mamzer* (a child born from adultery or incest, or the descendant of such a child who is born to a Jewish mother). That child, through no fault of their own – the parents are the ones at fault for sinning – is restricted in whom they may legally marry. The Rabbis deeply lamented the plight of the *mamzer*, who suffers because of the sins of parents; but they make clear that they cannot find a way to render the law inapplicable. See *Lev. Rabbah* 32:8. That *midrash* applies the verse in Eccles. (4:1) "Behold the tears of the oppressed, they have no comforter" to the *mamzer* – remarkably, identifying the Sanhedrin as the oppressor. Ultimately God will be the comforter of the *mamzerim*.

[80] See Sagi 1994; Stern 2004; Carmy 2007; Korn 2021, ch. 4.

[81] See Rabinovitch 1993, Ross 2013, Gellman 2016, 2019, and Lebens 2020b, part II. See also Lamm 2006d, 343–52, and Berkovits 1990, 27–37.

[82] See Lebens 2020b, part III.

There are many challenges to such a view, key among which is how to distinguish societal trends that are part of the ongoing revelation and hence have normative clout, from those that are not and perhaps should be shunned. Also, *whose* moral stances will be normative? Those who use the approach must explain, for example, how secularism's being so widely embraced could be part of the ongoing revelation; Orthodox advocates must explain why the other denominations outnumber them. Are these sociological facts telling the relevant parties that they are on the wrong side? Or, for that matter, why shouldn't the advent and success of Christianity be viewed as part of the ongoing revelation? Note, finally, this logical consequence: that prior to Jews coming to the evolved, morally correct viewpoint, God, at the bottom line, had issued commands that were immoral.[83]

It's not feasible here to sort through the many additional cases across history that have raised questions about how authorities dealt with ostensibly immoral laws, but the foregoing presents the general direction inquiry and debate have taken.

QUESTION 5: WHAT IS THE CONTENT OF JEWISH ETHICS?

Much has been written on the tensions in Jewish ethics between the opposing ethical theories of utilitarianism and deontologism;[84] likewise, about whether Judaism believes in rights or only duties.[85] I want to discuss here another aspect of the content of Jewish ethics, namely, the role of virtue considerations. I'm not speaking of the immense moralistic literature that identifies and teaches about virtue, such as Maimonides's *Eight Chapters* and literature of the nineteenth-century "Mussar" movement founded by R. Israel Salanter.[86] I refer instead to the point that virtue considerations may account for certain laws in the Torah – and, more strikingly, that considerations of virtue, often presented as *imitatio Dei*, sometimes override the technicalities of law.[87]

---

[83] See Korn 2021, ch. 4.
[84] See, e.g., Sokol 2013c.
[85] Compare, for example, the "only duties" view in Cover 1987 with Rosensweig and Mermelstein 2022.
[86] See Claussen, Green, and Mittleman 2023.
[87] See Blau 2000; Shatz 2019c. A good example of virtue ethics at work is Maimonides's understanding of the Talmud's teaching that Jews must help support the gentile poor and visit their sick "because of the ways of peace" (*Gittin* 61b). Many commentators understand the provision of support for the sake of peace to be a pragmatic strategy for keeping good relations with gentile neighbors and influencing them to reciprocate our

Question 5: What Is the Content of Jewish Ethics?   235

This invocation of virtue raises two issues about the extent to which Judaism embraces a virtue ethic as commonly understood.

First is, once again, the *ineluctability of heteronomy*. The mandate to utilize virtue as a consideration in decision-making about conduct, such as by following the mandate to imitate God's ways and to act supererogatorily (*lifnim mi-shurat ha-din* [beyond what duty requires], and to exemplify *middat hasidut* [way or trait of the pious]), was given by God – more precisely, by the rabbis invested with the authority to interpret Scripture. So, too, as argued by R. Judah Loew of Prague (Maharal, 1524-1609; see *Tiferet Yisrael* 6), the imperatives to be humble, kind, honest, and not cruel – the table of virtues and vices – are *dictated* or *imposed*. Hence in Judaism the imperative to have certain virtues, and the imperative not to stick to legal technicalities but to integrate virtue considerations, are just that – imperatives. Heteronomy seems ineluctable in Jewish virtue ethics; we cannot find independent reason to endorse the virtues that we endorse.

But is heteronomy *truly* ineluctable? I don't think so. After all, the question of whether heteronomy is ineluctable is not whether the permission or mandate to have certain virtues and set aside technicalities *is* given by God, but whether the permission or mandate *must* be given by God in order to be properly grounded. One may argue that a permission or mandate to have certain virtues and utilize virtue considerations in conduct is evident to reason – "had they not been written, they should have been written," as the rabbis said about *mishpatim*. God's command may not be *needed* to ground the permission or mandate to follow God's ways, even though de facto Judaism grounds the norms that way. Likewise with supererogation: The very notion that one is commanded to go beyond laws is itself mandated by a law. But it doesn't follow that there is no independent reason for supererogatory action. What I would claim, as I did earlier, is that the *religious character* of the conformity to law depends on recognizing its *ultimate* heteronomy within the system.

---

charity. But Maimonides interprets "ways of peace" to refer to emulating God's compassion. For the psalmist declares "His compassion is on all His works" (Ps. 145:9). Thus for Maimonides, supporting gentiles is an exercise in *imitatio Dei* (*Mishneh Torah*, Laws of Kings 10:12).

In another oft-quoted text, the Jerusalem Talmud (*Bava Metzi'a* 2:5) relates a story about the students of Shimon ben Shetah, who brought their teacher an animal that was wearing a precious jewel and that technically he was allowed to keep because it was lost by a gentile. He refused, exclaiming "Do you think that Shimon ben Shetah is a barbarian?" However, the text goes on to say that He wanted to hear the God of Israel praised, which suggests that more than ethical virtue is involved.

An alternative response to the ineluctability of heteronomy is: "Yes, heteronomy is ineluctable. So what?" Is there some problem with utilizing a virtue ethics just because the reason to acquire and cultivate certain virtues is that God commanded us to do so? While both of these replies are cogent in themselves, they concede that virtue ethics and rule-following are not antitheses. To have virtue and act virtuously, and to have these-or-those specific virtues – these duties are imposed heteronomously as rules. In Judaism, rules about virtue are far less specific and determinate than rules about action, and leave a good deal up to human interpretation as to what inner states and behaviors certain virtues entail. The same is true in the realm of secular virtue ethics: Perhaps there are rules we can devise about what virtues one should have, but we remain unclear as to what those virtues require.

So much for the ineluctability of heteronomy. A second issue is the instrumentality of virtue. Are Jewish virtues good because they lead to right actions, or are they good independently of whether they produce proper actions? On the first view, an unexercised virtue (an unactualized disposition), or a virtue that because of insuperable obstacles consistently fails to attain its intended results, is not of much value. On the second view, being forgiving or courageous or benevolent only as a disposition to act in certain ways in certain situations, without having had opportunities to be forgiving or courageous or benevolent, is still a very good thing. I leave this question unresolved, but note that the second view weakens the soul-making theodicy (see Chapter 3). To wit: If an unexercised virtue is good, then less evil would be needed for moral growth. People would develop virtue through encountering evils, but once they have the virtue they would not have to express their virtue through actions that combat evil; they would just need the virtue.

In whatever way we qualify or temper Jewish virtue ethics, however, virtue clearly has a place within Judaism's framework of obedience to divine law. Jewish ethics shows an interest not only in what we should do – but in what we should be.

SUMMATION

Biblical and rabbinic sources seem to support not only the existence of an independent standard of ethics, but its knowability by humans. The standard is knowable pre-Sinai (as in Genesis narratives) and even post (as in the story of Tzelofḥad's daughters.). Some sources, however, deny either the existence of the standard or its knowability.

Regarding motivation, some argue that motivation for ethical conduct should (ideally) be either an independent ethic or natural feeling, not obedience. But this position takes a specifically *religious* motivation out of the picture – which could be problematic, unless an agent recognizes an *ultimate* heteronomy.

Next, we saw that morality plays a role in halakhic decision-making, but it is controversial whether the morality used is internal to the legal system or external. Finally, virtue plays a role in determining Jewish law, but here too we must confront the ineluctability of heteronomy: It is God or the rabbinic authorities who command that virtue operate in decision-making – and who identify the virtues.

9

One God?

Judaism and Religious Diversity

People who subscribe to a particular religious worldview believe that the tenets of their religion, at least the core ones, are true.[1] At a certain point, however, they may – and arguably should – reflect on the existence of other religions and belief systems. In recent times, such reflection has generated a more liberal, pluralistic, ecumenical perspective than in the past. Famously, in a 1965 document titled *Nostra Aetate* (*In Our Time*), the Second Vatican Council altered the classic Church teaching of "no salvation outside the Church" and advocated a new perspective on other religions. The Church stressed that other religions contain truth and holiness, urged mutual understanding and respect, and exhorted "her sons" to collaborate with other religions for the benefit of humanity.[2] Since that time, there has been a proliferation of interfaith dialogues and an explosion of "isms" on the philosophical scene: exclusivism, inclusivism, pluralism, and relativism. You can, of course, be an exclusivist regarding some claims of your religion but, say, an inclusivist with respect to others.[3]

These "isms" represent not different approaches to which religion is true, but rather to how people who regard theirs as a (or the) true religion should view other religions.[4] Setting aside the epistemological question

---

[1] Someone might believe that their religion contains some noncore statements that are false (e.g., historically or scientifically inaccurate), but it would appear to be tautological that they believe the *core* tenets are true. There are nondoxastic conceptions of faith (conceptions that marginalize or dismiss the role of belief in faith; see Chapter 10), but I think even such a faith will contain *some* beliefs – e.g., about values and proper conduct.

[2] For changes in the Church's perspective regarding Jews in particular, see Korn 2011.

[3] See also Goshen-Gottstein 2021, 354.

[4] See Brill 2010 (which cites many Jewish sources), McKim 2012, Runzo 1988, and esp. the essays in Meister 2011.

of how one is justified in believing that one's religion is correct and others incorrect, there are several key questions that adherents of various religions might ask vis-à-vis other religions *from the standpoint of their own* – that is, starting with the assumption that their religion is correct.

(1) Truth: Are there religious/spiritual truths in other religions? Now, several religions hold overlapping beliefs, such as belief in a personal God who created the world and exercises providence over it. Our question needs refinement, therefore: Do (or might) other religions have religious truths *that I don't have in mine*? If they might have such truths, then should I try to find them (through reading, conversation, attending lectures, or formal interfaith dialogues), or should I instead rest content with the truths I have in my own religion? Should I ever modify my religion's beliefs and adopt a syncretic set of beliefs? Especially important is whether some *core* claims of another religion that do not appear in mine are true or at least worth investigating even from the standpoint of my religion.[5]

(2) Salvation in the hereafter: Can adherents of other religions achieve salvation (and spiritual bliss) in the hereafter even if they do not convert to my religion?

(3) Spiritual value: Bracketing the previous question (about potential spiritual bliss in the hereafter), what spiritual benefits in *this* world are enjoyed by, or are open to, people of other faiths? (For that matter, one might ask: What about secularists – can they, despite themselves [that is, notwithstanding their atheism or agnosticism] perhaps relate to God unwittingly via ethical living?) What about adopting figures from other religions as spiritual exemplars, or internalizing other religions' stories for the purpose of spiritual nourishment? Would it make sense to adopt certain *rituals* of another religion?

(4) Eschatology: What religious views and practices will be accepted by the world at the end of days, according to my religion? Will all religions become one (namely, mine)? Will all remain as they are? Will religions as we know them disappear even while monotheism prevails? Will adherents of "wrong" religions be punished by God?

(5) Explaining multiplicity: Why does God allow so many religions, if they have false and possibly harmful core and noncore beliefs? Do these religions perhaps serve in a divine plan for the present or future?

---

[5] See Gellman 2012a, 31–36.

(6) Practical societal issues: Should adherents of my religion seek proselytes, thus saving people spiritually? Should we participate in social action? What about interfaith dialogues?

In what follows, I explore most of these questions, doing so from the perspective of Jewish thought. I hope to show that resources are available in classical and other sources to forge a Jewish perspective that accords to a noticeable degree with modern sensibilities that affirm a set of related values – equal worth and dignity, tolerance, pluralism, diversity, and the rights of all to equal treatment. (Of course the definition and scope of these concepts is not straightforward.) As is the case with numerous other issues in Jewish thought, though, a defense of any position about other religions necessitates privileging certain sources. Indeed, many texts militate *against* the "liberal" position. Numerous of these contravening texts are reactions to the negative, often horrific experiences that Jews have endured as a minority interacting with other societies and religions. Sometimes an Us/Them dichotomy is the natural effect of social separateness, especially ghettoization, on a group's perception of the Other.[6] These approaches are also obviously affected by the doctrine of the chosen people and election of Israel (Exod. 19:5; Deut. 7:6,14:2, 26:18; Isa. 41:8), which are core parts of Judaism.[7] Despite all this, intensely particularist and binary perspectives are far from being the tradition's only voice.

As we shall see – once again – the ancient evidence on many pertinent questions consists not of broad, systematically stated theories, but of fragmentary and often ambiguous statements, whose content and motivation we can seek to fathom only through educated conjecture.[8]

---

[6] See Katz 1961.

[7] Jewish thinkers have grappled with the doctrine of chosenness, presenting accounts that dissociate it from racist doctrines. See Frank 1993, Kaminsky 2008, Kellner 1991, Novak 1995, Gellman 2012a, Carmy 2013. Cf. Wyschogrod 1983; Schweid 2005. See also Gluck 2015.

[8] In this chapter, my focus is Christianity, for the simple reason that the overwhelming majority of Jewish writings about other religions focus on it. My questions might be further broken down into questions about specific denominations of Christianity. Parallel questions arise regarding other denominations of one's own religion – how does one assess them? For a brief account of Jewish and Muslim attitudes to each other's faith, see Fenton 2012. For a contemporary perspective on Buddhism, see Gellman 2012b. On Hinduism, see Goshen-Gottstein 2016 and cf. Berger 2019.

Brill 2004 and 2010, presents many valuable sources and important discussion. My focus on classical sources, combined with limitations of space, unfortunately precludes consideration of some important and stimulating thinkers of the past two centuries, such as Hermann Cohen, Franz Rosenzweig, and Abraham Joshua Heschel.

DOES JUDAISM BELIEVE THAT OTHER RELIGIONS ARE TRUE?

Jews, Christians, and Muslims generally agree on certain propositions: that God exists, that He is the creator, and that He exercises providence. Similarly, they accept that the Torah has a divine origin. Equally clearly, Judaism, Christianity, and Islam differ profoundly over many issues: Is God a trinity? Was Jesus the incarnation of an element in the Godhead? Is Jesus the Messiah? Did he rise from the dead? Have the laws of the Hebrew Bible been abrogated? Who are God's elect? Is Mohammed a true prophet? Which narratives in the respective Scriptures of the Abrahamic religions are true? It is difficult to see how the various answers to these questions that have been proffered by different religions can all be true.[9] Indeed, we saw in Chapter 1 that people with sharply different views of God may not even be referring to, and believing in, the same God. There are also disputes between different denominations of the same religion.

Furthermore, if all religions (or even more than one) were true, it would make no difference what belief system one adopts – making it difficult to fathom, for example, why Judaism demands martyrdom when a Jew is faced with a choice between dying at a coercer's hands and violating the prohibition of *avodah zarah* (foreign worship). (See *Sanhedrin* 73a.) On a nonexclusivist view, switching from one religion to another should make little difference.[10] Indeed, if all religions were true, it would be simple to justify not only syncretism, but even apostasy, no matter how whimsical (unless criteria other than truth are introduced). A nonexclusivist way of thinking goes contrary to the principles of various religions and violates their self-understanding.[11] Pluralism has also been thought to entail relativism.[12]

More needs to be said here, however, by way of qualification. Few Jewish thinkers embrace the well-known pluralistic view of religions championed by the British philosopher John Hick (1993). For Hick, all religions are diverse culturally conditioned responses to the one divine reality, a reality that, like Kant's things-in-themselves, cannot be known.[13]

---

[9] See Margalit 1996.
[10] See also M. Soloveichik 2007.
[11] But cf. McKim 2012, ch. 8.
[12] See Kellner, 2006b, 110–11, 146–47; cf. Jospe 2012 and the reply by J. Kellner and M. Kellner 2012.
[13] This is different from the thesis that God actively reveals Himself differently to different peoples, which was held by the early medieval thinker Nethanel ibn al-Fayumi (see Jospe 2012). Hick (and to a lesser extent Kook) instead stresses the *human* role in creating religions.

Nonetheless, a view somewhat like Hick's was embraced by Rabbi Abraham Isaac Kook (1865–1935). As a Kabbalist, Kook believed that all existence emanates from a single divine source. All things are therefore holy, and every idea and movement has at least an element of spiritual worth. All world religions are therefore in some way manifestations of the divine. Kook found values to extract even from idolatrous religions, such as those whose adherents passed their children through fires as sacrifices (cf. Deut. 18:10). Those religions are morally and intellectually odious, but they exhibit some worthy characteristics from which other religions could learn; they manifest infinite, intensely passionate commitment to the divine.[14] Kook further believed – reminiscent of Hick – that the supernal infinite cannot be captured in our conceptual categories. Different religions exemplify different efforts to respond to and represent the same transcendent reality, but in terms of metaphysical truth, *all* are inadequate. This approach would support a notion that we will encounter later in this chapter: that different people may legitimately, within limits, persist in worshipping God in their own way.[15]

But if all religions are thus inadequate in their metaphysical representations, why should anyone prefer one over the other? (Notice the reverse pluralism at work – all views are equally *wrong*.) One answer could be that the *practices* of one religion possess greater value than others on some metric. In Kook's case, there is the following cognitive difference: Other religions contain areas of truth and value, but there is a particular religion that takes a comprehensive, inclusivist approach to reality and thus "gets it right" – namely, Judaism. In addition, although Kook believes that in absolute terms, all formulated religions are off the mark, "religious claims are not a total free-for-all," as Tamar Ross (1997, 493) puts it. In Kook's thought, Ross suggests, choices can be made between religions based on criteria besides, or in addition to, evidence in the normal sense: comprehensiveness, psychological impact (Kook valued optimism and growth), moral influence, and effect on human welfare. In this vein, Kook critiques specific religions: Christianity for fleeing the physical world, Buddhism for breeding despair.[16] Judaism will purify and elevate other religions, he maintains. Hick, too, ends up conceding that some religions "mediate God

---

[14] Kook 1985a, 3 1985d, 131. See Gellman 1994, 106.
[15] For a much fuller account of Kook's positive views about other religions, as well as their qualifiers and limitations, see Shapiro 2025, 130–55. Shapiro takes into heavy consideration the most recent publications of Kook's writing.
[16] See Rappoport 2004.

to mankind better than others" and are "more adequate than others." Thus, for both Hick and Kook, there is a hierarchy of religions. For Kook, the values that put some religions in a higher rank may be tied to *ontological* truth, though I think this concession creates inconsistency within his system.

Some Jewish theologians, such as Irving Greenberg (2004), have put forth pluralistic theologies that posit multiple covenants and at the least flirt with the idea of plural truths. Notwithstanding its advocates' strong efforts to argue otherwise, critics appear to be correct that pluralism entails relativism and that, in Jewish tradition, support for multiple covenants (other than the Noahide covenant) is slim.[17]

Truth and value should not be equated, of course. Thus, even if other religions are false by Judaism's lights with regard to fundamental matters of doctrine, these religions may have value by dint of playing a critical, positive role in the dramatic unfolding of history. Using an analogy between Israel and a seed, Judah Halevi (1075–1141) portrayed Christianity and Islam as preparation for the fruit of the historical process – the Messiah's arrival – after which the tree will become one and others will esteem the root that they formerly despised.[18] Similarly, Maimonides – although he had angry and stinging words about Jesus and Mohammed – asserted that Christianity and Islam have familiarized the world with the concepts of Torah, *mitzvot*, and the messiah. In this way, they serve "to pave the way for the King Messiah and to prepare the whole world to serve the Lord together."[19] One could even say that in some sense, God – allowing ourselves here a rather un-Maimonidean anthropopathic expression – *wanted* Christianity and Islam to arise and spread, although His reasons for doing things that way are hidden.

Some Jewish thinkers, among them individuals who were exiled in the Spanish Expulsion, described Christianity as a healthy moral and religious force and a vital influence upon Jewish behavior and faith: so much so, that they expressed gratitude to God for having situated their exile in

---

[17] See Berger 2005b; Kellner and Kellner 2012; Kimelman 2007. Cf. Jospe 2012; Goshen-Gottstein 2012.

[18] Halevi, *Kuzari* 4:23; cf. ibid. 2:36 (analogy to a heart).

[19] Maimonides, *Mishneh Torah*, Laws of Kings, 11:4 (in uncensored editions). However, Maimonides adds that at the end of days other religions will repudiate their past. The view of Christianity and Islam as preparation for the Messiah seems to be a foil to the Christian view that Judaism was a preparation for Christianity, albeit with a qualification noted later: that according to some Jewish schools of thought, non-Jews will not convert *to Judaism* at the end of days. Lasker 2008 connects Halevi and Maimonides.

places where Christians could exert salutary moral influence on them.[20] Note further that prominent Jewish theologians of recent vintage have seen value in integrating ideas from Christian theologians in developing their own, often by modifying them.[21]

Of course these appreciative and at times deeply grateful assertions of value in other religions do not establish pluralism in the sense of "all religions are true." In what follows, I argue that although Judaism is exclusivist with regard to truth, one overall attitude in Jewish law and thought can be labelled "live and let live." I'll explain this attitude by considering a series of further questions.

CAN ADHERENTS OF OTHER RELIGIONS ATTAIN SALVATION IN THE HEREAFTER?

Even if only one religion can be true, it hardly follows that only one can effect salvation. A *mishnah* declares that "all Israelites have a share in the World-to-Come," except for three categories of heretics (*Sanhedrin* 10:1). What about gentiles, though? A simple quotation would appear to settle this question: "*Tzaddikei ummot ha-olam* (righteous gentiles) have a portion in the World-to-Come." Salvation in the hereafter, we are here told, extends from Israelites to the rest of humanity. Embracing Judaism is not necessary for entry into the World-to-Come.[22]

What could be the rationale for this inclusive approach? For one thing, from the fact that all humans are created in God's image, including all the progeny of Adam, whether Jew or gentiles, it stands to reason that God, a just being, would afford gentiles, like Jews, opportunities for reward.

---

[20] R. Isaac Arama, *Akedat Yitzḥak*, Va-Ethanan 88, 16a–b; R. Isaac Abravanel (1437–1508), commentary to Deut. 4:25 (both were exiled in the Spanish Expulsion). I take them to be speaking sincerely, though suspicions of political motivations are understandable. See also discussions of R. Jacob Emden in Miller 2008, Falk 1982, and B. Greenberg 1978.

[21] The two-sidedness is especially intriguing in Soloveitchik (opposition to dialogue on, inter alia, the grounds that faith is incommunicable, yet philosophical study of Kierkegaard, Barth, etc. who highlighted incommunicability). See Shatz 2019b.

[22] See the view of R. Joshua in Tosefta *Sanhedrin* 13:2 and BT *Sanhedrin* 105a. Maimonides, *Mishneh Torah*, Laws of Kings 8:11, follows this ruling, but with a significant proviso discussed at later. Although the two cited talmudic passages cite a contrary view, Maimonides's ruling is widely accepted, albeit often without the proviso. See also S. R. Hirsch 2018b, 225–27. An important work on Noahide laws is Novak 1983.

As noted in Chapter 7, the term "World-to-Come" is subject to differing interpretations. In the Talmud, it refers to a certain period in history, while Maimonides maintained that it refers to the continued existence of an individual's soul after the death of the body.

Can Adherents of Other Religions Attain Salvation? 245

All people get what they deserve. God would not consign most of the world to hell or nihility without taking into account whether they are righteous or wicked. He would give all deserving people opportunities for salvation.

This would explain why righteous gentiles have a share in the World-to-Come. Exactly what is righteousness in this connection? Most commonly, the term is interpreted as referring to those gentiles who observe the Noahide laws:

> Seven *mitzvot* were commanded to Noahides [gentiles]: the prohibitions against illicit sexual relations, murder, theft, blasphemy, *avodah zarah*, and eating the limb of a living animal, and the duty to establish a court system. [*Sanhedrin* 56a][23]

But now we run into a complication. Note the prohibition against foreign worship. If worshipping Jesus as a divine being constitutes foreign worship, then Christians would not attain the World-to-Come. However, in the modern period, explicit statements emerge, based on a particular reading of a major medieval source,[24] that Christianity is considered foreign worship *only for Jews*. Non-Jews who adopt Christianity do not violate the Noahide prohibition against *avodah zarah*, and are thus eligible for salvation. Other rabbinic authorities dispute this contention.[25] Emden declared that Christians (and Muslims) "act for the sake of Heaven, for their goal is to promote Godliness among the nations." Hence, "they will not be denied reward for their benevolent intentions."[26]

The thesis that, in Judaism, "Judaism is for Jews, Christianity for non-Jews" yields a correct representation of one modern-period approach to the laws of *avodah zarah* (again, that Christianity is foreign worship for

---

[23] Since commandments are the major means through which *Jews* relate to God, therefore, as R. Dov Linzer pointed out to me, the existence of commanded Noahide laws suggests a concern on the part of the talmudic rabbis to afford gentiles an opportunity to achieve closeness via commandments. In this regard, it is noteworthy that a view in the Talmud asserts that a non-Jew who studies Torah (generally understood in this context to refer to study of Noahide laws) is like the High Priest (*Avodah Zarah* 3a). This suggests further, optional modes through which non-Jews can relate to God. The view cited did not prevail, however. There was a period in which non-Jews adopted certain Jewish practices without converting; later this was forcefully discouraged. See Hirschman 2000, Linzer 2005, and Blidstein 1990.
[24] The text cited is Tosafot *Sanhedrin* 63b, s.v. *asur*.
[25] Most authorities agree that Islamic worship is not *avodah zarah*, even for Jews, though it is not permitted for them.
[26] Translated by Miller 2008, 130–31.

Jews but not for gentiles).²⁷ But it generates perplexity. How could it be that particular beliefs and worship can be considered *avodah zarah* for Jews but not for Christians? If Christianity constitutes foreign worship for Jews – worship of a being other than God – why would it not be considered equally wrong for non-Jews? Eugene Korn (2011) concludes that *avodah zarah* is not a matter of theology; in Judaism, different theologies are acceptable for different people. This observation follows from the thesis under discussion, but it seems to reformulate rather than remove a conundrum.

In considering modern "liberal" Jewish attitudes toward adherents of other religions, a precursor much discussed in our day in the context of interfaith relations is R. Menaḥem ha-Meiri (1249–1316).²⁸ Meiri drew a groundbreaking distinction, unmatched in medieval rabbinic literature, between "nations that are restricted by the ways of religion" and nations that are not. This distinction, not that between Jew and gentile, nor that between true religion and false religion, was central in Meiri's philosophical and legal thought.²⁹ Meiri advocated equality (under Jewish law) of juridical status, rights and duties for those gentiles who are "restricted by the ways of religion." In fact, notwithstanding the phrase "restricted by the ways of *religion*," it has been argued that Meiri's true principal category is civilized, ethical behavior.³⁰ Meiri, in this account, mentions religion as the criterion because he assumes that belief in a cosmic providential God who created the world *ex nihilo* is a prerequisite for ethical behavior. In Meiri's time, secularism was not a significant phenomenon. But the tight ethics–religion nexus does not hold in our time. Ethics, not theology, should (on this understanding) be determinative if Meiri's view is adopted. This is not to say that Meiri would himself have gone this far.

An important figure in our discussion must be Moses Mendelssohn (1729–1786), the most prominent figure in the Jewish Enlightenment (*Haskalah*), and considered its father. Cherishing equality and tolerance,

---

²⁷ B. Greenberg 1978, 363. Cf. Miller 2008.
²⁸ Meiri's view became well known only in the nineteenth to twentieth centuries.
²⁹ Meiri's concept of "nations circumscribed by the ways of religion" appears in his commentaries to several tractates. See, e.g., *Beit ha-Beḥirah*, *Gittin* 62a. However, Meiri did not apply his distinction to all aspects of Jewish law that govern how Jews act toward gentiles. For the multifarious details, see esp. Katz 1961, ch. 10, Halbertal 2000a, 2000b, Berger 2005a. Meiri states that only nations at the "extremities" of the world qualify as "*not* restricted by the ways of religion."
³⁰ For discussion, see Halbertal (2000a, 2000b) and Berger (2005a, 96–99). Berger understands Meiri to consider Christianity "non-pagan *avodah zarah* in a monotheistic mode."

Can Adherents of Other Religions Attain Salvation? 247

Mendelssohn reveled in the egalitarianism implied by the talmudic passage about non-Jews attaining the World-to-Come. In correspondence with the millenarian cleric Johann Caspar Lavater, who had sought to convert him through logical argument, Mendelssohn emphasized with pride that whereas Christianity believes that salvation can come only through the Church, Judaism believes that those who do not embrace Judaism may be saved if they act morally, and he argued that moral truth is accessible to everyone by reason. Correct theology is not necessary for salvation. His logic is: "Convert a Confucius or a Solon? What for? ... It seems to me that anyone who leads men to virtue in this life cannot be damned in the next" (Mendelssohn 1975, 269).

Apart from the question of *avodah zarah*, one obstacle to Mendelssohn's view is a qualification that Maimonides placed on the talmudic statement about righteous gentiles. Maimonides had written in the Laws of Kings section of his legal code (8:11) that non-Jews who observe the Noahide laws attain *olam ha-ba* only if they observe those laws because God commanded them, through Moses, to do so. If they arrive at the laws by reason, they have no share in the World-to-Come.[31] Mendelssohn was deeply troubled. Could it be, he asked, that ethical paragons like Confucius and Solon would be deprived of their share in the hereafter because they never heard of Moses, let alone accept his authority? Some have reinterpreted the Maimonidean passage, bringing it closer to Mendelssohn's sensibilities.[32] In fact, other texts by Maimonides exude a different spirit. Maimonides declares that "anyone from among the world's inhabitants" – apparently, not necessarily a Jew or formal convert – whose intelligence and spirit move him to consecrate himself to God is regarded as holy, indeed, as like the "holy of holies."[33] Although he does not say so explicitly, it would seem fitting that a person who becomes like "the holy of holies" would attain the World-to-Come.[34]

Furthermore, Maimonides's portrait of the founding patriarch Abraham as one who came to know God through reason prior to the legislation at Sinai suggests the possibility of reaching spiritual heights on the basis of reason and character. These other Maimonidean texts do not allay Mendelssohn's worries about Confucius and Solon – after all,

---

[31] In effect, the gentile must accept the authority of Moses as a universal lawgiver.
[32] See Kook, 1985b, 99–100; Korn 1994 (citing Kook); Kellner 2006a, 241–47.
[33] *Mishneh Torah*, Laws of Sabbatical and Jubilee Years 13:13.
[34] Although Maimonides sees possibilities for great devotion to God on the part of non-Jews, he opposed the formation of new religions. See *Mishneh Torah*, Laws of Kings 10:9. See also Blidstein 1990 and the section later on proselytizing.

Maimonides is speaking only of monotheists – but they do blunt *somewhat* the effect of Maimonides's proviso in Kings 8:11.

The willingness of rabbis to declare that salvation is not limited to Jews is manifest in a passage by Rabbi Israel Lifshitz (1782–1860), a highly significant commentator on the Mishnah:

> And we see many of their pious ones who, aside from recognizing the Creator of the Beginning and believing in the divine origin of the Torah, also engage in benevolent acts for the Jewish People ... Many of them made especially great improvements for all people, such as [Edward] Jenner, who created the smallpox vaccine ... and [Francis] Drake, who brought the potato to Europe, which at times has prevented famine, as well as Guttenberg, who invented printing. Many did not receive reward in this world, such as the pious one Reuchlin, who endangered his own life to prevent the burning of the Talmud ... and due to this he was pursued and persecuted by his enemies the priests, until he died in his misery and with a broken heart. And could one possibly think that these great benefactors will not be recompensed in the next world after death? Is it not the case that God does not withhold the reward from any creature?[35]

Although Reuchlin put himself at risk for Jews, Lifshitz is not being parochial here; Jenner and Drake aided *all* humanity, not just Jews. Furthermore, Reuchlin's Christian allegiances did not disqualify him from the World-to-Come. If Christianity is not *avodah zarah* according to Lifshitz, Christians enter the world-to-come. If he holds that Christianity is *avodah zarah* for both Jews and gentiles, we may conclude that in his view a perfect record (fulfillment of all seven Noahide laws) is not required of gentiles.

In one regard it is easier for a righteous non-Jew to enter the next world than it is for a Jew: There is a large list of heresies and sins that can deprive a Jew of a share in the hereafter.[36] Yet, since most *mitzvot* (commandments) bind Jews but not non-Jews, Jews would have an added benefit: The additional *mitzvot* provide whatever spiritual boons performance of *mitzvot* bestows, along with greater opportunities to exhibit devotion, obedience, and sacrifice. However, Lifshitz mentions as well the counterpoint – that ethical non-Jews are superior to ethical Jews in that they freely choose their paths, on their own, while Jews have divine assistance in the form of revelation.

---

[35] See his commentary, *Tiferet Yisrael*, to *Avot* 3:14 and *Sanhedrin* 10:1. The translation is by Moshe Miller (unpublished) with an addition of my own. See also Resh Lakish's view in *Midrash Tanḥuma*, Lekh Lekha 6. (The credit given to Drake is incorrect.)

[36] See Maimonides, introduction to Mishnah *Sanhedrin* 10 (where he enunciates the Thirteen Principles of Faith); *Mishneh Torah*, Laws of Repentance, ch. 3.

The ultimate moral of the preceding discussion is that ethics has come to carry significant weight for some religious authorities, sometimes greater than theology, as a criterion for inclusion in the World-to-Come. This is hardly a consensus, however, and there are various interpretive issues.

DOES JUDAISM AIM AT CONVERTING GENTILES?

Jewish tradition ascribes great achievements to converts. These include the biblical character Ruth, ancestor of King David, and Onkelos, traditionally said to have translated the Bible into Aramaic during the talmudic period. And yet, according to talmudic law, when individuals seek to convert, the court that hears the request (Jewish conversions take place before judges) probes their sincerity in a way that seems calculated to discourage: "Do you not know that the Jews at this time are persecuted and oppressed, despised, harassed and overcome by afflictions?" If a prospective proselyte answers with an apparently sincere affirmative, the court impresses upon that candidate that acts which are of no consequence for a non-Jew carry heavy punishments when performed by a member of the Jewish faith (*Yevamot* 47a). This approach seems aimed at accepting only those with the sincerest motives, a very low likelihood of backsliding, and a true willingness to take on the burdens of Jewish law and the existential risks of joining the Jewish people. Jews welcome such converts; but they don't seek them. Certainly there is no doctrine of mission as in Christianity. Indeed, Judaism's attitude to other religions is largely, as I said, live-and-let-live, except where those religions threaten the welfare of society. In Michael Broyde's words, Judaism emphasizes inreach – "the process by which Jews make Jews into better Jews" – but not outreach.[37]

The reluctance to proselytize is a striking feature of Judaism, and at first blush reflects an admirable tolerance of and respect for others. Nonetheless, such a stance on proselytizing confronts a dual charge of unfairness. First, there is a divine unfairness: What could justify God's excluding the overwhelming majority of humanity from valuable spiritual

---

[37] Broyde 1999, 45. That Jews should not proselytize has long been the dominant opinion. Cf. Robert Goldenberg (1997, 93): "Overall, the rabbinic corpus [in the talmudic period] presents a wide variety of attitudes toward the value of proselytism ... these diverse opinions cannot be homogenized into a single 'normative' rabbinic view." In the early centuries after Christianity arose, some Jews did proselytize while others were opposed or indifferent to the practice. See Berger 2010c, 367–68.

experience and accomplishment, granting this only to a single group that constitutes 0.3 percent of the world population? And there is seemingly human unfairness: Is it right of Jews to be indifferent to others' spiritual welfare? Why don't Jews act benevolently to others by communicating and arguing for what they regard as truth, as the Church does?[38] Not only would proselytizing convey *truth* but it can also bring those who are proselytized to salvation. Salvation and truth aside, religion is so bound up with basic questions of how to live and find meaning, that, by the lights of a proselytizer, convincing the other will benefit that person in the here and now.

We may refer to our questions, collectively, as *the problem of indifference* (to others' spiritual welfare). Why don't Jews want to bring others the opportunity to be part of the religion they deem true? The quick answer is that non-Jews who observe the Noahide laws attain salvation without converting. But there are other dimensions to refraining from proselytizing, and the "quick answer" itself can be made wider and deeper.

I divide arguments against proselytizing into three categories: practical, ethical, and philosophical.

Practical Considerations: Interfaith Relations

Historically, it was dangerous for Jews to aggressively proselytize, and the chances for success were small. Worse, Jewish proselytizing could encourage Christian proselytizing, an undesirable outcome for Jews.[39] (Christians who proselytize will not be comparably fearful of Jews proselytizing.) Proselytizing can also "poison intergroup relations" (Berger 2010c, 376).

Such explanations in terms of historical *realia* are very plausible. Is there, in addition, a coherent, compelling theoretical reason not to proselytize, which would hold even when relations are and will continue to be amicable?

---

[38] The benevolence argument and other arguments for (and against) proselytizing, are assessed in Thiessen 2011 and Marty 1999. The famed logician Willard van Orman Quine, who seldom ventured into theology, summed up the benevolence argument admirably: "If someone firmly believes that eternal salvation and damnation hinge on embracing his particular religion, he would be callous indeed to sit tolerantly back and watch others go to hell" (Quine 1987, 208).

[39] See Berger 2010c, 367–70. Berger notes that because of persecutions, some Jews may have wanted gentiles to remain unconverted in order that they not be saved.

Practical Considerations: Particularism as a Means to Universalism

Some have argued that God "chose" Abraham because having seen humanity thrice sin – first, Adam and Eve, then the generation of the Flood, and next the Tower of Babel – God took a different route. He chose a particular people – Abraham and his descendants – who would be commanded to teach and inspire others to act ethically and follow the path commanded by God. Choosing this people with universalist goals in mind "is God's way of taking a longer, slower, surer path to the achievement of His universal objective" (Berger 2005a, 84).[40] This objective can be attained only by keeping the particular character of the people charged with actualizing that objective.[41] God is satisfied to wait till the end of days to be widely recognized. It is true that Abraham, in Jewish tradition, sought to win adherents to his worldview. It can be argued, though, that the conversion of his followers was only to monotheism and ethical conduct.

Ethical Considerations: Group Identity

To proselytize, it may be argued, is to jar and impair individual and group identity, which is ethically wrong. Proselytizing also interferes with other people fulfilling a duty to carry out their traditions (still another ethical violation). In a phrase of Samuel Lebens (2021b), it does "epistemic violence." This argument has its limits as an explanation of an aversion to proselytizing. It does not militate strongly against proselytizing *secularists* or those who, like the Khazar, the king in Judah Halevi's *Kuzari*, are *seeking* another religion.

Ethical Considerations: Preserving Freedom

Martin Marty (1999, 2) speaks of "the freedom to be alone and to choose one's own opinion, belief, creed, or party without intrusion."[42] Soloveitchik (1964, 23) uses a freedom argument as well.

---

[40] Allen Friedman made a similar point in correspondence.
[41] Jewish law goes further by prohibiting gentiles from adopting the most prominent Jewish practices. But cf. Hirschman 2000, Linzer 2005.
[42] Cf. Nietzsche 1991 #82: "He who wants to desert a party or a religion believes it incumbent upon him to refute it. But this is a very arrogant notion. All that is needed is that he should be clear as to the nature of the bonds that formerly tied him ... and to the fact that they no longer do so."

The freedom argument ties in with the one about preserving group identity. So long as the freedom is unharmful, it can be used to ground a live-and-let-live policy.

Ethical Considerations: Privacy

It has been argued that proselytizing intrudes on the privacy of faith.[43] But what does "privacy" mean, and can it really ground an objection to proselytizing?

One understanding is that religious beliefs (or some of them) are private insofar as they are not supportable by reasons, and may not be defeasible by reasons. Rather, they are a matter of faith, of existential choice. But privacy in this sense does not extend across the board to all believers, and it does not militate against proselytizing someone whose religious commitment is evidence-based and who may be persuaded by hearing or reading other people's opinions and arguments. Additionally, there are arguments for and against particular religions or particular denominations that use premises shared by the interlocutors (e.g., a common text like the Bible, used heavily in Jewish-Christian polemics), which makes persuasion possible. Of course, a largely fideistic approach can ground a privacy argument *for those who have no supporting reasons*. But privacy construed as the absence of reasons cannot generate an objection to any and all proselytizing.

One further question about this notion of privacy: Couldn't the same be said about moral argumentation in certain cases – namely, where moral disagreements trace to opposing rock-bottom ethical intuitions, between which rational argument will not adjudicate? Yet to rule out proselytizing in *moral* argumentation would be a virtual *reductio ad absurdum* of the privacy theory regarding participation in public discourse.

There is, however, another understanding of privacy. To wit, what makes religious belief private or intimate is that it involves not just belief but a *relationship* (with God).[44] People often prefer staying reticent about their innermost feelings in a relationship, and others ought not try to talk them out of those relationships; in fact, perhaps others ought not discuss them at all with the people who are in the relationship. We often wonder,

---

[43] See Soloveitchik 1964.
[44] Aaron Segal raised this suggestion. On the concept of having a relationship with God, see Golding 1993.

"How could B ever marry A? What did she see in A?" But we know it is improper to ask B that question.

True, there are instances in which it is proper to talk someone out of a relationship, such as the case of an abusive family member or a deceitful or dangerous friend. Nonetheless, and despite Richard Dawkins's oft-repeated and oft-challenged remarks to the effect that indoctrinating children into religion is a form of child abuse,[45] an atheist or member of another religion usually will have a hard time persuading a believer that a relationship with God (as that believer conceives it) is abusive or harmful. The current suggestion covers many cases and, I think, fares well as an explication of privacy.

In sum, privacy can refer to (i) the absence of reasons for religious belief or (ii) the fact religion involves the feeling of relationship. The absence-of-reasons understanding of privacy works (if at all) only when the potential proselytizee believes in some measure on faith. The suggestion about relationship works well, but it would not apply if belief in a relationship with God is thought by an atheist or an adherent of another religion to be harmful to the believer or to others.

Ethical Considerations: Reciprocity

Consider this Immanuel Kant-inspired principle: Do not proselytize others, because you would not want to be proselytized yourself. Unfortunately, this argument does not explain why one should not be *open* to being proselytized, nor why it is wrong to proselytize in cases in which you yourself would not mind being proselytized. Nonetheless, it goes some distance toward explaining the dominant Jewish approach, especially since our questions included cases of people who want to continue adhering to their religion and therefore are *not* willing to be proselytized.

Philosophical Considerations: Pluralism

Trends like pluralism, relativism, perspectivism, and postmodernism (which on some readings entails relativism) ostensibly provide a ready answer to our question. These schools of thought, whatever differences exist between them, promote the idea that each belief system is, in

---

[45] Dawkins 2006, 348.

Wittgenstein's phrase, "in order as it is."⁴⁶ Persuasion thus seems unnecessary and inappropriate.⁴⁷ Abraham Unger (2010, 138) makes the point this way:

> Philosophically then, we are living in a period that presumes a confidence in the authenticity of one's own cultural context, obviating the need to negotiate one's particularistic convictions.

As Martin Marty (1999, 2) puts it, conversion efforts "violate at least the implicit rules of the pluralist game."⁴⁸ So pluralism, along with relativism, perspectivism, and postmodernism, cuts against an ethic that encourages, let alone mandates, proselytizing.⁴⁹

Many dismiss this objection to proselytizing by dismissing pluralism, relativism, perspectivism, and postmodernism. This rejection would invoke matters like (i) the self-defeating character of the views (e.g., is the thesis of relativism itself true only relatively?); (ii) the fact that pluralists themselves maintain strong views about many topics, including strong opposition to others' views, contrary to their stated approach;⁵⁰ and (iii) what one believes becomes, on the cited views, a matter of indifference – why should I care what I believe? (*A fortiori*, pluralism cannot explain the mandate in Judaism to martyr oneself rather than perform certain acts.⁵¹) There are more matters for pluralists to address, such as (iv) explaining the role of argumentation and polemics in their framework. Pluralists might have resources to handle these problems. All I can do here is call attention to them and state my belief that the objections will stand.⁵²

Philosophical Considerations: The Value of Diversity

Another argument is not so much an ethical objection to proselytizing as an attempt to find positive ethical significance in leaving other faiths alone. Mendelssohn and Jonathan Sacks (2003) suggest that aversion to

---

⁴⁶ Wittgenstein 2009, 1:98 (in a different context).
⁴⁷ As many have noted, to be a pluralist is not to *tolerate*. I tolerate a belief when I think it's false; when I think it's equal in "truth-hood" to mine, I am not tolerating it, because I am not even contradicting it.
⁴⁸ As mentioned earlier, however, Marty suggests at one point that precisely because people confront so many choices of beliefs, the proselytizer does them a favor by leading them to accept one rather than remain overwhelmed.
⁴⁹ See also Thiessen 2011, 62–71.
⁵⁰ See similarly Williamson 2019.
⁵¹ See also M. Soloveichik 2007.
⁵² See, however, Rynhold 2019.

proselytizing is a result of Judaism's appreciation of diversity and desire to cultivate it. The moral advantage of living with diversity, with different ways of relating to God, is that it makes possible the virtue of tolerance, which cannot thrive in uniformity. Mendelssohn wrote, "Brothers, if you care for true godliness, let us not pretend that conformity exists where *diversity is obviously the plan and goal of Providence.*"[53] The existence of other religions creates a breeding ground for virtue. Refraining from proselytizing is deciding that it is more important for Jews to cultivate tolerance and respect for the other than to share with others that which one regards as truth. The diversity argument is difficult to defend, however, if some other religions are prohibited even to gentiles, as they constitute *avodah zarah* for them.[54]

Philosophical Considerations: Ethnicity and Nationhood

Judaism, unlike Christianity and Islam, is rooted not only in beliefs, practices, and attitudes, but in ethnicity. Ruth declared to her mother-in-law Naomi: "Your people are my people, and your god is my god" (Ruth 1:16). She both joined Naomi's people existentially and embraced the Jewish God. Accepting some converts – those who are truly devoted and who identify with the people – is one thing. But seeking converts is another, because at least theoretically these efforts threaten to pry ethnicity and religion apart on a fairly large scale.[55]

Philosophical Considerations: It's Not Broken

Finally, we come to a family I call the "It's not broken" arguments. The general idea behind this approach is that other religions do not have defects that would necessitate proselytizing; they are in order, or sufficiently in order, as they stand. Proselytizing is pointless. There are several variants of this view.

One variant amounts to pluralism: If all religions are true, proselytizing is unnecessary. We've seen that this approach confronts notorious

---

[53] As quoted in M. Gottlieb 2013, 112. Given Gottlieb's analysis, Mendelssohn's argument is more complicated than my introduction of it here suggests. But the quotation is useful.
[54] This was pointed out by David Berger.
[55] See also Berger 2010c, 368; Goshen-Gottstein 2012, 27–28. Lebens 2022a, 3–37, argues, based on the Book of Ruth, that attachment to community and nation is necessary for commitment to God.

problems. A different form of pluralism (and of "It's not broken") maintains that, although not all religions are true, adherents of other religions already have a suitable relationship with God by virtue of subscribing to their religions. This notion is presented sharply by the twelfth-century Yemenite rabbi Nethanel Ibn al-Fayumi, who maintains that God sends prophets to each nation, establishing every religion's relationship with the deity.[56] On such a view, there is no reason for Jews to proselytize.

As we discussed, another attempt to acknowledge that adherents of other religions enjoy relationships with God by means of their religion is suggested by Abraham Isaac Kook and John Hick.[57] Religions are culturally conditioned responses to the indescribable divine reality.[58] In his book *Jerusalem*, Mendelssohn makes a claim that is paraphrased by Michah Gottlieb as follows: "[M]ultiple representations of religious truth help prevent people from imagining that their particular religious symbols adequately signify the unconditional."[59] Diversity is therefore desirable.

Yet even Hick and Kook concede, as was pointed out earlier, that some religions are better than others in their representations of the divine and their ethical conduct. Why, then, shouldn't Jews proselytize to give others what by their lights is a *better* religion? And is it fair that only Jews have this assumed superior religion? Jews "proselytize" nonreligious Jews, so why not proselytize non-Jews?

Another form of the "It's not broken" argument is closely related to the preceding one, suggesting that all people have the potential to relate to God, even without conversion. This argument refers to spiritual *possibilities* – potential connections to God – for non-Jews. Indeed, a *midrash* tells us, "If a person wants to be a *tzaddik*, he may be one even if he is a gentile, because it is not a title determined by ancestry."[60] As noted previously – but now I'll quote in full – Maimonides affirms that:

Each and every human being, from anywhere in the world, whose spirit has moved him and whose knowledge has given him understanding to set himself apart in order to stand before the Lord, to serve Him, to worship Him, and to know Him, who walks upright as God created him to do, and releases himself

---

[56] See Jospe 2012, 107–9.
[57] Their view resembles a form of Hinduism.
[58] For Kook, though, this may be true with the exception of Judaism, which is based on the Sinaitic revelation.
[59] Gottlieb 2013, 100. This fleshes out a Mendelssohnian view mentioned earlier.
[60] *Bemidbar Rabbah* 8:2. See also *Tanna de-Bei Eliyahu* 10.

from the yoke of the many foolish considerations which trouble people – such an individual is as sanctified as the Holy of Holies (*kodesh kodashim*), and his portion and inheritance shall be in the Lord forever and ever.[61]

Apparently, such a person need not even adopt a formal religion. (In fact, Maimonides did not want people inventing their own religions.[62])

The argument against proselytizing that Mendelssohn presents in his letter to Lavater can be represented as yet another version of "It's not broken." Mendelssohn's words (quoted earlier) were: "Convert a Confucius or a Solon? What for? ... It seems to me that anyone who leads men to virtue in this life cannot be damned in the next." One need not be Jewish to achieve spiritual heights.

But the following question arises. According to Judaism, doesn't Judaism afford a *higher* level of relationship with God than do other religions, and with it a correspondingly higher reward? The argument from salvation that is under discussion makes it appear that people take religion and either pass or fail rather than getting a letter grade reflecting their level of achievement. A gentile's gaining access to the hereafter would not negate the fact that while alive, the gentile did not attain all that he or she could have spiritually. Why aren't there more opportunities for gentiles to embrace the "true" religion in this life? The notion that we can lower the demands for gaining reward (allowing ethics as the criterion, per our earlier discussion) does not address the question of why we don't focus on bringing the person up to an optimal level.

A possible reply is that according to the midrashic and Maimonidean texts cited earlier, non-Jews can rise to the *highest* spiritual levels such as *tzaddik*, "God-fearer," and "as sanctified as Holy of Holies." Thus, we are not ipso facto bringing X to a *higher* level by *converting* X. The encomia ("God-fearer" etc.) suggest that non-Jews can reach the *highest* levels. And even if they cannot, some of the other considerations against proselytizing are strengthened if non-Jews can attain salvation without converting.[63]

In this context, a word is in order about conversion in Jewish eschatology. Jewish texts about the *eschaton* supply a variety of visions. Some

---

[61] *Mishneh Torah*, Laws of Sabbatical and Jubilee Years 13:13. (The translation, with small changes, is from Kellner 2006a, 247.)

[62] See n. 34.

[63] David Berger made this point. Another question is why Jews need to observe all the commandments if others can attain salvation and the highest levels of religiosity without observing all the commandments. This question requires a close look at chosenness and covenant.

emphasize vengeance, retribution, and destruction; others highlight acknowledgment of the truth of Judaism or even conversion by the rest of the world at the end of days.[64] Several biblical texts are relevant to this topic (Isa. 2:1–4, Mic. 4:1–5, Zeph. 3:9, Zach. 14:9). Maimonides's formulation is that at the end of days, "the earth will be filled with knowledge of the Lord" (quoting Isa. 11:9), and all people "will accept the true religion."[65] But what he intends by "the true religion" has been debated.[66] For Maimonides, it may be that conversion to a full Judaism would not be necessary given three of his views: (i) Judaism aims ultimately at knowledge of God; (ii) Abraham knew God even prior to the legislation at Sinai;[67] (iii) anyone with the proper orientation can be among the "Holy of Holies."

Philosophical Considerations: The Role of Religions in History

We saw earlier that Halevi, Maimonides, and others affirmed that Christianity and Islam produced positive effects for world and/or Jewish history. This would explain why God allows the other religions to flourish. Arguably, we can turn this claim into a reason for not proselytizing. Perhaps God implements His ends by means of *other* religions because these religions can best produce positive effects if they operate as non-Jewish endeavors rather than Jewish ones (especially assuming that only a small part of the gentile world would convert to Judaism if Jews would in fact proselytize).

Initially, Jewish tradition's reluctance to proselytize seemed to violate the duty of benevolence. But although not every putative justification we considered was convincing, we have found several that are.

SUMMATION

Despite ambiguities in key Jewish sources, often profound disagreements, and the existence of stingingly deprecatory attitudes toward other peoples and religions – attitudes that must be acknowledged even though

---

[64] On texts concerning these scenarios and how scholars have approached them, see Berger 2010b, 121–35.
[65] *Mishneh Torah*, Laws of Kings 12:1.
[66] See Rapoport 2008 and Kellner 2008.
[67] *Mishneh Torah*, Laws of Foreign Worship, ch. 1.

they were not elaborated upon here – we find Jewish texts that allow for multiple paths to salvation; texts that respect, within limits, the integrity of other religions; and texts that find value in other religions, whether historical, social, or even ideological. These approaches, old though they are, generally accord with sensibilities that are functioning in today's globalized world.

PART IV

FAITH AND REASON

10

Reason, Faith, and Some Spaces in Between

The dichotomy of faith and reason is among the most famous of the "great divides" in philosophy, right up there with rationalism and empiricism, dualism and materialism, utilitarianism and deontologism, and natural law and positivism. But as is often the case with great divides, this one can be narrowed. In this chapter I want to look at various ways to build hybrid views of faith-and-reason within rationalism (which stresses the value of reason) and within fideism (which stresses the value of faith). Views that stress reason may incorporate faith, and views that stress faith might incorporate reason. In all we will have fourteen models for hybrids. In the words of George Mavrodes (1988, 4), "no simple dichotomous distinction is likely to be deeply illuminating in the field of religious epistemology."

To carry out my aim, I will formulate different types of rationalism and fideism, and explore their motivations, their consequences, and in many cases the difficulties they face. I also of course identify the hybrid models and relate them to Jewish sources. I argue not only that there are hybrids that grow out of arguments in medieval Jewish philosophy for what I'll call "prescriptive rationalism," but that certain arguments of medieval rationalists in truth support a more fideistic view.[1]

It is important to realize that conceptions of the nature of faith, the justification of faith, and the place of faith in religious life have undergone

---

[1] Ideally a section on faith and reason should consist of three chapters. The first would deal with Jewish approaches to proofs of God's existence, the second with the material in this chapter, and the third with what faith requires and how it can be justified. A draft of that trilogy grew unfeasibly long, and I chose to use only the middle chapter here, with a small amount from the other two chapters.

much nuancing in recent philosophical literature. Novel, often contested, claims have been advanced. Space considerations preclude my elaborating in this chapter on more than a few aspects of the state of the art, but among the most widely discussed theses concerning faith, some of them old but receiving renewed attention, are:

- that belief is not truly a requirement of faith
- that even if *some* cognitive orientation is required for faith, orientations other than belief can serve: "accepting," "being confident," "assuming" (e.g., for the sake of practical reasoning), "having a 'belief-like' attitude," "thinking it likely that," "assigning a certain credence level," or "believing in" (as opposed to "believing that")
- that faith is a matter of risk-taking or plunge-taking – "Faith is the courage to take risks, to walk on ahead. Faith is not certainty; it is the courage to live with uncertainty" (Sacks 2023, x)
- that orthopraxy[2] is a viable position
- that faith is compatible with doubt but belief is not
- that, as Blaise Pascal and William James thought, faith can be justified by its pragmatic benefits
- that faith requires resilience in the face of counterevidence
- that a cognitive orientation, assuming one is required, must be conjoined with certain affective states (e.g., passion, humility, awe, gratitude, optimism, trust) and certain behavior (e.g., compliance with God's commands), and perhaps participation in community
- that although faith requires passion, passion may lead to fanaticism and violence, and it must be held in check by reason and morality.[3]

While some of these elements will enter our discussion, the conception of faith used in this chapter sounds as old-fashioned as it is stereotypical: faith is a propositional belief. You believe that p while believing

---

[2] I.e., practice without belief; see also Lefkowitz 2014 on "social Orthodoxy."
[3] Among key writings about one or another of these claims are: Clegg 1979; Alston 1996; Halbertal 2005; Audi 2011; Buchak 2012, 2014, 2017a, 2017b; Howard-Snyder 2013; Kvanvig 2013; Muggs 2016; Wettstein 2019; Jackson 2023a, 2023b; Lebens 2023a, 17–28; Rosenberg 2023. The Talmud and Midrash (e.g., *Sotah* 37a) tell a story about Naḥshon ben Aminadav, who in this rabbinic narrative took the first plunge into the waters of the Sea with the Egyptians in hot pursuit (Exod. 14). Some commentators consider the possibility that Naḥshon's plunge exemplifies a willingness to take risks (and quite literally a plunge), rather than a fully confident belief that God would spare him from death. (My thanks to Aaron Segal for noting this midrash.) On religion and violence, see Sacks 2017, where, inter alia, he responds to those who post-9/11 indicted religion on moral grounds.

you don't meet certain epistemic standards. ("Believing what you know ain't so," in Mark Twain's sardonic paraphrase.) I concede this conception's primitiveness, incompleteness, and infirmities from the get-go. But despite their vices, simplistic conceptions often help focus issues, both interpretive and conceptual, and repay study.

So, to put the question: Does "the righteous person live by his faith" (Hab. 2:4)? Or by reason? Or perhaps by both?

SIMPLE FAITH VERSUS RATIONALISM

There exists in Judaism the concept of *emunah temimah* or *emunah peshutah* – a simple, pure, or perfect faith, not anchored in rational considerations, perhaps free of and immune to doubt,[4] impregnable no matter what contrary evidence has been or will be produced. One "inherits his belief from tradition, and does not wish to develop it, to refine it, or to elevate it"; this, as opposed to one who "is not satisfied with the simple faith, but wishes to establish his faith and to enhance it by using a coherent and systematic philosophy."[5] Many Jews have embraced the former model, especially but not only in *haredi* (ultra-Orthodox) society. In Jewish history, a simple-faith model has frequently been accompanied by hostility to philosophy – hostility not only to non-Jewish philosophy but also to bold philosophical works of Jewish provenance like Maimonides's *Guide of the Perplexed*.

This antagonism arose because in response to the question, "Do the righteous live by their faith or by their reason?," Maimonides and the medieval Jewish philosophers known as rationalists, as well as some later thinkers, answered: by their reason.[6] It is not that religious experience, tradition (including but not restricted to claims of divinely revealed truths), and faith have no positive role to play in religious life according to any of the rationalists. Rather, it's that the highest level of religious achievement requires immersion in the activity of proving the existence of God, as well as His unity and other attributes, in the strictest sense of the word "proof" – and in establishing and elucidating other beliefs, such as belief in providence, in accord with philosophical and scientific reasoning. Most but not all of these philosophers assign some epistemic

---

[4] I say "perhaps" because some Hasidic thinkers see room for doubt within faith; see later on R. Nahman of Bratslav.
[5] Brown 2005. The translation is from Hershkowitz 2013, 457.
[6] I am speaking of *religious* rationalism, not, for example, rationalism as the foil to empiricism.

weight to traditions and to faith, but not as much weight as they assign to demonstrations (roughly, ironclad proofs);[7] moreover, traditions are reinterpreted in the light of what makes sense to reason. Jewish rationalists also believed, as did Muslim counterparts, that there is a religious obligation to establish religious truths by reason and to understand God philosophically.[8] Some rationalists, notably Baḥya ibn Pakuda, go further and disparage the epistemic credentials of beliefs based on tradition.[9] Notably, Jewish tradition, especially after the medieval period, pays far less attention to the classic arguments than does Christian thought.[10] Daniel Rynhold (2009, 27) writes even that "arguments for the existence of God are not central in the syllabus of medieval Jewish thought, or indeed in the history of Jewish philosophy." Yet rationalism may be the best-known *movement* concerning faith and reason.[11]

In many of the texts we will examine, disputes about faith and reason are really about *traditions* and reason as sources of belief. Therefore, while I will use the word "faith" to position the discussion in the philosopher's framework of rationalism vs. fideism, I will use it to cover not faith arising in a vacuum from a sudden inspiration, but rather certain positive

---

[7] More technically, arguments that use only self-evidently true premises and propositions logically entailed by them.

[8] On Islamic religious epistemology and its numerous nuances, see Doko and Turner 2023.

[9] See Baḥya ibn Pakuda 1970, 63 (*Sha'ar Ha-Yiḥud* 2).

[10] Exceptions include Moses Mendelssohn.

[11] It has been argued that the Bible contains arguments for God's existence (see, e.g., D. Shapiro 1963). Many "arguments," however (e.g., Isa. 40:26, Jer. 5:22, 31:35–36), are addressed to people who already believe, and arguably they seek only to increase the audience's appreciation of God's creations and of His greatness. (Cf. Barr 1993, Manekin 2017.) A *midrash* sees Abraham as coming to God by reasoning that looks like either a design or cosmological argument (*Gen. Rabbah* 39:1), and R. Akiva wields a design argument against a heretic (*Midrash Temurah* 1:5). In the Abraham *midrash*, the patriarch arrives at God on his own, by reason, whereas in the biblical text, God reveals Himself to Abraham; this suggests that the Rabbis were making a point of assigning value to arriving at God by reason. But cf. Crescas 2018, 119 (1:3:6), who thinks that although Abraham used reasoning, attaining certainty required prophecy – via the revelation in Gen. 12:1 – showing reason is limited. (See Harvey 2018b.) Interestingly, some Orthodox rabbinic figures who one would think are fideists maintain that the design argument is so clearly cogent that only being bribed by desires could prevent someone from accepting it. (See Wasserman 1962, ch. 1)

Contrary to the conventional wisdom that after Hume and Kant natural theology is dead, arguments for God's existence are very much alive among analytic philosophers though hotly contested. As just one of countless examples, see the essays in Walls and Doughtery 2018, a collection that picks up on Alvin Plantinga's twenty-four "indicators" of God's existence.

attitudes to traditions. In some cases, tradition is accepted without sufficient evidence; in others, a sophisticated epistemological argument shows that the tradition's very existence functions as *some* evidence of its truth.

DESCRIPTIVE RATIONALISM, DESCRIPTIVE FIDEISM

Both rationalism and fideism come in two variations: descriptive and prescriptive (or, if you will, normative). The descriptive versions make empirical claims, and state (*roughly*) either:

Descriptive rationalism: People believe the tenets of their religion based on reason, or
Descriptive fideism: People believe the tenets of their religion based on faith.

The prescriptive versions state (likewise roughly) either:

Prescriptive rationalism: People ought to believe the tenets of their religion based on reason, or
Prescriptive fideism: People ought to believe the tenets of their religion based on faith (prescriptive fideism).

Establishing the descriptive rationalist claim that "people" – as a general matter – believe the tenets of their (theistic) religion based on good or bad reasons seems hopeless. Many religious people have no arguments for God's existence, let alone for other propositions their religion endorses, such as *God created the world* or *God exercises providence over individuals*, and many do not even *think* they need one. Jewish prescriptive rationalists are under no illusions about this; that is, about the role that reason actually plays – or, better, doesn't play – in religious life. They think that many among the masses believe on some basis other than reason, like unquestioning faith. They, the rationalists, accept descriptive fideism. In their view, lack of reasoning keeps the masses encrusted in false beliefs. Prescriptive rationalism is a critique of the *norm* of *emunah temimah*, not of descriptive claims about how much *emunah temimah* exists in Jewish circles.

The claim that religious belief is based on faith is often invoked for normative purposes – as a rebuff to demands for a rational defense of religious belief. The thought is that one who demands reasons of a theist is not comprehending what faith *is*, and not understanding that the demand for reasons is inappropriate. This line of thought is a glaring variation of an is-ought (or fact-norm) fallacy: empirically, people believe the tenets of their religion based on faith, therefore one cannot demand reasons of the faith-holder.

The answer to "Is religion based on reason, or is it based on faith?" is singularly unexciting: for some people it's reason, for others (probably the majority) faith. Not to mention my central claim that there can be numerous hybrids. Now, it is hardly a waste of time for philosophers to gather facts about trends in religious belief. Pew studies furnish interesting data and are invaluable for understanding the sociology, psychology, and politics surrounding religion at given times. But pumping philosophical theses out of that data is difficult.[12]

THE HYBRID MODELS

The hybrid models, to which we now turn, are built either by inserting a rationalist element into faith or vice-versa (inserting faith into reason). Note that numerous of these models might not have been conceptualized as hybrids by those presenting them. These individuals may have viewed themselves as pristine rationalists or pristine fideists. *The models are not mutually exclusive.* I start with the simplest, and matters then get more complicated. We need to grant second-order uses of reason or tradition in bestowing epistemic status. That is, the various forms of rationalism and fideism are argued for by means of reason and/or tradition.

Model 1: Believing the Absurd

The first model comes from a surprising place: the thesis that (in the words of Church Father Tertullian, 160–240) "I believe because it is absurd." The model is also embraced by Søren Kierkegaard.

---

[12] One attempt at pumping, however, is the argument from *consensus gentium* (common consent). This argument moves from "All (or most) people believe that God exists" to "It is true that God exists." Once widespread, the argument is now seldom heard and is not taken seriously – it's basically absent from course syllabi, journals, critical surveys, and the voluminous ranks of philosophical handbooks/companions. Thomas Kelly (2011), however, thinks that the *consensus gentium* argument is better than it's given credit for. It is often used when *p* lies outside the religious sphere, so why should religion be treated differently? Ultimately, after engaging with various objections, Kelly suggests that the sociological-cum-psychological question "What do people really believe about God?" is the critical one. Kelly ends inconclusively but notes such issues as the possibility of self-deception and conflicting conceptions of God. Another use to which empirical research could be put is determining how people understand what faith is and what reason is; see Citron 2014.

Believing the absurd sounds like fideism par excellence. But doesn't Tertullian's and Kierkegard's model for faith require the believer to engage in rational assessment in order to determine that certain beliefs are absurd? (I raised objections to the allure of the absurd in Chapter 8.)[13]

Model 2: Expansion by Inference

This model is exceedingly simple: Someone may infer certain propositions (by reason) from propositions contained in the tradition.[14] This practice is rather common in Judaism, since the biblical and rabbinic belief system needs expansion.

Model 3: Confirming or Strengthening Faith

If you believe that p on faith in a tradition, having an argument *in addition to that* raises the subjective confidence level of your belief. In the case of one who already holds to their faith/tradition with *subjective certitude*, the argument could raise the level of confidence to which the person is *entitled*. Someone might hold that tradition lends further support even when you have a proof, but it's not obvious how, if the proof is thought to yield 100 percent certainty.

Model 4: Overdetermination – the Consistency of Having Faith and Having Reasons

Daniel Howard-Snyder (2013, 368–70) notes that the philosophers and scientists called "neoatheists" maintain that faith requires the absence of evidence – and on that ground attack theism as irrational. The neoatheists would seem to be wrong that having faith and having evidence are incompatible, for there are cases where a belief is overdetermined. Imagine that a defense attorney's son is accused of a terrible crime.[15] The attorney might believe on faith, from the outset, prior to viewing any evidence from the case, that her son is innocent. But to successfully defend her son in court, she must eventually construct a convincing evidential argument for his innocence. She does so and finds the argument logically compelling.

---

[13] It is commonly thought that Judaism has very few affirmations of "I believe because it is absurd." I'm not sure about this; a lot depends on what is meant.
[14] See Mavrodes 1988, 32.
[15] A case inspired by Lehrer 1971 (which is not about religious belief).

Model 5: Belief "Based on" Faith but Having Reasons

Suppose that although the lawyer has good exculpatory arguments, her love is so strong that she would continue to believe in her son's innocence *even if* she had no rebuttal of the condemning evidence. Is the lawyer's belief that her son is innocent "based on" faith? Yes, in two senses. Sense one pertains to etiology, the *genesis* of the belief: it *originated* in faith. Sense two pertains to the *strength* of the belief: Even if the person would not have good reasons, or even would have good reasons for not believing, she would still believe on faith. So someone may endorse an argument for *God exists* and yet believe *God exists* on faith. Of course if the attorney were to surrender her "faith" in her son were the evidence to point the other way, then her belief, while not based on reason etiologically, is based on reason in terms of strength. In the case of overdetermination, the lawyer's view is etiologically based on faith, but in terms of strength of support is based on both. If a conflict arises, she may have to suspend belief.

In sum, believing that *p on faith* is compatible with possessing evidence for *p*, but distinctions should be drawn between cases with regard to strength of belief.

Model 6: Grounding the Tradition

This model harks back to model 4. Someone might use a rational argument based on neutral premises to establish the reliability and truth of tradition. "Reason does not generate revelations, but it vouches for the truth of them" (Mavrodes 1988, 24, discussing Locke[16]). Now, one's reason might seek to establish the truth of the *content of* the tradition on a tenet-by-tenet basis; but alternatively, it might establish the epistemic right to believe that the tradition is true just because it is one's tradition. One way to do this is to advocate for a principle of doxastic or epistemic conservatism, as articulated by Joshua Golding (2022, 61):

> Given a certain tradition, those individuals who are brought up in that tradition have a reason for adhering to the tradition, until and unless they find reason to believe that the tradition is flawed, incoherent, or based on erroneous doctrines.

This principle does not claim that the tradition is true, only that a person who has received the tradition is rational in continuing to believe its claims unless new, undermining reasons emerge. Some would go further and say it is *irrational not to continue* to believe those claims.

---

[16] Locke, *Essay Concerning Human Understanding*, 4:19:4

The Hybrid Models 271

In general, making tradition a source of knowledge without assessing its content tenet by tenet is something that some contemporary epistemologists would accept. Conservatism yields a hybrid model, but one different from the tenet-by-tenet blend of faith and reason.[17]

Model 7: Resilience, Recalcitrance, Conservatism

Numerous philosophers import into the very definition of faith a condition that the faith be resilient.[18] Resilience implies continued belief and/or commitment in the teeth of contrary evidence.[19]

However, we should distinguish resilience from epistemic recalcitrance, and both of these from conservatism. Resilience (this is my own stipulative definition) involves a disposition to seek *plausible* ad hoc hypotheses to accommodate contrary evidence. As I am using the term, it is not consistent with making *no* effort to accommodate the evidence, and also not consistent with moving to *wild* ad hoc hypotheses. So when there is resilience, reason plays a role in reformulating faith, and that is where hybridness enters. When the person makes no effort at reconciliation (e.g., rejects reason in order to salvage a literal construal of tradition) or uses wild ad hoc hypotheses – that is, has a come-what-may approach to handling contrary evidence – that sort of believer is recalcitrant. Think of resilience as a soft recalcitrance.

Suppose, though, that we adopt a general epistemic conservatism like Golding's, cited earlier. Resilience requires engaging with contrary evidence, but on one understanding of conservatism, no engagement needs to take place for the conservative's belief to be justified. One simply says: I have an epistemic right to believe the tradition. Golding's

---

[17] An argument rooted in the *Kuzari* by the medieval poet and philosopher Judah Halevi (1:25) has recently won the surprising support of several analytic philosophers. (It also received the imprimatur of Jonathan Edwards – see Goldschmidt 2019). The "*Kuzari* argument" attempts to show that the revelation at Sinai occurred, based on the premise that reports of the revelation to a huge number of people were not contested in the period after they originated. The reported event is what has been called a "national unforgettable." This argument from uninterrupted tradition is not an argument for trusting traditions generally, but for a particular people believing their particular tradition because their tradition meets certain conditions. It is not a tenet-by-tenet justification of content. See Gottlieb 2017; Goldschmidt 2019; Lebens 2021b, 189–98. See also Golding 2022, 61–65. Cf. Gellman 2016, 73–90. Saʿadyah Gaon (Saadia Gaon 1948, 29–31 [introduction: 6]) uses a *Kuzari*-style argument to verify biblical reports of miracles.

[18] See, e.g., Howard-Snyder 2013, Buchak 2017b.

[19] The contrary evidence could be evidence against *p* or evidence that undermines one's earlier evidence that *p*.

formulation rejects this understanding: he writes, "until and unless they find reason to believe that the tradition is flawed, incoherent, or based on erroneous doctrines." In *this* version of conservatism, engagement is needed when counterevidence arises. (Whether a conservative should advocate *seeking* counterevidence with which to engage is another question.)[20]

We seem to have several types of reaction by faith-holders to counterevidence, then: (i) resilience where some effort at reconciliation with contrary evidence is made, but using plausible rather than wild ad hoc hypotheses; (ii) a recalcitrance where no effort at reconciliation is made; (iii) a recalcitrance where effort is made but wild ad hoc hypotheses are introduced; (iv) the resilience required by epistemic conservatism, which, depending on one's formulation, may or may not require engagement with contrary evidence and therefore may or may not be covered by (i).

The theistic beliefs of medieval rationalists have a nonrationalistic etiology: They were taught Judaism as children before they encountered or constructed proofs. That gives rise to this question: Would *they*, when intellectually mature, have continued to believe even in the absence of what they considered good arguments, or in the presence of contrary reasons? When they interpret certain verses and rabbinic dicta as figurative, this is a way of conserving dicta of the tradition. What if they had not found a way to interpret a verse or dictum figuratively? Maimonides at one point writes (1963, 330 [*Guide* 2:25, end]) that Aristotle's view that the world is eternal is incompatible with the Torah, and were eternity proved, "the Law (the Torah) would become void and a shift to other opinions would take place." Seemingly this illustrates the limits of figurative interpretation as a solution to conflicts between Torah and philosophy. But there are other possibilities: It could be a way (a) of impressing upon readers why Aristotle must be rejected, or (b) of saying that there could not be a convincing proof of Aristotle's view, because it would destroy Torah. Or, (c) is Maimonides saying (in an esotericist fashion) that contrary to his stated view, eternity and Torah are in truth compatible? Knowing the answer would help us detail the relationship between faith and reason – and the functioning of resilience – in Maimonides's thought.

---

[20] For a conservative, an antecedent belief allows one to explain away certain contrary evidence using hypotheses that someone without the antecedent belief is not likely to use and in fact should not use. Lebens (2020b, 209–12) uses this reasoning to explain how an Orthodox theist may deflect the challenge of biblical criticism. However, it is likely that the evidence for the antecedent belief should enter into the justification somewhere.

For those who find conservatism an affront to rationality, a euphemism for dogmatism and a rationale for confirmation bias, consider that in one of the most famous scholarly books of the twentieth century, Thomas Kuhn (1962) showed that scientists often hold on to a "paradigm" even in the face of evidence that seems to falsify it; "ad hoc hypotheses" will be constructed to explain that evidence away. The advice "Maximize coherence and minimize change," formulated by Gilbert Harman (1986), is a rule a lot of us follow.

Conservatism also has the support of common practice. Suppose that the renowned twentieth-century psychologist B. F. Skinner had delivered a lecture on behaviorism for the zillionth time. An audience member raises a novel objection to behaviorism – and Skinner, stymied, announces that he's giving up his career-long commitment to behaviorism as a result of the objection. Not only is this repudiation strange psychologically (aside: since it's Skinner, I should say "behaviorally"), but many would think – intuitively – that it's unwarranted epistemologically *for him* to abandon his view, even though for a novice, abandonment of the view may be right.

Additionally, on a view made famous by W. V. O. Quine, all epistemic justification is relative to an assumed set of beliefs. Conservatism also undergirds such approaches as Bayesian conditionalization, John Rawls's notion of reflective equilibrium and William James's idea that certain logical possibilities may be ignored because they are not "live options" for the person who is considering what to believe. And doesn't our powerful tendency to hold on to common-sense views about the external world, induction, memory, and other minds rescue us, happily, from the jaws of skepticism? Conservatism also inhibits us from discarding true beliefs prematurely.

But what could justify the principle of conservatism? We can't justify the approach as I just seemed to attempt – namely, by pointing to our embrace of it in our practice; that would be circular. Alternatively, perhaps the basis for conservatism is pragmatic: the principle rescues our belief systems from instability and frequent changes of view that are cognitively inefficient and could be disruptive to our existence. The principle is a form of self-preservation – it has survival value; pragmatically, it's better to hold on to the antecedently held theory for a while. Sa'adyah Gaon (Saadia Gaon 1948, 7 [introduction: 2]) sees instability as disruptive and as frustrating the development of correct belief.[21]

---

[21] On justifications for conservatism, see further Shatz 2004, ch. 3.

Yet suppose we have a justification for conservatism. Clearing the site isn't building the house. How should we balance any appeal conservativism enjoys with the desirability of innovation, revision and retraction? Where does conservatism end and dogmatism begin?

Let me move on to recast resilience vs. recalcitrance using the terms "moderate prescriptive fideism" and "extreme prescriptive fideism." According to moderate prescriptive fideism, a person who believes on the basis of tradition should show resilience by, say, reinterpreting the tradition; this, as opposed to extreme prescriptive fideism, which countenances recalcitrance. In moderate fideism, reason controls faith insofar as belief in tradition taken literally is acceptable *provided* it does not contradict the deliverances of reason.

Let's return briefly to the atheist charge that theists are recalcitrant fanatics: that they tenaciously retain their beliefs no matter how much evidence there is against them. It is fairly easy to refute the descriptive claim that theists do not give up theism in the face of contrary evidence, and also the more restricted claim that *when* they give up theism, it is not because they are presented with evidence that their beliefs are not justified (but instead for other reasons). All you need for this refutation is a Google search, or conversations with clerics about attrition in their flock. But the epistemic recalcitrance objection also has a normative version – that notwithstanding widespread talk of resilience among philosophers, according to religions religious beliefs must be held unconditionally. Resilience would then be contrary to a religious norm. Elsewhere (Shatz 2013b, 37–43) I have laid out and assessed ways in which a theist could reply. Inter alia, there is a *tu quoque* argument: atheists criticize theists using moral principles that they admit they would not ever surrender; also, if God wants people to be committed, it makes sense He would give them a norm to be unconditionally committed, lest they lose the truth and a relationship with Him. But some theists, like Robert Merrihew Adams (1977, 235), argue against a norm of unconditional commitment.

Model 8: The Cognitive Heritage Model

Isaac Hershkowitz (2013) has shown that some rabbinic thinkers in the modern period (to be sure, minor figures) adopted versions of a "special cognitive heritage" model. The central idea, which then splinters into variations, is that one who believes certain propositions has faith "as an act of commitment to and trust in the cognitive endeavors of previous generations to prove the truths of faith" (Hershkowitz 2013, 463). In some variants of this approach, those who have the requisite trust, rather than merely knowing that generations of yore reasoned to their conclusions, also study and rehearse these bequeathed reasonings in some circumstances.

Hershkowitz presents this model as a foil to Alvin Plantinga's Aquinas-Calvin ("A/C") model (Plantinga 2000). For Plantinga, faith involves a "properly basic belief" – a belief whose justification (or warrant) is not evidence and inference, but rather (in broad terms) the causal connection between the belief and an external source, and the nature of the belief-forming process. The person whose religious belief is properly basic forms that belief by a *sensus divinitatus*, a faculty for experiencing the divine. Tradition is not part of Plantinga's model of proper basicality. Perhaps having a tradition and a community helps activate the requisite faculty, but this is not Plantinga's emphasis. In this regard he differs from the cognitive heritage model significantly. (Plantinga stipulates, shades of Halevi [1964, 1:67], that what is believed must not *contradict* reason.)

The cognitive heritage model is clearly a hybrid.

Model 9: Prescriptive (normative) Rationalism – Medieval Versions

At this point, I want to examine a group of arguments presented by Jewish rationalists that, contrary to first appearances, and probably to their intention, generate a hybrid model.

Prescriptive religious rationalism can be stated in various ways. The versions in which I'm interested in this chapter start with this claim:

(1) That God exists, and other truths in Judaism, can be established by reason.

Those who accept claim 1 can now head in several directions:

(2) *Mild prescriptive religious rationalism*: It is *beneficial* for a person (Jew or non-Jew, let's suppose), religiously or otherwise,[22] to try to establish the existence of God by reason or to study arguments that others have given for this conclusion. (One candidate benefit could be intellectual integrity, but we believe many things without arguments, as Wittgenstein and many contemporary philosophers point out.)

---

[22] The "or otherwise" is a bit sneaky, and how to fill it out is best ignored in our context. A historian has reasons to study arguments, but these are not reasons that rationalists had in mind. Nor should we include "you need to study or develop arguments because you need to pass your orals."

(3) *Strong prescriptive religious rationalism*: To satisfy religious norms, one's belief that God exists *must be* based on reason, and a person, even one who already is a believer, is *obligated* to search for (and maybe to find) reasons.

(4) *No benefits and no duty*: This approach says that although 1 is true, 2 and 3 are both false. The fact that there *are* good reasons (claim 1) is for this approach irrelevant.

There are two other forms of rationalism.

(5) *Moderate Hermeneutic rationalism*: If a canonical text (biblical or rabbinic) conflicts with reason it must be interpreted so as not to conflict with reason. Thus, since reason dictates that God does not have a body, Scriptural texts that imply otherwise must be interpreted figuratively. And so on for most or all other religious beliefs.

(6) *Extreme hermeneutic rationalism*: Not only should the texts of tradition be interpreted so as to make sense scientifically and philosophically, but even in the absence of a scientific or philosophical problem, science and philosophy should be read into the text. For example, several Jewish commentators, such as Gersonides (1998), saw *Song of Songs* as an allegory, aimed at the elite, involving the human intellect and the Active Intellect, not, as in midrashic tradition, an allegory about the historical relationship between Israel and God.[23]

Note that you might deny 2–3 (embracing 4 instead) – and even deny 1 – but think it religiously beneficial to accept 5 and 6.

At least two questions confront such rationalisms: standards and scope.

Standards: What is "Reason"? What is the rationalists' standard of rational belief? Medieval prescriptive rationalists, we noted, thought that one must one have ironclad proof (a.k.a. demonstrations). But in a more expansive rationalism, more congenial to contemporary epistemology, probabilistic arguments would suffice. Questions about other options ensue: Is believing that p because one's tradition affirms that p – a standard situation – a case of having a prima

---

[23] See also Maimonides's understanding of the book as an allegory about the individual's love of God (Laws of Repentance 10:3). Since Maimonides opposes the notion that God has emotions, it's hard to see how the other lover in Song of Songs can love.

facie good reason (or evidence) for believing that *p*? Or, on the contrary, are traditions the embodiments of illegitimate prejudice?[24] Is having a tradition that affirms that *p* a good reason, all by its lonesome, for believing that *p*, or is that the case only if the belief in the general reliability of this specific tradition (and/or its transmitters) is *independently* justified?[25] Is communal epistemic practice a good source of justification?[26] What about intuition – does that qualify as evidence? If so – is it *adequate* evidence? As a general matter: Do evidential reasons exhaust the possibilities for rational support? Can justification be noninferential? Is Plantinga's "Reformed epistemology" viable? Are pragmatic and moral reasons for belief admissible as well? In other words, is the tent of reason large or small?

Scope: Judaism includes many beliefs besides *God exists*, such as those about God's providence, the revelation at Sinai, the accurate transmission of the *masorah* (tradition), the messiah, the afterlife, and more. It may not be possible to carry out a project of establishing *all* these beliefs by reason. Some beliefs are delivered by revelation and cannot be shown true by reason.

This limitation of the reach of reason[27] generates (if not necessitates) a hybrid view we may call "separate spaces," on which certain beliefs should be reasoned through and others taken on faith. The faith-based (or tradition-based) beliefs might include, for example, belief that the messiah will come and that the resurrection will occur. If we take at face value Maimonides's (1963, 327–30) claims in *Guide of the Perplexed* 2:25, then he endorses creation *ex nihilo* because, even though (contrary to, e.g., Saʿadyah) creation *ex nihilo* cannot be proven, Genesis 1 affirms the view and he has no reason not to understand the text literally.[28]

One question for prescriptive rationalists who adopt "separate spaces" is this: if it is epistemically and religiously permissible for *some* specified beliefs to be based on faith, why is it not epistemically and religiously permissible for every *other* belief of the tradition to be based on faith?

---

[24] Such questions call to mind the Continental dispute between Hans-George Gadamer and Jurgen Habermas about traditions. See Vaddiraju 2024.
[25] See Buchak 2022.
[26] See Alston 1993.
[27] A phrase used by Sztuden 2018a.
[28] Gen. 1:2, however, when read literally, sounds as if God created the world from preexistent materials; see the exchange between a philosopher and R. Gamliel in *Gen. Rabbah* 1:9. Not everyone interprets Maimonides's claim about Gen. 1 at face value, and some think he secretly believes that the world is eternal.

Why is it better that only certain beliefs are/should be based on faith, and only certain others on reason? Also, how does one know which beliefs should be based on faith and which on reason?

For rationalists there appears to be some sort of pecking order, in which beliefs based on reason are more important than beliefs based on faith/tradition. There is a difference between (a) saying that believing in God is more important than believing in the coming of the messiah and (b) saying that it is better to hold a given individual belief on the basis of reason than to hold that same belief on the basis of tradition. In the next section, I explore why rationalists thought that it is better to hold a belief, or at least some beliefs, on the basis of reason.

Models 10, 11, and 12: Fideistic Aspects of Rationalism

To develop other hybrid models we need to discern fideistic aspects of rationalism. We may do so by scrutinizing the reasons given by prescriptive rationalists for positions 2 and 3 and seeing how certain of these reasons make faith prominent enough to generate a hybrid. To reiterate, I will here construe "based on faith" as "based on tradition" because "tradition" is the coin of the rationalists' realm.

Sa'adyah Gaon's most famous work, written in Arabic, was titled *Kitāb al-Amānāt wa'l-I'tiqādāt*. It is best known by its Hebrew title, *Sefer ha-Emunot ve-ha-De'ot* – the book of *emunot* and *de'ot*. What are *emunot* (*amānāt*) and what are *de'ot* (*i'tiqādāt*)? *Emunot* are what we might loosely call beliefs based on faith, but more exact would be "based on tradition," on hearing. *De'ot*, in contrast, are beliefs that can be grounded in reason.[29] Sa'adyah's aim in the book is to transform *emunot* into *de'ot*. He wants to show by reason that which Jews already believe on the basis of faith and tradition: the existence of God, the creation of the world out of nothing (*ex nihilo*), resurrection of the dead and other traditional beliefs. And he believes that a religious Jew *ought to* seek such rational grounds for those beliefs besides drawing on tradition. Baḥya ibn Pakuda held likewise.

The Bible, Sa'adyah and Baḥya aver, provides prooftexts for their position: "Do you not know? Have you not heard? Has it not been told to you from the beginning? Have you not understood the foundations of the earth?" (Isa. 40:21). Knowing, hearing and understanding are

---

[29] See A. Altmann's explanation in Saadya Gaon 1981, 19: "an attitude of firm belief as a result of speculation [philosophy]."

required. Bahya (1970, 33 [introduction]) invokes the verse "And you should know this day (*ve-yadata ha-yom*) and take to your heart that the Lord is God, in heaven above and earth below, there is no other besides Him" (Deut. 4:39). Knowing, says Bahya – explicating here the notion of *ve-yadata* – requires rational argument that goes beyond tradition. This already gives us a hybrid note here, that the argument for the necessity for exercising reason is based on revelation – tradition![30]

Sa'adyah and Bahya both offer an analogy to illustrate their view.[31] In Bahya's formulation, if a king orders his subjects to add up themselves a pile of coins, then basing one's belief as to the number of coins on testimony is not adequate compliance. Just so, Jews are *commanded to calculate, to take the long way*. To use an analogy, you can answer a question in math by looking up the answer in the back of the textbook, or by the long way – solving the problem by hand. (In this analogy, however, the quicker method, looking at the textbook's answers or using a computer, is usually more reliable.)

The upshot, in any event, is that there is a religious obligation to study philosophy and apply it to religious questions. In a striking comment, Bahya says (1970, 113 [*Sha'ar ha-Yihud*, on the Unity of God, ch. 2]) that one who bases one's belief solely on tradition is blind; and if one received that tradition from one who based their belief solely on tradition, it's a case of the blind leading the blind.

Question: If tradition is so epistemically inferior to proof, is Bahya accepting that even *Jewish* tradition is not a good source of justification? This isn't to say the tradition is *false*, only that it is not a justifier. But might Bahya reject Jewish tradition? It depends what you mean by the question. If you mean by tradition "the statements most Jews of his time believed, *as they understood them*," the answer is yes; he in fact rejects those views. If you mean "the texts of the tradition, the words of the Bible and of the Sages, which need not and sometimes must not be understood literally, as most Jews of the time did," the answer is no – Bahya accepts tradition (see 1970, 31–33). While Bahya engages far less in creative biblical reinterpretation than Sa'adyah or Maimonides, he thought that traditional Jewish belief needs purification or rectification; traditional formulations when understood as the masses do are inaccurate, but the tradition itself is accurate, when properly understood.[32]

---

[30] My thanks to Aaron Segal for this observation.
[31] Bahya 1970, 29–31 (introduction); Saadia Gaon 1948, 32–33 (introduction: 6).
[32] For a defense of the epistemic status of traditions, see Buchak 2022.

The notion that a religious person should/must pursue philosophical arguments is interesting. But why is this elaborate philosophical method *required*? A variety of answers are proffered by rationalists, and most face objections. But they afford a glimpse into the value of tradition in a rationalistic theory.

Model 10: *Answering the Heretic*

"Know how to answer the heretic," states a *mishnah* (Avot 2:19). To refute the heretic you need rational arguments. But if a person invents arguments *only* to refute the (perhaps not yet existing) heretic, then the arguer believes antecedently on a basis other than arguments, presumably tradition. The heretic's respondent must *start from* a position of knowing what the truth is, at least to the extent of knowing that the heretical belief is false. If the respondent has not yet devised the reply to the heretic, the respondent's position must be based on tradition. Further, when engaging the heretic (even an imagined one!), people rooted in traditional beliefs must retain belief even if the argument falls apart. Or so one assumes the *mishnah* holds.[33] This rationalist view is therefore a hybrid.

Model 11: *Attaining Honest-to-Goodness Knowledge*

Sa'adyah uses an additional argument: that through proofs "it will become a matter of actual knowledge to us."[34] This phrasing resonates with a historically central idea that there is a difference between true belief and knowledge, and that justification or rational argument turns true belief into knowledge.[35] But this distinction isn't quite the key to Sa'adyah's claim. For in his discussion he recognizes tradition as a source of *knowledge* and by implication what we would call justified belief. For Sa'adyah the key distinction is not between belief and knowledge but between two levels of knowledge. For him "actual knowledge" requires ironclad premises from which conclusions follow by ironclad deduction. Thus, as Samuel Lebens points out (Lebens 2023b), we may view moving from

---

[33] Cf. Golding 1992, 36.
[34] Saadya Gaon 1981, 45, n. 1 offers this translation of the passage from Sa'adyah's introduction, part 6, in his introduction to the work. In Altmann's actual translation, as opposed to this formulation found in a footnote, Altmann renders the text as "in order that we may find out for ourselves." Rosenblatt (Saadia Gaon 1948, 27-28) has: "to have verified in fact what we have learned from the prophets theoretically."
[35] Famously, Edmund Gettier (1963), in a two and a half page article, rejected the idea that adding justification to true belief produces necessary and sufficient conditions for knowledge, thereby spawning a staggering literature that now is old hat but was for a long period the center of attention in epistemology.

emunot to *de'ot* (by means of proofs) as moving not from belief to knowledge, but from one kind of knowledge (tradition-based) to a deeper kind.

Model 12: Purifying (or Rectifying) Belief

This model is closely related to the preceding one. Explaining the value of philosophy for faith, Augustine spoke of "faith seeking understanding." One starts with faith, and then philosophizes about that which is believed, establishing the view and explicating it in response to objections and perplexities. (This model sets the context for Anselm's generation of the ontological argument.)

Sa'adyah's view is roughly analogous. Tradition is the starting point; reason operates on tradition. Sa'adyah is well aware that the ancient Sages prohibited inquiry into metaphysical questions (Mishnah Ḥagigah 2:1). But Sa'adyah maintains (in introduction part 6: Saadya Gaon 1981, 45; Saadia Gaon 1948, 27–28;) that the Sages' strictures were directed only at someone who brushes aside Scriptures and relies entirely on personal judgments:

> One who speculates after this manner may sometimes find the truth and sometimes go astray; until he has found the truth, he will be without religion; and even if he finds the truth of religion and clings to it, he is never sure that he will not depart from it should doubts arise in his mind and weaken his belief. All of us agree that one who acts in this way is a sinner, even though he may be a genuine philosopher.

In speaking of the reasoner's fixed starting point, Sa'adyah neglects to mention something that is virtually definitive of rationalist Jewish philosophy, including his own – the hermeneutic aspect of rationalism. (I repeat a point made already in the Introduction.) At points the result of philosophy may be to dramatically alter one's faith-based starting point, such as by figurative interpretation. Example: If the proposition *God exists* is interpreted in light of the literal meaning of Scripture, the believer will think God is corporeal. Philosophy will purify the belief and stimulate the believers to interpret biblical anthropomorphic expressions and implications figuratively. Sa'adyah himself, earlier in the work (Saadia Gaon 1948, 3–8), identifies the process of successively eliminating doubts, and it seems this process would lead to purifying belief. Bahya and Maimonides likewise stressed such purification. With *emunah temimah*, one merely "inherits his belief from tradition, and does not wish to develop it, to refine it, or to elevate it."[36] In rationalist thought

---

[36] Brown 2005, as translated by Hershkowitz 2013, 457. Brown is not examining medieval rationalism.

more is needed.³⁷ So one reason that people should seek reasons for that which is already believed is that their belief will become more accurate as they think about how to establish it. Faith is the starting point, and the resultant view is hybrid.

To be clear, not every reason that medievals give in support of prescriptive rationalism exemplifies a hybrid view. But some of their additional reasons, I think, may serve the cause of tradition better than reason. Consider the argument from stability: that a belief based on tradition is (to its detriment) more easily abandoned than one based on reasoning. For some people and some societies tradition is psychologically firmer and is *supported* (not undermined) by the need for stability.

Another rationalist argument that actually better supports fideism is the argument from affect. For Maimonides, the value of studying science and metaphysics is not only that these disciplines expand knowledge and correct false notions, but that the *knowledge* they yield *leads to love and awe*. Maimonides's descriptions of the love of God are among the most passion-centered descriptions of knowing God in Jewish literature,³⁸ notwithstanding that he elsewhere has negative things to say about emotion.³⁹ This affective fruit motivates the hunt for arguments. But aside from the fact that a *bad* argument can also produce affect,⁴⁰ *does* reasoning produce affect? Judah Halevi belittled the religious significance of philosophical proofs because they were abstract and rendered God impersonal, distant, and uninvolved. Those who prove the existence of an abstract God, he claimed, are themselves emotionally unengaged. They would not martyr themselves for the sake of sanctifying God's name.⁴¹ R. Joseph Yavetz (1438–1539), exiled in the Spanish Expulsion, reported (Yavetz 1953, ch. 2, 30), that it was the learned philosophers in Spain who converted to Christianity under coercion, while the uneducated masses remained faithful even at the cost of life and possessions. Kierkegaard, too, maintained that reason cools the passions.

---

³⁷ See Saadia Gaon 1948, 265–67 (7:2), where he lays out four situations in which a verse should not be interpreted literally.
³⁸ *Mishneh Torah*, Laws of the Foundations of the Torah 1:2; Laws of Repentance 10; *Guide of the Perplexed* 3:51.
³⁹ "All passions are evil" (*Guide of the Perplexed* 1:54 [126]).
⁴⁰ The pursuit of arguments could be viewed as a spiritual exercise of the sort depicted by Pierre Hadot. Stern 2013 attributes such a position to Maimonides: that, while Maimonides was a skeptic about metaphysical knowledge, philosophical thinking is for him a spiritual exercise.
⁴¹ See *Kuzari* 4:15. Halevi prized experience, and the "Kuzari argument" had the epistemic value of experience.

Such complaints about philosophy's failure to instill passion survive to the present day.[42] The pro-rationalist argument based on affect can therefore be used to *defeat* prescriptive rationalism. Can't tradition create passion even better than proofs can? If not tradition, then what about religious experience as a source of affect? (A similar criticism weakens the argument that philosophical argument produces compliance with God's law: In fact, in the Middle Ages philosophers were faulted for not obeying the Torah law.) Excessive affect spells fanaticism, so, as Aaron Segal noted in correspondence, the affect must be apt – that is, informed by understanding.[43]

It has proved a challenge to find a good argument for favoring the acquisition or construction of proofs and other arguments (other than Judaism having a rationalist tradition advocating that).[44] The best arguments seem to be: Seek honest-to-goodness knowledge; purify beliefs to make them more accurate; and confirm certain prior beliefs (those that don't need revision). All these generate hybrid views; the views begin with faith (tradition). We have also seen that some rationalist arguments undermine themselves: the arguments inadvertently support reliance on tradition.

Model 13: Dialectical Faith – A Hybrid Model in Ḥasidic Thought

In the eighteenth century, Ḥasidic thinkers raised a variety of objections to rationalism.[45] Some Ḥasidic thinkers maintained that if one seeks proofs and is not content with faith, "it is as if you are confessing, heaven forbid, that you are not a link in the genealogical chain of Abraham's descendants."[46] The soul of the Jew does not pursue philosophizing.[47]

---

[42] See Kepnes 2021, Heschel 1955, Berkovits 1959.
[43] See Shatz 2009b.
[44] One other pro-rationalist argument: Maimonides believed that the ultimate perfection of a human being is the perfection of intellect. Since knowledge of God is the highest cognitive achievement, it is the highest level of perfection.
[45] Lamm 1999, ch. 3, provides a collection of Ḥasidic texts about faith, which present their numerous reasons for rejecting the use of proofs.
[46] R. Tzvi Elimelekh of Dinov, *Benei Yissaskhar*, Adar 3, discourse 2, translated in Lamm 1999, 74.
[47] R. Tzvi Elimelekh of Dinov, *Mayan Gannim* to *Or ha-Ḥayyim*, ch. 4, #20 (Lamm 1999, 77). Some texts in Lamm illustrate how the Ḥasidim sought to reconcile their negative attitude with the fact that venerable medieval forebears engaged in proofs. Yitzhak Melamed (2025, 200) has shown that "the intellectual leadership [of Ḥasidism] frequently engaged in this study [philosophy] and at times developed philosophical and theological positions that were far bolder than what one would find among the

An especially striking motif in Ḥasidism, however, is doubt. The topic of faith and doubt is prominent in Ḥasidism and underwent much development, the precise nature of which has been disputed by historians.[48] I will try to connect this attention to doubt to hybrid modelling of faith and reason.

Daniel Howard-Snyder (2013) advances an uncommon idea, seconded by Samuel Lebens (2022b, 253–61): belief is incompatible with doubt, but faith is compatible with doubt – the opposite of the conventional view.[49] A particularly significant Ḥasidic leader named R. Naḥman of Bratslav (1772–1810) fits in well with the Howard-Snyder/Lebens thesis; in fact, R. Naḥman goes further – doubt is part of faith. R. Naḥman does not argue, as they do, that faith does not require belief.

R. Naḥman is usually associated with the notion of *emunah peshutah* – defined earlier as "a pure or perfect faith, impregnable, not anchored in rational considerations, free of and immune to doubt."[50] "Our principal purpose and perfection lies in serving the Lord in complete simplicity ... We fulfill our purpose only and specifically by means of simplicity, i.e. the fear of the Lord and the practical observances, in utter artlessness."[51] In one of his well-known "tales," R. Naḥman depicts a simple, ordinary man and a wise (or clever) man. Both receive an invitation from the king. The simple man accepts forthwith; the wise/clever man refuses because he reasons out that the king couldn't possibly be summoning him. The wise man's sophistication works to his detriment. He doesn't get to see the king.[52]

So it appears that R. Naḥman stands staunchly opposed to the notion that philosophical thinking provides positive religious value, and certainly to the notion that doubt has positive religious value. As is common in Ḥasidism, however, this rabbi's thought is far more complex than it looks.[53] First of all, as Aaron Segal explains (2021b, 243), "it wasn't just

---

bourgeoisie of the German-Jewish *Haskalah* [Enlightenment]." Their activity included study of and admiration for Maimonides's *Guide of the Perplexed*, which they even quoted, though sometimes with criticism. Their approach was meant for the elite.

[48] See Margolin 2013, Garb 2022. "As modernity progressed, doubt occupied a more prominent and challenging place in Kabbalistic writing" (Garb 2022, 81).

[49] Howard-Snyder distinguishes having doubts, being in doubt and doubting. My analysis will not incorporate these interesting distinctions.

[50] Brown as translated in Hershkowitz 2013, 457.

[51] *Likkutei Moharan* 2:19, translated in Lamm 1999, 90–91.

[52] The tale is found in Band 1978, 139–62. Note the parable in part 3, ch. 51 of the *Guide of the Perplexed*, where only those "plunged into speculation [philosophy]" have a chance of seeing the king (Maimonides 1963, 623).

[53] Melamed (2025, 203) notes that R. Naḥman studied Maimonides's *Guide* even while telling those of lesser intellect to have pure faith. This might fit a dialectical model, described later.

in his own life that the path to theological simplicity was paved with deep philosophical reflection; his advocacy for that simplicity was buttressed by a philosophically compelling defense." Second, R. Naḥman was, in the title words of Arthur Green's 1979 study, a "tormented master": tormented by sin and tormented by doubt.

At the core of R. Naḥman's doubt is the Kabbalistic doctrine of *tzimtzum*, that the Infinite (*Ein Sof*) contracted in order to make room for the world. (*Likkutei Moharan* 64.) Given the fact of withdrawal, how could people not feel God is absent? How could they not doubt? "If God's absence is necessary for our existence," writes Segal (2021b, 244), "then so too is doubt." In other words, "religious doubt is constitutive of, and so certainly entailed by, a relationship with God" (245).[54]

How should doubt be dealt with? If I hold a certain view about the mind–body problem, I know that I can strengthen my argumentation if I think of how to try refuting it. A well-done critique by a journal referee or a colleague can force an author to make salutary changes. The very act of thinking about one's position involves entertaining objections to it. As each doubt arises, it produces a revision, and then a new doubt arises, necessitating another response, and so on. Here, then, are two models: simple and dialectical. For R. Naḥman, simple faith is for the masses, dialectical faith for the elite. Yet the process culminates in simple faith.[55]

The dialectical model injects a rationalistic element into a fideist approach. It is a hybrid. In fact, reason takes over the process by challenging faith. Because doubts of a certain sort benefit the successive articulations of one's position, one will welcome them. (Interestingly, Sa'adyah likewise described the successive removal of doubts) Notably, Moses Naḥmanides (Nachmanides 1963, 468) believed that grappling with the problem of evil is religiously prescribed, because understanding God's ways is needed to form knowledge of God. An objection, a doubt, can lead to a deeper, more robust belief, in that one doesn't simply announce "God is just" but truly understands that claim. Faith seeks understanding through rational challenges.

Model 14: Pragmatic Arguments – a Jewish Pascal?

My final example of a hybrid view is a special case of rationally justifying a belief that one knows is not adequately justified by the evidence taken

---

[54] See also Rosenberg 2023.
[55] So argues Green 1979, 285–332. Green speaks of a "spiralling ascent." My formulation is patently minimalist and hyper-simplified. Cf. Brown 2005, 423–29.

alone. But it involves *pragmatic* rationality, as distinct from theoretical rationality. A belief that *p* is pragmatically rational for a person if and only if holding it leads to certain goals the person has, besides the goal of acquiring truth. This characterization of rational belief is modelled after the characterization of rational action: A person is rational in performing an action A if and only if doing A leads to the attainment of goals that the person has. The pragmatic formulation in terms of goals needs ironing out – shouldn't the person (in the action case) have a good reason to believe that A leads to the desired goal, shouldn't the goal itself be rational to pursue, and the like. But the core idea is that when it comes to justified belief, the stakes matter.

The classic use of pragmatic justification to justify belief that God exists is Blaise Pascal's Wager. Pragmatic justification is also used by William James in "The Will to Believe" and, less often noted, by Immanuel Kant in the concluding part of the second edition of *Critique of Pure Reason*, where he gives pragmatic arguments for his Postulates of Practical Reason – God, Freedom, and Immortality. Pascal (1941) starts with the thesis that the evidence for belief in God and the evidence against are equibalanced and will remain that way' but one must decide (what James called a forced option).[56] Then he formulates the benefits and drawbacks of belief and unbelief. If you believe and God exists, you stand to gain infinite bliss, while giving up just a few earthly pleasures; if you believe and God does not exist, you will have lost only some earthly pleasures. If you don't believe, and God exists, then you stand to incur infinite torment, while having a few more pleasures than you would if you believed; if God does not exist, you gained only a few earthly pleasures. The smart money is on God.

Pascal's Wager, or at least pragmatic arguments, has attracted recent Christian analytic philosophers.[57] But Jewish philosophers such as Golding (2003) and Lebens (2022a) have enlivened the prospects for pragmatic justification vis-à-vis Judaism. Shalom Rosenberg (2023), who was a major figure in Jewish philosophy, proposes that Jewish

---

[56] It isn't clear why pragmatic reasons may kick in only when the evidence cannot decide the matter; see later in this chapter. Avnur 2020 argues that when evidence is equibalanced one need not remain agnostic but rather is rational in taking one side, even when pragmatic considerations are not taken into account. And a current school of thought called epistemic permissivism allows that there can be more than one rational doxastic response to given evidence. These positions work to the benefit of theists, as in Jackson 2023a.

[57] See the articles by Lara Buchak and Elizabeth Jackson in the bibliography.

commitment involves "bets," three in particular: faith; Halakhah and ethics; and expectation of redemption. Nadav Berman Shifman (2019) has shown that Eliezer Berkovits, too, adopted a form of pragmatic argument, where the caring God is a pragmatic postulate. Lebens (2022a; see also Lebens and Statman 2023) and Golding (2003; 2022, 68–73) have made important contributions to "Judaizing" the Pascalian wager. (Lebens uses the name "Baruch Pascalberg" in describing his wager!) They explain how such considerations as rhythm of the calendar, framework for family life, a weekly Sabbath retreat from technology ("freedom from the tyranny of social media and email," in Jonathan Sacks's phrase), feeling good that one is doing what God wants of us – all these incentivize accepting Judaism. Other considerations, such as the material losses caused by observance of law and moral difficulties in Torah law, deincentivize. Golding (2022, 69–73) helpfully distinguishes external benefits (which accrue if but only if the relevant propositions about God and Israel are true; e.g., you as a Jew will have a relationship with God) from internal ones (which accrue regardless of whether the propositions about God are true, e.g., more stable family life).

The pragmatic approach is a hybrid because it fuses faith and reason as follows: You believe that *p*, whose probability is not more than 0.5; therefore, believing that *p* is from an evidential standpoint an article of faith. You use practical reason to justify this leap beyond the evidence. In Pascal's and James's versions, a person uses the pragmatic consideration only when the evidence is stalemated. But the "expected utility" method in decision theory combines probability with utilities, and allows that sometimes the benefits brought by believing that *p* can make belief in *p* justified even if its probability is below 0.5, even well below. Lebens adopts this perspective.[58]

There are numerous objections to "Pascalberg's" wager. (1) Its scope is limited; it does not encompass more than a minimal Judaism. (2) Pascalian arguments seem to assume "doxastic voluntarism" – that a person can will to believe.[59] Pascal himself raised this challenge. He replied that even if you can't bring yourself to believe as an act of will, you can achieve belief in the way others have: by participating in ritual and other activities of a group. "Acting as if" can induce propositional

---

[58] See also R. M. Adams 1977, 242.
[59] *Affective* voluntarism – the thesis that *emotions* are subject to the will – has many supporters in Jewish tradition, given the number of biblical commandments that prescribe or prohibit certain emotions.

belief. In today's parlance, "Fake it till you make it." A more delicately worded adage is from the author of the fourteenth-century *Sefer ha-Hinnukh*, commandment 16: "the hearts follow the actions."[60] (3) It appears that the wagerer's motivation is a desire to believe. Is such self-brainwashing coherent? And is it proper? One can affect one's belief by choosing to read certain materials and avoid others, hanging around certain people, and the like. These suggestions, though, likewise require self-brainwashing – is that coherent and proper? (4) There is the notorious "many gods" objection: How does Pascal know which God to worship? What if the God of Judaism would send Christians to hell? What if the true God doesn't reward people who come to Him via a wager, and even gets angry at their self-interested motivation? (5) If you use the bet, doesn't your practice lack authenticity? (6) A Pascalian-style wager may not justify *believing* but rather living a certain way, or having hope, or becoming open to a certain kind of experience. It may justify risk-taking or calling off inquiry. But that's not the same as justifying a belief (or believing).

I will not explore the objections further,[61] but I would like to register three points.

First, the use of pragmatic considerations in ascribing states like knowledge and justified belief is now legitimized by epistemologists, who put the matter in terms of pragmatic considerations "encroaching" on the epistemic status of a belief.[62] These discussions of encroachment, to be sure, have a trajectory opposite to that of the encroachment of pragmatic considerations on religious belief. Epistemologists who advocate encroachment in secular contexts argue that when the stakes of holding a true belief are high, *the standards of evidence are raised above what is required when the stakes are low*. In the pragmatic approach to the *religious* case now under consideration, though, the stakes of being right are high, but this fact is regarded as allowing a *lower* standard of evidence than if the stakes were low. So current discussions of encroachment are

---

[60] Maimonides seems to be a voluntarist; Ḥasdai Crescas, an opponent of the view. The hub of this dispute is Maimonides's formulation of the first commandment listed in *The Book of Commandments*. See Crescas 2018, 26–29 (preface), 200–204 (2:5). Some hold that Crescas was misreading Maimonides; Maimonides wasn't requiring *belief* that God exists (as the Hebrew translation suggests), but rather *knowledge* that God exists attained through demonstration. Therefore, he was not saying that one can will to believe. On voluntarism see also Benatar 2001, Goldschmidt 2015.

[61] For critical discussions, see Bartha and Pasternack 2018; Buchak's works; Golding 1990, 2003; Jordan 2006; Lebens 2022a, 51–75; Rizzieri 2013.

[62] See, e.g., Kim and McGrath 2018.

not entirely applicable. Even so, the standards for being an *atheist or agnostic* might be raised as a result of pragmatic encroachment.[63]

Second, despite the use of pragmatic arguments by contemporary Jewish philosophers, there isn't much Jewish precedent for them. Dawid al-Muquammis (1989, ch. 20) (d. 937) used a Pascal-like argument in his *Twenty Chapters*.[64] So did the author of *Kol Sakhal* [*Voice of a Fool* (1:10)].[65] There are differences between these pragmatic arguments and Pascal's, which makes them even less of a precedent. The rise of Jewish pragmatic arguments today is an example of creative Jewish theology.

Third, whereas some medieval philosophers think, as we've seen, that it is religiously obligatory to search for evidential reasons for religious beliefs, and others that it is religiously obligatory to believe without reasons or even against reason, I suspect that few hold it is religiously obligatory to arrive at belief using the pragmatic method. It's not hard to guess why: Pragmatic arguments appeal to self-interest, and to think it is obligatory to occupy one's mind with such arguments is rather awkward. But is this consideration decisive? The Bible itself states that performing commandments is for "our good always" (Deut. 6:24). Maimonides, despite wanting to draw people out of self-interest, stresses this verse.[66] Moreover, as Golding (2003) stresses, pondering what to believe using pragmatic considerations focuses you on the rewards of religious life – not just rewards like a place in Heaven or providence in this life, but salutary effects that arise naturally like feeling closeness to God and having strong family bonds. If, as seems correct, it is religiously imperative to appreciate the value that one's religion carries, a Pascalian approach will be helpful.

In addition to pragmatic reasons now being accorded epistemic status by epistemologists today, some philosophers have held that the epistemic status of a belief may be affected by moral considerations. If I have evidence that my friend is cheating me, evidence good enough to convince a stranger, morality might dictate that I not so readily join the stranger

---

[63] I thank Aaron Segal for this last point. Rizzieri (2013) argues that because in pondering the question of religious belief the stakes are high, both sides need a more secure epistemic foundation.

[64] As noted by Sarah Stroumsa in her edition, 302–3 (citing Georges Vajda).

[65] The author is sometimes thought to be Leon de Modena (1571–1648) – like Pascal, someone who gambled. But Golding noted in correspondence that its authorship is uncertain, *pace* Rosenberg (2023, 6).

[66] *Guide of the Perplexed*, 3:31.

in believing the friend is cheating. The moral virtue of trusting makes disbelieving the report the right epistemic stance, at least for a while. Trusting God can be a virtue that affects the rationality of trust. Trusting ancestors and having fidelity to them – remaining part of a tradition – is virtuous too.[67]

CONCLUSION

I believe I have made good on my claims that many hybrid theories of faith and reason are possible, that models in medieval rationalism may be parsed as hybrid, and that the logic of some rationalist arguments places faith before reason even if rationalists didn't recognize that point. The upshot is that there is a dynamic between faith and reason, and observing it in action leads to a more textured and robust notion of the epistemology of religious commitment than rationalism or fideism in their pristine form.

[67] Cf. Nietzsche cited in Chapter 9, n. 42.

PART V

CONCLUDING REFLECTIONS

11

Features of Jewish Philosophy

A Closing Assessment

What general features of Jewish philosophy have emerged from our inquiry?

First – probably the most glaring fact we encountered – is that Jewish thought comprises a rich, at times dizzying, multiplicity of conflicting views. Competition between ideas, both at a given time (synchronically) and even more so across time (diachronically) is common in any culture, but the extent to which Jewish sources *extol* controversy and validate multiple interpretations (accept interpretive pluralism) stands out. "The Torah has seventy faces" (*Be-Midbar Rabbah*, 13:15–16); "just as a hammer breaks a rock into pieces, so too one verse can be explained several ways [glossing Jer. 23:29]" (*Sanhedrin* 34a); "the Torah is not in Heaven" (but rather decisions are in the hands of humans, who *debate* matters; *Bava Metzi'a* 59b); "these and these are the words of the living God" (*Eruvin* 13b, said about legal disputes between the House of Hillel and the house of Shammai).[1] Some sources dictate (sometimes hyperbolically) that jurists be able to justify both a legal judgment and its opposite and understand opposing perspectives; for example, to grasp forty-nine reasons on each side of a legal issue. (See *Midrash Tehillim* 12:3; Jerusalem Talmud, *Sanhedrin* 4:2; *Ḥagigah* 3b.) We are told that if every issue were ruled upon in the Torah, if Torah were given cut and dried, "no foot could stand" [Jerusalem Talmud, *Sanhedrin* 4:2]. Dispute (*mahaloket*) and argumentation is *expressly prized and encouraged*. "Every

---

[1] For a critical analysis of the many ways this phrase has been understood, see Sagi 2008. Understanding disagreement is an objective many philosophers have pursued. See, e.g., Feldman and Warfield 2010, Machuca 2013.

controversy that is for the sake of heaven will endure" (*Avot* 5:17). There are even countless disputes about how to interpret particular disputes. The old joke, "Two Jews, three opinions," captures a central facet of the tradition, not just an empirical observation.

In some chapters, the presence of debate has been more glaring than in others; I have had to choose between mounting a case and surveying the field of positions and reasons, and sometimes opted for the latter (recall Robert Merrihew Adams's [1994, 5] statement quoted in the introduction: "Progress in philosophy is more likely to consist in understanding possible alternatives than arriving at settled conclusions."). But let us ask: What advantage does Judaism see in being a culture of controversy? Why do the Rabbis speak warmly about *milḥamtah shel Torah*, "the war of Torah" and "the war of ideas"? Is there an assumption that it is through the *collision* of ideas, as opposed to a proliferation of echo chambers, that truth emerges, as John Stuart Mill contended in his defense of free speech in chapter 2 of *On Liberty*? Or, again in the spirit of Mill, is it that confronting challenges forces you to recognize the strengths and weaknesses of your argument, and then you learn how to sharpen it or instead let go of it? Is it that seeing many sides of an issue inculcates tolerance, humility and mutual respect, notwithstanding the potential for frayed relations in intellectual combat? Is dispute meant as a way of ensuring that the Torah will remain vital and dynamic in the life of the people? Or simply: Multiplicity is encouraged because there truly *are* multiple perspectives and multiple ways to reason. Perhaps all of the above.[2]

Importantly, with the High Court (Sanhedrin) existing no longer, Judaism does not have a central authority for resolving legal disputes, let alone philosophical ones. In fact, one position is that matters of theology are not subject to *pesak halakhah*, legal ruling.[3] Precedent and authority play a far clearer role in arriving at legal positions than arriving at philosophical positions.

---

[2] Minority opinions are preserved (*Eduyot* 1:5–6). To be sure, not all agree that disagreement is good: see *Sotah* 47b, *Sanhedrin* 88b; Tosefta *Ḥagigah* 2:9; and Maimonides' introduction to his Commentary on the Mishnah.

[3] See Shapiro 2012, 136–39. Shapiro notes (131–35) that even Maimonides, who in his Introduction to his commentary on the tenth chapter of Mishnah *Sanhedrin*, formulated thirteen beliefs requisite for attaining the World-to-Come (see also Laws of Repentance 3), declared numerous times that a dispute with no practical implications is not subject to a halakhic ruling. Naḥmanides holds otherwise, and some talmudic sources imply there is *pesak* in matters of thought. So here too is yet another dispute, or meta-dispute.

This point is well illustrated by the case of Maimonides, the most celebrated and significant of Jewish philosophers. Although pretty much any Jewish thinker feels obliged to *address* Maimonides's view, and his thirteen principles of faith have become normative, his name is not a conversation-stopper. He has not only sympathizers but antagonists, such as in the cases of divine impassibility, intellectualism, and negative theology. Certainly, as Samuel Lebens remarked in correspondence, "Jewish folk belief is far away from Maimonidean thought." (Granted, in large part this is because many people are not truly familiar with Maimonidean philosophical texts.) Within this perspective, it is easy – and justified – to adopt eclecticism, embracing some views of a thinker while discarding others, as long as consistency is maintained in the belief system as a whole.[4]

We have seen that, given the multiplicity of views, anyone who stakes out a position and wants to appeal to authority to support it will have to do some privileging of texts. To be sure, a harmonizing urge is often found in commentators on classical texts. But some or many attempts at reconciling views are unconvincing and the putatively harmonized views are recognized by rabbinic interpreters as bedrock disagreements. Why should views of different Sages about *philosophical* matters be harmonized, if disagreement is at the heart of the Jewish *legal* system? Privileging is often a more plausible approach than claiming compatibility.

A second salient fact in the preceding chapters is that at times there is a lack of historical continuity in Jewish thought, a sense of rupture. Numerous aspects of the biblical and rabbinic views of God, as we saw, appear to clash with later Perfect Being Theology. The immutable, affect-less, distant God of the rationalist medieval philosophers ("the God of Aristotle") seems so different from the dynamic God of the Bible, Talmud, and Midrash ("the God of Abraham"). If God is outside of time, He becomes even more removed from exercising providence (not responsive to prayer, for example). Additionally, the naturalistic metaphysics of numerous Jewish thinkers, whose motivations we have explored (Chapter 2), appears to contrast sharply with the metaphysics of the Bible and the Rabbis. To take another topic, the doctrine of *gilgul* (transmigration) is not strongly rooted in early texts, but in the Middle Ages, under the influence of Kabbalah, it becomes regarded by many as true, or even an article of faith. Intellectual history is full of such twists, turns, and leaps in traditions, and it isn't clear how to

---

[4] See Kellner 2021, 50–52. Maimonides's legal rulings are not universally followed either.

speak of preserving a single Jewish philosophical tradition when there is sharp diachronic disagreement. In point of fact, the later thinkers often write as if nothing new had arrived. Although I have tried to somewhat reduce the gap between ancient and medieval Judaism (e.g., there are biblical and rabbinic supports for Perfect Being Theology, and the Rabbis' belief in the truth of astrology opened the door somewhat to naturalistic accounts of events), still, *pace* Ecclesiastes 1:9, "there *is* something new under the sun." Lenn E. Goodman (2012, 34–35) writes aptly, however:

> But disruptions have been frequent, and continuity is hard won. Repeatedly, Jewish thinkers have had to rediscover or reinvent what was lost or forgotten, reframing the old stories to live again and light up a new context, rediscovering old meanings, and plumbing the old texts for meanings not yet brought to light.

This captures how traditions grow, especially those that combine fidelity with creativity and innovation (*ḥiddush*). At the same time, many later views can legitimately claim to be rooted in precedent and tradition, even when the thinkers are searching for a "usable past."[5]

A third point pertains to systematicity. It is often said that the predominance of analytic philosophy in the twentieth and twenty-first centuries means that the days of system building, exemplified by the nineteenth-century movement called Idealism, are long gone. But in recent years analytic philosophers have turned to studying systematicity – what it is, why it might be valued or not valued.

What makes a body of ideas into a systematic philosophy? One answer is that a body of ideas is systematic if it provides a comprehensive or nearly comprehensive view of large intellectual territory, covering many subjects in that area. Jewish philosophy qualifies as systematic on this definition: It addresses both issues in general philosophy of religion and issues endemic to Judaism. On another conception, however, a philosophy is systematic by virtue of architecture: The ideas can be ordered – that is, structured and organized under broad categories, such as God, humanity, and the relationship between God and humanity; or God's existence, Revelation, Reward and Punishment (as in Joseph Albo's *Book of Roots*); or Creation, Revelation, and Redemption (as in the thought of Franz Rosenzweig's [1886–1929] *The Star of Redemption*). Jewish philosophers across the ages were often systematic in this sense, too, as they

---

[5] Cf. Hughes 2012, J. Harris 2007. The phrase comes from Brooks 2018.

sought a comprehensive and well-structured ordering of topics, especially as regards the formulation of dogma.⁶

A third sense of "systematic," however, relates to how extensively and how well the parts of a thinker's philosophy interrelate. I mean not only how much the parts are *compatible* (simple coherence), but how often and how deeply the answer to one question affects treatment of other questions. How much system have we seen in this third sense? A goodly amount. This is why numerous sources in the book do double or triple or quadruple duty: They figure in discussion of several topics.

The simplest illustration of this third sense of systematicity is Perfect Being Theology. Its effects in generating the foreknowledge–free will problem and the problem of evil hardly need mention. Another example of systematicity: How one approaches the problem of evil affects how one views laws that strike us as immoral. For example, skeptical theism (which says that our intelligence is too limited to understand God's ways) dissolves, if successful, *both* the problem of evil *and* the problem of ostensibly immoral laws. But it also renders human ethical intuitions unreliable, and this generates difficulties for integrating moral considerations into legal decisions. So, systematicity weakens under pressure, albeit not without ways of overcoming the pressure. Again, philosophers often have a sensibility that impacts several topics: for example, a naturalistic sensibility affects one's beliefs about resurrection and miracles generally. I dealt with systematicity most explicitly in Chapter 7 on the afterlife, where I argued that some reasons for preferring one conception over another are a matter of fit rather than logical deduction or probabilistic inference. Another example, not discussed in this book, is how conceptions of God affect conceptions of the human ideal. If we value most *God's* wisdom, it makes sense that the ideal for the *human being* is wisdom. If we value most God's ḥesed (lovingkindness), it makes sense that the human *summum bonum* is ḥesed. If we value both wisdom and ḥesed equally, we get a hybrid human ideal. The high number of cross-references between chapters is an indicator of systematic connections.

If every part of a system derives from a single principle, there should be no internal contradictions. But freedom from contradiction could be a pipedream in a large system.⁷ Moreover, sometimes systematicity can shrink philosophy's agenda. If we accept apophaticism, there's no

---

⁶ See Kellner 2004.
⁷ See Segal 2020.

problem of evil, no problem of foreknowledge, perhaps (in some versions) no problem of morally objectionable laws or actions by God, and no ready way to explain the praises of God in prayer. Theological activity will be stopped at the door. (This example is similar to the one about skeptical theism.[8])

* * *

The overarching moral of our discussions, however, is that Jewish philosophy and analytic philosophy can interact in interesting ways. My framing of certain topics and arguments, and much literature I cite, are derived from analytic philosophy. Reciprocally, Jewish philosophy has much to contribute by way of exploring apophaticism, protest against God, antitheodicy, sufferings of love, divine control, restrictions on free will, models of the afterlife, ethical practice, moral motivation, religious diversity, faith and reason, and more. Additionally, biblical narratives, as well as talmudic and midrashic stories – all accompanied by mountains of rich exegesis – provide stimulating, heavily nuanced ways to think about philosophical questions. The views of Martha Nussbaum (1986) and Eleonore Stump (2010a) on the value of narratives are very much on point, as is Jonathan Sacks's (2005, 11) trenchant depiction of the superiority of narrative over law in conveying moral complexity.[9] More generally, to repeat a point made in the introduction, and is abundantly manifest in the book, many of the sources of Jewish philosophy are not usually perceived as containing "real" philosophy, but in fact do. Many who are not trained philosophers – and may even not want the label philosopher – have had much to say through alternative mediums. Judaism is hardly the only religion of which such things could be said.

I could say more, but let me conclude with this. We analytic philosophers are living through a "moment" in which religion interacts with our specialty, just as it interacted with schools and methods in prior times. Knowing how cultures change may place in our minds the specter of historicism; but the rigorous methods of analytic philosophy, sans the name, really run through the whole history of philosophy. The excitement of such thinking brings robust rewards. I express the hope that the joining of analytic philosophy and Jewish tradition in this work has yielded engaging and fruitful insights – and will inspire others to move matters further forward.

---

[8] Cf. Hick 1978, 6–11.
[9] See also Weiss, 2018, esp. ch. 7.

Bibliography

Abravanel, Isaac 2013. *Naḥalat Avot*, ed. Oren Golan (Oren Golan [publisher]).
Adams, Marilyn M. 1999. *Horrendous Evils and the Goodness of God* (Cornell University Press).
Adams, Robert Merrihew 1977. "Kierkegaard's Arguments against Objective Reasoning in Religion," *The Monist* 60: 228–43.
  1985. "Involuntary Sins," *Philosophical Review* 94: 3–31.
  1987. "Autonomy and Theological Ethics," in *The Virtue of Faith* (Oxford University Press), 123–27.
  1994. *Leibniz: Determinist, Theist, Idealist* (Oxford University Press).
Al-Muqammis, David 1989. *Twenty Chapters*, ed. and trans. Sarah Stroumsa (E. J. Brill).
Albo, Joseph 1929. *Sefer Ha-ikkarim: The Book of Principles*, trans. Isaac Husik (Jewish Publication Society).
Allen, Diogenes 1980. "Natural Evil and the Love of God," *Religious Studies* 16: 439–56.
Alston, William 1989a. *Divine Nature and Human Language: Essays in Philosophical Theology* (Cornell University Press).
  1989b. "Referring to God," in Alston 1989a, 103–17.
  1989c. "God's Action in the World," in Alston 1989a, 197–222.
  1993. *Perceiving God: The Epistemology of Religious Experience* (Cornell University Press).
  1995. "Realism and the Christian Faith," *International Journal for the Philosophy of Religion* 38: 37–60.
  1996. "Belief, Acceptance, and Faith," in *Faith, Freedom and Rationality: Philosophy of Religion Today*, ed. Daniel Howard-Snyder and Jeff Jordan (Rowman & Littlefield), 10–27.
  2005. "Two Cheers for Mystery?," in Dole and Chignell 2005, 99–114.
Alter, Robert 1981. *The Art of Biblical Narrative* (Basic Books).
Angel, Hayyim 2017. "Afterlife in Jewish Thought," *Conversations* 27: 61–71.
Anscombe, Elizabeth 1958. "Modern Moral Philosophy." *Philosophy* 33(124): 1–19.

Arbour, Benjamin H. (ed.) 2019. *Philosophical Essays against Open Theism* (Routledge).
Audi, Robert 1996. "Theism and the Mind–Body Problem," in Jordan and Howard-Snyder 1996, 155–69.
  2011. *Rationality and Religious Commitment* (Oxford University Press).
Avnur, Yuval 2020. "What Is Wrong with Agnostic Belief?" in *Agnosticism: Explorations in Philosophy and Religious Thought*, ed. Francis Fallon and Gavin Hyman (Oxford University Press), 47–80.
Bachya ibn Pakuda 1970. *Duties of the Heart*, trans. Moses Hyamson (Feldheim).
Band, Arnold (ed. and trans.) 1978. *Nahman of Bratslav: The Tales* (Paulist Press).
Barbour, Ian 1990. *Religion in an Age of Science* (HarperCollins).
Barer, Deborah 2018. "Law, Ethics, and Hermeneutics: A Literary Approach to Lifnim Mi-shurat Ha-din," *Journal of Textual Reasoning* 10 https://scholarworks.wm.edu/cgi/viewcontent.cgi?article=1033&context=jtr
Barnes, Jonathan 2007. Review of Bernard Williams, *The Sense of the Past: Essays in the History of Philosophy*, *Journal of Philosophy* 104: 540–45.
Baron, Marcia 1984. "The Alleged Repugnance of Acting from Duty," *Journal of Philosophy* 81: 197–220.
Barr, James 1993. *Biblical Faith and Natural Theology* (Oxford University Press).
Bartha, Paul and Pasternack, Lawrence (eds.) 2018. *Pascal's Wager* (Cambridge University Press).
Basinger, David and Basinger, Randall 1986. *Philosophy and Miracle: The Contemporary Debate* (Edwin Mellen Publishers).
Batnitzky, Leora 2009. "From Resurrection to Immortality: Theological and Political Implications in Modern Jewish Thought," *Harvard Theological Review* 102: 279–96.
  2011. *How Judaism Became a Religion: An Introduction to Modern Jewish Thought* (Princeton University Press).
Benatar, David 2001. "Against Commanding to Believe," *Shofar* 19: 87–104.
Bennett, Jonathan 1984. *A Study of Spinoza's Ethics* (Hackett).
Benor, Ehud 1995. *Worship of the Heart: A Study of Maimonides' Philosophy of Religion* (SUNY Press).
Berger, David 1999. Review of Kellner 1999, *Tradition* 33(4): 81–89.
  2001. *The Rebbe, The Messiah, and The Scandal of Orthodox Indifference* (Littman Library).
  2005a. "Jews, Gentiles, and the Modern Egalitarian Ethic: Some Tentative Thoughts," in *Formulating Responses in An Egalitarian Age*, ed. Marc Stern (Rowman & Littlefield), 83–108.
  2005b. "Covenants, Messiahs, and Religious Boundaries," *Tradition* 39(2): 66–78.
  2010a. *Persecution, Polemic and Dialogue: Essays in Jewish-Christian Relations* (Academic Studies Press).
  2010b. "On the Image and Destiny of Gentiles in Ashkenazic Polemical Literature," in Berger 2010a, 109–38.
  2010c. "Reflections on Conversion and Proselytizing in Judaism and Christianity," in Berger 2010, 367–77.
  2010d. "Dominus Iesus and the Jews," in Berger 2010a, 378–84.

2011. "Miracles and the Natural Order in Nahmanides," in *Cultures in Collision and Conversation: Essays in the Intellectual History of the Jews* (Academic Studies Press), 129–51.
2019. "Perspectives on Avoda Zara" (Review of Goshen-Gottstein 2016). *Tradition* 51(2): 106–15.
Berkovits, Eliezer 1959. *God, Man and History* (Jonathan David).
1964. "A. J. Heschel's Theology of Pathos," *Tradition* 6(2): 67–104.
1973. *Faith after the Holocaust* (Ktav).
1990. *Jewish Women in Time and Torah* (Ktav).
2002. *Essential Essays on Judaism*, ed. David Hazony (Shalem Press).
Berman, Saul 1975 and 1977. "Lifnim Mishurat Hadin," *Journal of Jewish Studies* 26 (1975): 86–104 and 28 (1977): 181–93. (In two parts.)
Berman, Todd 2022. "Berkovits, Heschel, and the Heresy of the Divine Pathos," *Tradition* 54(4): 50–90.
Black, Andrew G. 1997. "Malebranche's Theodicy," *Journal of the History of Philosophy* 35: 27–44.
Blau, Yitzchak 2000. "The Implications of a Jewish Virtue Ethic," *Torah U-Madda Journal* 9: 19–41.
2001. "Body and Soul: *Tehiyyat ha-Metim* and *Gilgulim* in Medieval and Modern Philosophy," *Torah U-Madda Journal* 10: 1–19.
Bleich, J. D. 1988. "Judaism and Natural Law," *Jewish Law Annual* 7: 5–42.
Blidstein, Gerald 1965. "Capital Punishment: The Classic Jewish Discussion," *Judaism* 14: 159–71.
1990. "Maimonides and Me'iri on the Legitimacy of Non-Judaic Religions," in *Scholars and Scholarship: The Interaction between Judaism and Other Cultures*, ed. Leo Landman (The Michael Scharf Publication Trust of Yeshiva University), 27–35.
2012. "On Death," in *Society and Self: On the Writings of Rabbi Joseph B. Soloveitchik* (Ktav), 139–51.
Bloom, Jeffrey, Alec Goldstein, and Gil Student (eds.) 2022. *Strauss, Spinoza and Sinai: Orthodox Judaism and Modern Questions of Faith* (Kodesh Press).
Blumenthal, David 1993. *Facing the Abusing God: A Theology of Protest* (John Knox Press).
Brafman, Yonatan 2018. "Jewish Philosophy and Contemporary Jewish Culture: Therapy, Ideology, Critique," in Samuelson and Hughes 2018, 99–114.
2019. "Neither Authoritarian nor Superfluous: A Normative Account of Rabbinic Authority," in Lebens, Rabinowitz, and Segal 2019a, 276–94.
Braiterman, Zachary 1998. *(God) After Auschwitz: Tradition and Change in Post-Holocaust Jewish Thought* (Princeton University Press).
Braithwaite, Richard B. 1955. *An Empiricist's View of the Nature of Religious Belief* (Cambridge University Press).
Brill, Alan 2004. "Judaism and Other Religions: An Orthodox Perspective," www.bc.edu/research/cjl/meta-elements/texts/cjrelations/resources/articles/Brill.htm.
2010. *Judaism and Other Religions: Models of Understanding* (Palgrave Macmillan).

Brody, Baruch 2016–2017. "Jewish Reflections on the Resurrection of the Dead," *Torah U-Madda Journal* 17: 93–122.
  2020–2021. "Varieties of Divine Providence in Medieval Jewish Philosophy," *Torah U-Madda Journal* 18: 60–93.
Brooks, Van Wyck 2018. "On Creating a Usable Past," *The Dial* 7(April 11): 337–41.
Brower, Jeffrey E. 2009. "Simplicity and Aseity," in Flint and Rea 2009, 105–28.
Brown, Benjamin 2005. "The Return of 'The Simple Faith': The Concept of Ḥaredi Faith and Its Growth in the Nineteenth Century" (Hebrew), in Halbertal, Kurzweil and Sagi, 403–43.
  2019. "Theoretical Antinomianism and the Conservative Function of Utopia: Rabbi Mordekhai Yosef of Izbica as a Case Study," *Journal of Religion* 99(3): 312–40.
Broyde, Michael 1999. "Proselytism and Jewish Law: Inreach, Outreach, and the Jewish Tradition," in Witte and Martin 1999, 45–60.
Buber, Martin 1958. *I and Thou*, trans. Ronald Gregor Smith (Scribner).
Buchak, Lara 2012. "Can It Be Rational to Have Faith?," in *Probability in The Philosophy of Religion*, ed. Jake Taylor and Victoria S. Harrison (Oxford University Press), 225–47.
  2014. "Rational Faith and Justified Belief," in *Religious Faith and Intellectual Virtue*, ed. Tim O'Connor and Laura Goins (Oxford University Press), 49–73.
  2017a. "Reason and Faith," in *The Oxford Handbook of The Epistemology of Theology*, ed. William J. Abraham and Frederick D. Aquino (Oxford University Press), 46–63.
  2017b. "Faith and Steadfastness in the Face of Counter-evidence," *International Journal for the Philosophy of Religion* 81(1): 113–32.
  2022. "Faith and Traditions," *Nous* 57: 740–59.
Burling, Hugh 2019. "The Reference of 'God' Revisited," *Faith and Philosophy* 36: 345–71.
Byrne, Peter 1995. "Omnipotence, Feminism and God," *International Journal for the Philosophy of Religion* 37: 145–65.
Cahn, Steven M. 1967. *Fate, Logic, and Time* (Yale University Press).
Campbell, C. A. 1951. "Is Free Will a Pseudo-Problem?" *Mind* 60: 446–65.
Carmy, Shalom 1997. "Paradox, Paradigm, and the Birth of Inwardness: On R. Kook and the Akeda," in Elman and Gurock 1997, 473–78.
  (ed.) 1999. *Jewish Perspectives on the Experience of Suffering* (Jason Aronson).
  2006. "Use It or Lose It: On the Moral Imagination of Free Will," in *Judaism, Science, and Moral Responsibility*, ed. Yitzhak Berger and David Shatz (Rowman & Littlefield), 104–51.
  2007. "The Origin of Nations and the Shadow of Violence: Theological Perspectives on Canaan and Amalek," in Schiffman and Wolowelsky 2007, 163–99.
  2013, "Love's Scandal," *First Things* 238: 51–54.
Carmy, Shalom and Shatz, David 1997. "The Bible as a Source for Philosophical Reflection," in *The Routledge History of Jewish Philosophy*, ed. Daniel Frank and Oliver Leaman (Routledge), 13–37.

Chalmers, David 1996. *The Conscious Mind: In Search of a Fundamental Theory* (Oxford University Press).
  (ed.) 2021. *Philosophy of Mind: Classical and Contemporary Readings* (Oxford University Press, 2021).
Chignall, Andrew 2011. "'As Kant Has Shown ...': Analytic Theology and the Critical Philosophy," in Rea and Crisp 2011, 117–35.
Citron, Gabriel 2014. "Belief in a Good and Loving God: A Case Study in the Varieties of Religious Belief," in *God, Mind, and Knowledge*, ed. Andrew Moore (Ashgate).
  2017. "Response to Michael Harris's 'But Now My Eye Has Seen You': *Yissurin Shel Ahavah* as Divine Intimacy Theodicy." www.theapj.com/wp-content/uploads/2017/06/111.pdf
Clark, Kelly James and Koperski, Jeffrey (eds.) 2022. *Abrahamic Reflections on Randomness and Providence* (Palgrave MacMillan).
Clarke, Randolph 2003. *Libertarian Accounts of Free Will* (Oxford University Press).
Claussen, Geoff, Green, Alex, and Mittleman, Alan L. (eds.) 2023. *Jewish Virtue Ethics* (SUNY Press).
Clegg, J. S. 1979. "Faith," *American Philosophical Quarterly* 16: 225–32.
Cobb, John B., Jr. and Griffin, David Ray 1976. *Process Theology: An Introductory Exposition* (Westminster Press).
Cohen, Gavriel 1973. "Introduction [to Esther]," *Five Megillot* (Heb.) (Mossad HaRav Kook), 3–22 (of the Esther section).
Cohen, Hermann 1995. *Religion of Reason Out of the Sources of Judaism*, trans. S. Kaplan (Oxford University Press).
Cohen, Shaye 2006. *From the Maccabees to the Mishnah* (Westminster John Knox).
Cohn-Sherbok, Daniel 1989. *Jewish Petitionary Prayer: A Theological Exploration* (Edwin Mellen Publishers).
Cover, J. A. and O'Leary-Hawthorne, John 1996. "Free Agency and Materialism," in Jordan and Howard-Snyder 1996, 47–71.
Cover, Robert 1987. "A Jewish Jurisprudence of the Social Order," *Jewish Law and Religion* 5: 65–73.
Crescas, Ḥasdai 2018. *Light of the Lord*, trans. Roslyn Weiss (Oxford University Press).
Crick, Francis 1994. *The Astonishing Hypothesis: The Scientific Search for the Soul* (Charles Scribners' Sons).
Cureton, Adam and Hill, Thomas E. 2015. "Kant on Virtue and the Virtues," in *Cultivating Virtue: Perspectives from Philosophy, Theology, and Psychology*, ed. Nancy Snow (Oxford University Press), 87–110.
Davidson, Donald 1973. "Radical Interpretation," *Dialectica* 27: 314–28.
Davison, Scott 2017. *Petitionary Prayer: A Philosophical Investigation* (Oxford University Press).
Dawkins, Richard 2006. *The God Delusion* (Houghton Mifflin).
Dennett, Daniel 1984. *Elbow Room: The Varieties of Free Will Worth Wanting* (Bradford).
  2006. *Breaking the Spell: Religion as a Natural Phenomenon* (Penguin).

Dessler, Eliyahu 1985. *Strive for Truth*, ed. and trans. Aryeh Carmell (Feldheim).
Diamond, James A. and Hughes, Aaron (eds.) 2012. *Encountering the Medieval in Modern Jewish Thought* (Brill).
Diamond, James and Kellner, Menachem 2019. *Reinventing Maimonides in Contemporary Jewish Thought* (Littman Library of Jewish Civilization).
Doko, Enis and Turner, Jamie B. 2023. "Islamic Religious Epistemology," in Fuqua, Greco, and McNabb 2023, 148–62.
Dole, Andrew and Chignell, Andrew (eds.) 2005. *God and the Ethics of Belief* (Cambridge University Press).
Dorff, Elliot 2018. "Jewish Philosophy and Public Policy," in Tirosh-Samuelson and Hughes 2018, 115–29.
Dorff, Elliot and Crane, Jonathan K. (eds.) 2013. *The Oxford Handbook of Jewish Ethics and Morality* (Oxford University Press).
Dougherty, Trent 2014. *The Problem of Animal Pain: A Theodicy for All Creatures Great and Small* (Palgrave MacMillan).
Dressler, Joshua 1987. *Understanding Criminal Law* (Lexis Nexis).
Dworkin, Ronald 1967. "The Model of Rules," *Chicago Law Review* 35: 14–46.
Ekstrom, Laura 2011. "Free Will Is Not a Mystery," in *The Oxford Handbook of Free Will*, ed. Robert Kane (Oxford University Press), 366–80.
  2013. "A Christian Theodicy," in *The Blackwell Companion to the Problem of Evil*, ed. Justin P. McBrayer and Daniel Howard-Snyder (Wiley Blackwell), 266–80.
Elman, Yaakov 1999. "The Contribution of Rabbinic Thought to a Theology of Misfortune," in Carmy 1999, 155–212.
Elman, Yaakov and Jeffrey Gurock (eds.) 1997. *Ḥazon Naḥum: Studies in Jewish Law, Thought, and History Presented to Dr. Norman Lamm on the Occasion of His Seventieth Birthday* (Yeshiva University Press).
Epictetus (1983). *The Handbook of Epictetus*, trans. Nicholas P. White (Hackett).
Fagenblat, Michael (ed.) 2017a. *Negative Theology as Jewish Modernity* (Indiana University Press).
  2017b. "Introduction: Delineation: Negative Theology as Jewish Modernity," in Fagenblat 2017a, 1–29.
Falk, Harvey 1982. "Rabbi Jacob Emden's View on Christianity," *Journal of Ecumenical Studies* 19: 105–11.
Feldman, Richard and Warfield, Ted A. 2010. *Disagreement* (Oxford University Press).
Fenton, Paul 2012. "The Banished Brother: Islam in Jewish Thought and Faith," in Goshen-Gottstein and Korn 2012, 235–61.
Finocchiaro, Maurice A. (ed.) 1989. *The Galileo Affair* (University of California Press).
Fischer, John Martin 1982. "Responsibility for Consequences," *The Journal of Philosophy* 79: 21–40.
  1994. *The Metaphysics of Free Will: An Essay on Control* (Blackwell).
  2011. "Why Immortality Is Not So Bad," in *Our Stories: Essays on Life, Death and Free Will* (Oxford University Press), 79–92.
Fischer, John Martin and Ravizza, Mark (eds.) 1993a. *Perspectives on Moral Responsibility* (Cornell University Press).

1993b. "Responsibility for Consequences," in Fischer and Ravizza 1993a, 322–48.
1998. *Responsibility and Control* (Cambridge University Press).
Fischer, John Martin and Todd, Patrick 2011. "The Truth about Freedom: A Reply to Merricks," *Philosophical Review* 120: 97–115.
Fishbane, Michael 1979. *Biblical Text and Texture* (Oneworld Publications).
Fisher, Cass 2012. *Contemplative Nation: A Philosophical Account of Jewish Theological Language* (Stanford University Press).
  2015. "The Posthumous Conversion of Ludwig Wittgenstein and the Future of Jewish (Anti)-Theology," *AJS Review* 39: 333–65.
  2018. "Reconceiving Jewish Philosophy: Aspirations for the Future," in Tirosh-Samuelson and Hughes 2018, 231–46.
  2020. "The Cosmic Eye and Its Pupil: Divine Perfection and the Mediation of Universal and Particular Truth in Rabbinic Theology," in Goshen-Gottstein and Korn 2020, 61–82.
  2021. "Theological Realism and Its Alternatives in Contemporary Jewish Theology," in Kepnes 2021, 392–422.
  2026 (forthcoming) *Jewish Theological Realism: Recovering Reference to God in Rabbinic and Modern Thought* (Cambridge University Press).
Fleischacker, Samuel 2011. *Divine Teaching and the Way of the World: A Defense of Revealed Religion* (Oxford University Press).
  2015. *The Good and the Good Book: Revelation as a Guide to Life* (Oxford University Press).
Flint, Thomas 2006. *Divine Providence: The Molinist Account* (Cornell University Press).
Flint, Thomas E. and Rea, Michael (eds.) 2009. *The Oxford Handbook of Philosophical Theology* (Oxford University Press).
Foster, J. 1991. *The Immaterial Self* (Routledge).
Fox, Marvin 1990. *Interpreting Maimonides* (University of Chicago Press).
  2003a. *Collected Essays on Philosophy and on Judaism*, ed. Jacob Neusner (University Press of America).
  2003b. "Maimonides and Aquinas on Natural Law," in Fox 2000a, vol. 1: 183–208.
  2003c. "The Philosophical Foundations of Jewish Ethics," in Fox 2003a, vol. 3: 51–74.
  2003d. "Theodicy and Anti-Theodicy in Jewish Thought," in Fox 2003a, vol. 3: 173–87.
Fox, Michael V. 1991. *Character and Ideology in the Book of Esther* (University of South Carolina Press).
Frank, Daniel H. (ed.) 1993. *A People Apart: Chosenness and Ritual in Jewish Thought* (SUNY Press).
Frank, Daniel 2004. "What Is Jewish Philosophy?," in *History of Jewish Philosophy*, ed. Daniel Frank and Oliver Leaman (Routledge), 1–10.
Frank, Daniel and Segal, Aaron (eds.) 2016. *Jewish Philosophy Past and Present: Contemporary Responses to Classical Sources* (Routledge).
  2021. *Maimonides' Guide of the Perplexed: A Critical Guide*, ed. Daniel Frank and Aaron Segal (Cambridge University Press).

Frank, Daniel, Leaman, Oliver, and Manekin, Charles B. (eds.) 2000. *The Jewish Philosophy Reader* (Routledge).

Frankfurt, Harry 1969. "Alternate Possibilities and Moral Responsibility," *Journal of Philosophy* 66: 828–39.

  1988. "Rationality and the Unthinkable," in *The Importance of What We Care About* (Cambridge University Press), 177–90.

  1993. "What Are We Morally Responsible For?" in Fischer and Ravizza 1993a, 286–95.

  2008. "What We Are Morally Responsible For," in *The Importance of What We Care About* (Cambridge University Press), 95–103.

  2013. "Reflections on My Career in Philosophy," in *Portraits of American Philosophy*, ed. Steven M. Cahn (Rowman & Littlefield), 105–28.

Franks, Paul 2005. *All or Nothing: Systematicity, Transcendental Arguments, and Skepticism in German Idealism* (Harvard University Press).

  2006. "What Is the Context?" *Jewish Quarterly Review* 96: 387–95.

Freddoso, Alfred J. 1988. "Medieval Aristotelianism and the Case against Secondary Causes in Nature," in Morris 1988, 74–118.

  1998. "The Openness of God: Reply to Hasker," *Christian Scholars' Review* 28: 124–33.

Freud, Sigmund 1961. *The Future of an Illusion*, trans. James Strachey (W. W. Norton).

Friedman, Shlomo 2020. "The Immortality Impulse and Jewish Tradition," *Tradition* 52(2): 32–48.

Fuller, Lon 1969. *The Morality of Law* (Yale University Press).

Fuqua, Jonathan, John Greco and Tyler Dalton McNabb 2023. *The Cambridge Handbook of Religious Epistemology* (Cambridge University Press).

Garb, Jonathan 2022. "Doubt and Certainty in Late Modern Kabbalah: A Tale of Two Schools," *Maimonides Review of Philosophy and Religion* 1: 79–106.

Geach, Peter 1973. "Omnipotence," *Philosophy* 48: 7–20.

  1994. "On Worshipping the Right God," in *God and The Soul* (Thoemmes Press), 100–16.

Gellman, Jerome 1977. "The Meta-Philosophy of Religious Language," *Nous* 11: 151–61.

  1981. "Theological Realism," *International Journal for the Philosophy of Religion* 12: 17–27.

  1991. "Radical Responsibility in Maimonides' Thought," in *The Thought of Moses Maimonides*, ed. Ira Robinson, Lawrence Kaplan, and Julien Bauer (Edwin Mellen Press), 249–65.

  1993. "Naming, and Naming God," *Religious Studies* 29: 193–216.

  1994. *The Fear, The Trembling and the Fire: Kierkegaard and Hasidic Masters on the Binding of Isaac* (Rowman and Littlefield).

  1997. "The Denial of Free Will in Hasidic Thought," in Manekin and Kellner 1997, 111–31.

  2012a. *God's Kindness Has Overwhelmed Us: A Contemporary Doctrine of The Jews as The Chosen People* (Academic Studies Press).

  2012b. "Judaism and Buddhism: A Jewish Approach to a Godless Religion," in Goshen-Gottstein and Korn 2012, 299–316.

2016. *This Was from God: A Contemporary Theology of Torah and History* (Academic Studies Press).

2019. *Perfect Goodness and the God of the Jews: A Contemporary Jewish Theology* (Academic Studies Press).

2021a. "A Constructive Jewish Theology of God and Perfect Goodness," in Kepnes 2021, 453–66.

2021b. "Theological Realism and Internal Contradiction: A Reply to Steven Kepnes," *Journal of Textual Reasoning* 12(1): 52–66.

Gericke, Jaco 2012. *The Hebrew Bible and the Philosophy of Religion* (Society of Biblical Literature).

Gersonides, Levi 1987. *Wars of the Lord*, trans. Seymour Feldman (Jewish Publication Society).

1998. *Commentary on Song of Songs*, trans. Menachem Kellner (Yale University Press).

Gettier, Edmund L. 1963. "Is Justified True Belief Knowledge?" *Analysis* 23(6): 121–23.

Gillman, Neil 1997. *The Death of Death: Resurrection and Immortality in Jewish Thought* (Jewish Lights).

Gingerich, Owen 1993. "Where in the World Is God?" in *Man and Creation*, ed. M. Bauman, M. Kalthoff, and R. L. Number (Hillsdale College Press), 209–30.

Ginzberg, Louis 1928. "Jewish Thought as Reflected in the Halakhah," in *Students, Scholars and Saints* (Jewish Publication Society), 163–73.

Glazner, Moses Samuel 1977. *Responsa Dor Reviʻi* (A. Klein).

Gluck, Andrew L. 2015. *Various Theories of Why the Jewish People Are Special: A Response to Jerome Gellman, David Novak and Michael Wyschogrod's Understanding of the Chosen People* (Edwin Mellen Press).

Goldenberg, Robert 1997. *The Nations that Know Thee Not: Ancient Jewish Attitudes toward Other Religions* (Sheffield Academic Press).

Golding, Joshua 1990. "Toward a Pragmatic Conception of Religious Faith," *Faith and Philosophy* 7: 486–503.

1993. "Jewish Ritual and the Experience of Rootedness," in Frank 1993, 229–44.

1992. "Faith and Doubt Reconsidered," *Tradition* 26(3): 33–48.

2001. "On the Limits of Non-Literal Interpretation of Scripture from an Orthodox Perspective," *Torah U-Madda Journal* 10: 37–59.

2003. *Rationality and Religious Theism* (Routledge).

2022. "Commitment to Judaism in the Modern Era," in Bloom, Goldstein, and Student 2022, 49–73.

Goldman, Eliezer 1986. "Responses to Modernity in Orthodox Jewish Thought," in *Studies in Contemporary Jewry* 2, ed. Peter Medding (Indiana University Press), 52–73.

Goldschmidt, Tyron 2015. "Commanding Belief." *Ratio* 27: 163–74.

2019. "A Proof of Exodus: Yehuda HaLevy and Jonathan Edwards Walk into a Bar," in Lebens, Rabinowitz, and Segal 2019a, 222–42.

2022. "What's So Bad about Worshipping Other Gods?" *Journal of Analytic Theology* 10: 39–53.

Goldschmidt, Tyron and Seacord, Beth 2013. "Judaism, Reincarnation, and Theodicy," *Faith and Philosophy* 30: 393–417.
Goldschmidt, Tyron and Segal, Aaron 2017. "The Afterlife in Judaism," in *The Palgrave Handbook on the Afterlife*, ed. B. Matheson and Y. Nagasawa (Palgrave MacMillan), 107–27.
Goltzberg, Stefan 2011. "Three Moments in Jewish Philosophy," *Bulletin du Centre de Recherche Francais a Jerusalem* 22: 1–11.
Goodman, Lenn E. 1996. *The God of Abraham* (Oxford University Press).
    2012. "Jewish Philosophy in America," in *Jewish Philosophy: Perspectives and Retrospectives*, ed. Raphael Jospe and Dov Schwartz (Academic Studies Press), 33–56.
    2017. "What Is Positive in Negative Theology?," in Fagenblat 2017a, 62–84.
Goodman, Micah 2015. *Maimonides and the Book that Changed Judaism: Secrets of the Guide for the Perplexed*, trans. Rabbi Yedidya Sinclair (Jewish Publication Society).
Goshen-Gottstein, Alon 2016. *Same God, Other God: Judaism, Hinduism, and the Problem of Idolatry* (Palgrave MacMillan).
    2021. "Jewish Theology of Religions," in Kepnes 2021, 344–71.
Goshen-Gottstein, Alon and Korn, Eugene (eds.) 2012. *Jewish Theology and World Religions* (Littman Library of Jewish Civilization).
    (eds.) 2020. *Religious Truth: Toward a Jewish Theology of Religions* (Littman Library of Jewish Civilization).
Gottlieb, Dovid 2017. *Reason to Believe* (Mosaica Press).
Gottlieb, Michah 2013. "Moses Mendelssohn's Metaphysical Defense of Religious Pluralism," in *Faith, Reason, Politics: Essays on the History of Jewish Thought* (Academic Studies Press), 98–121.
    2020. "Does Judaism Have Dogma? Moses Mendelssohn and a Pivotal Nineteenth Century Debate," *Yearbook of the Maimonides Centre for Advanced Studies* 2019 (deGruyter), 219–42.
Green, Arthur 1979. *Tormented Master: A Life of Rabbi Nahman of Bratslav* (Schocken).
    2010. *Radical Judaism: Rethinking God and Tradition* (Yale University Press).
Green, Ronald 1988. *Religion and Moral Reason* (Oxford University Press).
Green, Alex 2025. "Miracles," in *The Routledge Companion to Jewish Philosophy*, eds. Daniel Rynhold and Tyron Goldschmidt (Routledge), 213–22.
Greenberg, Blu 1978. "Rabbi Jacob Emden: The Views of an Enlightened Traditionalist on Christianity," *Judaism* 27: 351–63.
Greenberg, Irving 2004. *For the Sake of Heaven and Earth: The New Encounter between Judaism and Christianity* (Jewish Publication Society).
Grossman, Avraham 2004. *Pious and Rebellious: Jewish Women in Medieval Europe*, trans. Jonathan Chipman (Brandeis University Press).
Guttman, Julius 1973. *Philosophies of Judaism* (Schocken).
Halbertal, Moshe 1993. "Halakhah and Morality," *S'vara* 3: 67–72.
    1999. *Interpretative Revolutions in the Making: Values as Interpretative Considerations in Midreshei Halakhah* (Hebrew) (Magnes Press).

2000a. *Between Torah and Wisdom: Rabbi Menaḥem ha-Meiri and Maimonidean Halakhists in Provence* (Hebrew) (Magnes Press).
2000b. "'Ones Possessed of Religion': Religious Tolerance in the Thought of the Me'iri," *Edah Journal* 1: 1 http://edah.org/backend/JournalArticle/halbertal.pdf
2005. "On Believers and Belief" (Hebrew), in *On Faith* (Hebrew), ed. Moshe Halbertal, David Kurzweil, and Avi Sagi (eds.) (Keter), 11–38.

Halbertal, Moshe and Avishai Margalit 1992. *Idolatry*, trans. Naomi Goldblum (Harvard University Press).
Halevi, Judah 1964. *The Kuzari*, trans. Hartwig Hirschfeld (Schocken).
Halper, Edward 2019. "Anger and Divine Perfection," in Hazony and Johnson 2019, 130–41.
Harman, Gilbert 1986. *Change In View* (Harvard University Press).
Harris, Jay 2007. "Preface," in *Maimonides after 800 Years: Essays on Maimonides and His Influence*, ed. Jay M. Harris (Harvard University Press), vii–xi.
Harris, Michael 2003. *Divine Command Ethics: Jewish and Christian Perspectives* (Routledge).
2016–2017. "'But Now My Eye Has Seen You': *Yissurin Shel Ahavah* as Divine Intimacy Theodicy," *Torah U-Madda Journal* 17: 64–92.
2017. "APJ Symposium Responses-June 2017." www.theapj.com/event/symposium-on-michael-harriss-but-now-my-eye-has-seen-you-yissurin-shel-ahavah-as-divine-intimacy-theodicy-the-torah-u-madda-journal-172015/

Harris, Sam 2005. *The End of Faith: Religion, Terror, and the Future of Reason* (W. W. Norton).
Hart, H. L. A. 1961. *The Concept of Law* (Oxford University Press).
Hart, W. D. 1988. *The Engines of the Soul* (Cambridge University Press).
Hartman, David 1976. *Maimonides: Torah and Philosophic Quest* (Jewish Publication Society).
1985. *A Living Covenant* (The Free Press).
1994. *Crisis and Leadership* (Jewish Publication Society).

Hartshorne, Charles 1984. *Omnipotence and Other Theological Mistakes* (SUNY Press).
Harvey, Warren Zev 1992. "Rabbinic Attitudes Toward Philosophy," in *"Open Thou Mine Eyes": Essays on Aggadah and Judaica Presented to Rabbi William Braude*, ed. Herman J. Blumberg et al. (Ktav), 83–101.
2008. "Why Philosophers Quote Kabbalah: The Case of Mendelssohn and Rosenzweig," *Studia Judaica* 16: 118–25.
2018a. "The Versatility of Contemporary Jewish Philosophy," in Tirosh-Samuelson and Hughes 2018, 43–59.
2018b. "Maimonides, Crescas, and the Parable of the Castle," in *Scepticism and Anti-Scepticism in Medieval Jewish Philosophy and Thought*, ed. Racheli Haliva (DeGruyter).
2025 (forthcoming). "A Century of the Historiography of Jewish Philosophy," in *Oxford Handbook of Jewish Philosophy*, ed. Yitzhak Melamed and Paul Franks (Oxford University Press).

Hasker, William 2004. *Providence, Evil, and the Openness of God* (Routledge).
  2011. "Materialism and the Resurrection: Are the Prospects Improving?" *European Journal for the Philosophy of Religion* 3: 83–103.
Haught, John 1995. *Science and Religion: From Conflict to Conversation* (Paulist Press).
Hazony, Yoram 2012. *The Philosophy of Hebrew Scripture* (Cambridge University Press).
  2015. "The Question of God's Imperfection," http://jerusalemletters.com/the-question-of-gods-perfection
  2019. "Is God a 'Perfect Being'?" in Hazony and Johnson 2019, 9–26.
Hazony, Yoram and Johnson, Dru (eds.) 2019. *The Question of God's Perfection: Jewish and Christian Essays on the God of the Bible and Talmud* (Brill).
Hebblethwaite, Brian and Henderson, Edward (eds.) 1990. *Divine Action* (T&T Clark).
Hecker, Joel 2005. *Mystical Bodies, Mystical Meals: Eating and Embodiment in Medieval Kabbalah* (Wayne State University Press).
Hefter, Herzl 2013. "In God's Hands: The Religious Phenomenology of R. Mordechai Yosef of Izbica," *Tradition* 46(1): 43–65.
Heinaman, Robert 1993. "Incompatibilism Without the Principle of Alternate Possibilities," in Fischer and Ravizza 1993a, 296–309.
Held, Shai 2013. *Abraham Joshua Heschel: The Call of Transcendence* (Indiana University Press).
Henson, Richard 1979. "What Kant Might Have Said: Moral Worth and the Determination of Dutiful Action," *Philosophical Review* 88: 39–54.
Herman, Barbara 1981. "Acting from the Motive of Duty," *Philosophical Review* 90: 359–82.
Hershkowitz, Isaac 2013. "The Strengthening of Faith in Orthodox Discourse: A Reevaluation of Models of Faith," in Sagi and Schwartz 2013, 457–77.
Heschel, Abraham Joshua 1955. *God in Search of Man* (Farrar, Strauss and Giroux).
  1962. *The Prophets* (2 volumes) (Harper & Row).
Hick, John 1978. *Evil and the God of Love* (Harper & Row).
  1993. *God and the Universe of Faiths* (Oneworld).
Hirsch, Eli 1999. "Identity in the Talmud," *Midwest Studies in Philosophy* 23: 166–80.
  2006. "Rashi's View of the Open Future: Indeterminateness and Bivalence," *Oxford Studies in Metaphysics* 2: 111–35.
  2019. "Talmudic Destiny," in Lebens, Rabinowitz, and Segal 2019a, 13–33.
Hirsch, Samson Raphael 2018a. "The Educational Value of Judaism," in *Collected Writings of Rabbi Samson Raphael Hirsch*, vol. 7, trans. Gertrude Hirschler (Feldheim), 245–75.
  2018b. "Talmudic Judaism and Society," in *Collected Writings of Rabbi Samson Raphael Hirsch*, vol. 7 (Feldheim), 209–44.
Hirschman, Marc 2000. "Rabbinic Universalism in the Second and Third Centuries," *Harvard Theological Review* 93: 101–15.
Hitchens, Christopher 2007. *God Is Not Great: How Religion Spoils Everything* (Twelve).

Howard-Snyder, Daniel 2013. "Propositional Faith: What It Is and What It Is Not," *American Philosophical Quarterly* 50: 357–72.
Howard-Snyder, Daniel and McKauhan, Daniel J. 2022. "The Problem of Faith and Reason," in *The Cambridge Handbook of Religious Epistemology*, ed. Jonathan Fuqua, John Green, and Tyler Dalton-McNabb (Cambridge University Press).
Howard-Snyder, Daniel and Moser, Paul (eds.) 2001. *Divine Hiddenness: New Essays* (Cambridge University Press).
Hughes, Aaron 2012. "Medieval Jewish Philosophers in Modern Jewish Philosophy," in *The Cambridge History of Jewish Philosophy: The Modern Era*, ed. Martin Kavka, Zachary Braiterman, and David Novak (Cambridge University Press), 224–51.
Hughes, Aaron W. and Wolfson, Elliot R. 2010. "Introduction: Charting an Alternative Course for the Study of Jewish Philosophy," in *New Directions in Jewish Philosophy*, ed. Aaron W. Hughes and Elliot R. Wolfson (Indiana University Press), 1–16.
Humphreys, W. Lee 1988. *Joseph and His Family: A Literary Study* (University of South Carolina Press).
Hutner, Yitzchak 1974. *Paḥad Yitzḥak: Rosh Ha-Shanah* (Hebrew) (Ha-Mosad Gur Aryeh).
  1991. *Paḥad Yitzḥak: Letters and Correspondence* (Hebrew) (Ha-Mosad Gur Aryeh).
Ibn Gabbai, Meir 1894. *Avodat ha-Kodesh* (Warsaw).
Idziak, Jeanine-Marie (ed.) 1980. *Divine Command Morality: Historical and Contemporary Readings* (Edwin Mellen Press).
Jackson, Elizabeth 2023a. "A Permissivist Defense of Pascal's Wager," *Erkenntnis* 88: 2315–40.
  2023b. "Faithfully Taking Pascal's Wager," *The Monist* 106: 35–45.
Jacob, Walter 1974. *Christianity through Jewish Eyes* (Hebrew Union College Press).
Jacobs, Louis 1964. *Principles of the Jewish Faith: An Analytical Study* (Basic Books).
  1973. *A Jewish Theology* (Behrman House).
Jantzen, Grace 1984. "Do We Need Immortality?" *Modern Theology* 1: 25–31.
John Paul II [Karol Wojtyla] 2006. *Man and Woman He Created Them: A Theology of the Body*, trans. Michael Waldstein (Pauline Books & Media).
Johnson, Dru 2021. *Biblical Philosophy: A Hebraic Approach to the Old and New Testaments* (Cambridge University Press).
Johnson, Patricia Altenbrend 1992. "Feminist Christian Philosophy?" *Faith and Philosophy* 9: 320–34.
Johnston, Mark 2009. *Saving God: Religion after Idolatry* (Princeton University Press).
  2010. *Surviving Death* (Princeton University Press).
Jonas, Hans 1987. "The Concept of God after Auschwitz," *Journal of Religion* 67: 1–13.
Jonas, Silvia 2021. "'Whereof One Cannot Speak,'" in Frank and Segal, 125–39.

Jordan, Jeff 2006. *Pascal's Wager: Pragmatic Arguments and Belief in God* (Clarendon).
Jordan, Jeff and Howard-Snyder, Daniel (eds.) 1996. *Faith, Freedom and Rationality* (Rowman & Littlefield).
Jospe, Raphael 2012. "Pluralism Out of the Sources of Judaism: Religious Pluralism without Relativism," in Goshen-Gottstein and Korn 2012, 87–122.
Jospe, Raphael, Madsen, Truman, and Ward, Seth 2001. *Covenant and Chosenness in Judaism and Mormonism* (Fairleigh Dickinson University Press).
Kagan, Shelly 2012. *Death* (Yale University Press).
Kaminsky, Alan 2008. *Yet I Loved Jacob: Reclaiming the Biblical Concept of Election* (Abingdon Press).
Kanarfogel, Ephraim 2008. "Varieties of Belief in Medieval Ashkenaz: The Case of Anthropomorphism," in *Rabbinic Culture and Its Critics*, ed. Daniel Frank and Matt Goldish (Wayne State University Press), 117–59.
Kane, Robert 1996. *The Significance of Free Will* (Oxford University Press).
  1999. "Responsibility, Luck and Chance: Reflections on Free Will and Indeterminism," *The Journal of Philosophy* 96: 217–40.
  2000. "The Dual Regress of Free Will and the Role of Alternative Possibilities," in *Philosophical Perspectives 14: Action and Freedom*, ed. James E. Tomberlin (Wiley-Blackwell), 57–79.
Kant, Immanuel 1997. *Grounding for the Metaphysics of Morals*, trans. Mary Gregor (Cambridge University Press).
Kaplan, Mordecai 1958. *Judaism without Supernaturalism* (Jewish Reconstructionist Federation).
  1967. *Judaism as a Civilization* (Schocken Books).
Karelitz, Avraham Yeshayahu 1997. *Ḥazon Ish al Inyanei Emunah u-Bittaḥon ve-Od* (Sh. Greinemann).
Kass, Leon 2001. "L'Chaim and Its Limits – Why Not Immortality?" *First Things* (May 2001): 17–24.
Katz, Jacob 1961. *Exclusiveness and Tolerance: Studies in Jewish–Gentile Relations in Medieval and Modern Times* (Behrman House).
Katz, Steven T. 1983. "Eliezer Berkovits's Post-Holocaust Jewish Theodicy," in *Post-Holocaust Dialogues: Critical Studies in Modern Jewish Thought* (New York University Press), 268–86.
Katzoff, Charlotte 2020. *Human Agency and Divine Will: The Book of Genesis* (Routledge).
Kaufmann, Yechezkel 1958. *Commentary to Joshua* (Hebrew) (Kiryat Sefer).
Kavka, Martin 2017. "The Politics of Negative Theology," in Fagenblat 2017a, 335–55.
Kellner, Jolene and Kellner, Menachem 2012. "Respectful Disagreement: A Response to Raphael Jospe," in Goshen-Gottstein and Korn, 123–33.
Kellner, Menachem 1991. *Maimonides on Judaism and the Jewish People* (SUNY Press).
  1999. *Must a Jew Believe Anything?* (1st ed., Littman Library of Jewish Civilization).
  2004. *Dogma in Medieval Jewish Thought: From Maimonides to Abravanel* (Littman Library of Jewish Civilization).

2006a. *Maimonides' Confrontation with Mysticism* (Littman Library of Jewish Civilization).
2006b. 2nd ed. of Kellner 1999.
2008. "Maimonides' 'True Religion': For Jews or for All Humanity? A Response to Chaim Rapoport," *Meorot* (September 2008). www.yctorah.org/content/view/436/10/
2021. "Today's Perplexed: Between Maimonidean Promise and Peril," *Tradition* 53(4): 23–52.
Kelly, Thomas 2011. "Consensus Gentium: Reflections on the 'Common Consent' Argument for the Existence of God," in *Evidence and Religious Belief*, ed. Kelly James Clark and Raymond J. VanArragon (Oxford University Press), 135–56.
Kepnes, Steven 2007. *Jewish Liturgical Reasoning* (Oxford University Press).
2013. *The Future of Jewish Theology* (Wiley-Blackwell).
(ed.) 2021a. *The Cambridge Companion to Jewish Theology* (Cambridge University Press).
2021b. "A Program for Positive Jewish Theology," *Journal of Textual Reasoning* 12: 9–41.
Kim, Brian and McGrath, Matthew (eds.) 2018. *Pragmatic Encroachment in Epistemology* (Routledge).
Kimelman, Reuven 2007. Review of Irving Greenberg, *For the Sake of Heaven and Earth: The New Encounter between Judaism and Christianity*, *Modern Judaism* 27: 103–25.
Koller, Aaron 2020. *Unbinding Isaac: The Significance of the Akedah for Modern Jewish Thought* (Jewish Publication Society).
Kook, Abraham Isaac 1983. *Arpelei Tohar* (Hebrew) (Mossad HaRav Kook).
1985a. *Orot ha-Emunah* [Lights of Faith] (Mossad HaRav Kook).
1985b. *Orot ha-Kodesh* [Lights of Holiness] (Mossad HaRav Kook).
1985c. *Iggerot Ha-Reayah* (Mossad HaRav Kook).
1985d. *Orot* (Mossad HaRav Kook).
1986. *Rav A. Y. Kook: Selected Letters*, trans. Tzvi Feldman (Ma'aliot Publications).
Koons, Robert and Bealer, George (eds.) 2010. *The Waning of Materialism* (Oxford University Press).
Korn, Eugene 1991. "Tradition Meets Modernity: On the Conflict of Halakhah and Political Liberty," *Tradition* 25(4): 30–47.
1994. "Gentiles, the World-to-Come, and Judaism: The Odyssey of a Rabbinic Text," *Modern Judaism* 14: 265–87.
1997. "Tselem Elokim and the Dialectic of Jewish Morality," *Tradition* 31(2): 5–30.
2001. "The Halakhic Debate over Women in Public Life: Two Public Letters of Rav Abraham Isaac ha-Kohen Kook and the Responsa of Rav BenZion Uziel on Women's Suffrage and Representation." *Edah Journal* 1(2). https://library.yctorah.org/files/2016/09/The-Halakhic-Debate-over-Women-in-Public-Life-Two-Public-Letters.pdf
2011. "Orthodoxy, Modern Pluralism, and the Christian Other: Rabbinic Positions and Possibilities," in *Mishpetei Shalom: A Jubilee Volume in Honor of Rabbi Saul (Shalom) Berman*, ed. Yamin Levy (Yeshivat Chovevei Torah), 307–39.

    2012. "Rethinking Christianity: Rabbinic Positions and Possibilities," in Goshen-Gottstein and Korn 2012, 189–215.
    2021. *To Be a Holy Nation: Jewish Tradition and Ethical Values* (Urim).
Kraemer, David 1995. *Responses to Suffering in Classical Rabbinic Literature* (Oxford University Press).
Kramer, Peter 1993. *Listening to Prozac* (Penguin Books).
Kreisel, Howard 2001. *Prophecy: The History of an Idea in Medieval Jewish Philosophy* (Kluwer).
Kretzmann, Norman 1966. "Omniscience and Immutability," *Journal of Philosophy* 63: 409–21.
Kripke, Saul 1980. *Naming and Necessity* (Harvard University Press).
Kugel, James 1999. *The Great Poems of the Bible: A Reader's Companion* (Free Press).
Kuhn, Thomas 1962. *The Structure of Scientific Revolutions* (University of Chicago Press).
Kushner, Harold 2004. *When Bad Things Happen to Good People* (Anchor Books).
Kvanvig, John 2013. "Affective Faith and People of Faith," *Midwest Studies in Philosophy* 37(2013): 109–28.
    1990. *Halakhot va-Halikhot* [Heb.] (Mossad HaRav Kook).
    (ed.) 1999. *The Religious Thought of Hasidism* (Ktav).
    2006a. *Faith and Doubt: Studies in Traditional Jewish Thought* (3rd ed., Ktav Publishing).
    2006b. "Faith and Doubt," in Lamm 2006a, 1–40.
    2006c. "The Religious Implications of Extraterrrestrial Life," in Lamm 2006a, 105–58.
    2006d. "Amalek and the Seven Nations: A Case of War vs. Morality," in Lamm 2006a, 321–57.
    2015. "Those Who Live and Those Who Live On," in *The Koren Yizkor*, ed. Joel B. Wolowelsky (Koren), 65–72.
Langermann, Tzvi 2004. "Maimonides and Miracles: The Growth of a (Dis)Belief," *Jewish History* 18: 147–72.
    2020–2021. "Aspects of Maimonides' Historiosophy," *Torah U-Madda Journal* 18: 94–113.
Lasker, Daniel 2008. "Tradition and Innovation in Maimonides' Attitude to Other Religions," in *Maimonides after 800 Years: Essays on Maimonides and His Influence*, ed. Jay M. Harris (Harvard University Press), 167–82.
Lebens, Samuel 2014. "Why So Negative about Negative Theology? The Search for a Plantinga-Proof Apophaticism," *International Journal for the Philosophy of Religion* 76: 259–75.
    2015. "God and His Imaginary Friends: A Hassidic Metaphysics," *Religious Studies* 51: 183–204.
    2020a. "Revelation Through Concealment: Kabbalistic Responses to Divine Hiddenness," *Eurtpean Journal for The Philosophy of Religion* 12(2): 89–108.

2020b. *The Principles of Judaism* (Oxford University Press).
2021a. "On Where God Isn't: Excrement and Philosophy of Religion; Two Jewish Perspectives," *Religious Studies* 57: 717–31.
2021b. "Proselytism as Epistemic Violence," *The Monist* 104: 376–92.
2022a. *A Guide for the Jewish Undecided: A Philosopher Makes the Case for Orthodox Judaism* (Yeshiva University Press/Maggid Books).
2022b. "Is God A Person? Maimonides, Crescas, and Beyond," *Religious Studies* 58: 534–560.
2022c. "Response to Critics," *European Journal for the Philosophy of Religion* 14(4): 340–58.
2023a. *Philosophy of Religion: The Basics* (Routledge).
2023b. "Amen to Daat: On the Foundations of Jewish Epistemology." *Religious Studies* 59 (special issue 3): 465–78.
2023c. "Does Judaism Recognize the Supererogatory?" in *Handbook of Supererogation*, ed. David Heyd (Springer).
Lebens, Samuel, Rabinowitz, Dani, and Segal, Aaron (eds.) 2019a. *Jewish Philosophy in an Analytic Age* (Oxford University Press).
2019b. Contribution to "Symposium: Jewish Studies and Analytic Philosophy of Judaism," in Lebens, Rabinowitz, and Segal 2019a, 330–35.
Lebens, Samuel and Statman, Daniel 2023. "The Unlikely Comeback of Pascal's Wager: On the Instability of Secular Post-Modernism," *Philosophia* 51: 337–48.
Lefkowitz, Jay P. 2014. "The Rise of Social Orthodoxy: A Personal Account," *Commentary* (April): www.commentary.org/articles/jay-lefkowitz/the-rise-of-social-orthodoxy-a-personal-account/
Leftow, Brian 2011. "Why Perfect Being Theology?" *International Journal for the Philosophy of Religion* 69: 103–18.
Lehrer, Keith D. 1971. "How Reasons Give Us Knowledge, or the Case of the Gypsy Lawyer," *Journal of Philosophy* 68(10): 111–13.
Leibniz, Gottfried Wilhelm 1989. "Discourse on Metaphysics (1686)," in *Leibniz: Philosophical Essays*, trans. Roger Ariew and Daniel Garber (Hackett Publishing Company).
Leibowitz, Aryeh 2014. *Hashgachah Pratis* (CreateSpace Independent Publishing).
Leibowitz, Nehama 1981. *Studies in Bereshit (Genesis)*, trans. Aryeh Newman (World Zionist Organization).
Leibowitz, Yeshayahu 1992. *Judaism, Human Values, and the Jewish State*, trans. and ed. Eliezer Goldman et al. (Harvard University Press).
Leiner, Mordechai Yosef 1995. *Mei ha-Shiloah*, ed. Elchanan Goldhaber and Yehudah Spigelman (Yitzhak Natan Naftali England).
Lerner, Berel Dov 2009. "RaMBaM and Middle Knowledge: A Puzzle in the *Lehem Mishneh*," *BDD* 21(March): 75–80.
2019. "God the Walker," in Hazony and Johnson 2019, 27–42.
Lerner, Ralph and Mahdi, Muhsin 1963 (eds.). *Medieval Political Philosophy: A Sourcebook* (Free Press).
Levenson, Jon 1988. *Creation and the Persistence of Evil: The Drama of Divine Omnipotence* (Harper & Row).
1998. "The Abusers of Abraham," *Judaism* 47: 259–77.

2008. *Resurrection and the Restoration of Israel: The Ultimate Victory of the God of Life* (Yale University Press).
Levinas, Emmauel 1996. *Proper Name*, trans. Michael B. Smith (Stanford University Press).
  2007. "Useless Suffering," in *Wrestling with God: Jewish Theological Responses during and after the Holocaust*, ed. Steven T. Katz, Associate Editors Shlomo Biderman, and Gershon Greenberg (Oxford University Press), 451–54.
Lewinsohn, Jed 2006–2007. "Philosophy in Halakhah: The Case of Intentional Action." *Torah U-Madda Journal* 14: 97–136.
  2016. "Ritual and Rationality," in Frank and Segal 2016, 243–55.
Lewis, C. S. 1962. *The Problem of Pain* (HarperCollins).
  1994. *God in the Dock: Essays on Theology and Ethics*, ed. W. Hooper (Wm. B. Eerdsmans).
Lewis, Hywell D. 1959. *Our Experience of God* (Collins).
Libet, Benjamin, Freeman, Anthony, and Sutherland, Keith (eds.) 1999. *The Volitional Brain* (Imprint Academic).
Lichtenstein, Aharon 1975. "Does Jewish Tradition Recognize an Ethic Independent of Halakhah?" in *Modern Jewish Ethics*, ed. Marvin Fox (Ohio State University Press), 62–88.
  1999. "The Duties of the Heart and Response to Suffering," in Carmy 1999, 21–61.
  2023. *Values in Halakha: Six Case Studies* (Maggid Books).
Linden, Ingemar Patrick 2022. *The Case against Death* (MIT Press).
Linzer, Dov 2005. "On the *Mitzvot* of Non-Jews: An Analysis of *Avodah Zarah* 2b–3a," *Milin Havivin* 1: 25–37.
Loeb, Louis E. 1981. *From Descartes to Hume: Continental Metaphysics and the Development of Modern Philosophy* (Cornell University Press).
Loose, Jonathan, Menuge, Angus J. L., and Moreland, J. P. (eds.) 2018. *The Blackwell Companion to Substance Dualism* (Wiley-Blackwell).
Lorberbaum, Yair 2015. *In God's Image: Myth, Theology and Law in Classical Judaism* (Cambridge University Press).
Lubarsky, Sandra B. and Griffin, David Ray 1996. *Jewish Theology and Process Thought* (SUNY Press).
Luzzatto, Moshe Chaim 1997. *The Way of God: Derech Hashem*, trans. Aryeh Kaplan (Feldheim).
  2004. *Mesillas Yesarim: The Path of the Just*, trans. Yosef Leibler (Feldheim).
Machuca, Diego E. 2013. *Disagreement and Skepticism* (Routledge).
MacIntyre, Alasdair 1981. *After Virtue: A Study in Moral Theory* (University of Notre Dame Press).
Mackie, J. L. 1977. *Ethics: Inventing Right and Wrong* (Penguin Books).
Maimonides, Moses 1963. *Guide of the Perplexed*, trans. Shlomo Pines (University of Chicago Press).
  1985. "The Essay on Resurrection," in *Epistles of Maimonides: Crisis and Leadership*, trans., Abraham Halkin, discussions by David Hartman (Jewish Publication Society), 209–45.
Malebranche, Nicolas 1992. *Philosophical Selections*, ed. Steven Nadler (Hackett).
Manekin, Charles 1997a. "Introduction," in Manekin and Kellner 1997, 1–19.

1997b. "Freedom within Reason? Gersonides on Human Choice," in Manekin and Kellner 1997, 165–204.
1998. "On the Limited-Omniscience Interpretation of Gersonides' Theory of Divine Knowledge," in *Perspectives in Jewish Thought and Mysticism*, ed. Alfred Ivry (Harwood Educational Publishing), 135–70.
2007. "Possible Sources of Theological Conservatism in Maimonides' Later Writings," in *Maimonides after 800 Years: Essays on Maimonides and His Influence*, ed. Jay M. Harris (Harvard University Press).
2016. "Warrants for Belief and the Significance of Religious Experience," in Frank and Segal 2016, 101–9.
2017. "Maimonides on the Divine Authorship of the Law," in *Interpreting Maimonides: Critical Essays*, ed. Charles Manekin and Daniel Davies (Cambridge University Press), 133–51.
2025 (forthcoming). "Free Will," in Melamed and Franks 2025.
Manekin, Charles H. and Eisen, Robert (eds.) 2008. *Philosophers and the Jewish Bible* (University Press of Maryland).
Manekin, Charles H. (ed.) and Kellner, Menachem (Associate Editor) 1997. *Freedom and Moral Responsibility: General and Jewish Perspectives* (University Press of Maryland).
Margalit, Avishai 1996. "The Ring: On Religious Pluralism," in *Toleration: An Elusive Virtue*, ed. David Heyd (Princeton University Press), 147–57.
Margolin, Ron 2013, "On the Essence of Faith in Hasidism," in Sagi and Schwartz 2013, 302–66.
Marty, Martin 1999. "Introduction: Proselytizers and Proselytizees on the Sharp Arete of Modernity," in Witte and Martin 1999, 1–14.
Mavrodes, George 1988. *Revelation in Religious Belief* (Temple University Press).
McCracken, Charles J. 1983. *Malebranche and British Philosophy* (Oxford University Press).
McKim, Robert 2012. *On Religious Diversity* (Oxford University Press).
Meister, Chad (ed.) 2011. *The Oxford Handbook of Religious Diversity* (Oxford University Press).
2017. "Ancient and Contemporary Expressions of Panentheism," *Philosophy Compass* 12(9): 1–12.
2018. *Evil: A Guide for the Perplexed* (Bloomsbury).
Meister, Chad and Moser, Paul (eds.) 2017. *The Cambridge Companion to the Problem of Evil* (Cambridge University Press).
Melamed, Yitzhak Y. 2025. "Hassidism and Philosophy: The Return to Nothingness," in *The Routledge Companion to Jewish Philosophy*, eds. Daniel Rynhold and Tyron Goldschmidt (Routledge), 200–210.
Melamed, Yitzhak, and Franks, Paul 2025. *The Oxford Handbook of Jewish Philosophy* (Oxford University Press).
Mele, Alfred 2014. *Free: Why Science Hasn't Disproved Free Will* (Oxford University Press).
Mendelssohn, Moses 1975. "Letter to Johann Caspar Lavater [1769]," in Talmage 1975, 265–72.
1983. *Jerusalem: Or on Religious Power and Judaism*, trans. Alan Arkush (Brandeis University Press).

Merricks, Trenton 2009. "Truth and Freedom," *Philosophical Review* 118: 29–57.
  2011. "Foreknowledge and Freedom," *Philosophical Review* 120: 567–86.
Mill, John Stuart 1996. "Sedgwick's Discourse," in *The Collected Works of John Stuart Mill*, vol. 10: *Essays on Ethics, Religion, and Society*, ed. John M. Robson (Routledge), 31–74.
  2009. "An Examination of Sir William Hamilton's Philosophy," in *The Collected Works of John Stuart Mill*, vol. 9: *Essays on Ethics, Religion, and Society*, ed. John M. Robson (Routledge).
Miller, Moshe 2008. "R. Jacob Emden's Attitude Toward Christianity," in *Turim: Studies in Jewish History and Literature Presented to Dr. Bernard Lander*, ed. Michael A. Shmidman (Touro College Press), 105–36.
Minas, Anne C. 1975. "God and Forgiveness," *Philosophical Quarterly* 25: 138–50.
Mittleman, Alan 2009. "Asking the Wrong Question," *First Things* 189: 15–17.
  2015. *Human Nature and Jewish Thought: Judaism's Case for Why Persons Matter* (Princeton University Press).
Moore, Michael 1997. *Placing Blame: A Theory of the Criminal Law* (Oxford University Press).
Morgenbesser, Sidney and Ullman-Margalit, Edna 1977. "Picking and Choosing," *Social Research* 44: 757–85.
Morris, Thomas V. (ed.) 1988. *Divine and Human Action: Essays in the Metaphysics of Theism* (Cornell University Press).
  1997. *Our Idea of God: An Introduction to Philosophical Theology* (Regent College Publishing).
Muffs, Yohanan 2005. *The Personhood of God: Biblical Theology, Human Faith, and the Divine Image* (Jewish Lights).
Muggs, Joshua 2016. "In Defense of the Belief-Plus Model of Faith," *European Journal for the Philosophy of Religion* 8: 201–19.
Murphy, Mark 1998. "Divine Command, Divine Will, and Moral Obligation," *Faith and Philosophy* 15(1): 3–27.
  2011. *God and Moral Law: On The Theistic Explanation of Morality* (Oxford University Press).
Nachmanides, Moses 1963. *Kitvei Ramban*, ed. Charles B. Chavel (Mossad HaRav Kook).
  2009. *Writings of the Ramban*, trans. and ed. Charles B. Chavel (Shilo Press).
  2010. *Ramban: Commentary on the Torah*, trans. and ed. Charles B. Chavel (Judaica Press)
Nadelhoffer, Thomas and Wright, Jennifer Cole 2018. "Humility, Free Will Beliefs, and Existential Angst: How We Got from a Preliminary Investigation to a Cautionary Tale," in *Neuroexistentialism: Meaning, Morals and Purpose in an Age of Neuroscience*, ed. Gregg Caruso and Owen Flanagan (Oxford University Press), 269–97.
Nadler, Steven 2011. *Occasionalism: Causation among the Cartesians* (Oxford University Press).
Nagasawa, Yujin 2017. *Maximal God: A New Defense of Perfect Being Theology* (Oxford University Press).
Nagelst Thomas 2012. *Mind and Cosmos: Why the Materialist Neo-Darwinian Conception of Nature Is Almost Certainly False* (Oxford University Press).

Newman, Louis 1989. "Law, Virtue, and Supererogation," *Journal of Jewish Studies* 40: 61–88.
Nietzsche, Friedrich 1991. *Human, All Too Human*, trans. R. J. Hollingdale (Cambridge University Press).
Novak, David 1983. *The Image of the Non-Jew in Judaism* (Edwin Mellen Press).
  1995. *The Election of Israel: The Idea of the Chosen People* (Cambridge University Press).
  2008. *Natural Law in Judaism* (Cambridge University Press).
  2014. "Interview," in *David Novak: Natural Law and Revealed Torah*, ed. Hava Tirosh-Samuelson and Aaron Hughes (Brill), 89–139.
Novick, Tzvi 2014. "Free Will/Judaism/Rabbinic Judaism." *Encyclopedia of the Bible and Its Reception*, vol. 9, ed. Joseph Davis. www.degruyter.com/database/ebr/html?lang=en
  2019. Contribution to "Symposium: Jewish Studies and Analytic Philosophy of Judaism," in Lebens, Rabinowitz, and Segal 2019a, 325–30.
Nozick, Robert 1981. *Philosophical Explanations* (Harvard University Press).
Nuland, Sherwin B. 1995. *How We Die: Reflections on Life's Final Chapter* (Vintage).
Nussbaum, Martha 1986. *The Fragility of Goodness: Luck and Ethics in Greek Ethics and Philosophy* (Cambridge University Press).
Oakes, Robert 1990. "The Wrath of God," *International Journal for the Philosophy of Religion* 27: 129–40.
Olson, Eric T. and Segal, Aaron 2023. *Do We Have a Soul? A Debate* (Routledge).
Oppy, Graham 2017. "Logical Problems of Evil and Free Will Defenses," in Meister and Moser 2017, 45–64.
Pascal, Blaise 1941. *Pensées and the Provincial Letters*, trans. W. F. Otter (Modern Library).
Peli, Pinchas 1979. "In Search of Religious Language for the Holocaust," *Conservative Judaism* 21(2): 3–24.
  (ed.) 1984. *Soloveitchik on Repentance* (Paulist Press).
Pereboom, Derek 2001. *Living Without Free Will* (Cambridge University Press).
Peterson, Michael, Hasker, William, Reichenbach, Bruce, and Basinger, David 2012. *Reason and Religious Belief: An Introduction to the Philosophy of Religion* (5th ed., Oxford University Press).
Pike, Nelson 1965. "Divine Omniscience and Voluntary Action," *Philosophical Review* 74: 27–46.
Pinnock, Clark, Rice, Richard, Sanders, John, Hasker, William, and Basinger, David 1994. *The Openness of God* (Intervarsity Press).
Plantinga, Alvin 1967. *God and Other Minds* (Cornell University Press).
  2000. *Warranted Christian Belief* (Oxford University Press).
  2011. *Where the Conflict Really Lies: Science, Religion, and Naturalism* (Oxford University Press).
Pleijel, Richard 2019. "To Be or to Have a Nephesh?" *Zeitschrift für die alttestamentliche Wissenschaft* 131: 194–206.
Pojman, Louis 1979. "Rationality and Religious Belief," *Religious Studies* 15: 159–72.
Putnam, Hilary 2008. *Jewish Philosophy as a Guide to Life: Rosenzweig, Buber, Levinas, Wittgenstein* (Indiana University Press).

Quine, Willard van Orman 1987. *Quiddities: An Intermittently Philosophical Dictionary* (Harvard University Press).
Rabinovitch, Nachum L. 1993. "The Way of Torah," *Edah Journal* 3(1): 1–29.
Rachels, James 1971. "God and Human Attitudes," *Religious Studies* 7: 325–37.
Ramal, Randy 2019. "On How Not to 'Sublime' God's Perfection," in Hazony and Johnson 2019, 169–88.
Raphael, Simcha Paul 2009. *Jewish Views of the Afterlife* (Rowman & Littlefield).
Rapoport, Chaim 2008. "'Dat Ha-Emet' in Maimonides's Mishneh Torah," Meorot, www.yctorah.org/content/view/436/10/
Rappoport, Jason 2004. "Rav Kook and Nietzsche: A Preliminary Comparison of their Ideas on Religions, Christianity, Buddhism, and Atheism," *The Torah U-Madda Journal* 12: 99–129.
Rea, Michael 2011. "Introduction," in Rea and Crisp 2011, 9–11.
  2018. *The Hiddenness of God* (Oxford University Press).
Rea, Michael and Crisp, Oliver (eds.) 2011. *Analytic Theology: New Essays in the Philosophy of Theology* (Oxford University Press).
Rizzieri, Aaron 2013. *Pragmatic Encroachment, Religious Belief, and Practice* (Pagrave).
Rogers, Katherin 2002. *Perfect Being Theology* (Edinburgh University Press).
Rosenberg, Shalom 2023. "A Narrow Bridge: Rabbi Nahman of Breslov's Faith in a World of Doubt," *Tradition* 55(3): 1–14.
Rosensweig, Itamar and Mermelstein, Shua 2022. "Rights and Duties in Jewish Law," *Touro Law Review* 37: 2179–209.
Rosenzweig, Franz 2005. *The Star of Redemption* trans. Barbara E. Galli (University of Wisconsin Press).
Ross, Tamar 1997. "The Cognitive Value of Religious Truth Statements: Rabbi A. I. Kook and Post-Modernism," in Elman and Gurock 1997, 479–528.
  2013. "Religious Belief in a Postmodern Age," in *Faith: Jewish Perspectives*, ed. Avi Sagi and Dov Schwartz (Academic Studies Press), 188–240.
  2014. *Expanding the Palace of Torah: Orthodoxy and Feminism* (Brandeis University Press).
Roth, Leon 1999a. *Is There a Jewish Philosophy? Rethinking Fundamentals* (Littman Library of Jewish Civilization).
  1999b. "Is There a Jewish Philosophy?" in Roth 1999, 1–14.
  1999c. "Imitatio Dei and the Idea of Holiness," in Roth 1999a, 15–28.
Rowe, William L. 1993. "Causing and Being Responsible for What Is Inevitable," in Fischer and Ravizza 1993a, 310–21.
  2004. *Can God Be Free?* (Oxford University Press).
Rubin, Israel Netanel 2016. *What God Cannot Do* (Hebrew) (Rubin Mass).
Runzo, Joseph 1988. "God. Commitment and Other Faiths," *Faith and Philosophy* 5: 343–64.
Rynhold, Daniel 2009. *An Introduction to Medieval Jewish Philosophy* (I. B. Tauris).
  2019. "Religious Diversity," in *Theism and Atheism: Opposing Arguments in Philosophy*, ed. Joseph W. Koterski and Graham Oppy (Gale), 227–41.
Saadia Gaon 1948. *The Book of Beliefs and Opinions*, trans. Samuel Rosenblatt (Yale University Press). [One of two translations cited in the book.]

Saadya Gaon 1981. *Book of Doctrines and Beliefs*, trans. Alexander Altmann in *Three Jewish Philosophers* (Atheneum). [One of two translations cited in the book.]
Sacks, Jonathan 2003. *The Dignity of Difference* (Continuum).
  2005. *To Heal a Fractured World* (Schocken Books).
  2017. *Not in God's Name: Confronting Religious Violence* (Schocken).
  2023. "Foreword," in Rabbi Nachum L. Rabinovitch, *Pathways to The Hearts: Torah Perspectives on the Individual* (Maggid).
Sagi, Avi 1994. "The Punishment of Amalek in Jewish Tradition: Coping with the Moral Problem," *Harvard Theological Review* 87: 323–46.
  2008. *The Open Canon: On the Meaning of Halakhic Discourse* (Continuum).
  2009. *Jewish Religion after Theology*, trans. Batya Stein (Academic Studies Press).
Sagi, Avi and Schwartz, Dov (eds.) 2013. *Faith: Jewish Perspectives* (Academic Studies Press).
Sagi, Avi and Statman, Daniel 1995. "Divine Command Morality and Jewish Thought," *Journal of Religious Ethics* 23: 49–67.
Samuelson, Norbert 2009. *Jewish Faith and Modern Science: On the Death and Rebirth of Jewish Philosophy* (Rowman & Littlefield).
Schechter, Solomon 1888. "The Dogmas of Judaism." *Jewish Quarterly Review* 1(1): 48–64.
Scheffler, Samuel 2013. *Death and the Afterlife*, ed. Niko Kolodny (Oxford University Press).
Schiffman, Lawrence and Wolowelsky, Joel B. (eds.), 2007. *War and Peace in The Jewish Tradition* (Yeshiva University Press).
Schimmel, Solomon 1977. "Free Will, Guilt, and Self-Control in Rabbinic Judaism and Contemporary Psychology," *Judaism* 26: 418–29.
Schlesinger, George N. 1988. *New Perspectives on Old-Time Religion* (Clarendon Press).
Schlossberger, Eugene 1992. *Moral Responsibility and Persons* (Temple University Press).
Schnall, Ira M. 2007. "Sceptical Theism and Moral Scepticism," *Religious Studies* 43: 43–69.
Schoenecker, Dieter and Wood, Allen W. 2015. *Immanuel Kant's Groundwork for the Metaphysic of Morals: A Commentary* (Harvard University Press).
Schreiber, Aaron 1979. *Jewish Law and Decision Making* (Temple University Press).
Schwartz, Dov 1999. *Astrology and Magic in Medieval Jewish Thought* (Hebrew) (Bar-Ilan University Press).
  2017. *Messianism in Medieval Jewish Thought* (Academic Studies Press).
Schwartz, Jeffrey M. and Begley, Sharon 2002. *The Mind and the Brain: Neuroplasticity and the Power of Mental Force* (HarperCollins).
Schweid, Eliezer 2005. "Is There a Religious Meaning to the Idea of a Chosen People after the Shoah?" in *The Impact of the Holocaust on Jewish Theology*, ed. Steven Katz (New York University Press), 5–12.
Sears, David 2003. *The Vision of Eden: Animal Welfare and Vegetarianism in Jewish Law and Mysticism* (Meorei Ohr).

Seeskin, Kenneth 1990. "The Positive Contribution of Negative Theology," in *Jewish Philosophy in a Secular Age* (State University of New York), 31–70.
  1991. "Jewish Philosophy in the 1980's," *Modern Judaism* 11: 157–72.
  1995. *No Other Gods: The Modern Struggle against Idolatry* (Behrman House).
  1999. *Searching for a Distant God* (Oxford University Press).
  2016. *Thinking about the Torah: A Philosopher Reads the Bible* (Jewish Publication Society).
  2017. "No One Can See My Face and Live," in Fagenblat 2017a, 48–61.
Segal, Aaron 2012–2013. "A Religiously Sensitive Jewish Philosophical Theology," *The Torah U-Madda Journal* 16: 186–200.
  2014. "Adam, Moshe, and the Desire to Live Forever," www.yutorah.org/sidebar/lecturedata/806736/Adam,-Moshe,-and-The-Desire-to-Live-Forever (audio)
  2016. "Immortality: Two Models," in Frank and Segal 2016, 151–61.
  2017. "Why Live Forever? What Metaphysics Can Contribute," *Erkenntis* 83(2): 185–204.
  2019a. "If This World Is an Anteroom, Why Be This Worldly?," in *Sefer Ha-Yovel of Yeshivat Har Etzion* (Kodesh Press), 319–32.
  2019b. "Metaphysics Out of the Sources of the *Halakha*, or a *Halakhic* Metaphysics?" In Lebens, Rabinowitz, and Segal 2019a.
  2020. "Lost at Sea: A New Route to Metaphysical Skepticism," *Pacific Philosophical Quarterly* 101(2): 256–75.
  2021a. "His Existence Is Essentiality: Maimonides as Metaphysician," in Frank and Segal 2021, 102–24.
  2021b. "Doubting God, Doubting Ourselves," *Tradition* 53(3): 240–49.
  2023. "Crescas, Hard Determinism, and the Need for a Torah," *Faith & Philosophy* 40(1): 70–89.
Septimus, Bernard 1982. *Hispano-Jewish Culture in Transition* (Harvard University Press).
Setira, Kieran 2022. "The Personal Is Philosophical: On the First English Translation of Wittgenstein's Early Private Notebooks," *Boston Review* (March 28). https://bostonreview.net/articles/the-personal-is-philosophical/
Shapiro, David 1963. "The Rationalism of Ancient Jewish Thought," *Tradition* 5(2): 205–24.
Shapiro, Marc B. 1993. "Islam and the Halakhah," *Judaism* 42: 332–43.
  2003. "Of Books and Bans," *Edah Journal* 3(2). www.edah.org/backend/JournalArticle/3_2_Shapiro.pdf
  2011. *The Limits of Orthodox Theology: Maimonides' Thirteen Principles Reappraised* (Littman Library).
  2012. "Is There a 'Pesak' for Jewish Thought?," in *Jewish Thought and Jewish Belief*, ed. Daniel Lasker (Ben-Gurion University Press), 119–40.
  2025. *Renewing the Old, Sanctifying the New: The Unique Vision of Rav Kook* (Littman Library).
Shatz, David 1985. "Free Will and the Structure of Motivation," *Midwest Studies in Philosophy* 10: 451–85.
  1988. "Compatibilism, Values, and 'Could Have Done Otherwise,'" *Philosophical Topics* 16: 167–75.

1991. "Practical Endeavor and the *Torah u-Madda* Debate," *Torah U-Madda Journal* 3: 98–149.
1997a. "Hierarchical Theories of Freedom and the Hardening of Hearts," *Midwest Studies in Philosophy* 21: 202–24.
1997b. "Irresistible Goodness and Alternative Possibilities," in Manekin and Kellner 1997, 33–73.
1997c. "Freedom, Repentance, and Hardening of the Hearts: Albo vs. Maimonides," *Faith and Philosophy* 14: 478–509.
(ed.) 2001. *Philosophy and Faith* (McGraw-Hill).
2004. *Peer Review: A Critical Inquiry* (Rowman & Littlefield).
2008. "Is There Science in the Bible? An Assessment of Biblical Concordism," *Tradition* 41(2): 198–244.
2009a. *Jewish Thought in Dialogue: Essays on Thinkers, Theologies, and Moral Theories* (Academic Studies Press).
2009b. "Does Jewish Law Express Jewish Philosophy? The Curious Case of Theodicies," in Shatz 2009a, 291–304.
2009c. "'From the Depths I Have Called to You': Jewish Reflections on September 11th and Contemporary Terrorism," in Shatz 2009a, 257–90.
2010. "Hashkafah and Interpretation," in *Mitokh ha-Ohel*, ed. Daniel Feldman and Stuart Halpern (YU Press/Maggid), 341–61.
2011. "Morality, Liberalism, and Interfaith Dialogue," in *New Perspectives on Jewish-Christian Relations*, ed. Elisheva Carlebach and Jacob J. Schacter (Brill), 491–519.
2013a. "Ethical Theories in the Orthodox Movement," in Dorff and Crane 2013, 241–58.
2013b. "So What Else Is Neo? Theism and Epistemic Recalcitrance," *Midwest Studies in Philosophy* 37: 25–50.
2013c. "On Constructing a Jewish Theodicy," in *The Blackwell Companion to the Problem of Evil*, ed. Justin P. McBrayer and Daniel Howard-Snyder (Wiley-Blackwell), 309–25.
2017. "Can Halakhah Survive Negative Theology?" in Fagenblat 2017a, 282–303.
2019a. "Should Theists Eschew Theodicies?" in Lebens, Rabinowitz, and Segal 2019a, 198–221.
2019b. "Rabbi Joseph B. Soloveitchik and Western Culture: An Enigmatic Dialogue," *Critical Inquiry* 45: 506–30.
2019c. "Law, Virtue, and Self-Transcendence in Jewish Thought and Practice," in *Self-Transcendence and Virtue: Perspectives from Philosophy, Psychology, and Theology*, ed. Jennifer A. Frey and Candace Vogler (Routledge), 95–124.
2021. "Maimonides and the Problem(s) of Evil," in *Maimonides' Guide of the Perplexed: A Critical Guide*, ed. Daniel Frank and Aaron Segal (Cambridge University Press).
2022. "Review of Samuel Lebens, *The Principles of Judaism*," *Journal of Analytic Theology* 10: 723–29.
Shifman, Nadav Berman 2019. "Pragmatism and Jewish Thought: Eliezer Berkovits's Philosophy of Halakhic Fallibility," *Journal of Jewish Thought and Philosophy* 27(1): 86–135.

Shilo, Shmuel 1978. "On One Aspect of Law and Morality in Jewish Law: *Lifnim Mishurat Hadin.*" *Israel Law Review* 13(3): 359–90.
Shmalo, Gamliel 2011–2012. "Orthodox Approaches to Biblical Slavery," *Torah u-Madda Journal* 16: 1–20.
Simkins, Ronald P. 2022. "Attitudes to Nature in the Bible and the Ancient Near East," in *The Oxford Handbook of the Bible and Ecology*, ed. Hilary Marlow and Mark Harris (Oxford University Press), 269–82.
Simon, Moshe D. 1997. "'Many Thoughts in the Heart of Man': Irony and Theology in the Book of Esther," *Tradition* 31(4): 5–27.
Slifkin, Natan 2010. *The Challenge of Creation* (Lamda Publishers).
Sokol, Moshe 2013a. *Judaism Examined: Essays in Jewish Philosophy and Ethics* (Academic Studies Press).
  2013b. "Is There a 'Halakhic' Response to the Problem of Evil?" in Sokol 2013a, 67–83.
  2013c. "Attitudes toward Pleasure in Jewish Thought: A Typological Proposal," in Sokol 2013a, 83–111.
  2013d. "Maimonides on Freedom of the Will and Moral Responsibility," in Sokol 2013a, 140–57.
  2013e. "The Allocation of Scarce Medical Resources: A Philosophical Analysis of the Halakhic Sources," in Sokol 2013a, 305–37.
  2013f. "Some Tensions in the Jewish Attitude toward the Taking of Human Life," in Sokol 2013a, 338–54.
  2013g. "How Do Modern Jewish Thinkers Interpret Religious Texts?," in Sokol 2013a, 481–508.
Soloveichik, Meir 2007. "Of (Religious) Fences and Neighbors," *Commentary* 123(3): 38–43.
Soloveitchik, Joseph B. 1964. "Confrontation," *Tradition* 6(2): 5–29.
  1965. "The Lonely Man of Faith," *Tradition* 7(2): 5–67.
  1975. *Shiurim le-Zekher Avi Mori* [Lectures in Memory of My Father and Teacher] (Akiva Yosef).
  1978a. "Majesty and Humility," *Tradition* 17(2): 25–37.
  1978b. "Redemption, Prayer and Talmud Torah." *Tradition* 17(2): 55–72.
  1979. "Surrendering Our Minds to God," in *Reflections of the Rav*, adapted by Abraham R. Besdin, 99–106.
  1983. *Halakhic Man*, trans. Lawrence Kaplan (Jewish Publication Society).
  1986. *The Halakhic Mind* (Seth Press).
  2000a. *Fate and Destiny*, trans. Lawrence J. Kaplan (Ktav).
  2000b. *Family Redeemed*, ed. David Shatz and Joel B. Wolowelsky (Toras HoRav Foundation and Ktav).
  2002. *Out of the Whirlwind: Essays on Mourning, Suffering and the Human Condition*, ed. David Shatz, Joel B. Wolowelsky, and Reuven Ziegler (Toras HoRav Foundation and Ktav).
  2005. *The Emergence of Ethical Man*, ed. Michael S. Berger (Ktav).
  2008. *And from There You Shall Seek (U-Vikkashtem mi-Sham)*, trans. Naomi Goldblum (Ktav).
  2017. *Halakhic Morality* (Maggid).
Speaks, Jeffrey 2018. *The Greatest Possible Being* (Oxford University Press).

Spiegel, Shalom 1979. *The Last Trial*, trans. Judah Goldin (Jewish Lights).
Statman, Daniel 2005. "Negative Theology and the Meaning of the Commandments." *Tradition* 39(1): 55–68.
Steiner, Mark 2000. "Rabbi Israel Salanter as a Jewish Philosopher," *The Torah U-Madda Journal* 9: 42–57.
  2017. "Philosophy and Subphilosophy in Maimonides: Two 'Perplexities,'" *Iyyun: The Jerusalem Philosophical Quarterly* 66: 27–57.
Steiner, Richard 2015. *Disembodied Souls: The Nefesh in Israel and Kindred Spirits in the Ancient Near East, with an Appendix on the Katumuwa Inscription* (SBL Press).
Steinmetz, Devora 1994. "The Vineyard, Farm, and Garden: The Drunkenness of Noah in the Context of the Primeval History," *Journal of Biblical Literature* 113: 193–207.
Sterba, James 2019. *Is a Good God Logically Possible?* (Palgrave Macmillan).
Stern, Josef 1987. "Language," in *Contemporary Jewish Religious Thought*, ed. Arthur Cohen (Charles Scribners' Sons), 543–51.
  1997. "Maimonides' Conceptions of Freedom and the Sense of Shame," in Manekin and Kellner 1997, 217–66.
  1998. *Problems and Parables of Law: Maimonides and Nahmanides on Reasons for the Commandments* (SUNY Press).
  2004. "Maimonides on Amalek, Self-Corrective Mechanisms, and the War against Idolatry," in *Judaism and Modernity: The Religious Philosophy of David Hartman*, ed. Jonathan W. Malino (Routledge), 371–410.
  2013. *The Matter and Form of Maimonides' Guide* (Harvard University Press).
  2017. "What a Jewish Philosophy Might Be (If It Exists): A View from the Middle Ages," *Iyyun: The Jerusalem Philosophical Quarterly* 66: 227–57.
  2019. "Maimonides and His Predecessors on Dying for God as 'Sanctification of the Name of God,'" in Lebens, Rabinowitz, and Segal 2019a, 149–80.
  2024 "A Guide to the AfterDeath: Maimonides on Olam ha-ba'," *Religious Studies* 60 special issue S1 (May 2024): S74–S90.
Stern, Marc (ed.) 2005. *Formulating Responses in an Egalitarian Age* (Rowman & Littlefield).
Stocker, Michael 1976. "The Schizophrenia of Modern Ethical Theories," *Journal of Philosophy* 83: 443–66.
Strawson, P. F. 1962. "Freedom and Resentment," *Proceedings of the British Academy* 48: 1–25.
Stump, Eleonore 1997. "Saadia Gaon on the Problem of Evil," *Faith and Philosophy* 14: 523–49.
  1999. "Orthodoxy and Heresy," *Faith and Philosophy* 16(2): 147–63.
  2009. "The Problem of Evil: Analytic Philosophy and Narrative," in Rea and Crisp 2011, 251–64.
  2010a. *Wandering in Darkness: Narrative and the Problem of Suffering* (Oxford University Press).
  2010b. "The Problem of Evil and the History of Peoples: Think Amalek," in *Divine Evil?: The Moral Character of the God of Abraham*, ed. Michael Bergmann, Michael J. Murray, and Michael C. Rea (Oxford University Press), 179–97.

2016. *The God of the Bible and the God of the Philosophers* (Marquette University Press).

2019. "The Personal God of Classical Theism," in Hazony and Johnson 2019, 65–81.

Sullivan, Meghan 2012. "Semantics for Blasphemy," in *Oxford Studies in the Philosophy of Religion*, ed. John L. Kvanvig, 4: 159–172.

Swinburne, Richard 1997. *The Evolution of the Soul* (Oxford University Press).

Sztuden, Alex 2012. "Naturalism and the Rav: A Reply to Yoram Hazony," *Meorot* 10(2012). https://library.yctorah.org/files/2016/07/3-sztuden-naturalism-and-the-rav.pdf

2016. "Naturalism within the Limits of Theism," *Daat* 81: vii–xliv.

2018a. "The Reach of Reason: Judaism, Halakhah, and Analytic Philosophy," in Tirosh-Samuelson and Hughes, 209–30.

2018b. "Judaism and the *Euthyphro* Dilemma: A New Approach," *Theologica* 2(1): 37–50.

2019. "Omnipotence Is No Perfection: Rabbinic Conceptions of God's Power, Knowledge, and Pursuit of Justice," in Hazony and Johnson 2019, 142–65.

Talmage, Frank (ed.) 1975. *Disputation and Dialogue: Readings in the Jewish-Christian Encounter* (Ktav Publishing House).

Tennant, F. R. 1962. *Philosophical Theology* (Cambridge University Press).

Thiessen, Elmer 2011. *The Ethics of Evangelism: A Philosophical Defense of Proselytizing and Persuasion* (InterVarsity Press).

Thomas, Owen C. (ed.) 1983. *God's Activity in the World: The Contemporary Problem* (Scholars Press).

Tillich, Paul 1960. *The Protestant Era*, trans. J. L. Adams (University of Chicago Press).

Tirosh-Samuelson, Hava and Hughes, Aaron W. (eds.) 2014. *Jewish Philosophy for the 21st Century: Personal Reflections* (Brill).

(eds.) 2016. *David Shatz: Torah, Philosophy and Culture* (Brill).

(eds.) 2018. *The Future of Jewish Philosophy* (Brill).

Trakakis, Nick 2008. *The End of Philosophy of Religion* (Continuum Books).

Turner, Jason 2009. "The Incompatibility of Free Will and Naturalism," *Australasian Journal of Philosophy* 87: 565–87.

Unger, Abraham 2010. "A Modern Orthodox Approach to Interfaith Dialogue," *Conversations* 8: 136–42.

Urbach, Ephraim 1987. *The Sages: Their Concepts and Beliefs*, trans. Israel Abrahams (Magnes Press).

Vaddiraju, Anil Kumar 2024. *Reason, Religion, and Modernity: Gadamer-Habermas Debate* (Springer).

Valabregue, Sandra 2017. "The Limits of Jewish Theology in Medieval Kabbalah and Jewish Philosophy," in Fagenblat 2017a, 30–47.

Vallicella, William F. 2010. "Divine Simplicity," in *Stanford Encyclopedia of Philosophy*. https://stanford.library.sydney.edu.au/archives/win2014/entries/divine-simplicity/

Van Inwagen, Peter 1978. "Ability and Responsibility," *Philosophical Review* 87: 201–24.

1989. "When Is the Will Free?," *Philosophical Perspectives* 3: 399–422.

2006. *The Problem of Evil* (Clarendon Press).
Van Inwagen, Peter and Zimmerman, Dean (eds.) 2007. *Persons: Human and Divine* (Clarendon).
Wainwright, William 2009a. "Theology and Mystery," in Flint and Rea 2009, 78–102.
  2009b. "One and a Half (or Two) Cheers for Perfect Being Theology," *Philo* 12: 228–51.
Walls, Jerry and Dougherty, Trent (eds.) 2018. *Two Dozen (or So) Arguments for God: The Plantinga Project* (Oxford University Press).
Wasserman, Elchanan 1962. *Kovetz Ma'amarim* (A. S. Vaserman).
Watson, Gary 1977. "Skepticism about Weakness of Will," *The Philosophical Review* 86: 316–39.
Weinberg, Jehiel Jacob 1977. *Seridei Esh* (Hebrew) (Mossad HaRav Kook).
Weiss, Dov 2016. *Pious Irreverence: Confronting God in Rabbinic Judaism* (University of Pennsylvania Press).
Weiss, Raymond L. and Butterworth, Charles (eds.) 1975. *Maimonides' Ethical Writings* (Dover Publications).
Weiss, Shira 2017. *Joseph Albo on Free Choice: Exegetical Innovations in Medieval Jewish Philosophy* (Oxford University Press).
  2018. *Ethical Ambiguity in the Hebrew Bible: Philosophical Analysis of Scriptural Narrative* (Cambridge University Press).
Westerkamp, Dirk 2008. "The Philonic Distinction: German Enlightenment Historiography of Jewish Thought," *History and Theory* 47: 533–59.
Westphal, Merold 2001. *Overcoming Onto-Theology: Toward a Postmodern Christian Faith* (Fordham University Press).
Wettstein, Howard 2012. *The Significance of Religious Experience* (Oxford University Press).
  2019. "The Fabric of Faith," in Rabinowitz, Lebens, and Segal 2019, 183–97.
  2020. "The Faith of Abraham," in *Swimming against the Current: Reimagining Jewish Tradition in the Twenty-First Century—Essays in Honor of Chaim Seidler-Feller*, ed. Shaul Seidler-Feller and David N. Meyers (Academic Studies Press), 55–67.
Widerker, David 1995. "Libertarianism and Frankfurt's Attack on the Principle of Alternative Possibilities," *Philosophical Review* 104: 247–61.
Wiederblank, Nathaniel 2018. *Illuminating Jewish Thought: Explorations of Free Will, the Afterlife, and the Messianic Era* (Maggid).
Wierenga, Edward 2011. "Augustinian Perfect Being Theology and the God of Abraham, Isaac and Jacob," *International Journal for the Philosophy of Religion* 69: 138–51.
Williams, Bernard 1973a. "The Makropulos Case: The Tedium of Immortality," in *Problems of the Self: Philosophical Papers 1956–1972* (Cambridge University Press), 82–100.
  1973b. "A Critique of Utilitarianism," in J. J. C. Smart and Bernard Williams, *Utilitarianism: For and Against* (Cambridge University Press).
  1986. *How Free Does the Will Need to Be?* (University of Kansas).
  2006. *The Sense of the Past: Essays in the History of Philosophy*, ed. Myles Burnyeat (Princeton University Press).

Williams, Patricia 2006. "Preface," in B. Williams 2006, ix–xii.
Williamson, Timothy 2019. "Morally Loaded Cases in Philosophy," *Proceedings and Addresses of the American Philosophical Association* 93(November): 159–72.
Witte, John and Martin, Richard C. (eds.) 1999. *Sharing the Book: Religious Perspectives on the Rights and Wrongs of Proselytism* (Orbis Books).
Wittgenstein, Ludwig 2009. *Philosophical Investigations*, ed. P. M. S. Hacker and Joachim Schute (4th ed., Wiley-Blackwell).
Wolbe, Shlomo 1986. *Alei Shur* (Mussar Institute).
Wolf, Susan 1990. *Freedom within Reason* (Oxford University Press).
Wolfson, Elliot R., and Hughes, Aaron 2010. "Introduction," in Hughes and Wolfson 2010, 1–16.
Wolpe, David 1997. "*Hester Panim* in Modern Jewish Thought," *Modern Judaism* 17: 25–56.
Wolterstorff, Nicholas 1982. "God Everlasting," in *Contemporary Philosophy of Religion*, ed. Steven M. Cahn and David Shatz (Oxford University Press), 77–98.
Wood, Allen W. 1984. "Kant's Compatibilism," in *Self and Nature in Kant's Philosophy*, ed. Allen W. Wood (Cornell University Press), 73–101.
Wood, William 2021. *Analytic Theology and the Academic Study of Religion* (Oxford University Press).
Wurzburger, Walter S. 1962. "Pluralism and the Halakhah," *Tradition* 4(2): 221–40.
  1969. "Va-yechi," in *Yavneh Studies in Parashat Hashavua*, ed. Joel B. Wolowelsky (Yavneh), 40–42.
  1989. "Confronting the Challenge of the Values of Modernity," *The Torah U-Madda Journal* 1: 104–12.
  1994. *Ethics of Responsibility* (Jewish Publication Society).
Wyschogrod, Michael 1983. *The Body of Faith: Judaism As Corporeal Election* (Seabury Press).
  2004. "Sin and Atonement in Judaism," in Wyschogrod, *Abraham's Promise: Judaism and Jewish-Christian Relations*, ed. R. Kendall Soulen (Eerdmans), 53–74.
Yavetz, Yosef 1953. *Or Ha-Hayyim* (A. Weinfeld).
Zimmerman, Michael J. 1996. "Responsibility Regarding the Unthinkable," *Midwest Studies in Philosophy* 21: 204–23.
Zimmerman, Dean A. 2010. "The Compatibility of Materialism and Survival: The 'Falling Elevator' Model," *Faith and Philosophy* 16(2): 194–212.
Zuckier, Shlomo 2023. "Resurrecting Rabbi Soloveitchik's Approach to Tehiyyat Ha-Metim," *Tradition* 55(2): 193–225.

Index of Biblical and Rabbinic Sources

Bible
  Genesis 129, 213, 236
    1 74, 127, 156, 197, 210,
      211, 277
    1:2 277
    1:31 197
    2 157
    2:17–18 210
    3:5 210
    3:6 120, 210
    3:11 211
    3:22 211
    3:22–24 158, 174, 197, 210, 211
    4 205, 211
    4:10 211, 212
    6:2 212
    6:5 156
    6:7 55
    9:6 212, 213, 221
    10:12–20 213
    12:1 266
    15:13–15 129
    18:14 28
    18:21 55
    18:23 106
    18:25 86, 209
    18:33 91
    21:12 208
    22 23, 206
    22:12 208
    25:8 174
    25:17 174
    27:41 120
    29:26 122
    30:14–21 129
    30:31–43 129
    31:4–13 129
    32:50 174
    34:30–31 213
    35:29 174
    37:14 131
    37:15–17 131
    37:18–36 120
    37–50 22, 125, 130–148
    39:2–5 133
    39:23 133
    40 122
    40:14 140
    41:9–13 140
    42:21 132
    45:5 136
    46:2–4 133
    49:33 174
    50:19–20 137, 144
  Exodus
    1 120, 129, 135
    1:8 131
    1:13–14 135
    3:6 110
    3:14 30, 31
    3:16 110
    7:3 121
    9:12 121
    10:1 121
    10:20 121
    11:10 121
    12:9 121
    14 264

Bible (cont.)
   17:14–16 233
   19 213
   19:5 240
   20:12 96
   32:10 55
   33:19 86
   33:20 45
   34:6–7 38
Leviticus
   14 216
   16 216
   18:4 215
   19:1 230
   19:14 70
   26 78
Numbers
   12:8 45n56
   13–14 69
   14:13–20 91
   16:32–36 213
   20:24 174
   27:1–11 213
   27:13 174
Deuteronomy
   1:22–45 69
   2:30 57, 121
   4:35 152
   4:39 279
   5:16 96
   6:4 35
   6:4–9 38
   6:24 289
   7:6 240
   7:8 31
   8:6 37
   8:17–18 76
   10:12 37
   11:12 37, 64
   11:13–21 143
   12:26–28 143
   13:5 37
   14:2 240
   15:7–8 232
   18:10 242
   18:11 174
   20:9 37
   20:16–17 233
   22:6–7 96
   22:7 96
   24:16 233
   25:5–10 216
   25:6 189
   25:17–19 233
   25:19 55
   26:18 240
   29:28 28
   30:6 158
   30:19 121
   31:17–21 105
   31:18 106
   32:4 28, 101
   32:20 106
   32:22 174
   32:39 187
   32:50 174
Joshua
   10:12–13 126
   11:20 121
I Samuel
   2:6 174, 175
   15 233
   15:11 55
   28:13 174
II Samuel
   22:31 28
I Kings
   2:6 174
   17:17–24 175
   18:37 122
II Kings
   2:11 175
   4:18–37 175
Isaiah
   2:1–4 258
   6:3 30–31, 32
   11:9 258
   14:9–15 174
   25:8 185, 198
   26:19 175
   40:18 45
   40:21 278
   40:26 266
   41:8 240
   45:15 107
   47:6 136
   54:8 106
   55:8 51
   59:2 106
   62–63 90
   64:6 106
Jeremiah

5:22 266
9:22–23 230
12:1–3 90, 86, 91
15:18 91
17:7 71
23:24 28
23:29 293
31:35–36 266
32:17 28
32:27 28
51:39 175
Ezekiel
 13:18 176
 18 91
 22 91
 37:1–10 175
Amos
 2:6 136
Jonah
 4:2 86
Mikhah
 4:1–5 258
 6:8 230
Ḥabakuk 90
 2:4 265
Zephaniah
 3:9 258
Malakhi
 3:6 30, 31, 57
 3:23–24 175
Psalms
 6 91
 8:2 63n2
 10 91
 12 91
 13:2 90
 16:11 175
 18:1 214
 18:31 28
 19:2–3 63n2, 75
 19:18 28
 23 91
 27:10 103
 33:13–14 28
 37 90
 37:23 68n17
 43 91
 44 91, 107
 65:2 47
 66:5 134
 73 90

73:28 103
74 91
80 91
89 91
94:12 99
104 63
104:24 74
115:17 195
136:1 214
139:12 28
145:9 235
146:5–9 177
Proverbs
 3:12 99
 25:11 127
Job 90, 94, 97, 189
 1:21 93
 4:20 175
 9 91
 13 91
 19:25–26 175
 23 91
 28:24 28
 34:21 28
 37:12 28
 37:16 28
 42:2 28
 42 94
 End 51
Ecclesiastes
 1:9 296
 4:1 233
 8:11–14 86
 9:2–3 95
Esther 133, 134,
   140, 143
 1 123
 4:13–14 139
Ruth 249, 255
 1:16 255
Song of Songs 276
Lamentations
 3:40 99
Daniel
 12:2–3 175–6, 178

Mishnah
 Arakhin 5:6 159
 Avot
  1:3 220
  2:1 220

Mishnah (cont.)
  2:16 200
  2:19 280
  3:15 123
  4:19 111
  4:21 197
  4:22 197
  5:3 223
  5:17 294
  Berakhot 9:5 135
  Eduyot 1:5–6 294
  Ḥagigah 2:1 281
  Sanhedrin 10:1 40, 176, 244

Tosefta
  Ḥagigah 2:9 294
  Sanhedrin 13:2 244

Jerusalem Talmud
  Bava Metzi'a 2:5 235
  Ḥagigah 2:1 96
  Sanhedrin 4:2 293
  Shekalim 6:3 76
  Sotah 5:5 102

Babylonian Talmud
  Avodah Zarah
    3a 245
    6a–b 70
    18b 95
    54b 77
  Bava Batra
    10a 100
    47b–48a 121
  Bava Kamma
    38b 224
    83b–84a 231
  Bava Metzi'a
    30b 230
    58b 97, 106
    59a–b 293
    85a 99
  Berakhot
    5a–b 97, 98, 99
    7a 86, 111
    10a 145
    17a 183
    32b 54
    33b 68
  Eruvin 13b 293
  Gittin
    36a 231
    61b 234
  Ḥagigah
    3b 293
    5a 98
  Ḥullin
    7a 68
    142a 96
  Ketubbot 110b 64
  Kiddushin 39b 96, 98
  Makkot 7a 231
  Menaḥot 29b 108, 111
  Mo'ed Katan 28a 79, 96, 98, 153n13
  Niddah 61b 196
  Pesaḥim
    8b 225
    64b 76
  Sanhedrin
    34a 293
    56a 212, 217, 245
    64b 127
    73a 241
    90a–b 176
    105a 244
  Shabbat
    32b–33a 95
    33b 98
    53b 75
    55a 95
    55b 197
    88a 143
    119b 112
    156a–b 79, 96, 153, 154
  Shevu'ot 39b 98
  Sotah
    5b 98
    14a 38
    37a 264
  Sukkah 52a 223
  Ta'anit
    7b–8a 95
    25a 69
  Yevamot
    47a 249
    50a 79, 96
    71a 127
    105a 98
    121b 98
  Yoma

Index of Biblical and Rabbinic Sources 333

9b 106
67b 216
69b 92

Minor Tractates
Avot de-Rabbi Natan 2:2 97

Midrash
Mekhilta de-Rabbi Shimon bar Yoḥai,
   Be-Shalaḥ 3 38
Mekhilta de-Rabbi Yishmael 13
Sifrei
   Numbers 112 127
   Deuteronomy 49 38
Bereshit (Genesis) Rabbah
   1:9 277
   9:5 197, 198
   9:7 157
   39:1 266
   40:6 122
   79:6 68
   84:13 131
   84:14 131
   89:1 69
   89:2 140
Va-Yikra (Leviticus)
   Rabbah 32:8 233
   37:1 95
   41:6 185
Be-Midbar (Numbers)Rabbah
   8:2 256
   13:15–16 293
Ruth Rabbah 6:4 96
Kohelet (Ecclesiastes) Rabbah
   5:4 95
Sifra, Kedoshim 9:12 223
Tanḥuma
   Lekh Lekha 6 248
   Lekh Lekha 9 122
   Va-Yeshev 4 135
Midrash ha-Gadol
   Gen. 37:1 37,135
Midrash Tehillim
   12:3 293
   24:2 31
Pirkei de-Rabbi Eliezer 38:11 136
Tanna de-Bei Eliyahu Rabbah
   10 256
Midrash Temurah 1:5 266

Biblical Commentaries
Isaac Abravanel
   Deut. 4:25 244

Isaac Arama (Akedat Yitzḥak)
   28:1 (Va-Yeshev) 137–38,146
   88 (Va-Etḥanan) 244
Baḥya ben Asher
   Gen. 22 208
   Gen. 18:19 79
   Exod. 17:13 74
   Deut. 25:9 189
Abraham Ibn Ezra
   Daniel 12:2 178
Samson Raphael Hirsch
   Gen. 6:5 156
Moses Naḥmanides
   Gen. 2:9 158–59, 210
   Gen. 6:2 212, 230
   Gen. 6:19 66
   Gen. 12:6 122
   Gen. 15:14 135–36, 144–47
   Genesis 18:19 79
   Gen. 38:28 189
   Gen. 42:6 145
   Lev. 19:1 230
   Lev. 26:11 71, 74, 79
   Deut. 6:18 230
   Deut. 30:6 158
   Job 64, 189
Ovadyah Seforno
   Lev. 13:47 79

Medieval Philosophical Works
Sa'adyah Gaon, Book of Emunot
   and De'ot
   Intro. 2 273, 281
   Intro. 6 15, 271, 280, 281
   2:8 52
   3:3 218
   3:4 219
   4:4 119, 121
   5:1 97
   6:8 179
   7 177
   7:2 282
   7:3 173
   9:1 97
   9:2 97
   9:5–11 177
Baḥya ibn Pakuda, Duties of the Heart
   Intro. 279
   Part 1 (Sha'ar ha-Yiḥud) 2 266
   Part 2 (Sha'ar ha-Beḥinah) 214
   Part 3 (Sha'ar Avodat Elokim),
      introduction 214
   Part 4 (Sha'ar ha-Bittaḥon) 71

Medieval Philosophical Works (cont.)
Judah Halevi, *The Kuzari*
  1:25 271
  1:67 275
  2:36 243
  4:15 282
  4:23 243
Moses Maimonides
  Commentary to the Mishnah
    Introduction 294
    Berakhot 9:5 135
    Sanhedrin 10 38, 248 (introduction to Helek)
    Eight Chapters (Introduction to commentary on *Avot*) 156, 223–226
  Book of Commandments
    Positive commandment 1 288
    Positive commandment 8 38
  Mishneh Torah
    Character Traits 1 38
    Divorce 2:20 159, 167
    Fasts 1 97
    Foundations of the Torah
      1:2 282
      1:7 35
      4:8–9 177
    Foreign Worship
      1 258
      11:16 79
    Kings
      8:11 244, 247
      10:9 247
      10:12 235
      11:6–7 243
      12:1 178
      12:3 178
    Murder 5:11 159
    Rebels 3:3 40
    Repentance
      3 248, 294
      3:7 40 (with Rabad)
      5:5 154 (with Rabad)
      6:3 167
      6:5 138
      8 172
      8:1 177, 183
      8:2 83, 184 (with Rabad)
      8:8 172, 179
      10 282
      10:1 196
      10:3 276
    Sabbatical and Jubilee Years 13:13 247, 257
  Guide of the Perplexed
    Intro. Part 1 126, 127
    1:2 210
    1:26 47
    1:34 156
    1:35 39
    1:46 47
    1:50 41
    1:50–60 46
    1:54 37, 54, 282
    1:58 47
    1:59 53, 54
    2:25 277
    2:29 65
    2:48 66
    3:8 155, 156, 178
    3:9 45
    3:10 197
    3:10–11 98
    3:10–12 89
    3:15 178
    3:22–23 89, 102
    3:24 101
    3:25 198
    3:28 39
    3:31 289
    3:32 64, 74
    3:41 161
    3:51 74, 183, 282, 284
    3:54 183
  Letter on Astrology 79, 170
  Letter/Essay on Resurrection 173, 175, 178, 183–4
Moses Naḥmanides, *Sha 'ar ha-Gemul* 97, 109, 176, 179, 182
Levi Gersonides
  Wars of the Lord
    3–4 34
    3:3 47
  Commentary on Song of Songs 127, 276
Ḥasdai Crescas, *Light of The Lord*
  1:3:6 266
  2:5 152, 288
  2:6:1 179
  3A:1:3 179
  3A:2–4 182
  4:7 190
Joseph Albo, *The Book of Roots* (*Sefer ha-Ikkarim*)

Index of Biblical and Rabbinic Sources 335

4:7 87
4:13–14 100
4:29 179
4:30–31 178

Other Rabbinic Literature
Abravanel, Issac
  Naḥalat Avot, Avot 1:3 82, 220
  Rosh Amanah 12 40
Abulafia, Meir, Yad Ramah, Sanhedrin
  90b 182
Bornsztayn, Avraham, Avnei Nezer,
  Yoreh De'ah 2:306 215
Duran, Shimon ben Tzemaḥ
  Ohev Mishpat 9 40
  Responsa Tashbetz #53 165
Emden, Jacob, commentary to
  Maimonides, Shemonah
  Perakim, chap. 6 226
Isserles, Mosheh, Torat ha-Olah 3:71
  218
Leiner, Mordechai Yosef, Mei ha-Shiloah
  152
Lifshitz, Israel, Tiferet Yisrael,
  commentary to the Mishnah,
  Sanhedrin 10:1 and Avot 3:14
  248

Loew, Judah ben Betzalel (Maharal)
  Tiferet Yisrael 6 235
Luzzatto, Moshe Hayyim (RamHal)
  Derekh Hashem 191
  Mesillat Yesharim (The Path of the
  Just) 197
Menaḥem ha-Meiri, Beit ha- Beḥirah,
  Gittin 62a 246
Nahman of Bratzlav
  Likkutei MahaRaN
  1:64 285
  2:19 284
  The Clever Man and the Ordinary
  Man (story) 284
Sefer ha-Bahir 189
Sefer ha-Ḥinnukh, commandment #16
  288
Shnayer Zalman of Lyadi, Tanya 152
Tzadok ha-Kohen, Tzidkat ha-Tzaddik
  42k
Tzvi Elimelekh of Dinov
  Benei Yissaskhar Adar 3 discourse 2
  283
  Mayan Gannim to Or ha-Ḥayyim
  4:20 243
Vital, Ḥayyim, Sha'ar ha-Gilgulim 189
Yavetz, Yosef, Or ha-Ḥayyim, chap. 2 282

Note: Once one enters the 20th century, the proliferation of books and journals renders the number of relevant citations unwieldy. For 20th and 21st century figures see the general index.

General Index

Purely bibliographic references in footnotes are not included.

Aaron (High Priest), 174
Abner of Burgos, 152
Abraham, 79, 86, 90, 106, 129, 130, 131, 138, 153, 206–9, 209, 212, 247, 251, 258, 266. *See also* akedah
Abraham ben David (Rabad), 154, 166, 170, 184
Abravanel, Isaac, 40, 82, 126, 220
Academy for Jewish Philosophy, 6
Adam and Eve, sin of, 23, 120, 158, 174, 197, 199, 209–11, 251
Adams, Robert Merrihew, 2, 8, 221, 274
afflictions of love, 98, 99–105, 112
afterlife, 20, 22, 65, 78, 171–200, 225, 277, 297, 298. *See also* immortality; reincarnation
Aggadah, 2
akedah, 206–9
akrasia, 168
R. Akiva, 79, 100, 102, 103, 108, 123, 154, 231, 232, 266
Albo, Joseph, 9, 40, 100, 126, 179, 296
Al-Farabi, 66
Alghazali, 68
Allen, Diogenes, 104
al-Muquammis, Dawid, 289
Alston, William, 8, 42, 46, 129
Alter, Robert, xiv, 22, 128, 129, 133, 147, 189
Altmann, Alexander, 4
Amalekites, 55, 87, 215, 233
Amidah, 176

anachronism, 5
androcentrism, 33
Anscombe, Elizabeth, 221
Anselm of Canterbury, 27, 28, 46, 58, 281
anthropocentrism, 88, 102
anthropomorphism, 35, 40, 46, 82
anthropopathism, 38, 46, 295
antifoundationalism, 16
antimaterialism, 181
antirealism, *See* realism and anti-realism
antitheodicy, 108–12, 113
Apocrypha, 176
apophaticism, 44–55, 297, 298. *See also* negative theology
Aquinas, Thomas, 46, 58, 166, 181, 228, 275
Arama, Isaac, 137, 146, 153
Aristotle, 3, 30, 119, 164, 182, 198, 272, 295
Association for the Philosophy of Judaism, 1
astrology, 79, 153–57, 170, 296. *See also mazzal*
atheism, 14, 44, 50, 51, 60, 64, 88, 124, 239, 253, 269, 274, 289
attributes, divine. *See also* Perfect Being Theology
of action vs. essence, 46, 49, 54
authority, 15, 17, 18, 19, 39, 61, 219, 229, 232, 294, 295
avodah zarah, 41, 42, 43, 62, 69, 165, 216, 217, 241, 245, 246, 247, 248, 255. *See also* idolatry

Ba'al Shem Tov, 107
ba'alei mahashavah, 12
Bahya ben Asher, 74
Bahya ibn Pakuda, 71, 266, 278, 279
belief. *See also* heresy
  error in, 37–43
  and reason, 261–90
Bennett, Jonathan, 4
Berger, David, 178, 232, 255, 257
Bergson, Henri, 7
Berkeley, George, 68
Berkovits, Eliezer, 31, 105, 106, 107, 203, 287
Berman Shifman, Nadav, 287
Bible, xiv, 1, 7, 10, 13, 15, 17, 22, 23, 30, 31, 32, 34, 35, 43, 44, 45, 55, 56, 57, 58, 63, 65, 66, 67, 71, 78, 85, 91, 107, 113, 117, 119, 120, 121, 122, 123, 124, 125, 126, 127, 128, 134, 143, 144, 147, 149, 174–76, 181, 183, 192, 200, 205, 206, 207, 209, 212, 214, 215, 221, 231, 232, 241, 252, 266, 269, 271, 272, 281, 289, 295, 296, 298. *See also* Index of Biblical and Rabbinic Sources for specific sources
  on afterlife, 174–76, 189, 190
  attributes of action in, 46
  on chosenness, 240
  continuity and discontinuity with medieval philosophy, 11, 55–59, 62, 126, 127, 128, 295
  and divine command morality, 203–14
  on divine glory, 74
  on divine perfection, 21, 28, 29, 43, 53, 55–59, 61, 62
  dual causality in, 125, 128, 129, 130, 131
  on eschatology, 258
  exegesis, 12
  figurative interpretation of, 126, 127, 128, 272, 276, 281
  and free will, 117–19, 120–23, 125–40, 159
  as God's anthropology, 117
  on *Hester Panim*, 105, 107
  on *imitatio Dei*, 37
  on imposition of death, 197
  on life of faith, 265
  literary approach to, 122, 125, 128, 129, 147

  medieval philosophical interpretations of, 120–23, 272, 276, 278, 279
  miracles in, 63
  nature in, 63
  and negative theology, 46, 51
  on ontology of human beings, 175, 176
  protest in, 84, 90
  and reincarnation, 189
  retributivist theodicy in, 86, 94, 95
  as source of philosophy, 13, 125–48, 266
  as support for rationalism, 276
  teleology in, 74
binding of Isaac. *See akedah*
bittahon, 69–71
bittul ha-yesh, 152
Blau, Yitzchak, 226
Blidstein, Gerald, 199
Boethius, 34
Borowitz, Eugene, 8
Brafman, Yonatan, 10
Brandom, Robert, 16
Broyde, Michael, 249
Buber, Martin, 9, 45, 53, 105, 107
Buddhism, 242
Bultmann, Rudolph, 15
Burling, Hugh, 42
Byrne, Peter, 33

Cain, 205, 211–13
cause and effect. *See* determinism; occasionalism
charity, 4, 5, 71, 195, 224, 225, 235
chosenness, 20, 240, 257
Christianity, 1, 234, 238, 240, 241, 242, 243, 245, 247, 248, 249, 250, 255. *See also* philosophy, Christian
Citron, Gabriel, 17
Cohen, Hermann, 9, 173, 192, 193, 240
commandments, 20, 23, 39, 74, 78, 82, 92, 96, 105, 121, 143, 194, 195, 196, 216, 220, 221, 225, 226, 227, 243, 245, 248, 257, 287, 289
  reasons for, 48, 80
compatibilism, 120, 129, 152, 160–69
conservatism (epistemic), 65, 270, 271, 272, 273, 274
Conservative Judaism, 8, 12, 179, 231
Copernican revolution, 169
creation, 52, 65, 74, 75, 77, 112, 187, 296
creation *ex nihilo*, 277, 278
Crescas, Hasdai, 9, 152, 179, 184, 288
Crick, Francis, 149

Daniel, 92
Darwin, Charles, 67, 169, 171
Darwinism. *See* Darwin, Charles
Dawkins, Richard, 253
death, reasons for, 197–200
deism, 65
deontologism, 234, 263
Dessler, Eliyahu, 69, 70, 157–60, 165, 170
determinism, 118, 119, 120, 124, 149–71. *See also* free will
Dewey, John, 60
Dinah, 213
divine command morality, 1, 55, 89, 90, 203–37. *See also* ethics
divine intervention, 39, 63, 67, 73, 78, 81, 82, 131, 148, 155, 173
divine providence, 63–83, 117, 124, 128, 152. *See also* divine intervention
general vs. individual, 65
dogma, 39, 40
Dostoevsky, 164, 204
double agency. *See* dual causality
dual causality, 128–48
dualism, 175, 263
Duran, Shimon ben Tzemah, 40
Durkheim, Emile, 60
Dworkin, Ronald, 229, 230, 232

egocentrism, 80
Egyptians, 122, 134, 135, 136, 137, 138, 139, 140, 141, 142, 144, 145, 264
Ein Sof, 48, 152, 285
Ekstrom, Laura, 103
Elijah, 2, 122, 174, 184
Elisha, 174
Elman, Yaakov, 98
Emden, Jacob, 245
empiricism, 263
emunah temimah, 265, 267, 281, 284
Enlightenment, 179, 246
Epictetus, 102, 137
Epicurus, 198
epistemic permissivism, 286
epistemology, 8, 14, 23, 37, 173, 263, 266, 276, 277, 280, 290
Esau, 120, 122
eschatology, 23, 239, 257. *See also* Messiah; messianic activism; resurrection
Esther, 123, 139, 140, 143
ethics, 30, 38

independent of God's command, 90–92
independent standard, 91
evil, 84–113
evil, problem of, 20, 29, 32, 33, 36, 56, 61, 65, 70, 72, 75, 78, 79, 190, 215. *See also* theodicy
psychological dimensions of, 88, 89
evil, protest against, 90–93
evolution, 74, 127
exclusivism, 238, 241, 244
exegesis, 17

Fackenheim, Emil, 4, 8, 9, 105, 107
faith vs. reason, 20, 261–90
fideism, 23, 261–90
Fischer, John Martin, 167
Fisher, Cass, 11, 13, 58, 60, 61
Flint, Thomas, 57
foreknowledge, 22, 32, 33, 34, 56, 57, 117, 118, 119, 120, 121–23, 124, 130, 144, 152, 162, 297, 298. *See also* God, omniscience of
Forking Paths principle. *See* Principle of Alternative Possibilities
Fox, Marvin, 8, 108, 206
Frankfurt, Harry, 7, 142, 143, 144, 162
Franks, Paul, 18
free choice. *See* free will
free will, 20, 22, 33, 34, 56, 65, 69, 70, 72, 89, 113, 117, 119, 120, 124, 125–48, 149–71, 297, 298. *See also* compatibilism; determinism; foreknowledge; materialism; restrictivism
and astrology, 153–55
Biblical silence about, 120–23
and divine action in history, 125–48
devaluation of, 157–60
in Hasidism, 152–53
historical perspective on, 169–70
Freud, Sigmund, 167, 169
future contingents, 34

Gadamer, Hans, 18
Galileo, 127
Gan Eden (Garden of Eden), 177, 180, 206, 209–11.
Geach, Peter, 33
Gehinnom, 100, 177, 180
Gellman, Jerome, 1, 33, 42, 56, 190
Gersonides, Levi, 9, 33, 47, 52, 62, 126, 153, 154, 156, 166, 276

Gettier, Edmund, 280
gilgul. *See* reincarnation
Gillman, Neil, 193
Ginzberg, Louis, 2
God. *See also* attributes, divine; Imperfect Being Theology; foreknowledge; divine intervention; divine providence; Perfect Being Theology
  action of, 20, 47
  as almighty, 33
  anger of, 31, 39
  attributes of, 29–62
  compassion of, 31, 38
  creator, 35
  emotions of, 46. *See also* God, impassibility of
  emulating. *See imitatio Dei*
  existence of, 48
  fallibility of, 43
  glory of, 32, 74, 75
  goodness of, 28, 84, 85, 88
  humility of, 36
  immanence of, 32, 59, 63, 64, 67, 152
  immutability of, 30, 31, 34, 55, 57, 128
  impassibility of, 30, 31, 38, 43, 55, 59, 128
  incomprehensibility of, 48
  incorporeality of, 15, 30, 43, 47, 48
  indescribability of, 43, 45, 46
  ineffability of, 45, 48
  infinitude of, 48
  knowledge of, 28, 47
  love of, 31
  multiple attributes of, 35
  mystery of, 50
  necessary existence of, 30
  omnibenevolence of, 30, 32, 36
  omnipotence of, 30, 32, 33, 36, 37, 55, 56, 57, 58, 84, 85, 88
  omnipresence of, 30, 31, 32, 63
  omniscience of, 30, 32, 33, 34, 36, 55, 56, 57, 58, 62, 84, 85, 88, 128, 144
  perfection of. *See* Perfect Being Theology
  power of, 28, 47, 75
  proper name, 42
  purposes and intentions of, 49
  simplicity of. *See* God, unity of
  timelessness of, 34, 37
  transcendence of, 32, 43, 44, 45, 53, 58, 59, 64, 67, 242
  trust in. *See bittaḥon*
  unity of, 35, 37, 40, 47, 48, 52
  unknowability of, 45
  will of, 68, 75
  wisdom of, 74, 75
God of the gaps, 67
Golding, Joshua, 1, 270, 271, 286, 287, 289
Goldman, Eliezer, 66
Goldschmidt, Tyron, 190, 191, 196
Goltzberg, Stefan, 7
Gottlieb, Michah, 256
Great Chain of Being, 198
Green, Arthur, 8, 61
Greenberg, Irving, 243

Haggadah, 63
Halakhah, xiii, 2, 10, 11, 13, 32, 48, 74, 76, 112, 167, 195, 203, 204, 212, 220, 231, 237, 287
halakhot. *See* Halakhah
Halevi, Judah, 9, 243, 251, 258, 271, 275, 282
ḥalitzah, 189
Haman, 123, 139
ha-Meiri, Menaḥem, 246
Ḥanina ben Dosa, 68
Harman, Gilbert, 273
Harris, Michael, 94, 103, 104, 158, 205, 206, 217
Hart, H. L. A., 229
Hartman, David, 6, 77
Hartshorne, Charles, 31, 32
Harvey, Warren Zev, 4, 11
Ḥasidism, 12, 32, 107, 152, 170, 206, 265, 283–85
Haskalah. *See* Enlightenment
Haugeland, John, 16
Haught, John, 170
Ḥazon Ish (Abraham Yeshayahu Karelitz), 218
Hazony, Yoram, 13, 55, 56, 57
Hebrew Union College, 8
Hegel, George, 7
Heidegger, Martin, 18, 48, 54
heresy, 12, 38, 39, 40, 41, 43, 50, 62, 110
  inadvertent, 40
Hershkowitz, Isaac, 274
Heschel, Abraham Joshua, 4, 8, 9, 31, 45, 107, 117, 240
ḥesed, 71, 297
Hester Panim, 105–7, 113
heteronomy, 221, 227, 235, 236, 237. *See also* obedience, value of
Hezekiah, 145

Hick, John, 43, 100, 108, 241, 242, 243, 256, 298
Hirsch, Eli, 1, 4
Hirsch, Samson Raphael, 77, 156
historicism, 8, 12, 298
history of philosophy, *See* philosophy, history of
Hitler, Adolf, 194
Hobbes, Thomas, 121, 169, 175
Holocaust, 10, 48, 85, 89, 91, 105, 106, 107, 108, 191, 215
homiletics, 10, 13, 232
Howard-Snyder, Daniel, 269
Hughes, Aaron, 18
ḥukkim, 216, 224
Hume, David, 68, 72, 120, 162, 167, 169, 266
humility, 50, 52, 158, 169, 170, 294
Humphreys, W. Lee, 140
Hutner, Isaac, 159
hypnosis, 169

Ibn al-Fayumi, Nethanel, 241, 256
Ibn Daud, Abraham, 9, 126
Ibn Gabirol, Solomon, 9, 126
idolatry, 21, 41, 42, 77, 165, 216, 242
  conceptual, 41, 52
imitatio Dei, 37, 38, 50, 62, 221, 234, 235
immortality, 22, 171–200
Imperfect Being Theology, 36, 55–62
inclusivism, 238
incompatibilism. *See* compatibilism
interfaith dialogue, 238, 240
interpretive charity, 4, 18, 126
Isaac. *See akedah*
Ishmael, 174
Islam, 240, 241, 243, 255. *See also* philosophy, Islamic

Jacob, 120, 122, 130
Jacobs, Louis, 193, 206
James, William, 264, 273, 286
Jeremiah, 92
Jewish law. *See* Halakhah
Jewish philosophy, 20
  analytic, 32
  definition of, 9–16
  history of, 6, 12, 19
  medieval, 7, 11
Jewish Theological Seminary, 8
Job, 28, 51, 64, 90, 91, 93, 94, 97, 175, 189
Jonah, 86

Joseph, 120, 122
Joseph and his brothers, 125–48

Kabbalah, 10, 12, 13, 32, 45, 48, 51, 88, 107, 126, 173, 179, 189, 285, 295
Kant, Immanuel, 7, 48, 52, 53, 54, 81, 90, 166, 169, 220, 221, 222, 223, 225, 227, 228, 241, 253, 266, 286
Kaplan, Mordecai, 60, 192
Karaism, 40
Karelitz, Avraham Yeshayahu. *See* Ḥazon Ish (Abraham Yeshayahu Karelitz)
karet, 183
Katzoff, Charlotte, 1, 121, 129, 131, 137, 140, 142, 144
Kaufmann, Yehezkel, 128
Kellner, Menachem, 11, 41
Kelly, Thomas, 268
Kepnes, Steven, 18, 61
Kierkegaard, Søren, 4, 23, 206, 207, 208, 209, 244, 268, 282
Kimḥi, David, 126
Koller, Aaron, 208
Kook, Abraham Isaac, 42, 43, 50, 169, 170, 209, 241, 242, 243, 256
Korn, Eugene, 231, 246
Kripke, Saul, 7, 18, 42
Krochmal, Nachman, 9
Kuhn, Thomas, 150, 273
Kushner, Harold, 36

Laban, 122
Lamm, Norman, 3, 107, 170, 192, 283, 284
Land of Israel, 64
Langermann, Y. Zvi, 135
Lavater, Johann Caspar, 247, 257
Lebens, Samuel, 1, 7, 13, 19, 31, 32, 40, 45, 46, 50, 52, 66, 81, 93, 152, 194, 203, 213, 251, 255, 272, 280, 284, 286, 287, 295
legacy conception of afterlife, 192–94, 200
Leibowitz, Isaiah, 32, 48, 64, 73, 77, 80, 206, 207, 226
Leibowitz, Nehama, 128
Leiner, Mordecai Joseph, 152
Leiter, Brian, 16
Lerner, Berel Dov, 88
Levenson, Jon, 57, 175, 192, 209
Levinas, Emmanuel, 9
Lewinsohn, Jed, 226, 227
Lewis, C. S., 76

Libertarianism, 151, 160, 164, 165
Libet, Benjamin, 151, 155
Lichtenstein, Aharon, 206
Lifshitz, Israel, 248
Linzer, Dov, 245
liturgy, 10, 11
lo lishmah, 80
Locke, John, 162, 182
Lucretius, 198
Luria, Isaac, 189
Luther, Martin, 163
Luzzatto, Moshe Ḥayyim, 159, 191, 197

MacIntyre, Alasdair, 221
Mackie, J. L., 87
magic, 67
Maimon, Solomon, 9
Maimonideans, 45, 173
Maimonides, Moses, 7, 12, 18, 19, 32, 35, 39, 41, 43, 45, 46, 47, 51, 52, 53, 54, 58, 64, 66, 73, 74, 77, 79, 97, 101, 102, 126, 127, 135, 138, 157, 165, 166, 167, 170, 173, 175, 178, 179, 197, 223, 234, 235, 243, 244, 247, 248, 257, 258, 265, 272, 276, 277, 283, 284, 288, 295
  on Abraham, 247
  on afflictions of love, 101
  on astrology, 153
  axiological shift in, 102
  as biblical commentator, 126
  on Christianity and Islam, 243, 258
  on compatibilism, 166–67
  on creation vs. eternity, 277
  on divine attributes, 39, 46, 47, 48, 49
  on divine emotion, 38, 39, 46, 47
  on divine unity, 35, 47
  on eschatology, 258
  on evil as privation, 98
  on gentiles and the World to Come, 247
  Gersonides' critique of, 47, 48
  on God causing sin, 135
  ideological uses of, 18
  on *imitatio Dei*, 37, 38
  on matter as cause of disobedience, 155, 156
  on motivation for observance of commandments, 196
  on motivation for observing commandments, 223–28, 289
  naturalistic understandings of miracles, prophecy, and providence, 65, 183
  on necessity of material things perishing, 199
  on negative theology, 39, 46, 47, 48, 53, 54, 295
  on *olam ha-ba*, immortality, and resurrection, 172, 173, 177, 178, 179, 181, 183, 184, 200
  as part of canon of Jewish philosophers, 9, 18, 295
  on Principle of Plenitude, 199
  on psychological elements in the problem of evil, 89
  on spiritual attainment, 247, 256
  on studying science and metaphysics, 281, 282
  teleological view of nature, 64, 74
  on theological error, 39, 40, 41, 42
  on thirteen principles of faith, 38, 40, 178, 294, 295
  on virtue, 223–28
  on voluntarism, 288
Malebranche, Nicholas, 68, 69, 70
mamzer, 233
Manekin, Charles, 51, 53, 65, 123, 138, 153, 154, 156, 166
Marques, Nichole, 93
Marty, Martin, 251, 254
martyrdom, 103, 199, 241, 254, 282
materialism, 149, 150, 151, 157, 160, 170, 172, 263. *See also* determinism
Mavrodes, George, 263
mazzal, 78, 95, 96, 153, 154
McCracken, Charles, 69
McDowell, John, 16
Men of the Great Assembly, 54, 92
Mendelssohn, Moses, 9, 40, 179, 246, 247, 250, 254, 255, 256, 257, 266
mental states, 63
Messiah, 176, 178, 241, 243, 277
messianic activism, 65
metaphysics, 8, 13, 14, 32, 37, 52, 53, 65, 68, 73, 78, 79, 80, 81, 82, 158, 172, 188, 282, 295. *See also* theology
  rejection of, 16, 48
middat hasidut, 235
Midrash, xiii, xiv, 10, 13, 17, 21, 22, 31, 37, 38, 41, 43, 55, 58, 63, 65, 69, 91, 108, 123, 135, 147, 173, 176, 209, 215, 216, 233, 256, 257, 264, 276, 293, 295, 298. *See also Index of Biblical and Rabbinic Sources* for specific sources

Mill, John Stuart, 33, 36, 72, 120, 214, 294
miracles, 57, 63–83, 127, 178, 183, 185, 186, 187, 189, 271, 297
mishpatim, 216, 218, 224, 227, 235
Mittleman, Alan, 59, 149
Molina, Luis de, 138
Molinism, 138, 139, 146
monism, 32
monotheism, 239, 251, 258
morality, 20, 77. See also deontologism; divine command morality; ethics; utilitarianism; virtue ethics
Morgenbesser, Sidney, 7
Moses, 46, 87, 91, 92, 108, 110, 174, 184, 213, 247
mourning, laws of, 172, 198
Mussar movement, 13, 234

Nagel, Thomas, 14, 151
Naḥman of Bratslav, 265, 284, 285
Naḥmanides, 64, 66, 71, 79, 109, 126, 135, 136, 144, 145, 146, 147, 158, 159, 170, 179, 182, 184, 189, 212, 230, 285, 294
natural law, 63–83, 228, 229, 263
naturalism, 21, 64, 65, 66, 67, 68, 72, 73, 75, 77, 78, 79, 80, 81, 82, 83, 183
   hard vs. soft, 72, 73, 75, 78, 81, 82
nature, 21, 27, 28, 39, 41, 46, 53, 60, 63, 64, 65, 66, 67, 68, 69, 70, 71, 72, 73, 74, 75, 76, 77, 78, 79, 81, 85, 104, 129, 151, 157, 158, 170, 178
negative theology, 21, 39, 44, 46, 47, 48, 49, 50, 51, 53, 44–54, 62, 295. See also apophaticism
Neoplatonism, 44, 126
Nietzsche, 4, 251
Nineveh, 86
Noah, 66, 212, 213
Noahide laws, 217, 245, 247, 248, 250
Nostra Aetate, 238
Novak, David, 10, 214
Novick, Tzvi, 8, 123
Nozick, Robert, 119, 159, 169

obedience, value of, 219–28
occasionalism, 67–72, 75
olam ha-ba, 172, 176, 179, 247
ontological argument, 27, 28, 56, 281
open theism, 33, 56

Orthodox Judaism, 8, 12, 41, 80, 128, 173, 180, 231, 234, 265, 266, 272
orthopraxy, 264

pagan belief, 69
panentheism, 32, 63
panpsychism, 151
pantheism, 31, 32, 63
paradise. See *Gan Eden*
Pascal, Blaise, 264, 286
Pascal's wager, 285–90
Perfect Being Theology, 21, 27–62, 82, 84, 87, 92, 93, 112, 113, 121, 295, 296, 297
perspectivism, 253, 254
Pharaoh, 120, 121, 122, 130, 131, 132, 135, 142, 159, 167
Pharisees, 176
Philo, 9, 125
philosophy. See also faith vs. reason
   analytic, 14–16, 36
   ancient, 30
   Anglophone, 7
   Christian, 8, 9, 16, 69, 91, 103, 194, 266, 286
   Continental, 2, 4, 9, 13, 15, 16, 52, 108, 277
   disputes in, 37
   experimental, 14
   Greek, 30
   history of, 3–8. See also historicism
   Islamic, 7, 16, 66, 68, 266
   of language, 8
   medieval, 30, 31, 35, 39, 44, 55, 58, 64, 66, 73, 179, 263, 276
   pre-Socratic, 6, 13, 149
   studying vs. doing, 3–6
   vs. theology, 13–15
physicalism. See materialism
Plantinga, Alvin, 8, 151, 275, 277
Plato, 27, 30, 97, 166, 179, 181, 183, 198, 203
Plotinus, 44
pluralism, 9, 40, 238, 240, 241, 242, 243, 244, 253, 254, 255, 256, 293
Pojman, Louis, 207
positivism, 228, 229, 230, 231, 263
postmodernism, 253, 254
prayer, 34, 39, 54, 60, 70, 71, 73, 92, 172, 176, 218, 295, 298
Principle of Alternative Possibilities, 142, 144, 162–69

Process Theology, 31, 33, 56
progressive revelation, 233
property-dualism, 150
prophecy, 31, 57, 65, 66, 73, 144, 145, 219
proselytizing, 249–58
punishment. *See* reward and punishment (divinely-administered)
punishment (humanly-administered), 161, 164, 212, 218, 229, 231, 232, 249
Purgatory. *See Gehinnom*
Putnam, Hilary, 1, 7, 16
Pythagoras, 189

quantum physics, 67, 109, 118, 160
Quine, Willard van Orman, 250, 273

Rabbi Isaac Elchanan Theological Seminary, 8
rabbinic authorities, 12
Rabinovitch, Nachum, 110
randomness, 67, 75, 78
rationalism, 12, 15, 23, 66, 71, 73, 126, 127, 261–90
Rawls, John, 273
realism and anti-realism. 16, 44, 59–62
Reconstructionism, 60
Reconstructionist Rabbinical College, 8
redemption, 65
Reform Judaism, 8, 12, 106, 173, 179, 183, 231
reincarnation, 22, 84, 172, 173, 180, 186, 189–92, 200. *See also* theodicy, reincarnationist
relativism, 16, 238, 241, 253, 254
religious diversity, 20, 43, 238–59
repentance, 39
restrictivism, 152, 153–57
resurrection, 22, 172, 173, 175, 176, 177, 178, 179, 180, 181, 182, 183, 184, 185–89, 195, 200, 277, 278, 297
retributivism. *See* theodicy, retributivist
revelation, 20, 48, 51, 65, 159, 204, 216, 217, 218, 219, 220, 228, 231, 248, 266, 279. *See also* Sinai, revelation at
reward and punishment, 68, 182
  collective punishment, 105–7, 113
reward and punishment (divinely-administered), 66, 75, 81, 82, 86, 87, 93, 101, 112, 121, 132, 135, 136, 143, 159, 174, 177, 190, 196, 197, 199, 220, 296. *See also* theodicy, retributivist

Ricoeur, Paul, 18
Rorty, Amelie, 7
Rosenberg, Shalom, 286
Rosenzweig, Franz, 9, 187, 240, 296
Ross, Tamar, 242
Rowe, William, 141, 142
Rynhold, Daniel, 266

Sa'adyah Gaon, xiv, 15, 45, 52, 119, 121, 126, 177, 179, 182, 200, 218, 219, 273, 277, 278, 279, 280, 281, 285
Sacks, Jonathan, 6, 107, 110, 254, 287
Sadducees, 173, 176
Sagi, Avi, 59, 89, 206, 218
Salanter, Israel, 13, 234
Samuel, 174
Samuelson, Norbert, 6, 8
Satan, 94, 216
Schechter, Solomon, 39, 40
Scheffler, Samuel, 193, 200
Schiller, Ferdinand, 222
Schimmel, Solomon, 157, 164, 168
Schwarzschild, Steven, 8
science, 12, 37, 60, 67, 68, 76, 77, 78, 80, 82, 109, 117, 124, 150, 156, 159, 160, 169, 170, 171, 276, 282
scientism, 150
Seacord, Beth, 190, 191
sefirot, 48
Segal, Aaron, 1, 3, 7, 34, 38, 39, 41, 42, 46, 51, 86, 98, 105, 149, 151, 175, 181, 185, 191, 196, 197, 264, 283, 284, 285, 297
selfhood, 167, 182, 185
Shapira, Kalonymus, 89
Shapiro, Marc, 40
Shneur Zalman of Lyadi, 152
Siḥon, 121, 159
sin, 33, 34, 40, 42, 93, 94, 95, 97, 101, 106, 135, 136, 155, 156, 157, 158, 165, 182, 191, 212, 214, 233, 285
sin of the spies, 69
Sinai, revelation at, 20, 214, 215, 233, 236, 247, 256, 258, 271, 277
skepticism, 37, 273
Skinner, B. F., 168, 273
Slifkin, Natan, 74, 75
Society of Christian Philosophers, 9
Socrates, 182
Sodom, 55, 90, 106, 209, 231
Sokol, Moshe, 88, 166

General Index

Soloveitchik, Joseph B., 3, 8, 9, 74, 75, 80, 108, 110, 157, 159, 193, 199, 219, 221, 225, 244
  on afterlife, 193
  and antitheodicy, 108
  on death, 194, 199, 200
  on free will, 156, 163
  on Halakhah as a floor, not a ceiling, 231
  on intimacy with God, 103
  on miracles, 74, 75
  on motivation for charity, 225, 226
  on proselytizing, 251
  on scientific advances, 77
soul, 175, 177, 182, 185
soul-making, 190. *See also* theodicy, soul-making
Spinoza, Baruch, 4, 9, 166
State of Israel, 10, 48
Statman, Daniel, 89, 218
Steiner, Mark, 12
Steiner, Richard, 175
Stern, Josef, 1, 5, 6, 14, 19, 166
Stocker, Michael, 224
Strauss, Leo, 8
Stump, Eleonore, 1, 9, 134, 298
substance dualism, 150
suffering, reward for, 100. *See also* afflictions of love
suicide, 196
Sullivan, Meghan, 42
supererogatory action, 235
systematicity, 185–87, 296–98
Sztuden, Alex, 1, 16, 58, 82, 212, 221

Talmud, xiii, xiv, 1, 2, 4, 8, 10, 13, 21, 38, 41, 43, 54, 55, 58, 63, 65, 68, 70, 76, 77, 78, 79, 91, 92, 95, 97, 98, 99, 100, 101, 102, 104, 106, 108, 123, 127, 145, 153, 154, 155, 157, 173, 176, 183, 197, 200, 215, 216, 217, 224, 226, 231, 244, 245, 247, 249, 264, 293, 294, 295, 298. *See also source index for specific sources*
technology, 65, 76, 77, 287. *See also* science
teḥiyyat ha-metim. *See* resurrection
Temple, 32, 54, 92, 93, 105, 106, 215
ten plagues, 63
Tennant, F. R., 76
Tertullian, Father, 268

theism, 1, 8, 14, 28, 30, 32, 33, 37, 57, 63, 64, 66, 67, 70, 72, 82, 88, 185, 263, 269, 274
  skeptical, 297, 298
theistic naturalism, 63–83
theodicy, 3, 17, 22, 48, 56, 70, 79, 84–113, 174, 175, 196, 198, 298
  axiological shift, 102, 103
  divine intimacy, 103–4, 112
  free will, 106, 107, 112, 143, 160
  objections to developing. *See* antitheodicy
  psychological import, 191
  reincarnationist, 190–92
  retributivist, 86, 87, 93–99, 105, 106, 107, 112, 190
  soul-making, 100, 101, 102, 103, 104, 112, 196, 200, 236
theology, 2, 3, 8, 9, 11, 13, 14, 15, 18, 19, 27, 38, 44, 48, 50, 52, 53, 55, 56, 59, 60, 61, 62, 72, 90, 91, 112, 117, 171, 180, 181, 187, 246, 247, 249, 250, 258, 266, 289, 294. *See also* God; Imperfect Being Theology; Perfect Being Theology; Process Theology; negative theology; theism
  biblical, 13
  errors in, 37–43
  feminist, 33
  vs. philosophy, 13–15
  rabbinic, 13, 55, 58, 59. *See also* Midrash; Talmud
Thirteen Attributes, 46
Thirteen Principles of Faith (Maimonides), 38, 40, 178, 295
Tillich, Paul, 187
Tirosh-Samuelson, Hava, 11
tolerance, 40, 50, 240, 246, 249, 254, 255, 258, 294
Tosafists, 79, 154
transmigration. *See* reincarnation
tree of knowledge, 197, 209–11
Twain, Mark, 163, 226, 265
Tzadok ha-Kohen of Lublin, 152
Tzelofḥad, daughters of, 213, 236
tzimtzum, 98, 107, 152, 285

Unger, Abraham, 254
universal reason, 13, 14, 15
univocal predication, 46
Urbach, Ephraim, 176
utilitarianism, 234, 263

Van Inwagen, Peter, 8, 22, 88
Vatican Council, 238
virtue ethics, 30, 234, 235, 236, 237
Vital, Chaim, 189
voluntarism, 287

Washington, George, 163, 226
Weinberg, Jehiel Jacob, 224, 226
Weiss, Dov, 91
Westphal, Merold, 53
Wettstein, Howard, 1, 58
Widerker, David, 162
Williams, Bernard, 5, 121, 169, 199
Wittgenstein, Ludwig, 12, 14, 18, 254, 275

Wolbe, Shlomo, 164
Wolfson, Harry, 4
Wolpe, David, 107
World-to-Come, 40, 87, 96, 172, 176, 177, 178, 179, 183, 184, 197, 244, 245, 247, 248, 249
Wurzburger, Walter, 32, 76, 145, 231
Wyschogrod, Michael, 8, 210, 211

Yavetz, Joseph, 282
Yeshiva University, 8
yetzer ha-ra, 156, 157
yibbum, 189

For EU product safety concerns, contact us at Calle de José Abascal, 56–1°,
28003 Madrid, Spain or eugpsr@cambridge.org.

www.ingramcontent.com/pod-product-compliance
Lightning Source LLC
LaVergne TN
LVHW041619060526
838200LV00040B/1342